Studies in Geography of Jammu and Kashmir

Studies in Geography of Jammu and Kashmir

A.K. KAUL

RAWAT PUBLICATIONS

Jaipur • New Delhi • Bangalore • Hyderabad • Guwahati • Kolkata

ISBN 978-81-316-0660-5 (HB)
ISBN 978-81-316-0661-2 (PB)

Published by
Prem Rawat for **Rawat Publications**
Satyam Apts, Sector 3, Jawahar Nagar, Jaipur 302 004 (India)
Phone: 0141 265 1748/7006 Fax: 0141 265 1748
E-mail: info@rawatbooks.com
Website: www.rawatbooks.com

New Delhi Office
4858/24, Ansari Road, Daryaganj, New Delhi 110 002
Phone: 011 2326 3290

Also at *Bangalore, Hyderabad, Guwahati* and *Kolkata*

Typeset by Rawat Computers, Jaipur
Printed at Nice Printing Press, New Delhi

Dedicated
to my tomorrow
Aakankhsha – Abhinay – Mohit

Contents

Preface

There has been a persistent demand, since long, on the part of students and laypersons, scholars and researchers, for a concise and a coherent account of geography of Jammu and Kashmir. This has been accomplished by attempting the present volume where, seemingly, the major emphasis is on its physical aspect. It is based on research findings and fieldwork and decades of experience in teaching and textbook writing.

In explanatory description of selected themes, care has been taken in finding cause and effect relationships, influence of physical processes and phenomena on the life and activities of the humans occupying that space and other biological responses. As the subject matter in geography is vast and varied and linked with diverse disciplines, a number of sources had to be tapped. All these are cited in the list of references given at the end of each chapter. To give credence to stated inferences, opinions of the distinguished authors had to be incorporated in the text, of course, not without proper attribution. Claim to originality in the book is manifest in the selection, organisation and presentation of its content.

In some chapters, where conclusions arrived at lack reasoned explanation, questions have been raised for the students and scholars of geography to answer. These and other implied topics are likely to serve as an inducement to attempting research papers and dissertations. Geography, it is averred, is the study of *place* and its raw materials are *places.* A wide range of places, features and occurrences alluded to in this volume tend to make geographical visits and tours meaningful and rewarding, an effort for grasping the soul of geography.

I am highly indebted to Shri Pranit Rawat of Rawat Publications, in the first instance, in accepting the manuscript for publication in spite of certain hurdles and then getting deeply involved in its production.

But for him, the book could not have seen the light of the day. His vast expertise and profound commitment in the publishing field is exemplary and laudable. I am also thankful to Shri Ravinder Kumar for copy editing the manuscript. Mention here has to be made of my brother, Shri K.L. Kaul, for prompting me and exerting himself in getting this manuscript printed. I also take this opportunity to express my gratitude to the authors and publishers of the books, articles/papers consulted in the preparation of this book. Thanks are due to respective commanding officers of the meteorological units of 23 Wing AF and 21 Wing AD c/o 56 APO for providing me the latest climatic data asked for. I am thankful to the librarians (may their tribe increase!) of various institutions with whom I had the occasion to interact throughout my working life.

A.K. Kaul

Introduction

The book, at the outset, deals briefly, with the political history of the Jammu and Kashmir state from its founding in 1846, through the valour and diplomacy of Maharaja Gulab Singh, and its fragmenting through political developments following partition of Indian subcontinent, in 1947, axing one-third of its territory by Pakistan to the illegal occupation of its vast area by China since 1962, thereby appraising its present status, bounds and concomitant impediments.

The second chapter traces its geological evolution which is akin to that of the Himalayan system of which it constitutes the western segment. It also bares the position of each one of its three regions – Jammu, Kashmir and Ladakh – occupying the three steps of a terrace and their resultant accessibility.

The succeeding four chapters on 'Physical Features and Drainage' unfold location, area, relief, rocks, minerals, drainage and natural vegetation of each region. Each chapter opens with its name and layout which are followed by a detailed presentation. Besides, in chapter 6 is highlighted the interaction between humans and their environment, in these regions.

A systematic treatment of various elements and factors of weather and climate in chapter 7 equips the reader for proper understanding of the basics of this significant constituent of physical environment. It also addresses a criterion for the classification of seasons tenable on quantitative grounds.

The next three chapters present the weather and climate at the regional and the sub-regional level. It comprise analysis and interpretation of the latest available climatic data of seven stations of the state – two each from Kashmir and Jammu and three from Ladakh. Here a link has been established between the climatic conditions with the major occupation of its people – agriculture – by reckoning, among other things, the length of the growing season and the ideal outdoors working period.

The last chapter on the geology includes stratigraphy of Jammu and Kashmir from the pre-Cambrian to the recent times as well as the schedule and impact of the Quaternary Ice Age and its regional distribution. Two cases, one each, for the presence of monsoon in Kashmir and the existence of pre-historic Karewa Lake (Satisara), are substantiated by ample evidence, both traditional and scientific.

In several chapters pertinent topics are discussed separately as annexures.

1

Jammu and Kashmir State

Its Founding and Fragmenting

A study of the modern history of the Indian subcontinent, pertaining to early nineteenth century, reveals that there was no state like Jammu and Kashmir in existence then. Instead, its constituent possessions comprised separate and individual realms. Jammu region consisted, traditionally, of twenty-two principalities, with Jammu as the leader, but often at loggerheads with one another. Kashmir was annexed by the Sikhs from the Afghans in 1819. Ladakh, a Buddhist kingdom, was governed by a local *gyalpo.* Gilgit, Baltistan and other adjoining areas were ruled by unruly native Muslim rajas. The political developments, during this period, in north-western India created a situation in which Gulab Singh, through his sagacity and statesmanship, succeeded in uniting, by 1846, these disparate but contiguous territories into a single entity called Jammu and Kashmir state.

Founding of the State

Jammu

Gulab Singh, a Dogra-Rajput of Jammu, joined services of Maharaja Ranjit Singh, the Sikh ruler of the Punjab, in 1809. Soon after his younger brothers, Dhian Singh and Suchet Singh, became members of the Sikh darbar. Gulab Singh, a soldier, with pluck and prowess, rose from the ranks and endeared himself to the maharaja. He consolidated the Sikh rule in Jammu and quelled the opposition to it. He accompanied the Sikh forces along with his troops in a number of campaigns in which he returned victorious. Pleased with his commitment and loyalty in strengthening and extending his kingdom, Maharaja Ranjit Singh appointed him Governor of Jammu in 1822 and honoured him with the title of Raja. The coronation took place on the right bank of the Chenab at Akhnoor. His brothers were also promoted to higher posts.

Moreover, Dhian Singh was handed over governance of Poonch and Suchet Singh that of Ramnagar.

Ladakh

Raja Gulab Singh, thenceforth, stayed, for most of the time, in Jammu with the objective of first strengthening and then extending his authority. He sent a strong force under his valiant and adventurous commander, Gen. Zorawar Singh, to capture Ladakh. After subjugating Kishtwar, he advanced through the Warwan valley, crossed the Botkol pass (4,490 m) and entered the Suru valley on his way to Leh. He had to traverse this difficult terrain, comprising vast glaciers within the Great Himalaya, as Kashmir at that time was part of the Sikh state. Several expeditions undertaken by him between 1834 and 1841 culminated in the annexation of Ladakh and Skardu (Baltistan). Contribution of Gen. Zorawar Singh in acquiring these territories for Jammu raj, as a result of his military exploits in the inhospitable and rugged trans-Himalayan region, is unrivalled and laudable. Besides territorial gains, the other objectives achieved were economic and strategic. Ladakh is the northernmost border district of India which is bounded by the neighbouring countries of Tibet and China. It lay on the carvan routes between Tibet, China and India. The valuable merchandise among other things, was Pashmina wool which fetched adequate revenue to the potentate.

Indian nation is indebted to this dauntless military strategist for extending the boundaries, in this part of the country, beyond the Himalaya. Next on his agenda was the conquest of Tibet. He died fighting valiantly, the Tibetian forces, in freezing temperatures of the cold bleak winter, on 12 December 1841.

The Treaty of Amritsar

The decline in the Sikh authority set in, soon after the demise of Maharaja Ranjit Singh in 1839, for want of competent successors. Anarchy prevailed in Lahore darbar where intrigues and murders were order of the day. In this confusion both the brothers of Raja Gulab Singh were killed. He, however, managed to stay away from this turmoil. He had by this time, become a powerful ruler of Jammu, Ladakh and Baltistan. In the First Anglo-Sikh War of 1845, he refrained from joining Sikh forces in the fight against the British. The political upheavals that followed the defeat of the Sikhs in the said war saw the end of one and rise of another ruling dynasty; the disintegration of one and the creation of another state. According to the Treaty of Lahore, of 9 March 1846, the British received from Lahore darbar the territories to the east of the Beas and the west of the Indus, including Hazara and Kashmir. Pleased with his non-partisan attitude during the Anglo-Sikh conflict, the British acknowledged Raja Gulab Singh as their ally and raised his status, on 15 March 1846, to that of a maharaja.

On 16 March 1846, Treaty of Amritsar was signed between the British government and Maharaja Gulab Singh whereby most of the ceded provinces of the Sikh state were transferred to the latter. As the Sikhs were unable to pay war indemnity of rupees one crore in cash levied on them, the maharaja offered to pay the same in lieu of the domains to be passed on to him. He was exempted payment of rupees twenty-five lakh as the British retained the Beas regions of Kulu and Mandi. The remaining amount of rupees seventy-five lakh was paid by the maharaja. According to Article 1 of this Treaty, 'the British government transferred in perpetuity to Maharaja Gulab Singh ... the hilly or mountainous country with its dependencies to the eastward of the Beas and westward of the Indus including Chamba but excluding Lahaul ...'. It is averred that the British policy and intent, in view of these occurrences, was more instrumental in the formation of Jammu and Kashmir state rather than the payment of rupees seventy-five lakh (Grover, 1955).

Kashmir

Gulab Singh became the ruler of Kashmir but he could not take its possession due to stiff resistance offered by its last Sikh governor, Sheikh Immamudin. The tact and shrewdness of the maharaja's prime minister, Dewan Jawala Sahi, at this critical juncture, and in the subsequent affairs, proved beneficial. He pleaded this case with the British who, in turn, took appropriate measures for the smooth transfer of Kashmir to the maharaja. Gulab Singh entered Shergarhi in Srinagar on 6 November 1846.

This was followed by a period of border adjustments. Places like Hazara, Sujanpur, Pathankote and Chamba were separated from the state. The replacements were Mandir, Garhi, Kathua, Suchetgarh, Bhaderwah, Lakhanpur and Chandgraon. The River Jhelum from Muzaffarabad to Jhelum town became the western boundary of the state. River Ravi formed its southern limit. The boundary with Tibet was fixed under the guidance of Alexander Cunningham.

Gilgit

In strife torn Gilgit subregion, the raja of Yasin, invaded Gilgit. Its defeated raja escaped to Gor wherefrom he sent an emissary to Sikh governor of Kashmir seeking help to restore his kingdom. A contingent of Sikh troops under the command of Syed Nathu Shah was dispatched to Gilgit from Kashmir. It captured Astore in 1841 and Gilgit in 1842. Nathu Shah did not hand over the conquered territories to its rulers but made these a part of the Sikh state. With the transfer of hilly tracts of the Sikh state to Gulab Singh, Nathu Shah switched his allegiance to the Dogras. (Figure 1.1)

Figure 1.1
Jammu and Kashmir: The State in Making

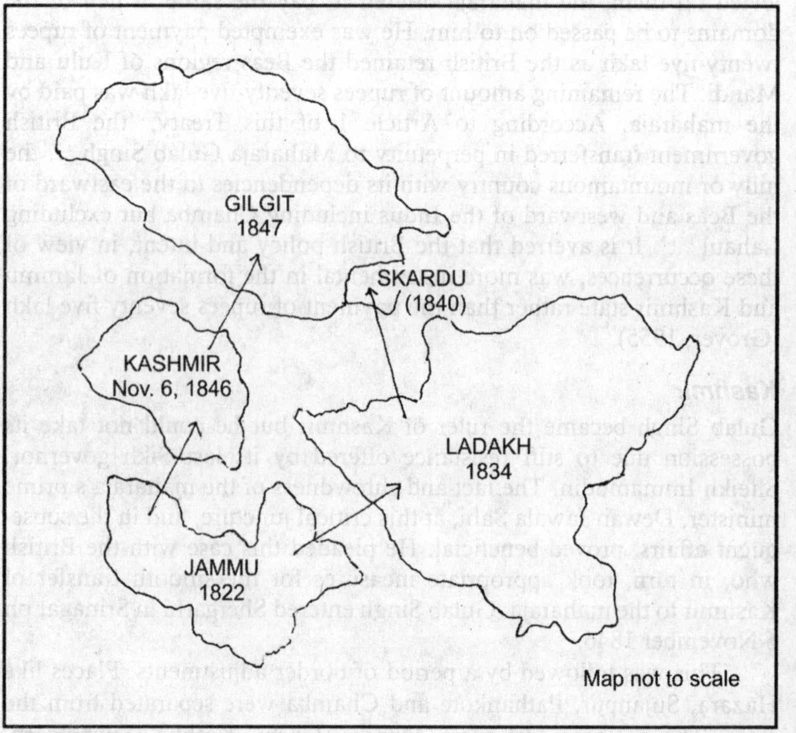

In the invasion of Central Asia by Russian Czarist forces in the mid-sixties of the 19th century, the British became apprehensive about the defence of their Indian empire. The strategic significance of Jammu and Kashmir in general, and its north-west in particular, captivated their attention – and their interference in the internal affairs of the state, at this juncture, became unavoidable. It began with the setting up of Gilgit Agency, under a British political agent, in 1877. A new force, called Gilgit Scouts, commanded by British officers, was raised in 1913. Under continued pressure, Maharaja Hari Singh leased the entire trans-Indus Gilgit to British India in 1935 for a period of 60 years.

Meanwhile, other areas of the Gilgit frontier region conquered by the state forces were Yasin, Punial, Chilas, Darel, Chitral, Hunza and Nagar, Kuh-Ghizer, Gor and Tangir mostly situated on the right bank of the Indus. These principalities though included in the Gilgit Agency were tributary to the maharaja. The state government had control only over Gilgit Wazarat.

The State of Jammu and Kashmir

The military exploits involved in subduing and the subsequent retention of far flung frontier regions of Ladakh, Baltistan and Dardistan characterized by rugged terrain, rigorous climate, sturdy and hostile inhabitants was possible because of the spirit of sacrifice, deep dedication, exemplary courage and enviable perseverance of the Dogra forces and their commanders and also the discreet leadership of their maharaja. The great struggle and strenuous efforts of Gulab Singh culminated in the founding

Figure 1.2

The State of Jammu and Kashmir (15 August 1947)

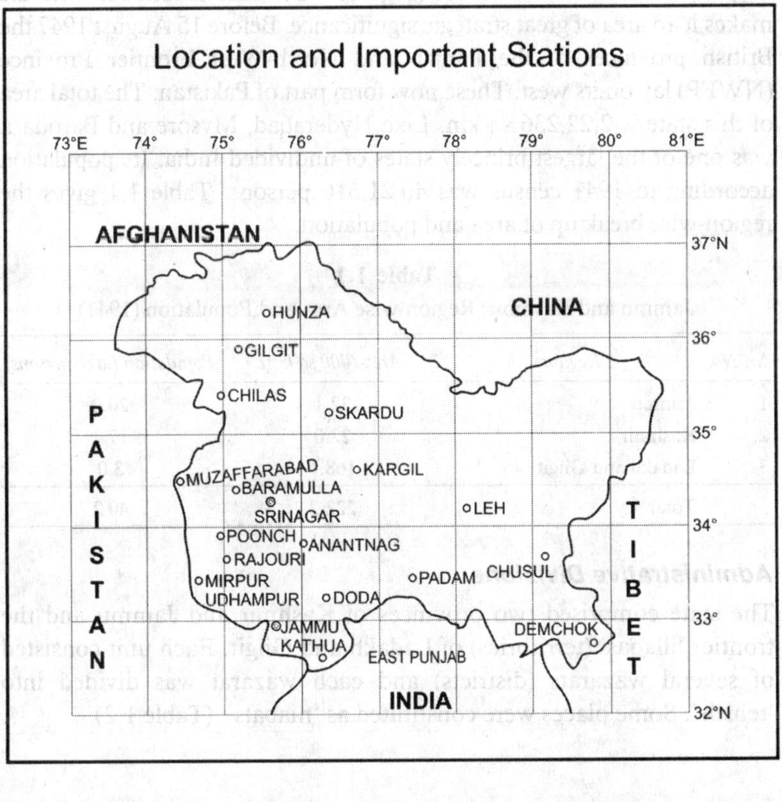

of the Jammu and Kashmir state. He integrated geographically, ethnically and culturally diverse regions and brought them under a single administration. The vast expanse of this new state can be judged by the then pony tract distances from Srinagar to Jammu, Gilgit and Leh of 305, 368 and 387 km respectively. In this connection Panikkar remarks, 'An area consisting of more than 80,000 sq miles (207 lakh sq km) including parts of Tibet as well as part of the Pamirs, besides genuinely Indian kingdom of Jammu and Kashmir, came into Gulab Singh's possession. This area had never been effectively united under one rule before and much of it, with of course, the exception of the valley of Kashmir, had never known settled government'.

Location and Size

Jammu and Kashmir state is located between the latitudes of 32°, 17′N and 37°6′N, and the longitudes of 73° 26′E and 80°30′E. Its east-west expanse is more than its north-south extent. It is the northernmost state of India and is bounded by Tibet in the north-east, China in the north and Afghanistan in the north-west (Figures 1.2). This locational attribute makes it an area of great strategic significance. Before 15 August 1947 the British provinces of the Panjab and North-West Frontier Province (NWFP) lay on its west. These now form part of Pakistan. The total area of this state is 2,22,236 sq km. Like Hyderabad, Mysore and Baroda it was one of the largest princely states of undivided India. Its population according to 1941 census was 40,21,616 persons. Table 1.1 gives the region-wise break up of area and population.

Table 1.1

Jammu and Kashmir: Region-wise Area and Population (1941)

Sr. No.	*Region*	*Area (000 sq km)*	*Population (lakh persons)*
1	Jammu	32.1	20.0
2.	Kashmir	22.0	17.2
3.	Ladakh and Gilgit	168.1	3.0
	Total	222.2	40.2

Administrative Divisions

The state comprised two provinces of Kashmir and Jammu and the frontier 'illaqas' (territories) of Ladakh and Gilgit. Each unit consisted of several wazarats (districts) and each wazarat was divided into 'tehsils'. Some places were constituted as 'niabats'. (Table 1.2)

Table 1.2
Jammu and Kashmir: Administrative Units – 1941

Provinces	*Wazarats*	*Tehsils*	*Niabat*
Jammu	1. Jammu	Jammu, Samba, Akhnoor, R.S. Pora	
	2. Kathua	Kathua, Basohli, Jasmergarh	
	3. Udhampur	Udhampur, Ramban, Ramnagar, Kishtwar, Bhaderwah	
	4. Reasi	Reasi, Rajouri	Gulabgarh
	5. Mirpur	Mirpur, Bhimber, Kotli	Naushehra
Kashmir	1. Anantnag	Anantnag, Kulgam, Awantipora, Srinagar	
	2. Baramulla	Baramulla, S.P.S. Pora, Uttar Machipora	Gurez, Sopore
	3. Muzaffarabad	Muzaffarabad, Karnah, Uri	
Frontier Illaqas	1. Ladakh	Ladakh, Kargil, Skardu	
	2. Gilgit	Gilgit, Astore	Bunji

The Partition of India

India, in the pre-independence era, consisted of two types of political entities – the provinces which were under the administrative control of the British crown and the states ruled by local maharajas and nawabs. Indian freedom struggle was restricted to the provinces and these were the object of the partition plan of India. The transfer of power, in mid-1947, involved the reorganization of these provinces into two dominions – India and Pakistan. The native states became free and sovereign with the lapse of British paramouncy. The rulers of these states were free to accede to either of these newly formed nations. From June to 15 August 1947, 562 out of 565 of these states had signed the Instrument of Accession either with India or Pakistan. Maharaja Hari Singh, of our state, was an exception. He offered, instead of accession, a 'Standstill Agreement' to both, on 12 August 1947.

Fragmenting of the State

Soon after its presentation, Pakistan violated this standstill agreement. In the first instance, it stopped the export of essential commodities to the state including food grains, salt and petrol for which it was the sole supplier. The people of the state were thereby exposed to tremendous hardships. Then, on 21–22 October 1947, the state was invaded by hordes of tribesmen of NWFP, fully armed by Pakistani military and commanded by its Maj. Gen. Akbar Khan. The invaders penetrated the long border of the state with Pakistan, at a number of places. The small numbers of state forces, inflicted by desertions, was unable to thwart this unexpected onslaught.

These tribal hordes entered Kashmir through the Jhelum valley road. They ravaged the enroute stations of Muzaffarbad, Uri, Baramulla and reached the outskirts of Srinagar. Their target was to capture Srinagar and its airport, which they had planned to attack on 27 October 1947.

Accession

Sensing the gravity of the situation Maharaja Hari Singh presented the Instrument of Accession to Indian government on 26 October 1947. His action was endorsed by Sheikh Mohammad Abdullah, President, J&K National Conference. The state, thus, joined the dominion of India formally and legally. Hari Singh also requested for military assistance to prevent the state from falling into the hands of Pakistan.

After accepting accession, the Government of India airlifted troops from Delhi to Srinagar on 27 October. The timely arrival of the defence forces saved Srinagar and its airport. In the counter operations the aggressors were pushed back when Baramulla was recaptured on 8 November, and Uri on 14 November. The intensity of thrust was increased in other sectors by the raiders when Bhimber, Rajauri, Nowshehra, Kotli and Mirpur fell into their hands. By March 1948, Pakistani regulars joined Pathan raiders and fought in coordination with them. It was by then, a full fledged war fought along the long border of the state with Pakistan. The places freed by the Indian army were Nowshera and Rajauri (April, 1948), Tithwal (23 May), Zoji la (1 November), Dras (15 November) and Kargil (24 November). Link was established with the besieged Poonch garrison on 24 November 1948.

To UN

As announced earlier by Mountbatten India lodged a complaint in the Security Council of the UNO, on 1 January 1948, against Pakistan regarding its invasion of the Indian state of Jammu and Kashmir. Much of the time in this council was spent on marathon speeches, loaded with allegations and counter allegations, by each delegation. The Security Council overlooked the Indian complaint and the outcome of its deliberations was equating of the aggressor with the aggressed. The role of the British Secretary of State for Common Wealth Affairs, Noel Baker, in this regard was damnable. The pro-Pakistan and partisan attitude of the Anglo-American block was manifest and resentful.

A five member United Nations Commission for India and Pakistan (UNCIP) was set up in April 1948. Its resolution of 13 August laid down terms for peace, called for a cease fire and withdrawal of Pakistani troops from the state. Its supplementary proposals, of 11 December, incorporated the peace plan of the earlier resolution and provided for plebiscite after cease fire and return to peace.

Cease Fire

A cease fire under the auspices of United Nations was effected on 1 January 1949. At that point of time, slightly more than one-third area of the erstwhile Jammu and Kashmir state remained under the occupation of Pakistan. The cease fire line divided the state into two parts – the Pak occupied and the rest of Jammu and Kashmir. Consequently, a large part of the state territory on the west and north-west got severed with the implementation of cease fire. The state of Jammu and Kashmir, founded in 1846, as a consequence of great sacrifices and heroism of Dogra forces under the leadership of Maharaja Gulab Singh, stood amputated as a result of Pak aggression in 1947.

Impact

Partition of Indian subcontinent and subsequent invasion of the state by Pakistan had great impact on its setting and communications. The state before Indian independence was mostly accessible through the west. The entire western border got sealed in October 1947 and was replaced by cease fire line in January 1949. An all-weather Jhelum valley road, beyond Uri, ceased to function as a highway for Kashmir. Similar road links between Jammu province with west Panjab got closed. A short but only railway line between Sialkote and Jammu city was cut off. The only direction in which the state could communicate with rest of India was the south. Here our neighbouring states are the Punjab and Himachal Pradesh. National Highway 1A, connecting Srinagar through Jammu with Pathankot has a north-south alignment. It traverses Lakhanpur-Madhopur corridor. Similar orientation is followed by the railways and airways.

Present Position

The resulting two segments of the princely state of Jammu and Kashmir became Pak-occupied Kashmir and Jammu and Kashmir, with an area of 83.2 and 139.0 thousand sq km respectively. (Figure 1.3)

Pak-occupied Jammu and Kashmir

Pak occupied areas have been further reorganized into two units of unequal sizes. The subunit with an area of 11.8 thousand sq km is

Figure 1.3

Jammu and Kashmir (1 January 1949): State Amputated

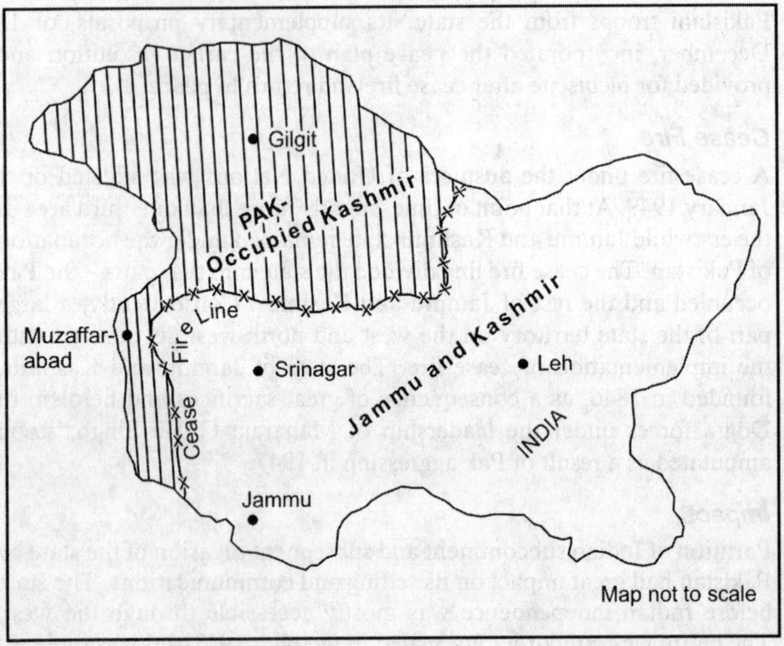

designated by them as 'Azad Kashmir'. It includes parts of the provinces of Kashmir and Jammu bordering Pakistan. In it the Muzaffarabad division consists of the districts of Muzaffarabad, Bagh, Poonch and Sudhnuti while the Mirpur division embodies districts of Mirpur, Kotli and Bhimber. Muzaffarabad is its capital.

The other subunit with a large area of 71.4 sq km is called Northern Areas. It includes the entire frontier illaqa of Gilgit and Baltistan. It consists of the districts of Gilgit, Diamer, Ghizer, Ghanche, Astore and Skardu.

Jammu and Kashmir

This part of the erstwhile state, post-1949, consisted of entire wazarats of Kathua, Udhampur, Jammu, Reasi, Anantnag and Baramullah. It also includes frontier illaqa of Ladakh excluding Skardu and parts of Poonch, Uri and Karnah. The number of districts, in 1960, was nine namely Kathua, Jammu, Udhampur, Doda, Poonch, Anantnag, Srinagar, Baramulla and Ladakh. In July 1979, the number of districts was increased to fourteen; six each in the provinces of Kashmir and Jammu and two in Ladakh as detailed below:

Jammu	Kathua, Jammu, Udhampur, Doda, Poonch, Rajauri
Kashmir	Anantnag, Pulwama, Srinagar, Budgam, Baramullah, Kupwara
Ladakh	Kargil, Leh

Figure 1.4

Jammu and Kashmir: Graph Showing Area and Population Relationship of its Three Regions

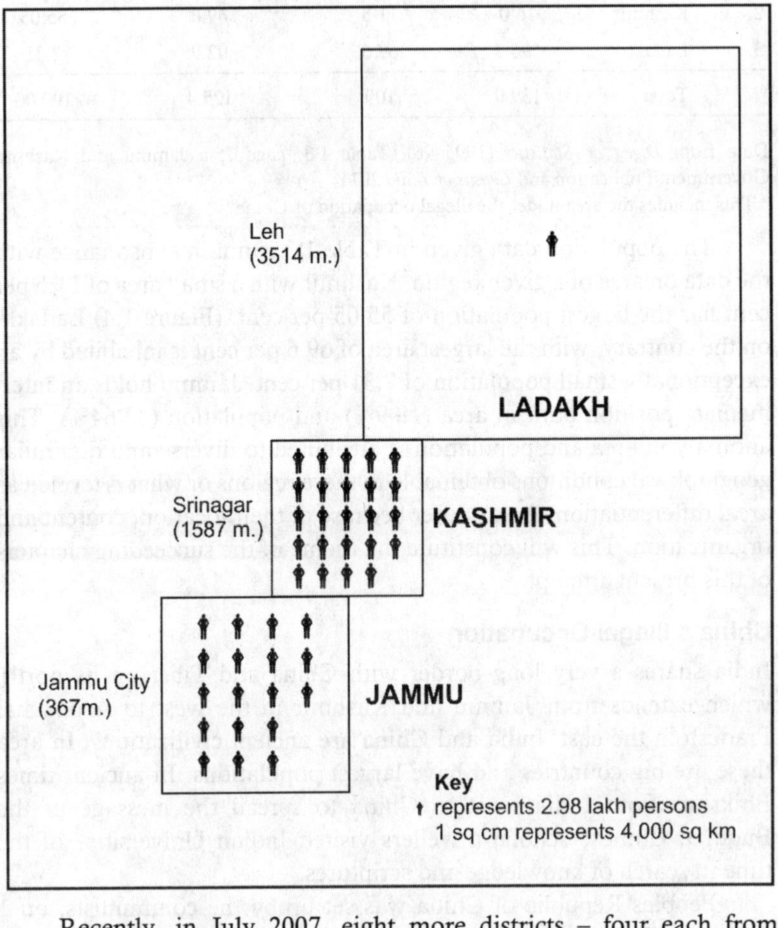

Recently, in July 2007, eight more districts – four each from Kashmir and Jammu divisions were carved. These are Kulgam, Shupiyan, Ganderbal and Bandipore in Kashmir; Ramban, Kishtwar, Reasi and Samba in Jammu division.

Area and Population

The break-up of the area of Jammu and Kashmir (1949) and its population according to the Census 2011 is given in Table 1.3

Table 1.3

Jammu and Kashmir: Area (1949) and Population (2011)

Sr. No.	*Region*	*Area (000 sq km)*	*Percentage*	*Population (lakh persons)*	*Percentage*
1.	Jammu	26.3	18.9	53.5	42.64
2.	Kashmir	16.0	11.5	69.0	55.05
3.	Ladakh	*96.7	69.6	02.9	2.31
	Total	139.0	100	125.4	100.00

Data from *Digest of Statistics* (1995–96), Table 1.3, page 7, a Jammu and Kashmir Government Publication and *Census of India* 2011.
* This includes the area under the illegal occupation of China.

The population data given in Table 1.3 is not in consonance with the data on area of a given region. Kashmir with a small area of 11.5 per cent has the largest population of 55.05 per cent. (Figure 1.4) Ladakh, on the contrary, with the largest area of 69.6 per cent is inhabited by an exceptionally small population of 2.31 per cent. Jammu holds an intermediate position both in area (18.9%) and population (42.64%). This anomaly in area and population is attributed to diverse and dissimilar geographical conditions obtainable in these regions or what is termed as areal differentiation. Areas differ because of their location, content and organization. This will constitute the theme of the succeeding chapters of this present attempt.

China's Illegal Occupation

India shares a very long border with China and Tibet on its north, which extends from Jammu and Kashmir in the west to Arunachal Pradesh in the east. India and China are ancient civilizations. In area these are big countries and have largest populations. In ancient times Bhikshus from India went to China to spread the message of the Buddha. Chinese scholar-travellers visited Indian Universities of the time in search of knowledge and scriptures.

Peoples Republic of China was set up by the communists, on 1 October 1949, under the leadership of Mao Zedong. The KMT (Chinese National Party) regime under Chang Kai Shak retreated to the island of Formosa (Taiwan). India was one among first few countries to recognize the new republic. It also endeavoured for the allotment of Security Council membership to communist China in place of KMT. In doing so India invited the displeasure of KMT as well as USA.

Tibet as an independent and sovereign country served as a buffer state between India and China. According to an early treaty with British India, India had its presence in Tibet. China sent its troops into Tibet after declaring sovereignty over it. A treaty was forced with representatives of the Dalai Lama in 1951.

Panchsheel Agreement

With India, China signed Sino-Indian (or Panchsheel) Agreement in 1954. The five principles of peaceful coexistence were incorporated in its preamble. With this was ushered in an era of *Hindi-Chini-bhai-bhai*, in our relationship with China. As a goodwill gesture and with the hope of building friendly relations, India conceded the sovereignty of China over Tibet. This, later on, turned to be a great political blunder on the part of India. When *Hindi-Chini-bhai-bhai* farce had reached its crescendo, India was in for another shock. Its sincerity was reciprocated by deceit. China declared that it recognized the McMohan Line as de facto not de jure boundary in the eastern sector. It also lay claim to a large chunk of Indian territory in the western sector. The argument advanced was that the boundary in Ladakh was only traditional and undemarcated on the ground. An ill-equipped Indian police party was outnumbered by the Chinese troops in the claimed area, near Kurnak fort, at an elevation of 4681 metres. Ten policemen were killed, on 21 October 1959, while others were taken prisoners. This was the first pinprick and show of strength on the part of China.

In the unguarded, high, vast dreary plain of Aksaichin, China built an easy to maintain short and strategic motorable road which linked Tibet with Xingjiang (Sinkiang) province of China in order to continue its hold on these two disturbed border regions. Within the Chinese territory such a road, normally, had to be built through a desert which could have been a longer road, difficult to keep up in desert landscape of shifting sand. Further, the desert was earmarked as a test site for nuclear devices, hence out of bounds for road traffic.

Two developments of the time contributed to the deterioration of Sino-Indian relations. First was revolt in Tibet where the locals vehemently opposed widening sphere of operations of the forces of occupation and the cultural invasion launched by Beijing. The second event that provoked Mao was the flight of the Dalai Lama from Tibet, alongwith twenty thousand followers, in March 1959, their safe arrival in India and the warm reception extended to them by the host country.

The Aggression

On 19 October 1962, China launched a massive attack on India, in violation of the Panchsheel Agreement, when wave after wave of Chinese troops overran our border posts. In the western sector they strongly defended what they had occupied illegally. In the eastern sector the thrust was very deep. Here they reached Tezpur in the Brahmaputra valley. China on 24 October declared unilateral cease fire. In the eastern sector, the Chinese army withdrew up to the McMohan Line, but in the western sector they stuck to the line of actual control. The humiliation inflicted, left the entire country and its leadership dazed. The apostle of peace lay bruised. This was the heaviest price India had to pay for its sincerity and probity.

Gains of the Aggressor

The aggressor gained a lot, as it continues to occupy, illegally, 37,555 sq km of our territory in Aksaichin, Ladakh (Table 1.4). The border problem continues to be unresolved to date.

China did not stop here, it put the maxim that the enemy of your enemy is my best friend into practice. Bridges of friendship were built with Pakistan. China strengthened the armed might of Pakistan by augmenting it with military hardware, nuclear and missile technology. Pakistan is backed and boosted as a strong adversary of India. Earlier, in 1959, China laid claims to Shaksgam Valley of Hunza, which was then under Pak occupation. In this connection China and Pakistan signed a provisional agreement in 1963, by virtue of which Pakistan ceded 5,180 sq km area, to the west of the Karakoram Pass, to China. In return China built 616 km Pak stretch of Karakoram highway from Thakot near Islamabad via Gilgit to Khunjerab pass (4,590 m). It provided an all weather dependable link between two friendly countries. This highway allows China access to the Arabian sea and also surrounds India on the west.

Outcome

The Chinese aggression also resulted in the sealing of our borders in Ladakh with it and Tibet and severance of centuries old trade links between India and these countries. Jammu and Kashmir with its lines of communication snapped on the west and the north, but south, acquired a terminal position. In form it can be likened to a bottle resting on its side with the neck opening to the south. The sealed boundaries of Ladakh form its bottom when the neck occupies Lakhinpur-Madhopur corridor. To defend its neglected borders in Ladakh, India had to deploy its armed forces in strength into this region.

Figure 1.5

Jammu and Kashmir (October 1962): State Further Truncated

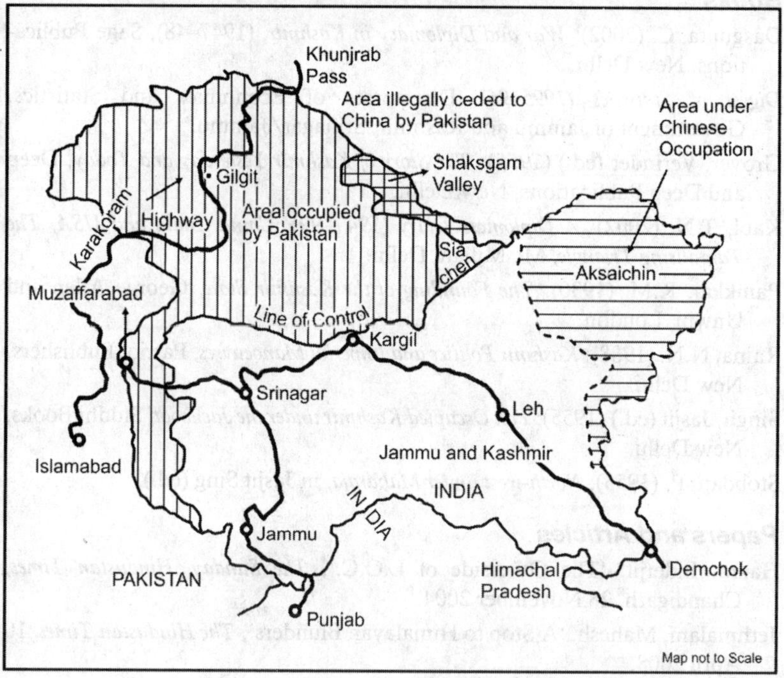

The outcome of the hostilities perpetrated on us by Pakistan in October 1947, and by China in October 1962, has been the illegal occupation of the territories of the erstwhile state of Jammu and Kashmir (Table 1.4) and consequent reduction in its area and disfigurement of its map as is revealed in Figure 1.5.

Table 1.4

Area of Jammu and Kashmir (in sq km)

(i)	Total Area* of Jammu and Kashmir on 15 August 1947	2,22,236
(ii)	Area under illegal occupation of Pakistan	78, 114
(iii)	Area illegally handed over to China by Pakistan	5,180
(iv)	Area under illegal occupation of China	37,555

* Represents provisional geographical area figures supplied by the Surveyor General of India, given in Table 1.3, Page 7 of the *Digest of Statistics, (1995–96),* a Jammu and Kashmir Government Publication.

References

Books

Dasgupta, C. (2002): *War and Diplomacy in Kashmir*, (1947–48), Sage Publications, New Delhi.

Digest of Statistics (1995–96): Directorate of Economics and Statistics, Government of Jammu and Kashmir, Srinagar/Jammu.

Grover, Verinder (ed.) (1955): *The Story of Kashmir Yesterday and Today*, Deep and Deep Publications, New Delhi.

Kaul, T.N. (2002): *A Diplomats Diary* (1947–99), *China, India and USA, The Tantalising Triangle,* Mc Millan, Delhi.

Panikkar, K.M. (1930): *The Founding of the Kashmir State,* George Allen and Unwin, London.

Raina, N.N. (1988): *Kashmir Politics and Imperial Manoeuvres,* Patriot Publishers, New Delhi.

Singh, Jasjit (ed.) (1955): *Pak Occupied Kashmir under the Jackboot,* Siddhi Books, New Delhi.

Stobdan, P. (1955): *North-west under Maharaja,* in Jasjit Sing (ed.).

Papers and Articles

Hazra, Inderjit. 'The Otherside of L.O.C.', *The Sunday, Hindustan Times,* Chandigarh, 28 November 2004.

Jethmalani, Mahesh. 'A Stop to Himalayan Blunders', *The Hindustan Times,* 10 April 2008.

Joshi, Arun. 'Azad Carves Out Eight New Districts', *The Hindustan Times,* 7 July 2007.

Sagar, Daya. 'Jammu and Kashmir as it looked before 1947 Divide', *The Daily Excelsior,* Jammu, 13 February 1994.

Saraf, Om. 'Azad Kashmir', *The Daily Kashmir Times*, Jammu, 17 June 1990.

Shukla, Saurabh. 'How China Duped Nehru', *The India Today*, Delhi, 16 July 2007.

2

Jammu and Kashmir and the Himalayas

The state of Jammu and Kashmir in the north is bounded by the high plateau of Tibet, with an average elevation of 5,000 metres and to its south lies the North Indian Plain with a mean altitude of 300 metres. The space between these landforms, of contrasting heights, is occupied by a series of six to seven mountain ranges, of varying elevations,

Figure 2.1

Jammu and Kashmir: Relief and Drainage

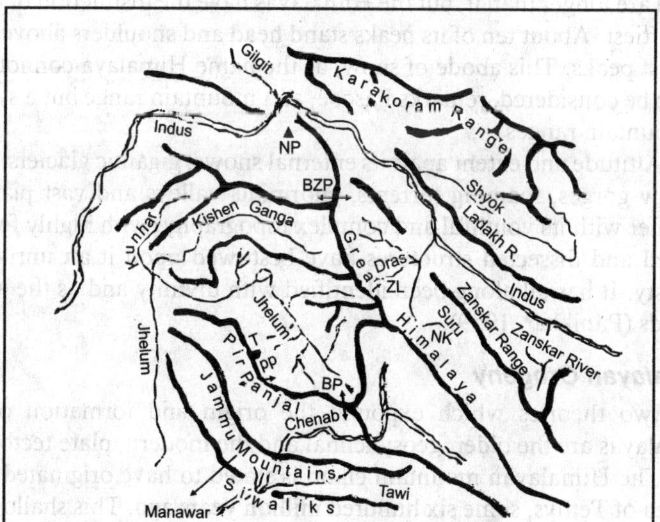

running in south-east, north-west direction, almost parallel to one another. In the southern half of the state stand, in succession and in an ascending order of altitude, the Himalayan foothills (or the Siwaliks), the Jammu mountains (or the Pahar), the Lesser Himalayas (or the Pir Panjal) and the Great Himalaya. In the northern half are the trans-Himalayan ranges of the Zanskar, the Ladakh and the Karakoram. A number of rivers like the Indus, Zanskar, Shyok, Suru, Dras, Kishenganga, Jhelum, Chenab, Tawi and Ravi have carved out their valleys through or between these ranges. All these rivers together give rise to the Indus drainage system.

With the exception of a narrow stretch of lowland in the south the entire state lies within the western Himalayas. The precincts of the state form a part of this mountain system. In order to comprehend the physical geography of the part it is essential to have a clear grasp of the evolution and structure of the whole.

The Himalayas

The Himalayas or *Himvat* of classical literature, the *Emodus* of Ptolemy, comprise an unbroken arc of a series of rugged, young fold mountains stretching in the north of Indian subcontinent, over a distance of 2500 km from the Indus to the Brahmaputra. Some mountain chains in the world are longer than it, but the Himalayas have the distinction of being the loftiest. About ten of its peaks stand head and shoulders above their highest peaks. This abode of snow, as the name Himalaya connotes, is not to be considered, remarks Pascoe, as a mountain range but a system of mountain ranges.

Altitude and extent apart its enternal snows, gigantic glaciers, deep narrow gorges, foaming torrents, enormous valleys and vast plateaus together with its youthful and complex topography, with highly folded, faulted and dissected structures have bestowed upon it an unrivalled majesty. It has all along been identified with divinity and as the abode of gods (Panikkar, 1959).

Himalayan Orogeny

The two theories which expound the origin and formation of the Himalayas are the older, geosynclinal and the modern, plate tectonics.

The Himalayan mountain chain is stated to have originated from the sea of Tethys, some six hundred million years ago. This shallow sea extended from the western edge of Europe to the south-eastern corner of Asia. It lay between and partly rested upon the ancient landmasses of Angaraland in the north and Gondwanaland in the south. In this intervening trench were poured enormous quantities of eroded materials by the rivers flowing down from either of these ancient continents. This process continued for millions of years when the floor of the sea sagged to give rise to a geosyncline. For another long period of time further stupendous infilling of the Tethyian geosyncline took place. A stage came when, probably, due to cooling and contraction, crustal shortening caused the movement of the Angaraland towards the Gondwanaland (Suess) or of both the super-continents towards each other (Kober). Consequently, the sedimentary deposits in the geosyncline, due to great tangential compression, buckled and the Himalayas rose, steadily and imperceptibly, out of the Tethyian sea some fifty to sixty million years ago. This process is believed to be still on.

The theory of Plate Tectonics, presented in the sixties of the last century, further elucidates this mountain building process. According to this theory continents and oceans are part of large lithospheric plates. When the plates move so do the continents and oceans above them. About a dozen big and small plates have been identified. The major plates are the Eurasian, African, Indian, Pacific, American and Antarctic. Smaller plates fill up the gaps between the larger ones.

The zones of contact of these plates are associated with tectonic activities. When the plates move in relation to each other huge compressional forces are released which have resulted in the formation of the mountain chains of the world. The movement of plates leads to building of stress within the plates and the continental rocks on the top leading to folding, faulting and igneous activity. Great mountain masses originate when a plate, which is almost static, pushes into the boundary of the other. The Himalayas, according to this theory, were formed because of the powerful lateral thrusts produced when the Eurasian plate moved towards the Indian plate. Consequently, sedimentary material deposited in the geosyncline was compressed in the form of rock waves which emerged from the sea to form the Himalayas and other associated ranges. The uplift took place in phases during various geological epochs like the middle Eocene, close of the Oligocene, middle of Miocene and the close of the Pliocene.

The uplift of the Karakoram is considered to have taken place earlier, during the Cretaceous period. Due to the conflicting movement of the Indian, African and Eurasian plates the mountain ranges of Eurasia including Alps emerged from the sea of Tethys, soon after the rise of the Himalayas, during the Miocene period. The Eurasian plate can be identified with the Angaraland and the Indian plate with the Gondwanaland of the earlier theory.

The main Himalayan range was subjected to intense igneous activity from time to time. Huge masses of granite forced its way into the sedimentary rocks which underwent a change due to metamorphism. The plutonic rocks formed the core and constitute the crystalline axis of the Great Himalaya. With the repeated upheavals, causing frequent folding, faulting and fracture, the structure of the Himalayas became more and more complex.

Soon after its emergence the Himalayas were exposed to various agents of denudation when huge quantities of eroded rock-waste were deposited in the estuary which lay to its south and along its longitudinal extent. These later on got folded and rose to form the Himalayan foothills in the post-Pliocene epoch. Finally, the finer material settled down in that part of the ancient depression which lay between the Himalayas and the Deccan plateau. This infilling gave rise to the Great Indian Plain.

The finishing touches to the mountain system were given by the Pleistocene Ice Age which dawned about a million years ago. In it, periods of ice-advance alternated with periods of ice-retreat characterized by strong erosion. There were minor upheavals during this time when the Pir Panjal attained its present height.

A constant struggle, thus, ensued between the tectonic forces on the one hand and the forces of erosion on the other over millions of years. Today, the Himalayas stand before us in all their youthfulness, complexity and glory.

Evolution of Himalayas

Let us now trace the evolution of the Himalayas with reference to Jammu and Kashmir through different geological eras. (For Geological Time Scale consult Table 11.1). On the basis of their dominant characteristics these eras can, as far as possible, be categorized into the phases of deposition and deposition-cum-elevation. To the former belong the Primary era and the Secondary era and to the latter the Tertiary era.

It is, by now clear that the space where the Himalayas, including the Jammu and Kashmir state, stand today was hundreds of million years ago, occupied by the sea of Tethys. The formation of Himalayas commenced in this geosyncline in the beginning of the Primary or the Paleozoic era. The pre-Cambrian rocks, of the Archaean and the Purana systems, formed the basement on which the sedimentation in the following epochs took place.

Primary Era

Marine sedimentation, is believed to have taken place, without break from the Cambrian (600 million years ago) through the Ordovician (500), the Silurian (440), the Devonian (400) and the Lower Carboniferous epochs of this era. This state of quiet sedimentation was followed in the Upper Carboniferous period by violent volcanic eruptions from shallow parts of the sea floor. The outcome of this volcanic activity was the formation of a group of islands. Kashmir, temporarily, acquired continental features and served as a land bridge between the Angaraland and the Gondwanaland. This facilitated transfer of land plants from the south to the north. Towards the close of primary era, the Permian sea inundated the land and re-deposition of the rock series came about.

Secondary Era

Marine sedimentation continued through the Triassic (225 million years ago), the Jurassic (180) and the Cretacious (135) epochs of this era. However, during the Cretaceous period the continued synclinal conditions, with some exceptions, came to a close. The sea of Tethys retreated when some portions of it were retained in areas now occupied by Ladakh and Jammu. These gulfs served as basins for further deposition of sediments till the middle of the Eocene (60). Marine sedimentation ceased in Kashmir after the Jurassic epoch.

Towards the close of Cretaceous an igneous activity of great magnitude was experienced when large masses of magma were either forced into the existing sedimentary rocks or pushed to the surface. This gave rise to plutonic and volcanic rocks which formed core of the main Himalayan axis as well as its high peaks. A mild tremor of the Tethyian sediments is likely to have taken place at that time.

The Tertiary Era

This era, which began about 65 million years ago, is of great significance with regard to the birth of Himalayas. Mid-Eocene onwards a series of earth movements caused compression and subsequent upheaval of marine deposits. It began some 50 to 60 million years ago and reached its climax in the Oligocene (38). The uplift continued in spasms separated by long intervals of time. This period saw the rise of the main Himalaya of ancient sedimentary and crystalline rocks. An orogenic movement of increased intensity followed about the middle of Miocene (26) when the sediment was warped and thrown into corrugations due to powerful lateral thrusts. The Himalaya by this time rose to become an effective barrier to isolate Tibet. This epoch also witnessed the creation of the Lesser Himalaya.

Towards the close of the Tertiary era retreat of the Tethyian sea was complete. By this time there existed a wide estuary extending from Sindh to Assam. In it were laid eroded matter from the main Himalaya by a river of immense size called the, 'Indo-Brahm' by Pascoe and 'the

Siwalik' by Pilgrim, up to the end of the Pliocene. The last phase, which took place during the Pliocene caused the folding of these alluvial deposits which resulted in the uplift of the Siwaliks and continued till after the middle of Pleistocene. This movement caused further rise of the Great and the Lesser Himalayas. Thus, the uplift of the Himalayas which began in post-Nummulitic (Mid-Eocene) period continued into the Pleistocene. The thrust movement still continues and is the cause of severe earthquakes which often frequent the Himalayas and the adjacent areas.

Given below is the plausible resume of the Himalayan Evolution.

Era and Period	*Other Activity*	*Activity related to the Himalayas*
Secondary		
Cretacious	Presumed rise of the Karakoram	The line of Himalaya may have been locus of a gentle, initial upheaval (Pascoe).
Tertiary		
Mid-Eocene to end of the Oligocene	—	**Phase I:** Rise of the main Himalayan axis of ancient sedimentary and crystalline rocks to a sufficient height and width to isolate Tibet.
Mid-Miocene	Rise of the Alps	**Phase II:** Strong compressional movement caused the buckling of the marine sedimentary deposits. Also appearance of the Lesser Himalaya.
Pliocene to **Quaternary** The middle of Pleistocene		**Phase III:** Rise of the Siwaliks. Further uplift of the Great and the Lesser Himalayas. Probably attained their present elevations.

The Quaternary Era

The era began about one million years ago. Its chief feature has been the Pleistocene Ice Age or Glacial Epoch when the Himalayas were covered by vast sheets of ice of great thickness. An indelible imprint has been left on the topography of the Himalayas by this glacial epoch which is discerned in the heaps of moraines, huge erratics, U-shaped valleys, cirques and glaciofluvial deposits of the Karewas. One evidence of great significance is the extinction of a variety of mammals which once roamed the Siwaliks and other heights. The extinction is ascribed to severe cold of the glacial epoch.

In Kashmir four distinct glacial periods were followed by three interglacial periods. At the advent of glaciation the physical geography of Kashmir was different than it is today. The Great Himalaya had almost acquired its present elevation but the Pir Panjal is deemed to have stood at an average altitude of 2,700 metres against the present elevation of 4,500 metres above sea level. Throughout the Pleistocene this lesser Himalayan range rose several times.

There was an uplift of this range towards the end of I Glaciation. During the II Glaciation the Pir Panjal underwent an effective rise when the Lower Karewas were elevated and tilted. By IV Glacial it had almost acquired its present height. The last uplift, probably, was post Karewa when the lake beds were tilted and folded. The direction of the tilt of Lower Karewa beds is everywhere towards the Valley. The presence of the plant beds at Laridura, Dangerpur, Botapathri, Gogjipathri and Ludrmarg ranging in altitude from 1,980 to 3,200 m provides palaeontological evidence in this regard.

First mild uplift of the Pir Panjal, during the First Interglacial, blocked the normal flow of the Jhelum. The backward flowing river filled the rocky basin forming a vast, deep lake. Kashmir climate during this interglacial period was warm and humid which, in addition to melting of glaciers, favoured the growth of trees like oak, box, cinnamon along with willow and poplar. Elephants of the Upper Siwalik type, deer and other mammals and birds inhabited the shores of this prehistoric lake. The lake deposits of the time are the Lower Karewas. The lake was of small size in the Second Interglacial and its deposits constitute the Upper Karewas. Towards the close of this stage the Jhelum excavated its spillway and the lake got drained. The Jhelum and its tributaries dissected the lake bed to shape their own valleys. The Karewas now stand as isolated mounds in the Valley floor and as foothills along the Pir Panjal range and represent older alluvium, when the rest of it is the recent formation of the Jhelum.

Main Features of Himalayas

Classification

The Himalayas comprise three, more or less, parallel ranges or longitudinal zones, like the Great or Main/Inner Himalaya, the Lesser or the Middle Himalaya, and the Sub or Outer Himalaya. The Great Himalaya has an average altitude of 6,100 m and is characterized by towering peaks like the Everest (8,848 m), Kanchenjunga (8,598 m) and Dhaulagiri (8,172 m). Its highest peak in Jammu and Kashmir is Nanga Parbat (8,119 m). The mean altitude of the Lesser Himalaya is 3,600 to 4,600 metres. It is designated here as the Pir Panjal range. The Sub-Himalaya or the Himalayan foothills or the Siwaliks has an average altitude of 600 to 1,220 metres. The above stated layout is well defined in the western sector because of its large width. Between the Great and the Lesser Himalaya are situated the longitudinal valleys, of tectonic origin, of Kashmir and Kathmandu. Within the Siwaliks are the strike valleys of smaller size called the 'Duns' like Udhampur and Sunderbani.

Configuration

The Himalayas extend in the shape of an arc in southeast-northwest direction, with the bulge protruding towards south. This arc undergoes a sharp bend at either extremity. This configuration of the mountain range is attributed to the resistance offered to southward advancing crest waves by the rigid ancient landmass of the Deccan plateau and the horn like structures in the form of the Aravalis in the north-west and Assam ranges in the north-east. The outer or the southern slopes of the Himalayas facing the North Indian plain are steep, devoid of snow cover and vegetation, except in sheltered valleys. On the contrary, the inner or the northern slopes fall gradually, bear snowfields and are forested.

Syntaxial Bends

At the western and the eastern ends of this mountain chain, where the Indus and the Brahmaputra have cut deep gorges, its usual direction gets altered as it undergoes a hairpin bend called syntaxial bend. Here a sharp change in direction of the strike of the mountains has taken place. The Himalayan peaks which overlook these gorges at the syntaxial bends are the Nanga Parbat in the west and the Namcha Barwa in the east. This structural features of the mountain ranges impacts the direction of flow of the rivers. The Indus undergoes such a bend near Gilgit, the Chenab at Kishtwar and the Jhelum at Domel. The main river at the syntaxial bend is invariably joined by a tributary stream. It is the Gilgit stream in case of the Indus, the Marwah for the Chenab and the Kishenganga for the Jhelum.

Climatic Barrier

This great mountain wall in the north, because of its high elevation, acts as a barrier for the free movement of the winds across it. In winter, it prevents the flow of cold and dry winds from Central Asia into the Indian subcontinent, thereby maintaining areas, on the same latitudes, at a higher temperature in India compared to Central Asia. In summer, it also acts as an obstacle in the path of the south-west monsoon. In the first instance it deflects the Bay of Bengal branch in a manner so that most of the subcontinent comes within the purview of monsoon rainfall. Further, its altitude deprives the onshore monsoon of its entire moisture content by causing snowfall in high Himalaya and rainfall in foothills and plains.

The Himalayan highlands and the Tibetian plateau cause the bifurcation of the Jet Stream. The shifting of its branches to the north and south of the Himalayas, as lately identified, plays a vital role in the onset of summer monsoon and the arrival of western disturbances in winter.

Irrigation

From the vast glaciers and snowfields of the Himalayas originate numerous streams which constitute three major drainage systems namely the Indus, the Ganga and the Brahmaputra.

Canals have been drawn from these perennial rivers of the north to irrigate the cropland in the Himalayan valleys and the fertile north Indian alluvial plain. To teeming millions of India agriculture provides work and food. Irrigation is a vital input in agriculture for increasing production and productivity. How important irrigation is in Ladakh can be judged from the fact that no plant or tree growth is possible here without it. Irrigation also plays a significant role in the farm economy of Kashmir and Jammu.

The Terrace

Within the bounds of Jammu and Kashmir the mountain ranges are arranged in a manner that resulting relief, in its broad outline, presents itself as a terrace with three large and distinct steps of unequal elevation (Figures 1.4 and 2.2). The upper step represents the trans-Himalayan Ladakh, the middle step the Himalayan Kashmir and the lower step, the sub-Himalayan Jammu. Consequently, each region is in possession of a varied quantum of environmental assets and constraints. Added to this is the interaction of the inhabiting human groups equipped with diverse cultural attributes which in course of millennia have transformed each physiographic entity into a discrete habitat. Coincidently, the three relief regions constitute the three different cultural units of Jammu and Kashmir.

Location

The three regions of the state have different locational perspectives. Jammu region, located in the south, is contiguous with the country through the states of the Punjab and Himachal Pradesh. Kashmir is placed to the north of Jammu, and Ladakh in the far north. The road distance between Jammu city and Srinagar is 294 km while Leh lies further inland by 434 km. Jammu city has the lowest altitude of 367 m,

Figure 2.2
Jammu and Kashmir – The Terrace

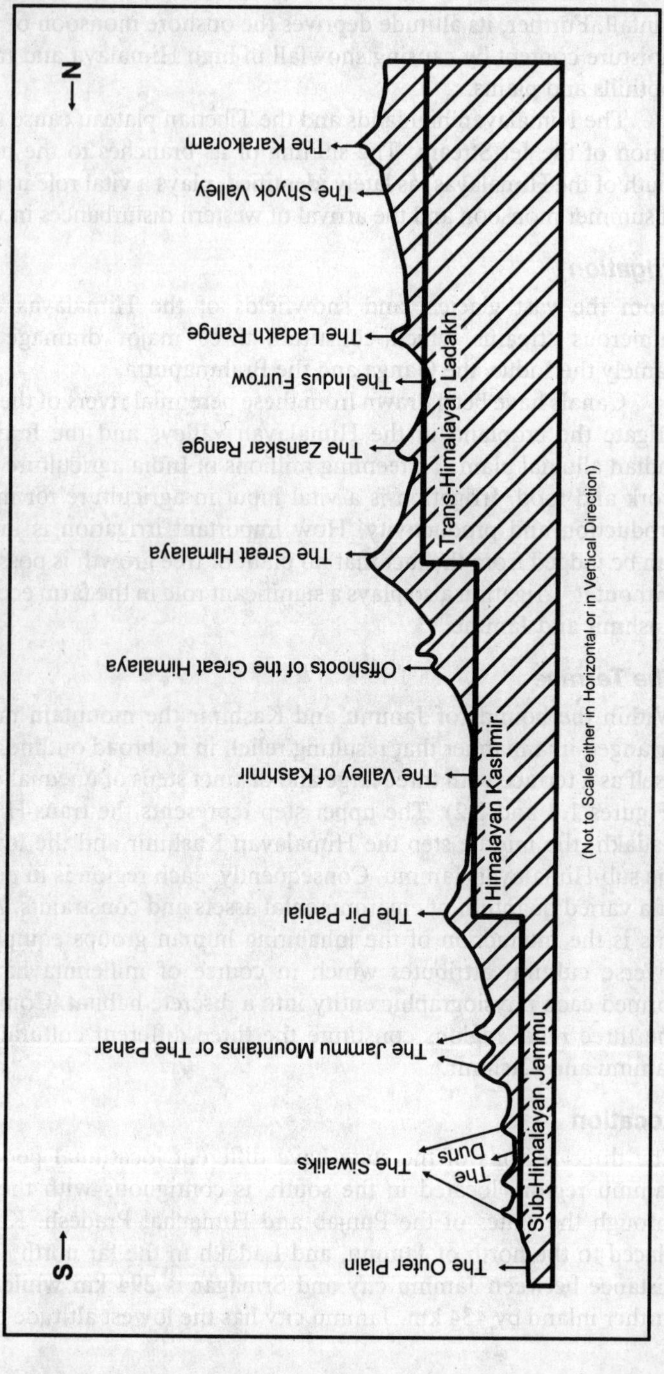

compared to other two regional centres. Srinagar is situated at a higher height of 1,587 m and Leh has the highest elevation of 3,514 m. This altitudinal variation has direct relationship with weather and climate of each region. Jammu region has uninterrupted, year-round, road and railway connectivity with rest of the country. The blockade of NH 1A due to heavy snowfall and landslides cuts off year-round road link of Kashmir for a few days or a week, but not without psychological and economic repercussions. For six months the road link between Srinagar and Leh gets snapped because of heavy snowfall in the Zoji la. The consequences of this long isolation on the life of the people of Ladakh is worthy of consideration.

The next few chapters deal with the content and organisation of these three regions.

References

Panikkar, K.M. (1959), *Geographical Factors in Indian History,* Bharati Vidya Bhawan.

Pascoe, Sir Edwin H. (1973), *A Manual of Geology of India and Burma*, Controller of Publications, Govt. of India, New Delhi.

Spate, O.H.K. (1967), *India and Pakistan*, Metheun, London.

Steers, J.A. (1950), *Unstable Earth,* Methuen and Co. Ltd., London.

Tirtha, Ranjit (2002), *Geography of India,* Rawat Publishers, Jaipur.

Wadia, D.N. (2004), *Geology of India,* 21st Reprint, Tata McGraw Hill, New Delhi.

3

The Sub-Himalayan Jammu

Physical Features and Drainage

The Name

The territory designated as Jammu was, according to the *Gulab Nama* of Dewan Kirpa Ram, ruled by the rajas of Raghuvanshi dynasty. One of its rulers, Agnivarman, had settled near Kathua. But his descendants extended the kingdom to Jammu. Two sons of Raja Agnigarb, Bahu Lochan and Jambu Lochan, founded the towns of Bahu and Jammu on the left and the right bank of the Tawi, respectively. There is an interesting incident connected with the selection of the site for the new city.

Raja Jambu Lochan, in search of a suitable site for the establishment of his capital town, rode far and wide, through the thick forests which then covered most of the right bank of the river. During his wanderings he sighted a pool of water where, to his great astonishment, he saw a lion and a goat drinking water simultaneously (this incident is captivated in a sculpture at Shiv Mandir Chowk, near New Secretariat). There cannot be a more auspicious site than this, he thought. The township came to be known as Jambu after its founder, which with the passage of time changed to Jammu.

Jammu and Duggar, writes Sharma (1955), are synonymous terms but Duggar or Dogra is much older than Jammu. The names of the rivers, mountains and places of Jammu region are found in Indian classical literature but there is no mention of the term Jammu as such. Panini, in his writings, speaks of an area in northern India, called Madra, which lies between the Chenab and the Ravi. Even, *Nilamatpurana* refers to it as Madradesh. Kalhana, in his *Rajatarangini,* calls the territories between the Vitasta (The Jhelum) and the Chanderbhaga (the Chenab) as *Darvabhisara* and the states located therein were *Rajapuri* (Rajauri), *Lohara* (Lohrin) and *Parnotsa* (Poonch). Other states situated to the south east of Kashmir mentioned are

Kasthavata (Kishtwar), *Campa* (Chamba) *Bhadravakasa* (Bhaderwah), *Vallapura* (Billawar), *Kanda* and *Visalata* (Banihal). The words Jammu and Duggar do not exist in this chronicle. To Stein, the original form of the name seems to be *Durgara.*

The origin of the name Duggar is believed to be a Sanskrit term *Dvigarta*, meaning the land of two hollows. The hollows are identified by some scholars, as the twin lakes of Mansar and Surinsar. But to Prof. Gauri Shanker (1962) the two hollows stand for the Ravi and the Chenab. He interprets the term as the land bounded and fed by the Ravi and the Chenab. The latter explanation appears more valid. A clear reference to Dogra and Dogri is found in Tuzuk-i-Jehangiri.

Prior to his coronation as the raja of Jammu and after it, Gulab Singh annexed and integrated all the principalities from Lakhinpur to Banihal and Kishtwar to Poonch whereby a composite state of Jammu was established which after 1846 became a province of Jammu and Kashmir state.

At present, Jammu is the name of the city which is the winter capital of the state, as well as that of the entire administrative division. In order to avoid confusion between the names of two distinct areal units, the former shall be referred to as Jammu city and the latter as Jammu or Jammu region.

Layout

Jammu region is bounded by the Pir Panjal range in the north and the Ravi in the south. The Ravi separates Jammu and Kashmir from the neighbouring states of the Punjab and Himachal Pradesh. Its elevation, above sea level, ranges between 325 metres at Kathua and 4,340 metres of Kalikundi peak overlooking Scoj. Thc terrain is marked by numerous undulations.

In its south, along the international border, is a narrow alluvial plain, which is an extension of the North Indian plain. It is called Jammu plain. Most of it is dissected by ravines and stream courses and covered with boulders and other rock waste. There are, however, some areas with deep fertile alluvial soils which, with the help of irrigation, constitute productive cropland. To its north stand the Himalayan foothills or the Siwaliks. The outer gentle slopes of these hills support a dry scrub forest which imparts them a green appearance. The lower slopes of these hills form the Kandi belt.

Jammu mountains or 'the Pahar' like the Siwaliks are part of sub-Himalayan Jammu but these differ from the latter in geology and physical features. The human response, too, is different. Main boundary fault sets the northern limit of the sub-Himalaya. The last physiographic unit is the zone of transition between the sub-Himalaya and the Lesser Himalaya.

The break up of the area under different physiographic divisions is given in Table 3.1. It reveals that 79 per cent area in Jammu region is hilly and mountainous.

Table 3.1

Jammu Region – Area under different Physiographic Units as on 15.08.1947

S. No.	*Physiographic Units*	*Area (sq km)*	*Percentage*
1.	Jammu Plain and Kandi	6,750	21
2.	Mountainous Area	25,370	79
3.	Total	32,120	100

(Courtesy Daya Sagar)

Physiographic Divisions

The Jammu Plain

It extends from Kathua in the south through Hiranagar, Bishnah, Ranbir Singh Pura, Jammu city, Akhnoor, Bhimber up to Mirpur in the west over a distance of 200 km. The width of the plain varies from eight to 25 kms. It has an elevation of 300 to 366 metres and runs to the south of the Himalayan foothills which act as its backdrop.

Terrain

Streams and ravines issuing from the Jammu mountains passing through this plain find their way into the Punjab. These have formed fans and spread out their load of detritus in this plain. These ravines and gullies have thus, badly dissected it. Their width varies between 0.35 to 1.5 km. These lie, compared to their high banks, at a depth of about 30 metres. The porous nature of the beds of these ravines together with their depth drains the area dry. Their beds exhibit a perceptible slope. For greater part of the year these ravines, called locally as *Khads*, remain dry but during spells of rain these get temporarily transformed into gushing torrents which transport huge quantities of brown clay, sand, gravel and boulders. On such occasions vehicular traffic on the highways gets disrupted. The frequency of these ravines can be assessed by the number of small and big bridges, totaling 200, constructed during the extension of 80 km long railway track from Kathua to Jammu. These dry ravines support a scant vegetation. At some spots of held-up soil a thick, tall, wild coarse grass called *Khar* grows which is used as thatch. These ravines are exploited for their contents of sand, gravel and boulders for construction purposes.

Margins of the ravines are marked by vertical bluffs. The intervening space between two ravines gives rise to a plateau-like feature which contributes land for cultivation and settlements. Except where the national highway has to pass over a bridge the entire road length presents a wavy appearance indicated by crests and troughs, the former being provided by intervening uplands and the latter by the ravines. It is a unique feature of this important single national highway of the state.

The main rivers flowing through this plain are the Ravi and the Chenab. Other streams are the Ujh, Basanter, Tawi, Manawar Tawi and Poonch. Canals drawn from these rivers provide the much needed water for irrigation.

Cropland

Apart from the parched, stony and brown wilderness of the ravines, the Jammu plain comprises large expanses of cropland with deep, fertile alluvial soils. The subtropical climate of the area permits year-round

Figure 3.1

Jammu Region: Important Stations

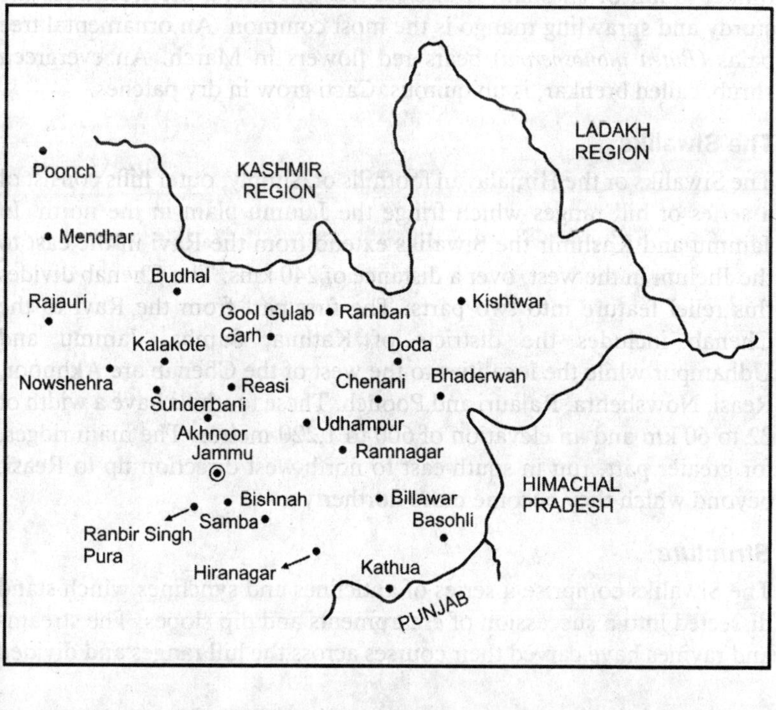

cultivation of crops subject to the availability of water for irrigation. The means of irrigation in use are wells, tube wells and canals. Some of the major irrigation schemes are the Ravi-Tawi link project, the Ranbir canal and the Pratap canal. This productive agricultural tract is locally referred to as *Anderwah* and *Bajwat.* Largest hectarage of this arable land is present in the tehsils of Kathua, Hiranagar, Bishnah, Ranbir Singh Pura (R.S. Pura), Jammu and Akhnoor. Chief crops raised are rice in Kharif and wheat in Rabi season. Fine and exportable variety of Basmati rice is cultivated in R.S. Pura and Bishnah.

Jammu plain supports a large population distributed in big villages and towns. Almost half of Jammu city is spread over this plain. Some of the important localities on the right bank of the Tawi are Talab Tiloo and Gole Gujral. Gandhi Nagar and Satwari are situated along the left bank of the river.

Natural Vegetation

In the alluvial plain and on the sections of uplands, bounded by ravines, trees and bushes, mostly evergreen, occupy the land not fit for cultivation, and contribute their share of greenery to the landscape. The trees found are banyan, pipal, simal and toon. The tree valued for its timber is tali or shesham *(Dalbergia sissoo).* Among the fruit trees the sturdy and sprawling mango is the most common. An ornamental tree palas (*Butea monosperma*) bears red flowers in March. An evergreen shrub, called brenkar, is ubiquitous. Cacti grow in dry patches.

The Siwaliks

The Siwaliks or the Himalayan foothills or, simply, outer hills consist of a series of hill ranges which fringe the Jammu plain in the north. In Jammu and Kashmir the Siwaliks extend from the Ravi in the east to the Jhelum in the west, over a distance of 240 kms. The Chenab divides this relief feature into two parts. The first part from the Ravi to the Chenab includes the districts of Kathua, Samba, Jammu and Udhampur while the localities to the west of the Chenab are Akhnoor, Reasi, Nowshehra, Rajauri and Poonch. These foothills have a width of 22 to 60 km and an elevation of 600 to 1,220 metres. The main ridges, for greater part, run in south-east to north-west direction up to Reasi, beyond which they become more northerly.

Structure

The Siwaliks comprise a series of anticlines and synclines which stand dissected into a succession of escarpments and dip slopes. The streams and ravines have carved their courses across the hill ranges and divided them into sections of short lengths. Some of these ridges run along the general strike of the Himalayas, while others stand at right angles to it. Such an arrangement creates an irregularity in the configuration of this relief feature. The presence of hill ranges, isolated hills, escarpments and dip slopes have given rise to a rugged and fractured terrain.

The Siwaliks slope gently towards the Jammu plain. These outer slopes are composed of boulders, sand and clay. A dry scrub forest covers these slopes up to the crest. On the other side of the crest the slopes fall almost vertically giving rise to escarpments of grey coloured sand rock. The inner slopes are bare because of the absence of the soil cover. Denudation plays havoc with these soft rock formations. The sub-aerial denudation is accelerated by high monsoon rainfall. The eroded material is carried to the streams and ravines.

Behind the outer ridges lies a stretch of badlands composed of the Tertiary Siwalik beds. A good section of the badlands is identified above Nagrota along the right bank of the Tawi. Beyond lies a succession of parallel high ranges separated by broad longitudinal flat valleys, called the duns or doons, with an average elevation of 550 to 730 metres. Some of the important duns are Udhampur, Dhansal and Sunderbani. Udhampur dun is 25 km long and 8 km wide. The Udhampur–Dhar road has been built through the Siwaliks. On either side of the level stretch of the road stand guard these hills with favoured slopes under a thick forest. The duns contribute their share of cropland.

Complexity of the Siwalik terrain can be perceived by the study of construction details of the railway line laid between Jammu and Udhampur. The 53 km track, inaugurated in 2005, passes through a series of short and long tunnels, totalling a length of 10 km bored through a succession of the Siwalik ridges. The broken nature of terrain of the outer hills is testified by the construction of 36 major and 122 minor bridges across the ravines, rivulets and the Tawi. The other physiographic details too are quite interesting. The boulder conglomerate beds continue from Jammu railway station to Bajalta, after which sand rock predominates. It is at places interspersed with brown clay. On bare precipices and escarpments erosion is intense, as is indicated by the presence of chunks of sand rock in the ravines. Some of these eroded rock faces appear smooth and shining. The remaining slopes have a thick forest cover with hues ranging from dark to light green and yellow. The lately introduced eucalyptus is found, not in clusters, but, in singles or twos at the lower margins. River terraces are observed at several locations. Ramnagar onwards the railway tract enters Udhampur where the hills stand wide apart to enclose a dun.

Rocks

The conspicuous younger tertiary strata from Jammu city to Nagrota, in the north, is boulder conglomerate. Nagrota bridge onwards, along the national highway it is sand rock. On approaching Udhampur town it is greyish-yellow sandstone. This sandstone has been used in the construction of temples, 'baolies' (springs), public and private buildings in and around Udhampur town. The temple complex at Babor, in Dhansal, now in ruins, is made of calcareous sandstone.

The Jammu-Srinagar national highway after winding uphill and downhill, for a distance of 35 km, crosses the Siwalik range at Nandini through a 200 metres long tunnel. The Jammu-Poonch road crosses the Siwalik range at Kali Dhar to reach Sunderbani. Akhnoor facing slope of this ridge, as is usual with this relief feature, is composed of boulders while on the inner side is an escarpment with a vertical height of 300 metres consisting of alternate layers of sand rock and clay. During a heavy downpour the grey coloured unconsolidated sand rock slips down leading to the interruption of vehicular traffic.

Kandi Belt

The lower slopes of the Siwaliks up to an altitude of 700 m from the Ravi to the Chenab and beyond to Reasi constitute the 'Kandi' area. 'Kandi' literally means an edge. But in common usage it stands for a dry, boulder encrusted hilly area characterized by thirsty soils, very low water table and scarcity of water. Before fifties of the last century, tanks storing rain water were the only sources of water for all purposes – drinking, washing and bathing. In the hot dry summer, when the tanks dried up, water had to be fetched from a distance of several kilometres. Erosion in this part is quite rampant and every shower of rain depletes the soil of its clay content. Exposed boulder beds constitute its ground surface. Cultivation is solely dependent on rainfall. Sustenance in such a harsh environment demanded strenuous efforts on the part of Kandi inhabitants. But now the face of Kandi has undergone a change through various Five-Year Development Plans. Piped water for drinking has replaced the tank water.

Lakes

In the Siwaliks, to the east of Jammu city, are the twin lakes of Surinsar and Mansar situated at an altitude of 600 to 666 metres and 15 km apart. Perhaps these lakes are situated within the same parallel ridges and are composed of the same strata. Of the two, Surinsar (604 m) is the smaller, with dimensions of 800 by 400 m and an area of 29 hectares. It has a maximum depth of 26 m. There is a small island in its middle. The sand rock slopes on its two sides bear a forest cover of chir pine. The lake, it appears, occupies a platform as is evident from the steep fall of the ground on its other two sides. Mango trees line its banks.

The Mansar lake (666 m) measures 1,200 by 800 metres and has an area of 50 hectares and a depth of 50 metres. It is surrounded on the three sides by forested hills, while in the north-west it opens into a ravine. A tourist complex has been set up and a garden laid out on the lake shore. Both the lakes are basins of sand rock interstratified with clay and both are spring fed. Mansar is the much frequented lake because of its religious sanctity and as a tourist spot. The first part of the name of each lake, Mansar in Jammu, Mansbal in Kashmir and Mansarovar in Tibet, is identical.

Siwalik Towns

In their lower courses, all rivers of Jammu region pass through the Siwaliks. The Chenab flows for a distance of 30 km from Reasi to Akhnoor through these outer hills. The run of the Tawi from Udhampur to Jammu city is 68 km. Where these rivers debouch into the plain stage towns have come up. These are Lakhinpur on the Ravi, Jasrota on the Ujh, Samba on the Basanter, Jammu city on the Tawi and Akhnoor on the Chenab. The strategic importance of these Siwalik towns, in the past, is endorsed by the presence of a fort at each location.

Jammu City

Jammu city is the winter capital of Jammu and Kashmir. The Dogra Maharajas who ruled the state for more than one hundred years belonged to this place. The old city was confined to the Siwalik slopes on the right bank of the Tawi. Like many capitals of the past, it was a walled city with a number of gates, out of which only one, the Gumat, stands in shape. The city is now spread over to both banks of the river and covers the Siwalik hills as well as the Jammu plain. In the Siwalik expanse the palaces of the Dogra rulers adorn the right bank of the Tawi, when the Bahu fort stands guard on the opposite side. Three bridges link the two parts of the city.

All but a few trains arriving from different stations of the country terminate here. All vehicular traffic to or from Ladakh, Kashmir, Kishtwar and Poonch has to pass through this city which establishes its locational significance. It is the starting point for the bus journey to Katra for the pilgrims to the cave shrine of Mata Vaisno Devi.

The fast expanding city is devouring the Siwalik slopes in the east and the north and swallowing the level land of the Jammu plain in the west and the south. It is the administrative, commercial and educational hub of the state.

Natural Vegetation

The Himalayan foothills are clothed with a dry scrub vegetation which imparts green appearance to the area. It comprises trees, thorny bushes and an evergreen shrub. The tree species are kikar *(Acacia arabica),* Phulai *(Acacia modesta)* and baer *(zizyphus jujube).* Khair *(Acacia catechu)* grows in Basohli. It is used for the production of 'Kaththa'. Clumps of bamboo are found at many places including Jasrota. The evergreen shrub is brenkar.

Montane sub-tropical forests occur on the inner and higher slopes, above an altitude of 900 metres. The important tree is Chir pine *(Pinus longifolia*). It is tapped for rosin, an important industrial raw material. The tree also yields good quality timber.

The Pahar or the Jammu Mountains

In Jammu region the space between the Himalayan foothills and the Lesser Himalaya is occupied by a mountainous tract which is locally termed as Pahar. Drew calls this Pahar subregion as the Middle mountains when the term Middle mountains is used by Wadia to denote the Lesser Himalaya. In order to avoid this mix-up of terms, the Jammu Mountains (or Pahar) is the appropriate, suggested name for this physiographic unit.

Two shades of opinion exist regarding the position of the mountain ranges of the Pir Panjal (of the Jammu and Kashmir) and the Dhauladhar (of the Himachal Pradesh). Some authors consider the Dhauladhar to be an extension of the Pir Panjal, beyond the Ravi. While others assert that the Pir Panjal extends into the Himachal Pradesh as a separate and a distinct range from the Dhauladhar. If the second viewpoint is worthy of acceptance then the Jammu mountains may be considered as a continuation of the Dhauladhar range in Jammu and Kashmir. Notwithstanding the fact that this relief division falls in the sub-Himalayan Jammu, its separate treatment is justified on the basis of its geology and geography.

Extent

Jammu mountains, like the Himalayan foothills, extend from the Ravi to the Jhelum. In the south-east the range has a width of 65 km which decreases to 15 km or more in the west. Westwards of the Ravi these mountain pass through Basantgarh, Dudo, Seoj, Bhaderwah, Kishtwar, Marothi, Sudh Mahadev, Chenani, Kud, Batote, Gool Golabgarh, Tangar, Barakh, Arnas, Darhal, Rajauri and Poonch. This mountain range also covers Basohli, Reasi, Nowshehra and Kalakote. Its northern limit is formed by the Chenab from Kishtwar to Arnas.

Beyond Arnas for its remaining length it runs parallel and close to the Pir Panjal range. The average altitude of these mountains is 1800 to 2450 metres.

Rocks

This highland tract is composed of older Tertiary rocks of the Miocene Murree series, like the red or purple sand stones, shales and clays. The other rock formations are limestones of the Eocene and Permo-carboniferous epochs.

Structure

Jammu mountains comprise ridges of varying irregular direction which branch again and again. The mountain mass is cut by ravines and water courses in a manner that very little flat space is left. In the physiography of this subregion, slopes predominate. This mountain range contrasts remarkably with the Siwaliks. In the latter, the ridges run almost parallel to one another overlooking flat valleys and sloping plateaus. The ravines and streams have badly dissected the Siwalik ridges, when in case of Jammu mountains the main ridges are also important watersheds. The streams like the Ujh, Basanter, Tawi and Manawar Tawi, in fact, originate from these mountains.

Distribution

At the foot of its highest peak, the Kali Kundi, lies the alpine meadow of Seoj. The undulating surface of the meadow is the result of past glaciation and the heaps of moraines left by it. Snowfields in the recesses of the surrounding ridges and forested lower slopes make it a charming spot. The Tawi originates from these snowfields. In the mountain rim is situated a lakelet called Kaplash kund. Every alternate year it becomes the destination of Wasiqi Nag Yatra which starts from Bhaderwah town.

Bhaderwah valley, situated at an altitude of 1645 m, is drained by the Neru stream. The presence of long batholiths speak of the association of the area with past igneous activity. With temperate climate, its vegetation, crops and fruit compare favourably with that of Kashmir valley. A hydroelectric power house at Sartangal generates 700 kw of electricity. In the vicinity of Bhaderwah are a number of scenic spots like Bhalesa, Desa, Jayi and Chinta.

The south eastern parts of the Jammu mountains, along the border with Chamba district of Himachal Pradesh, are inhabited by a Hindu pastoral community called the 'Gaddis'. In winter they move down to the outer hills or the Jammu plain with their flocks of sheep and goats.

In spring their upward march begins till they reach their habitations where they stay for the major part of the year. Unlike Gaddis, the Gujjars and Bakerwals have their homes at lower elevations but move to highlands in summer for several months. The Gaddis are concentrated in the eastern part of the Pahar region while the remaining stretch, in the west is inhabited by the Muslim Gujjars and Bakerwals.

At Kishtwar the Chenab cuts through the Pir Panjal range which, this station onwards, forms its right hand rampart. The town is situated on a plateau and is surrounded by mountains on all sides except on the west where the river flows. Batholiths are exposed in this area also. Like Bhaderwah, it shares some features of Kashmir like climate and vegetation. Outside Kashmir, Kishtwar is the only place where saffron is cultivated.

Kud and Batote are the two hill stations in the Pahar region, perched on either side of the range. Patni top, at an elevation of 1950 m, is the highest point over which the Srinagar-Jammu national highway passes. The tourist complex here is thronged by visitors throughout the year. In summer they come to enjoy its cool comfort and sylvan surroundings and in winter to experience snowfall. Higher up, towards north-west, is the forest girdled meadow of Sanasar (2,029 m).

Patni top onwards number of spurs branch out from the main ridge towards the Chenab. The spurs alternate with narrow valleys, filled with huge boulders and fallen rock over which rills tumble down. The upper slopes of these spurs carry a forest of coniferous trees, whereas the lower slopes – bare, steep and rocky – are found jutting towards the river. In this section, the right bank side is formed by the unbroken wall of the Pir Panjal range. The left bank formed by the Jammu mountains presents a broken appearance. The river here flows in a deep narrow valley between the interlocking spurs of either range. Ramban onwards both the mountain ranges run in east-west direction. At Reasi the river cuts a deep gorge through Jammu mountains and flows south.

A branch ridge at Tangar runs south-west and terminates in the Trikuta mountain. The three-peak summit, with an elevation of 2,200 m, is in view from Jammu city. In this mountain of the Permian limestone is located the cave shrine, of Mata Vaisno Devi, at an altitude of 1,615 metres. More than one crore pilgrims visited the cave shrine in the year 2013. The impact of this year-round pilgrimage on the economy of the region is discernible. 'Garbhvhu' at Adh Kunwari (1,485 m), halfway on the holy cave route, a cavern with a number of stalagmites and stalactites, is a typical feature of Karst or limestone topography. The base station for this 14 km trek is at Katra town (914 m).

The Trikuta ridge runs west with a descending altitude up to Reasi where at the point of its termination stands the Zorawar Singh fort. The Pauni ridge, which lies to the north of Reasi, is an escarpment which comprise a series of limestone cliffs. A road winding uphill leads, on the opposite side, to Kalakote and Rajauri. The only coal reserves of the state are found in Kalakote. Several kilometres downhill are the hot water springs, 'Tatapani', at Barmandal.

In the Pahar region are situated a number of scenic spots. One in the eastern section near Basohli is Bani. A pony track links it with Bhaderwah. At Patyarna, in Bani block, is located Sewa Hydel Project. The snow clad Panchari part of the Jammu mountains is known for its forested slopes and lush green meadows. It is likely to be developed as a para gliding centre. The valley of Surankote, in Rajauri district is known for its 20 m high waterfall of 'Noorichamb'. It used to be an important camping site on the old Mughal road. The Jammu mountains stretch beyond Poonch to Uri. Here a pass of low elevation, called Haji Pir, allowed year-round communication between Poonch and Kashmir in the past.

Minerals

The area within the Jammu mountains in Reasi district is known for its mineral wealth. In the Eocene Nummulitic limestones are found deposits of iron ore, coal and bauxite. The coal reserves, situated in Kalakote area, at a height ranging between 883 to 990 m, consist of six blocks, namely Metka, Bargna, Sair, Jigni, Moghla and Chainpur. These were estimated to contain 200 lakh tons of semi-anthracite coal. Mining operations were started in 1961 in only three blocks – Bargna, Metka and Jigni. A thermal power station with a capacity of 22.5 MW of power generation was set up at Kalakote, to utilize this coal. On actual mining the quality and the quantity of the coal was found far below expectations. During the time of Dogra rulers iron ore found was smelted locally on a modest scale, for making of the then military hardware. It also went into the construction of the suspension bridge over the Chenab at Ramban. The vast reserves of bauxite remain unutilized for want of cheap electricity. Deposits of sulphide ores of nickel, zinc, lead and copper are found in the Permian limestone of Reasi. Gypsum deposits occur in Batote-Asar-Ramban belt. At presents it is obtained from Batote. Deposits of magnesite are found at the eastern end of the Riasi dolomite dome at Chipprian in Panthal area.

Climate

Altitude of this highland tract modifies the climate at many places from subtropical to temperate, which in turn affects its vegetation. Human response to these environmental conditions is also different compared to the Siwaliks. The Pahar subregion is well placed as regards precipitation. It receives ample amounts of summer as well as winter precipitation. This climatic attribute aids dense forest growth on the northern slopes. The southern slopes too have a cover of herbages except where the ground is stony or the slopes are vulnerable to land slips. Either of the vegetal mantles, the forests and the undergrowth, make the landscape verdant but for the environment degradation processes of deforestation and overgrazing. Winter precipitation takes the form of snow which at lower elevations melts soon but in the higher reaches and mountain recesses it stays for a bit longer. The occurrence and duration of the snowfall and the sloping nature of the terrain influence the life and activities of the humans. At places where snow stays on the ground for a long time use of woollen garments, generally made of home spun *pattu*, is a must. Slopes are cut into terraces for the location of the dwellings and the cropland. The small plots of arable land are cultivated for raising altitude determined crops. Maize is the major cereal. Rice is restricted to lower elevations with facilities of irrigation. Temperate fruit, like apples, pears, peaches and plums, also grow in these highlands.

Landslides

The national highway 1A traverses the Jammu highlands from Udhampur to Ramban bridge for a distance of 82 km. This stretch of the sole traffic artery of the state is prone to landslides, which become a constant source of anguish for those responsible for its maintenance. Most of these, including the largest and oft repeated one at Nashri, near Batote, are caused by the seepage of rainwater or snowmelt into the rocks of Murree series. The water, serving as a lubricant, aids the sliding down of the strata comprising clay, shales and sandstones, enmasse on the steep slopes. The landslides bury the road and disrupt regular flow of traffic. The clearance operations, despite use of heavy earth removing machinery, are time consuming. Till then, the road traffic is brought to a standstill thereby delaying movement of passengers and goods in either direction. A similar sliding area is located on the Batote – Kishtwar road at Mallori where during spells of rain, landslides occur and the road gets blocked.

Natural Vegetation

The vegetation of the Pahar sub-region is of montane temperate type and comprises broad leaved and coniferous species. On the lower slopes of these mountains grow such deciduous trees as oak, maple, horse-chestnut and walnut. In Rajouri district, in the Pahar areas of Darhal, grows box, a tree valued for its timber which goes in the making of combs and other decorative wood carving articles. On higher slopes the forests consist of such coniferous species as blue pine (*Pinus wallichiana*), silver fir (*Abies pindrow*), spruce (*Picea symthiana*) and deodar (*Cedrus deodara*). Chir pine also grows in this area up to an altitude of 1,525 metres.

The Transition Zone

The change from the sub-Himalayan to the Himalayan region can neither be sudden nor sharp but gradual and irregular. In Jammu and Kashmir, like any other place, it is marked by a transition zone, where Himalayan attributes predominate at some places.

Extent

This physiographic division extends from Sansari in the south-east on the state's border with the Himachal Pradesh to Poonch in the west. It comprises three sections. The first section includes the valley of the Chenab up to Kishtwar. The second, the southern slopes of the Pir Panjal stretching up to the right bank of the Chenab. The third, the western slopes of the Pir Panjal running parallel to the Jammu mountains beyond Arnas.

(a) In the first part the area included is Padar where Chenab flows through a narrow gorge with the Great Himalaya forming the right and the Pir Panjal the left wall. Here the Sickle Moon (6,574 m) is the highest peak. Some distance downstream of Sansari are the twin villages of Atholi (1,938 m) and Gulabgarh (1,920 m) located on the left and the right bank of the Chenab, respectively. At Gulabgarh the main river is joined by the Bhot or the Machil stream. The path along this stream ascends to the pass of the Umasi la and thence leads to the Zanskar valley in Ladakh. To the north of Gulabgarh, above the village of Sumjum are situated sapphire mines at an altitude of 4,500 metres. The mines remain snowbound for most part of the year and the working season lasts from July to September. This blue coloured corundum, famous for its colour and brilliance, is valued as a gem and is next only to diamond in hardness. This gem occurs in Pegmatite rocks. The amount of corundum collected in 2004–2005 was 3,125 grams.
Presence of *roches moutonees* in Padar valley above Hamuri at an altitude of 2,300 m and the grooves on the gneiss rocks confirm the impact of the Pleistocene glaciation in the area. The climate of Padar is harsh. Snow falls in winter and stays on the ground from four to five months in a year. Avalanches cause much damage and even bury the dwellings. Crops, at times, do not ripen due to lack

of sunshine. Maize is the main crop. The leeward slopes of the mountains have a forest cover of pine, deodar and fir. Interspersed among the forest trees is the edible pine *(Pinus gerardiana)*. Jammu region in the Padar valley can, rightly, boast of a slice of main Himalayas on account of the presence in it of both Great as well as Lesser Himalayan ranges.

(b) The second part includes the localities of Warwan, Ramban and Banihal. In Kishtwar district, in the angle formed by the Eastern range of Kashmir and the Great Himalaya lies the long narrow valley of Warwan. The major inhabitations of the valley are Inshan (2,480 m), Warwan and Dacchan. The area is drained by the Marwah, a stream of great volume. Botkol pass in the Great Himalaya links Warwan valley with the Suru valley of Ladakh. Margan pass in the Eastern range of Kashmir connects Warwan with the Valley.

The slopes of the Pir Panjal facing Jammu region are steep, bare and even devoid of soil cover. These slopes bear the brunt of strong monsoon currents and are badly eroded. Consequently, the hard older rocks stand exposed and at places take the form of precipitous cliffs.

Ramban, with a low altitude of 651 m, constitutes a subtropical tract within the temperate, mountainous, region. Here the spurs branch out from the Pir Panjal range and descend towards the river. In these intervening valleys slopes, at the lower level, are terraced for cultivation and are irrigated. At higher elevations, these are forested while the open spaces are covered with herbages. Olive cultivation has been introduced into the area, lately. The strata here comprises Dogra slates.

From Banihal town (1,630 m) situated at the foot of the Pir Panjal range, the national highway winds uphill to cross the Jawahar tunnel. Ramban to Banihal is another landslide prone stretch of the highway particularly at Magarkote and Ramsu. The southern slopes of the Pir Panjal including the spurs branching out from it are bare except some sheltered pockets where open coniferous forests are found.

(c) The third section of the transition zone lies to the west of Arnas where the spurs originating from the Pir Panjal run close to the Jammu mountains, making the topography of the area quite complex. This includes the eastern parts of the districts of the Rajauri and Poonch. Important stations are Budhal, Behramgalla and Mandi. The mountain slopes are clothed with coniferous and deciduous forests.

Passes

There are about fifteen passes and 'galies' in the Pir Panjal from Banihal to Apharwat. In fact, each peak is followed by a pass or a 'gali'. These passes in the past served as the routes of ingress and egress between Kashmir on one side and Jammu and the Punjab on the other.

The pass with the lowest altitude of 2,835 m is Banihal. It connected the Valley of Kashmir with the upper Chenab valley, Jammu and east Punjab. A 320 km long Banihal cart road was constructed to link Jammu city with Srinagar. It was thrown open for public in 1923. It passed through a 67 m long tunnel at an elevation of 2,740 m. The road remained closed for several months in a year due to heavy snowfall. A second, low level, 2.56 km long, Jawahar tunnel, at an elevation of 2,210 m, was inaugurated in December 1956. In addition to the reduction of 28 km in the road distance and two hour journey time, this two bore tunnel has enabled this sole strategic highway to remain open throughout the year. Another tunnel, 11 km long and 440 metres below the Jawahar road tunnel has been constructed across the Pir Panjal range by the Indian railways. This, now is the longest and the highest railway tunnel in the country.

Pir Panjal pass (3,490 m) route functioned as an important and busy highway of travel and trade in the past. It provided a direct link between Kashmir and west Punjab and passed through Rajouri. In ancient times it was used, among other things, for the import of rock salt and got the appellation of salt road. During the medieval period, when Kashmir was part of the Mughal empire, it shot into prominence as the imperial road. It was subsequently called the Mughal road. A motorable road over it, which was thrown open for light vehicles since November 2009, provids an alternate link between Kashmir and Jammu. The other passes are Golabgarh (3,812), Budhal (4,270) and Tosmaidan (3,960 m). The routes over the first two passes connect Kashmir with Reasi. Tosmaidan route is the shortest link between Srinagar and Lohrin (in Poonch).

Transhumance

The Pir Panjal range also offers routes of transhumance when pastoral communities of Gujjars and Bakerwals move from the plain and foothill areas of Jammu province to the alpine meadows of Kashmir with their livestock. Two such major streams of these graziers cross the passes of Banihal and Pir Panjal in spring and autumn for their to and fro oscillations respectively. Those belonging to Manwal, Dudhar, Kirmchi and Thakurdwar, etc., (districts of Jammu and

Udhampur) cross the Banihal pass. The second stream which originates from Darhal, Rajauri, Thanamandi, etc., (Rajauri and Poonch districts) uses the Pir Panjal pass.

Drainage

The main rivers of Jammu region are Chenab and Ravi. The Manawar Tawi and the (Jammu) Tawi are the tributary streams of the Chenab.

The Chenab

This snow fed, perennial river of large volume and length has a vast hydroelectric potential, but being one of the three east flowing rivers, only run-of-the-river projects can be constructed on it.

Two streams, the Chandra and the Bagha rise from the snowfields on either side of the Bara lacha la (4,876 m) in the Great Himalaya, in Lahaul district of Himachal Pradesh. These two streams join together near Tandi. The combined river called Chanderbhaga after flowing through Pangi valley enters Jammu and Kashmir at its south-eastern corner, in Kishtwar district. The ancient name of this river as mentioned in the Rigveda is *Asikini*. The Mahabharata refers to it as Chanderbhaga and so does the Nilamatpurana of Kashmir. Ptolemy calls it as *Sandabhaga*. It is during the medieval period that the river came to be called Chenab. Up to Kishtwar the river occupies a structural trough bounded by the mountain ranges of the Great Himalaya in the north and the Pir Panjal in the south. Throughout its length in the state the river undergoes a number of bends and flows both in longitudinal and transverse valleys. It follows the strike of the Himalayas for the first 90 km of its course length up to Kishtwar and passes through a longitudinal valley. The first bend in the river is observed at Bhanderkote, where it is joined by the Marwah stream coming from the north. It makes a detour round the Kishtwar plateau and flows in south-east direction. Here it cascades down, in steps, with a loud roar through a height of 200 m. This large drop in elevation has been utilized for the generation of 390 MW of electricity in the Dul-Hasti project.

The river then flows in a 25 km long transverse gorge, resembling a canyon, formed of massive rocks of siliceous mica schist, up to Jangalwar. Between Jangalwar and Reasi it again adopts a longitudinal course and flows towards west. In this section of the river Baglihar hydel project has been constructed, with power generation capacity of 450 MW. It was commissioned in October 2008. Below Ramban the valley of the river widens.

The next bend of the Chenab takes place near Reasi, where it is joined by the Ans stream. The main river flows south through the limestone mountains of the Pahar subregion, through a transverse course. The river formed a loop round the hillock on which stood the Dhiangarh fort. Here the first large scale hydel project was constructed at Salal. Both stages of this project, producing 690 MW of electricity, are operational since 1987. After passing through the Siwaliks the river enters the plain stage at Akhnoor. (Figure 6.1)

The fast flowing ice-cold water of the Chenab carries an ash coloured sediment loaded with specks of mica. Even at Akhnoor it is a swift flowing river navigable only for country craft. Two canals have been drawn from the river on its either bank. These are the Ranbir canal from the left and the Pratap canal from the right bank. These irrigate the cropland in the Jammu plain and some parts of the Kandi tract. A small power house, second in the state after Mohara (Kashmir), with an installed capacity of 1 MW, is located on the Ranbir canal in Jammu city. The canal, after the power house, is carried across the Tawi, below its bed, through a siphon.

The ancient site at Manda, situated on the right bank of the Chenab, with its Harappan relics, presents, till date, the northernmost limit of the Indus Valley Civilization. These finds confirm a close link between the Chenab valley and this great river valley civilization of ancient India, circa 2500 to 1700 B.C.

The Ravi

Like the Chenab and the Jhelum, the Ravi is a major river of Indus basin. It rises in the Chamba district of Himachal Pradesh and flows through Brahmur, Dalhousi, Basohli and Madhopur. A road bridge and a railway bridge over the Ravi connect Jammu and Kashmir through Madhopur corridor with the rest of the country. Ranjit Sagar Dam or Thein Dam Hydroelectric project, constructed on the Ravi, with a power generating capacity of 600 MW, was commissioned in the year 2000.

A major irrigation scheme linking the Ravi with the Tawi has been completed to irrigate 0.6 lakh hectares of cropland in the Jammu plain and the Kandi areas. It consists of a 76 km long canal which utilizes the state's share of the Ravi water and carries it up to Vijaypur, where it is linked with the Tawi lift irrigation scheme. In this connection a barrage has been constructed across the Ujh stream.

The Manawar Tawi

It originates from the southern slopes of the Rattan range in the Rajauri district. The upper catchment area of the Manawar Tawi is snow bound hence the water, in varying proportions, continues to flow in it throughout the year. It passes through Thana Mandi, Rajauri and Nowshehra and finally joins the Chenab near Manawar town, hence the name.

The (Jammu) Tawi

The Tawi rises in the glaciated alpine meadow of Seoj. It has a total length of 140 km and a catchment area of 2,160 square kilometres (Angural). A fraction of the catchment in the upper part is snowbound by virtue of which the Tawi maintains a certain volume of water throughout the year. The lower part of the catchment area is rain fed. Like other Himalayan streams it frequently changes its direction. It is joined by nine tributaries mostly dependent on rain water. One important tributary which joins it on the right bank is the Jajjar nala. On it has been constructed a tourist complex at Jajjar Kotli.

From its source to Chenani, a distance of 48 km, the Tawi flows through a longitudinal valley. Here it passes through 3000 to 6000 m

Figure 3.2

Jammu Region: The Tawi Basin

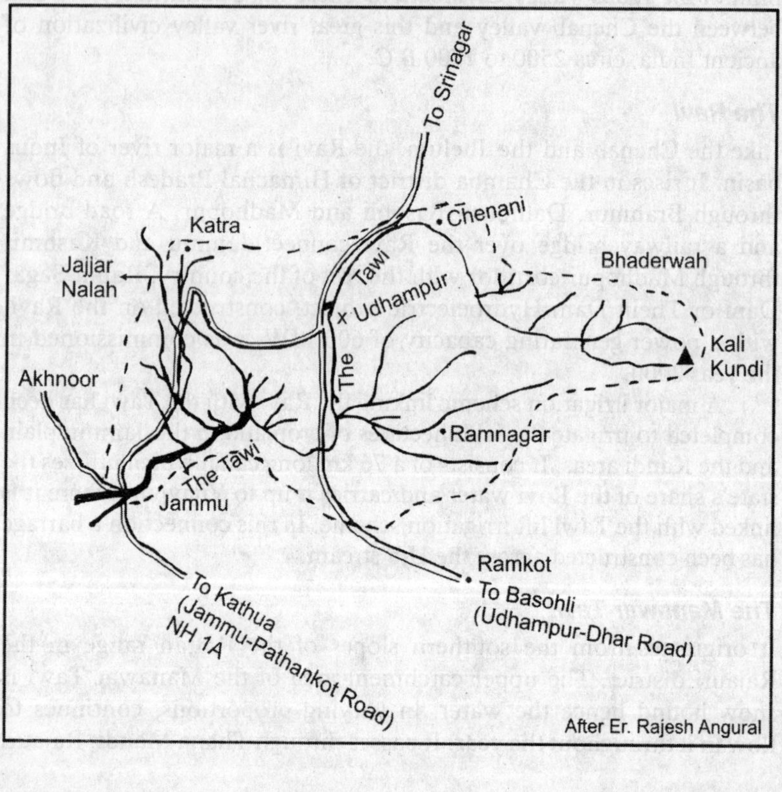

high and rugged ridges of the Jammu mountains. The mountain slopes are either forested or under pasture while the summits are bare.

At Chenani it undergoes a right angled bend and then onwards it passes through a transverse valley. It flows in south-west direction up to Udhampur. The Chenani Hydroelectric Project, running on the water drawn from the Tawi, produces 18 MW of electricity when the production in Udhampur power house, built on Udhampur canal, is 800 KW.

Width of the Tawi in Jammu city is 300 m and its bed is strewn with boulders. The shifting and meandering water course covers, hardly one-third of its bed in normal conditions. Below the first (the oldest) bridge the stream bifurcates into the *Waddi Tawi,* and *Nikki Tawi.*

Steep gradient of its catchment together with the absence of vegetation cover causes quick runoff and consequent severe floods. Erosion on such occasions is enormous and large quantities of eroded material are transported downstream which finally rests on the river bed and increases its level.

Tawi water through gravity canals irrigates the cropland in the districts of Udhampur and Jammu. The Tawi Lift Irrigation scheme, with pump station installed at the foot of the Bahu spur, lifts Tawi water to feed a 29 km long canal constructed from Jammu city to Vijaypur. More than half of the drinking water requirements of Jammu city are provided by the Tawi. It joins the Chenab in Pakistan.

References

Books

Drew, Frederic (1875): *The Jummo and Kashmir Territories,* E. Standford, London.

Grover, Verinder, (ed.) (1955): *The Story of Kashmir, Yesterday and Today,* Vol. I to III, Deep and Deep Publications, New Delhi.

Kaul, A.K. (1987): *Home Geography (J&K),* Ambanju Publications Srinagar/Vinod Publications, Ludhiana.

Kapadia, Harish (2001): *High Himalaya unknown Valleys,* Indus Publishing Company, New Delhi.

Mehta, R.L. (1963): *Elements of Physical Geology,* Hari Chand Mehta, Jammu.

Spate, O.H.K. (1964): *India and Pakistan,* Methuen.

Ram, Diwan Kirpa (1977), *Gulabnama,* Translated by Sukhdev Singh Charak, Light and Life Publishers, New Delhi.

Sharma, Hans Raj (1955): *Through Corridors of Jammu's Past* in Ref. No. 2, Verinder Grover, (ed.)

Wadia, D.N. (21st Reprint, 2004): *Geology of India,* Tata McGraw Hill, New Delhi.

Papers and Articles

Angural, Er. Rajesh, 'River Tawi – A Synoptic View', *The Daily Excelsior,* Jammu, 20 April 1997.

Bukhari, Safeer Hussain Shah, 'Beautiful Valley of Surankote', *The Daily Excelsior,* Jammu, 23 September 2007.

Dhar, B.L. et al., 'Geomorphological Studies of Chipprian Magnesite Deposits, Panthal (Jammu Himalayas)' in *Indian Geomorphological Diversity,* Rawat Publications Jaipur, 1994.

Faridi, Nasir, 'A Day with Chanderbhaga, I & II', *The Daily Excelsior,* 17 and 24 September 2003.

Khajuria, G.L. 'Enchanting Chenab Valley', *The Daily Excelsior,* Jammu, 30 September 2007.

Khanna, A.K. 'The Mighty Chanderbhaga', *The Daily Excelsior,* 19 October 2008.

Rana, Jaswant Singh, 'Sapphire Stones of Padder', *The Daily Excelsior,* 14 November 2010.

Sagar, Daya, 'Jammu and Kashmir As It Looked Before 1947 Divide', *The Daily Excelsior,* 13 February 1994.

Saraf, Suraj, 'Beauty Spots in Jammu', *The Kashmir Today,* November 1956.

Shankar, Prof. Gauri, 'The People of Jammu and Kashmir: Their Languages and Culture', *The Kashmir Today,* July 1962.

Sharma, G.D. 'Banihal Tunnel', *Kashmir,* Published by Ministry of Information and Broadcasting, Government of India, April 1956.

Zutushi, D.P. et al., 'Limonology of Nine Lakes of Jammu and Kashmir Himalayas', *Hydrobiologia,* The Hague, Netherlands, February 1980.

4

The Himalayan Kashmir (I)

Physical Features

The Name

Kashmir has the distinction of having a complete historical record from the ancient to the modern period. In this connection contribution of Kalhana is outstanding. His *Rajatarangni* (River of Kings), in Sanskrit verse, presents unbroken narration of Kashmir history from the ancient times to the middle of 12th century AD. This tradition was continued by Jonaraja, Srivara, Suka and Prajabhatta up to the close of 16th century. In the mediaeval and later epochs the historians of repute, who wrote in Persian, were Haider Malik (of Chaudura), Mohammad Azim (of Diddamar), Mulla Shah Muhammad (of Shahbad, Doru), Narayan Kaul Ajiz, Pir Ghulam Hassan (of Khuyihom, Bandipore), Dewan Kripa Ram and others. There have been a number of historical noticcs in Sanskrit, Persian and English by non-local writers, whose contributions vouch for the authenticity of Kashmir history.

The original Sanskrit form of the name of this region, according to Stein, is *Kashmira* which in Persian spelling becomes Kashmir. The name *Kashmira* has remained unchanged and used without interruption throughout its history by the locals as, well as by the outsiders ... for more than 23 centuries. The names recorded by Ptolemy are *Kaspira* or *Kaspiria* which are based on its Prakrit form *Kasvira*. The inhabitants of the region call it *Kashir* which is a direct phonetic derivative of *Kasmira* through Prakrit *Kasvir*.

The name *Kasmira* has been interpreted differently by different scholars. In one version the term is split into two parts where *ka* means water and *smira* stands for 'to desiccate', denoting thereby land desiccated from water. Regarding Kashmir, Humboldt, a German geographer, states that its primeval name was *Casyapamar* signifying the habitation of Kasyapa. The Chinese scholar-traveller, Hiouen Thsang (7th century AD) called it *Kia-shi-mi-lo.* Haider Malik considered

Kasmira as the contraction of the term *Kasyapamir,* meaning the sea or mountain of Kasyapa. This version has been adopted by a host of Persian chroniclers. Even foreigners like Burnouf and Wilson have used it. Kasyapa *rishi* has been responsible for changing the lifestyle of early settlers from migratory graziers to settled agriculturists.

For the last more than six decades, most of the writings on this territory have used the name Kashmir for the entire state in place of Jammu and Kashmir. Such a usage, in a book on geography, often proves misleading. The name Kashmir, in this volume, is restricted to the great fertile valley through which flows the Veth (Upper Jhelum) and the valley facing slopes of the surrounding mountain girdle. Here, Kashmir is Kashmir and the state is Jammu and Kashmir. Kashmir valley is frequently shortened to 'the Valley', (with capital V). The Valley together with the localities of Uri, Gurez, Keran and Karnah constitute Kashmir region as well as Himalayan Kashmir.

Layout

The situation of Kashmir within the Himalayas is explicitly given by Kalhana when he writes, 'In the three worlds, the Jewel producing earth be extolled; on that the region of Kubera (the north); there (next) the mountain range, the father of Gouri (the Himalayas) and lastly the country Kashmir that is encircled by that mountain range'. In the western section of the North Indian mountain system the Great Himalaya with its concave face and the Lesser Himalaya with its convex bulge stand some distance apart from each other. This peculiar configuration of the mountain ranges has created an oblong basin with its long diagonal parallel to the main Himalayan axis. This rocky basin is filled with alluvium, both ancient and recent. This alluvial plain, encircled by a mountain girdle, constitutes Kashmir Valley.

In its physical setting and content Kashmir is unique, and without a parallel, in the entire expanse of the Himalayas. Kathmandu, in Nepal, may be cited as another example of the Himalayan valley. It has many features similar to Kashmir but it is different from Kashmir with regard to its size and some of the outstanding attributes of its physical environment. On global level, Kashmir is often compared with Switzerland but the basic plan of their physiography is different. Switzerland for the most part is a high plateau bounded in the north and the south by still higher mountain ranges.

Kashmir, thus, is a mix of two types of landforms – highlands enclosing a lowland. Through, the latter flows the sole drainage artery, the Veth, in its middle, which assigns it a distinct geographical personality. The highland component comprises the off shoots of the Great Himalaya, forming the eastern and the northern walls whereas the

Figure 4.1
Jammu and Kashmir: Physical Map

southern and western ramparts are formed by the Pir Panjal range. The Valley floor includes the Veth (or the Jhelum) flood plain and Karewa uplands. On a physical map (Figure 4.1) Kashmir Valley looks like an oval patch set in a ring of mountains. Geologically, Kashmir boasts of an uninterrupted record of the strata from the Pre-Cambrian to the Jurassic period.

A number of transverse valleys, big and small, open into the main longitudinal Valley contributing their share of arable land, water resources, forests, alpine meadows, hydroelectric potential and scenic splendour. These important side valleys are the Lidder, the Sindh and the Lolab. Projecting ridges and receding valleys have made the outline of the oval irregular.

The surrounding mountain girdle has a gap in the west through which the Jhelum leaves the Valley. In this Jhelum gorge is situated the township of Uri. An important tributary of the Jhelum, outside the Valley, is the Kishenganga. On its left bank are situated the localities of Gurez, Keran and Karnah.

'Kashmir', writes Stein, 'owes its historical unity and isolation to the same facts which give to its geographical position a distinct and in some respects almost unique character. We find here a fertile plain embedded among high mountain ranges, a valley large enough to form a kingdom for itself and capable of supporting a highly developed civilization'.

Table 4.1

The Himalayan Kashmir

	Area of the Physiographic Divisions (in sq km)		
(a)	Total Area of Himalayan Kashmir		**15,948**
(b)	Area of the Peripheral Mountain Tract		
	(i) Gurez	1,854.67	
	(ii) Karnah	406.63	
	(iii) Uri	697.23	
	Total (i+ii+iii)		**2,958.5**
(c)	Area of Kashmir Valley (a-b)		**12,989.5**
(d)*	Break up of the area of Kashmir Valley according to its physiographic divisions		
	(i) Mountain Girdle	8,354.5	
	(ii) Sloping Karewas	820.0	
	(iii) Karewa Table lands	1,615.0	
	(iv) Veth Lowland	2,200.0	
(e)	Total Mountainous Area b(i+ii+iii) + d(i)	2,958.5 + 8,354.5	**11,313.0**
(f)	Percentage of the mountainous area (e/a)		**70.9**
(g)	Total Valley floor (Lowland + Upland) d (ii+iii+iv)		**4,635.0**
(h)	Percentage of the valley floor area (g/a)		**29.1**

* Data from: (a) *Digest of Statistics* (1995–96), J&K Govt., Table 1.03, (b) *Census of India*, 1981, District Directories.

* Area of Physiographic Divisions computed manually by the present writer from the Map of Kashmir appended as plate LV with the book 'Studies in the Ice Age ...' by H. de. Terra and T. T. Paterson, 1939. (Figure 4.2)

Physiographic Divisions

The Mountain Girdle

Parimu, a present-day historian of Kashmir, avers, 'Perhaps in no region in India has geography so amply influenced its history as in case of Kashmir, the largest and the loveliest valley enclosed in the womb of the Himalayas'. One of the geographical features that has shaped Kashmir society most is the mountain girdle around the Valley. Kashmir in this connection may be likened to a huge fort with high and massive ramparts. These lofty ranges made the realm secure against outside invasions. In such a safe location it could preserve and pursue its culture and develop an indigenous social and economic system. The highlands, with manifest barrier functions, guided its political history. Thus, in the past, its mountain fortification bestowed upon it a distinct geographical, historical and cultural existence (Stein).

This huge, natural fort had several doors in the form of passes, above 3,000 metres in altitude. These remained snowbound for half the year hence impassable. During the pass-open period these served as the routes of trade and travel. These also became vulnerable spots for outside incursions. On a number of occasions an early snowfall at the time of harvest destroyed standing crops which resulted in severe famines. With snowbound passes the import of food grains, to mitigate human sufferings and miseries, was not possible. Great loss of life was followed by the agony of the famished survivors. The cumulative effect of such repeated afflictions, over generations, on the psyche of its people, as indicated by their distinctive behavioural patterns, is justifiable. This is conspicuous in one of their practices of laying in store, in bulk, not only provisions but also other necessaries of life. Further, the closed passes converted this 'heaven on earth' into a natural prison subjecting its occupants into forced isolation.

Classification

With the Veth (or Upper Jhelum) as the base, Kashmir Valley is divisible, roughly into two triangles which, for the sake of convenience, may be called the Pahalgam triangle and the Gulmarg triangle. In the former the other two sides on the east and the north are formed by the offshoots of the Great Himalaya. In the Gulmarg triangle the remaining two sides, in the south and the west are formed by the Pir Panjal range. In this way the Veth along its right bank is flanked by the Himalaya and along the left bank by the Pir Panjal. Srinagar lies close to the Himalayan range. This classification is presented in the following tabular form.

MOUNTAIN GIRDLE OF KASHMIR

(South and West)	(East And North)
The Lesser Himalaya or the Pir Panjal Range	**The Great Himalaya** or The Himalaya (i) The Eastern Range (ii) The Northern Range

The Pir Panjal Range

Proceeding towards north, beyond the three relief features of sub-Himalayan Jammu stands first impressive high mountain range of the Pir Panjal. From Jammu region its view, on a haze free day, is superb both from Bari Brahmana and Patni top. This is the only high Himalayan range of Jammu and Kashmir seen from the North Indian plain. This Lesser Himalayan range, as the name implies, stands at a lower altitude compared to the offshoots of the Great Himalaya in the east and the north. Its average elevation is 4,000 metres. It is composed of rocks that range from the Purana to the Eocene. Its axial zone is formed of the Upper Carboniferous series comprising the Panjal traps and Agglomeratic slates. On the Valley side it extends from the peak of Kaukut (4,110 m) to Uri over a distance of 128 km. In the first instance from Kaukut peak to Darhal pass it runs in the east-west direction. At Darhal pass it undergoes the first bend to acquire south-east to north-west direction. The next bend takes place near the peak of Shin Mahinyuv (4,610 m) when it again aligns in the east-west direction up to Uri. (Figure 4.2)

Crestline

The serrated crestline of the Pir Panjal range in Banihal pass dips to the lowest elevation in the entire rim of the Kashmir bowl. To the west of the Golabgarh pass the crestline rises to an elevation of 4736 m at Brahma Shikhar, which consists of three peaks. At the foot of these peaks is the tarn of Kounsernag. In the south-east to north-west part of the range the first pass is the Pir Panjal which links Shupiyan in Kashmir with Rajauri in Jammu. Next to it lies the Sunset peak or Romshi Thong (4,745 m). Overlooking the valley of Dudhganga, in this section, is the highest peak of this range called Tratakuti (4,752 m). The Pir Panjal watershed maintains itself at a high altitude between the peaks of Brahma Shikhar and Tratakuti. The crestline decreases in height on either side of this elevated region, towards Chenab in the east and towards Jhelum in the west. In the last east-west part of the range the highest peak is Apharwat (3,930 m) above Gulmarg.

Slope Structure

The orthoclinal structure of the inner slopes of the Himalayas is best illustrated in the Pir Panjal range. Its Valley-facing slopes fall gradually giving rise to several conspicuous steps. For a clear comprehension of their structure and other characteristics it is worthwhile to select a

Figure 4.2
Kashmir Region: Landforms

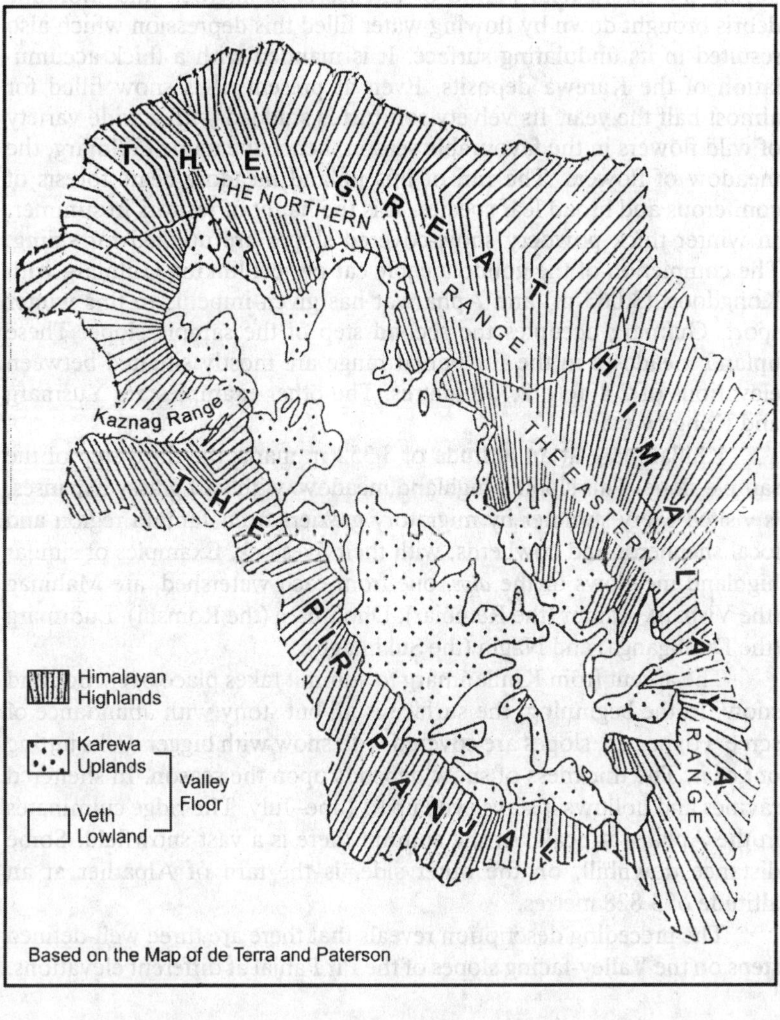

sample slope, in Gulmarg section, which in turn can serve as a model for the entire range.

Proceeding from Srinagar in the Valley floor upwards, Tangmarg (2,225 m) denotes the first step in the Pir Panjal incline. Here rocky spurs of the range are mantled by the Karewas. These bear a thick forest of blue pine and Himalayan spruce. Human habitations and irrigated cropland are its other features. (Figure 4.3)

Gulmarg (2,655 m) is located at the meeting place of the Lower Karewa foothills and silver fir clad rocky spurs branching out from the Pir Panjal. This saucer shaped basin was scooped by a glacier. Later on, during the interglacial period of intense erosion, rock and morainic debris brought down by flowing water filled this depression which also resulted in its undulating surface. It is mantled with a thick accumulation of the Karewa deposits. Even at present, it is snow filled for almost half the year. Its velvety soft turf is studded with a wide variety of wild flowers in the favourable season, hence the name Gulmarg, the meadow of flowers. The rim of this upland meadow bears forests of coniferous and broad leaf species. It is the haunt of visitors in summer. In winter thick powdery snow-covered slopes are utilized for skiing. The completion of the gondola cable car project linking Gulmarg with Kongdoori (3,063 m) and Apharwat has given impetus to this winter sport. Gulmarg occupies the second step of the sample slope. These upland meadows in the Pir Panjal range are mostly situated between elevations of 2,400 to 2,750 metres. The other examples are Yusmarg and Kongawattan.

Khillanmarg at an altitude of 3,352 m marks the third step of the sample slope. This sloping highland meadow, with vast grassy expanses, is visited every summer by migratory graziers from Jammu region and local shepherds and cowherds, with their livestock. Examples of similar highland meadows or the *alps*, one from each watershed, are Mahinag (the Vishau), Rainur (the Rembiar), Dholimarg (the Romshi), Ludrmarg (the Dudhganga) and Nagin (the Sukhnagh).

The ascent from Khillanmarg to summit takes place over rock and snow. In the beginning, the surface is all but stony with abundance of scree. Higher up, slopes are covered with snow with bigger rocks jutting out of it. The thickness of snow depends upon the season. In sheltered ravines and hollows it stays even up to June–July. The ridge culminates in the Apharwat peak. At the summit there is a vast snowfield. Some distance downhill, on the other side, is the tarn of Alpather at an altitude of 3,828 metres.

The preceding description reveals that there are three well-defined steps on the Valley-facing slopes of the Pir Panjal at different elevations.

The space between these steps has a thick forest cover. The second step, comprising an upland meadow, has become a significant tourist spot. Pasturage for the transhumance is offered by the third step of alpine meadows. Above the *alps* is the stony wilderness while the summit has a snow cover. The tarn is reminiscent of past glaciation.

Branching Ridges

A number of spurs and ridges branch out from the watershed range and descend towards the Valley. Some of these end in the Valley floor, as isolated hills, as those at Shupiyan, Beerwah, Pushker and Magam. A pair of branching ridges, close to the crestline, form the headwater region of a stream, emanating from the Pir Panjal, flowing downhill to join the master stream on its left bank. Canals have been drawn from these mountain streams, in their upper stretches, to irrigate the cropland on the Karewas and in the Veth plain, at lower elevations. Streams draining the Pir Panjal slopes, from south to north, are the Vishau, Rembiar, Romshi, Dudhganga, Sukhnag, Ferozepur and Ningle.

Natural Vegetation

About 40 per cent of total forest area of Jammu and Kashmir is claimed by Kashmir. It is the single largest land use in this region. In addition to yielding timber, fuel wood and minor produce, forests contribute their share in imparting and enhancing natural charms of Kashmir. These occupy the slopes of the enclosing mountain girdle. Forests of the Pir Panjal range are known for their quality and quantity. The gentle gradient of these slopes, their northern aspect, deep soils and longer stay of snow cover favour growth of natural vegetation. Vertical zonation of vegetation is sharp and well defined in these forests. The vegetation zones identified are:

1. Kashmir Valley zone below 2,133 metres.
2. Coniferous zone from about 2,133 to 3,200 metres.
3. White birch zone above the coniferous forests from about 3,200 to 3,645 metres.
4. Alpine zone from about 3,645 to 4,014 metres.

In these dense temperate forests the conifers consist of deodar (*Cedrus deodara*), blue pine (*Pinus wallichiana*), Himalayan spruce (*Picea smythiana*) and silver fir (*Abies pindrow*). The broad leaved species present are maple, hazel, bird cherry, alder, elm, ash, horse-chestnut and walnut. The undergrowth, among other species, includes Kilun (*Viburn nervosum*) and Patr (*Skimmia laureoula*). The dominant conifer is silver fir which is spread over 65 per cent of the forested area. It is followed by blue pine with an area of 26 per cent. These coniferous forests because of their quality, compactness and excellent regeneration are the finest forests in the entire Jammu and Kashmir. The vegetation of the Alpine zone comprises Juniper (*Juniperus recurva*) and (*Juniperus communis*), rhododendron (*R. companulatum*) and (*R. anthropogon*), birch (*Betula utilis*) and stunted willow (*Salix sp.*)

The Great Himalaya

The main Himalayan axis, in its western part, extending from Bara lacha la in Himachal Pradesh to Nanga Parbat in Gilgit subregion, with an average elevation of 6,100 m has a perpetual snow cover. In it, on the latitude of Pahalgam are situated the twin peaks of Nun and Kun in Ladakh region. From this lofty range branch out ridges of lower elevation which enclose the Valley on the east, north and north-west. These mountain ranges stand at an average elevation of 4,267 m.

The Eastern Range

The Eastern Himalayan range in Kashmir has a north-south alignment and acts as a watershed between the Jhelum and the Chenab. From its point of bifurcation, near Zoji la, up to Kohenhar peak, above Sheshnag, its crestline maintains a height of 5,000 m. To the south of this peak a marked decline in its elevation is noticed. It is in the southern part of this range that access to Warwan valley and Kishtwar is possible through the passes of Margan (3,619 m) and Smithan (3,784 m) respectively. (Figure 4.3)

The Kolahoi Massif

The mountain mass along the latitude of 34° 10′N and forming the north-eastern corner of Kashmir rhomboid has a maximum width of 60 km. (Figure 4.2). In it lies Mt. Kolahoi (*Gwashibror*) at an altitude of 5,425 metres. This, the highest peak of Kashmir Himalayas, stands 618 m above Mont Blanc, the highest peak of the Alps. The peak made of the Panjal volcanics is needle shaped, with black precipices from the point downwards, which looks like 'an isolated lancet piercing the sky'. On the shoulders of the Kolahoi ridge rests the largest and fully developed valley glacier of the same name. It used to be 8 km long and its snout descended to a height of 3,565 m. Another glacier, smaller in size, lies on the Kohenhar ridge at an altitude of 3,400m. The mountain mass here bears in cirque basins, a total of ten, big and small glaciers distributed in an asymmetrical manner. Those directed towards north are 2 to 6 km long while those facing south have a length of less than a kilometre (Kaul, 1994). He, further, reports that the Kolahoi glacier retreated 1,900 metres from 1857 to 1988 and the Sheshnag glacier diminished by 510 m.

Presence of towering mountains, craggy peaks, lake filled cirques, recurring snowfields, speeding brooks, gushing torrents and wooded slopes impart truly alpine character to the area. The Himalaya, in this part of Kashmir, stands in its wildest and awe-inspiring grandeur.

To the east of the Kolahoi is the Amarnath peak (5,279 m). To the south-east the Mahagunas (4,350 m) ridge acts as a watershed between the drainages of the Lidder and the Sindh. Triassic limestones constitute the ridges at Pahalgam along the left bank of the Lidder and form number of peaks towards Amarnath side. The Panjal volcanics are widely distributed, along the right bank of the Lidder, at and below Pahalgam and in the ridges towards Kolahoi.

The Lidder Valley

Basically, the Lidder stream consists of two branches, the east and the west, which drain two separate catchment areas of the same Eastern range.

The east Lidder has its source in the highland tarn of Shishram or Sheshnag (3,658 m) some 21 km above Pahalgam. The lakelet measures 1.5 by 0.75 km, occupies a cirque and stretches in east-west direction. The ridge that surrounds the tarn, culminates in the Kohenhar peak (5,181 m). A small glacier descends from this ridge towards the surface of the lakelet. The area lies above the treeline and the vegetation comprises bushes of Juniper and rhododendron. The stream from Sheshnag to Chandenwari flows through narrow gorges including that of Pissu *ghati*. The east Lidder passes beneath a snow bridge at Chandenwari. Here slopes are covered with coniferous forests. It flows through a narrow valley, past Pahalgam village and tourism complex, to join the west Lidder below race course.

The west Lidder is formed when three narrow valleys, in the western gorge, meet close to the forest girdled meadow of Lidderwat (3,048 m). One is occupied by a torrent issuing from the snout of the Kolahoi glacier. Through the second, flows the rivulet of Satlanjan which rises at the foot of the Basmai anticline. The third, carries the discharge of the tarn of Tarsar (3,810 m). This tarn is surrounded on three sides by mountains which are treeless but abound in pastures. To the west of it, separated by a low ridge, is another highland lakelet of Marsar, the source of the Marsar stream which flows westwards to Srinagar. The west Lidder receives a number of affluents as it passes through Aru to Pahalgam.

All stream valleys comprising the east, the west and the combined Lidder at Pahalgam are encased in a Y-shaped amphitheatre of mountains mostly with forested slopes and snow-covered peaks. Most of the valleys are U-shaped and littered with moraines, the result of the Pleistocene glaciation. A huge heap of morainic matter belonging to II Glacial and Second Interglacial forms a high terrace, near the race course, on right bank of the east Lidder, where stone tools of prehistoric man were found by H.D. Sankalia in 1969 (Chapter 11, Annexure–II).

The mountains in Pahalgam stand some distance away from the left bank of the Lidder. These rise gradually with a gentle slope offering a wide stretch of space which has been utilized for the development of tourism-related infrastructure. Along the right bank, the basaltic ridges stand vertically close to the stream. The Lidder valley at Pahalgam, 400 m wide, is open and terraced but below Pahalgam it narrows down again except at Nunwan. At Ganeshbal are the headworks of the Martand canal. Below Langabal the valley acquires a maximum width of 2 to 3 km.

Pahalgam, meaning the village of shepherds, with an altitude of 2,130 m, is the most frequented tourist resort in Kashmir. Its scenic charms together with bracing air, even at the height of summer, is alluring for the tourists and the local people. It serves as a base camp for the annual pilgrimage to Amarnath. The thirty-nine km pony track from Pahalgam to Mahagunas pass involves a traverse at an elevation of 2,200 to 4,267 metres. It passes through the eastern defile, with night halts at Chandenwari, and Wawjan (above Sheshnag). The last halt takes place at Panchtarni, across the Mahagunas ridge. The route from Sheshnag onwards passes through a highland tract which lies above the treeline. The mountain slopes though bare of trees sporadically support flower bedecked pastures. The trek becomes arduous because of rarefied air, at these high altitudes and the unfair weather, associated with the onshore monsoon during the period of pilgrimage, July-August.

Radiating Ridges

The highland mass of north-eastern Kashmir, covering a large area, is characterized by a complex topography on account of the steep divides and branching ridges, which originate from around the Kolahoi massif. A series of ridges and spurs radiate towards the Valley and partially occupy the space on the east of the highway from Wayil on the Sindh to Sangam on the Veth. Some of these prominences extend as far as the Veth at Awantipore, Sombhur, Barus and Pantachok. Others give rise to semi-circular valleys of Tral, Awantipore, Khrew, Badami Bagh and Srinagar.

Tral is situated on a Karewa at an altitude of 1,710 metres. At Awantipore deep incursion of the Wasterwan spur into the Valley floor has reduced its width to about 3 km. The limestone projection at

Sombhur extends up to the right bank of the Veth. In Vihi area, the limestone ridges are thrown into folds which lend them a wavy appearance. The mountains are bare but the slopes at the foot are dotted with almond orchards. The adjacent Karewa tablelands are under saffron cultivation. The ridges are the sources of Triassic limestone. Two raw materials required in the manufacture of cement, limestone and clay, are available in abundance in this area. The former is quarried from nearby mountains and the latter obtained from Karewas. The first cement factory in Kashmir was set up at Wuyan, in 1962, with a production capacity of 60 tonnes per day. The second, large scale, factory at Khrew produces 350 tonnes of cement per day. Iron used to be smelted, in the past, at village Shar where heaps of slag are encountered. Vihi area provides several ideal sites, for the study of geological strata, at Zewan, Khonamuh and Barus. Rhyolite, an acidic volcanic rock is quarried at Pantachok. All these valleys from Tral to Vihi receive meagre rainfall. The mountains are too low to bear snowfields. Unlike other parts of Kashmir, Vihi area is lacking in a natural stream. The sources of water here are springs, like Zewan, Khonamuh and Khrew.

Another ridge from Kolahoi massif extends westwards to form the left bank mountain flank of Marsar stream. The ridge near Harwan turns south to form the amphitheatre of mountains on the east and the south of the Dal lake. It terminates in the isolated hill of Shankaracharya (1,860 m). One more ridge leaves the massif, again westwards, to form the right bank mountain wall of the Marsar stream. In it lies the peak of Mahadev (3,970 m) which overlooks the city of Srinagar. Upstream of Harwan reservoir is the world famous Dacchigam wild life sanctuary, in the Marsar valley, spread over an area of about 143 sq km. The sanctuary is the habitat of musk deer, black bear, and also the endangered Kashmir stag (*Hangul*). Mahadev ridge forms the northern wall of the Dal lake with the isolated hill of Hari Parbhat (1,728 m) on its west. The same ridge on its north forms the left bank mountain wall of the Sindh stream.

In the southern part of the Eastern range, upstream of Sangam, the projecting spurs enclose the valley of the Lidder, Arpath, Ahlan, Brengi, Nowbug and Sandren. At the foot of these limestone hills issue springs of large volume like Mattan, Anantnag, Achabal, Kokernag, Vethavathur and Vering. There is a mineral water spring, one each in Nagbal and Malakhnag in Anantnag town and at Kokernag. It is the presence of numerous (*anant*) springs, big and small, fresh water and mineral, that have given the name Anantnag to the district. The Mughals adorned the springs at Achabal and Verinag with their style of gardens. At Kokernag a botanical garden has been laid out recently. In

Verinag spring, situated at the foot of the Pir Panjal range, the aquifer consists of the pervious Triassic limestone which is enclosed in the crystalline rock of the Panjal trap. At village Sof, in Brengi valley, iron was produced in the past, from the local ore using forest wood as fuel.

The Sindh Valley

The Sindh stream has its source in Panchtarni, on the north face of the Mahagunas watershed. Panchtarni is a circular level tract, surrounded by high rugged mountains, through which flow five rills, fed by meltwater of the snowfields. Heaps of moraines dot the tract. To its north lies the Amarnath cave (3,880 m) in the side of a steep cliff of the Mesozoic limestone, a white coloured dolomite. This colossal structure is cubical in shape. A rivulet, the Amaravati flows along the foot of the cave. Sangam, the place of confluence of the Panchtarni with the Amravati, is also the meeting point of the traditional (Pahalgam) route and the new (Baltal) route to the holy cave.

Sangam onwards the Sindh tumbles down a narrow gorge, a bare wilderness, towards west to reach Baltal. The fall in elevation from holy cave to Baltal in a distance of 15 km is 1,045 metres. The Sindh valley widens at Baltal, where the ground and the surrounding slopes are treeless but covered with herbages. The mountains in this part rise vertically from the ground forming a canyon like feature. It then passes through Sonamarg.

Sonamarg, an alpine meadow at an altitude of 2,668 m, is almost triangular in shape. The 1.5 km long base of this triangle lies on the west and its apex 4 km distant in the east. It is joined at the north end of the base by the Lashimarg nar (rivulet) and the Thajwas nar joins it at the southern end. The whole area is an anticlinal cut into the Triassic shales and limestones. The surrounding mountains are covered with coniferous forests at lower and snow at higher elevations. Where the crestline is ice free peaks are pointed and pyramidal, well chiseled by frost action.

It is joined on the south-west by a wider, undulating transverse valley called Thajwas. In the latter, a rivulet flows in a wide bed which has divided the surface into a number of islets. In the west facing mountain slopes, hollows stand scooped by moving ice and frost action which are occupied by glaciers. These hanging glaciers are about 120 m above the ground. A low central ridge with a forest cover of silver fir and white birch separates Sonamarg from Thajwas.

The Sindh valley from Sonamarg to Gagangir assumes the form of a narrow gorge through which the stream descends as a foaming torrent through a number of rapids. Below Gagangir it occupies a boulder

Figure 4.3

Kashmir Valley: Peaks, Passes, Ridges and Places

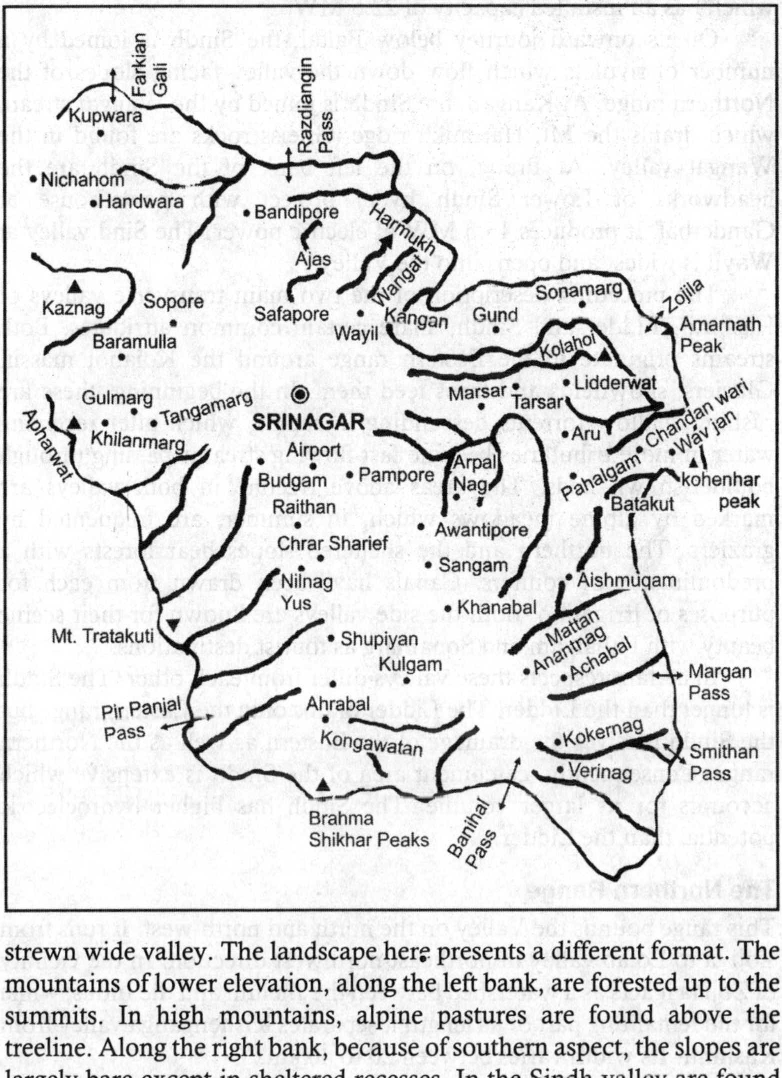

strewn wide valley. The landscape here presents a different format. The mountains of lower elevation, along the left bank, are forested up to the summits. In high mountains, alpine pastures are found above the treeline. Along the right bank, because of southern aspect, the slopes are largely bare except in sheltered recesses. In the Sindh valley are found such landforms as alluvial plain, alluvial fans and plateaus which constitute its arable land. Rice cultivation ceases at 2,130 m and Gagangir marks the upper limit of walnut trees.

A part of the stream at Kulan is diverted into a 7.3 km long conductor to carry water to the Upper Sindh hydel project. The powerhouse at Sumbal produces 18 MW of electricity in summer. Tail-end water of this project is carried to the powerhouse at Kangan which has an installed capacity of 22.5 MW.

On its onward journey below Baltal, the Sindh is joined by a number of rivulets which flow down the valley facing slopes of the Northern range. At Kangan, the Sindh is joined by the Wangat stream which drains the Mt. Harmukh ridge. Gneiss rocks are found in the Wangat valley. At Prang, on the left bank of the Sindh are the headworks of Lower Sindh hydel project with powerhouse at Ganderbal. It produces 13.5 MW of electric power. The Sind valley at Wayil is widest and opens into the Valley.

The preceding description of the two main transverse valleys of Kashmir, Lidder and Sindh, share certain common attributes. Both streams originate in the Eastern range around the Kolahoi massif. Glaciers, snowfields and tarns feed them. In the beginning, these are rushing shallow torrents descending in rapids, which after receiving water of more tributaries become fast flowing streams passing through boulder-strewn beds. The areas above treeline in both valleys are marked by alpine meadows which, in summer, are frequented by graziers. The northern and the sheltered slopes bear forests with a predominance of conifers. Canals have been drawn from each for purposes of irrigation. Both the side valleys are known for their scenic beauty with Pahalgam and Sonamarg as tourist destinations.

In certain respects these valleys differ from each other. The Sindh is longer than the Lidder. The Lidder drains only the Eastern range but the Sindh receives the drainage of the Eastern as well as the Northern range. Consequently, catchment area of the Sindh is extensive which accounts for its larger volume. The Sindh has higher hydroelectric potential than the Lidder.

The Northern Range

This range bounds the Valley on the north and north-west. It runs from Zoji la to Lolab valley in northeast-northwest direction. In the vicinity of Zoji la it acts as a watershed between the Jhelum and the Indus, while for the remaining part of its length it separates Kishenganga valley from Kashmir. Its width varies between 20 to 40 km.

The Harmukh Massif

The crestline of this range Zoji la westwards increases in elevation and attains the highest altitude in Harmukh massif. It has five peaks, one of which rises to 5,143 metres. The massif teems with glaciers, snowfields and tarns. A large glacier 3.2 km long, occupies its northern slope. Its snout lies at 3,688 metres and its meltwater finds its way into the highland lake of Gangabal. It is the largest of all the tarns in the mountain rim of Kashmir. Situated at an elevation of 3,570 metres it has a circumference of 8 km. Some distance below Gangabal is the tarn of Nandkol. Other highland lakes on the northern side of the Harmukh are Vishensar (3,850 m), Krishensar (3,818 m), Gadsar (3,962 m) and Satsaran (3,680 m). Like the Kolahoi, Harmukh glacier has all the attributes of a valley glacier. The ridges that branch out from Harmukh enclose the valleys of Wangat, Erin and Madhumati. The Wular lake is surrounded on the east and the north by ridges which radiate from the Northern range. A spur reaches as far as Mansbal. The grandeur of the Wular lake is enhanced by these towering mountains and in stormy conditions these make the lake look more dreadful. Beyond Lolab the range turns south up to Chowkibal where it joins the Kaz Nag range.

Passes

The first important pass in the Northern range is Zoji la (3,505 m) which connects Srinagar with Kargil and Leh through a motorable road. In the past it served as a carvan route to Leh, and beyond it, to Central Asia and Tibet. The ridge on Kashmir side stands like a vertical wall and is composed of soft rocks like the Jurassic limestones and shales which make the maintenance of the road rather difficult in unfair weather.

On the north and the west the Kishenganga skirts the entire length of this range. The first pass that links Kashmir with the Kishenganga valley is Razdiangin or Tragbal (3,530 m). A motorable road from Bandipore crosses this pass, at present, to reach Gurez. In the past a pony track, Gurez onwards, crossed another pass, the Burzil (4,199 m) in the Great Himalaya to reach Gilgit. This pony track from Kashmir to Gilgit was then called Gilgit transport road.

In the north-western corner of Kashmir, in Kupwara, there are a number of low altitude passes, called 'galis'. The Pharkian gali and Sonapind gali each leads into Keran. The Nestichuen or the Sadhna pass (3,238 m) connects Chowkibal, at the head of the Kahmil valley, with Karnah or Tangdhar by a motorable road.

The Lolab Valley

Bounded by the Northern range and its branching spurs is the picturesque side valley of Lolab. On its south and west the mountains rise to an elevation of 915 m above ground level but those in the north-west are taller. These highlands are marked by the absence of glaciers and snowfields and the winter snow does not stay beyond May or June. It is drained by the Lolab (or Manchar) stream which is joined by a number of affluents, most of which dry up as summer advances, except the Shrant and the Klaroos. Water from springs is used for drinking purposes. Some of these of large volume are those at Chandigam, Sadhuganga, Shumbrial and Tritsch.

This verdant, undulating valley is 19 km long and has a width varying between 0.3 and 5 km. The two tree species that dominate its landscape are deodar and walnut, both of exceptional girths. The uniqueness of this valley lies in its sylvan surroundings. This rocky basin of Lolab valley, with its gorge like opening near Kupwara, resembles Kashmir valley in shape and scenic charm.

There is a deep cave in the mountain range above Klaroos, the rock formations of which are said to contain copper ore. In Kupwara district, marble of grey and light brown colour is quarried at Zirhama, Oura, Trehgam and Drugmulla. One industrial unit for cutting and polishing it has been set up at Hiri in Zirhama.

Isolated Hills

Two significant orographic features of Kashmir Himalayas, the Eastern and the Northern ranges, deserve to be highlighted. First, the highest peaks of Kolahoi and Harmukh are not situated on the main watershed ranges but on the ridges that project from those towards the valley. Second, is the termination of ridges branching from the main range in isolated hills. Examples of such isolated hills are Kanjdoori (Lidder valley), Baal (Anantnag), Sosanwar (Achabal), Barus (Vihi), Brein spur (the eastern shore of the Dal), Shankaracharya and Hari Parbat (Srinagar), Ahateng (Mansbal), Baba Shakur-ud-Din hill (Watlab, Wular lake).

Natural Vegetation

The heavy exploitation of the forests on the Himalayan flank in the past has resulted in numerous bare slopes as, for example, those that skirt the Dal and the Wular. Some of the problems for regeneration of the forest species are created by the southern aspect of their Valley-facing slopes. The re-creation of forest cover on Shankaracharya hill is worthy of admiration. However, there are rich montane temperate coniferous forests at a number of places like the valleys of the Lidder, Arpath, Brenghi, Wangat, Erin, Madhumati, Sindh, Lolab, Langet and Handwara. The tree species are the same as those on the Pir Panjal range. The Alpine meadows also have a similar vegetal cover.

The Valley

The rocky basin of Kashmir bounded by the Great and the Lesser Himalayas was occupied by a fresh water lake during the first

Interglacial period of the Quaternary Ice Age. The lake got drained at a later date. The Veth and its tributaries carved out a flood-plain out of this, otherwise, continuous lake bed. This is the Veth lowland. Sections of lake bed are left as isolated mounds or in the form of terraces which constitute the *Wudars* or the Karewa uplands. These occupy more than half the area of the Valley floor (Table 4.1) and form a peculiar feature of Kashmir landscape. When viewed from air, the uplands with their browns or yellows contrast sharply with the greens and greys of the lowland.

From Verinag in the south-east to Kupwara in the north-west the Valley measures 168 km. It has a maximum width of 40 km. The heights above sea level of Anantnag (in the south), Srinagar (in the middle) and Baramulla (in the west) are 1,600; 1,587 and 1,585 m respectively. The average elevation of the Veth plain is 1,585 m. The Karewa uplands range in elevation from 1,645 to 3,800 m.

Kashmir Valley according to Wadia, is an exaggerated instance of a dun or a longitudinal Valley. He has shown the Valley occupying a synclinal on the back of the great Kashmir Nappe. The Himalayan Valleys of Kashmir and Kathmandu and the duns in the outer Himalayas are synclinal troughs enclosed between contiguous anticlinal features. deTerra, on the other hand, opines that structurally the Valley of Kashmir is an inter-montane fault with a sinking tendency relative to the general rising of the mountain belt.

The Veth Lowland

The Veth occupies a deep furrow in the valley floor at an elevation of 1,582 m and flows close to the Himalayan flank, thereby allowing a wide plain along its west bank. This asymmetrical position of the master stream causes great variations in the altitude of the valley outlets on either side of the basin. Whereas, Himalayan streams (the Lidder, Sindh, etc.) enter the Valley at an altitude of 1,615 m, the streams flowing down the Pir Panjal debouch into the Valley at 2,614 m.

The Veth lowland is of the width ranging between 3 to 40 km. It is wide above Sangam and below Srinagar, narrow between these two stations and narrowest near Awantipore. It appears to be a level plain but it slopes from south towards north-west. It comprises water bodies, wetlands and cropland.

Water bodies include stream courses, lakes and canals. The Veth and its tributaries constitute the stream courses. The lakes are Dal, Anchar, Mansbal and Wular. The chief government owned canals of

Kashmir, with lengths in km given in parenthesis, are Zainagir (33), Lar Kol (33), Babul (24), Martand (40), Nandi (20), Dadi (25) and Padshah Kol (14). To this list may be added numerous canals managed by the farmers.

'Nambals' or wetlands get water filled in spring and summer which renders these swampy. Some of these dry up in winter. Examples of such wetlands are Malangpora, Shalun, Lasjan, Batmaloo, Barangoura, Naranbagh and Trigam. Wetlands also abound in deltaic portion of the Sindh, the southern and western shores of the Wular, which support extensive willow plantations. In addition there are the lakelets of Hokarsar, Haigan, Mirgund, Nowgam, etc. The presence of these features indicate that the Valley still is not completely drained (Pascoe, 1973) and the undrained remnants are little more than inundation hollows in the river alluvium. The total area under water bodies, wetlands and lakelets sums up to about 250 sq km. The remaining area of the Veth lowland is formed of recent alluvium which gets renewed due to recurrent floods. This contributes the main cropland of Kashmir. The soils, clay loams, are deep and fertile. These have been cultivated for millennia for raising paddy. Climatic conditions of Kashmir do not permit cultivation of paddy without irrigation. A network of gravity canals serves this cropland. Lift irrigation schemes are also operational at several places. Rice is not only the staple food of the inhabitants of the Valley but also a crop of prestige value to a Kashmiri farmer. Hence, most of the hectarage of this irrigated lowland is under this crop. It is also used for growing temperate fruit like apples, peaches, plums, pears and cherry. A small percentage of this cropland is brought under *rabi* cultivation. The matter of great concern about this fertile, *abiaval*, arable land is its loss, at an unprecedented scale, to the urban sprawl.

Aquifers have been identified in the Valley floor which have aided in the construction of tube wells under artesian conditions. In Srinagar such tube wells were sunk at Bemina (near Govt. College) and Soura east. Aquifers are also traced in Pattan-Palhalan area. At Wanigam, drilling to a depth of 124 m has resulted in the ejection of 900 gallons of water per hour. A similar tube well has been constructed at Kanihama. Artesian conditions have been located in the area to the south of Bijbehara. Here a tube well, each, has been drilled at Sheikhpora and Kuchpora. The popularly believed spring in the Mughal garden of Cheshma Shahi is, in reality, an artesian well.

Srinagar

It is one of the ancient cities of India and its present site has remained unchanged for the last fourteen centuries. At the time of Hiouen

Thsang's visit, in 631 AD, it was confined to the right bank of the Veth, around the Hari Parbat hill and was called the 'new city'. It lay some distance to the north of the old capital, Asoka's Srinagri, which extended from Pandrethan to Atigaj gap.

King Pravarasena II, who ruled Kashmir in second half of 6th century founded the new city which was named Pravarasenpora or Pravarapora, after him. The two capitals, the old and the new, existed side by side for a long time. The new city in due course of time came to be known as Srinagar, meaning, the glorious city. The royal residence, probably shifted to the left bank during the reign of king Ananta (AD 1028–63). New quarters were added by the later kings. These, for example, to quote a few, are Kutubudinpora (Sultan Kutub-ud-Din), Now Shahr (Sultan Zain-ul-Abdin), Nagar Nagar (Mughal emperor, Akbar), Sher Garhi (Afghans), Munshi Bagh and Ram Munshi Bagh (Dogras).

The city occupies a central position in the Valley. It is almost equidistant (50 km) from the major urban centres of Kashmir like Anantnag, Shupiyan, Sopore, Baramulla and Bandipore. It lies more to the east as this is the position taken by the Veth in its wanderings in its alluvial plain. Other stations of Kashmir can be arranged in concentric rings of equal radii with Srinagar as the centre. On the first ring of 15 km radius lie Budgam, Chadura, Pampore, Khunamuh, Nishat and Narabal. The fast spreading tentacles of the capital city have reached these satellite towns. The second ring of 28 km radius comprises Awantipore, Pulwama, Chrari-Sharief, Patan and Sumbal. The last ring consists of Kupwara and Sonamarg.

Contiguity of the Dal lake with the city and penetration of its waters into its land area has resulted in the formation of a number of waterways, bays, inlets, peninsulas and islands. The other water bodies like the Veth, Tsunt Kol, Kuta Kol and Dudganga too have contributed their share of some of these features which for smooth and easy communication had to be connected by bridges (or Kadals). This accounts for the frequent use of the suffix Kadal in the place names of the different quarters of the city like the Amira Kadal, Kani Kadal, Saida Kadal, etc.

One such large island constitutes the commercial, educational, recreational, electronic and other media hub of Srinagar. In it are located the Tourist Reception Centre in the east, Maisuma locality in the west, Government Transport Yard in the north and the Main Branch of State Bank of India in the south. It is bounded in the south and the west by the Veth and on the east and the north by the Tsunt Kol. Nine bridges connect this island with the surrounding areas. But for the high embankments on all sides, this island is prone to the floods in the surrounding water courses. T.R. Swinburne, the author of the book *The Holiday in the Happy Valley* (1907), went to Nedous hotel in a *shikara* as the island was water filled due to breaches in its embankments. The present writer along with other college students, during the devastating flood of September 1950, waded through the rushing water in the Polo ground due to the overflow of flood water at the Tourist Reception Centre bund. The ground level of this island is 3 metres below the highest flood level in the Veth.

On the Veth front from Head Post Office to Sheikh Bagh the stretch of the embankment is called 'The Bund'. The mart on it comprises shops and other commercial establishments which largely cater to the needs of the tourists. Tourists travelling by air or by road first arrive in Srinagar and then disperse to various destinations in the Valley. The return journey also commences from here. In either case they stay in the city where sufficient infrastructure related to tourism has been developed for their comfortable sojourn. During their shopping spree their preference is for Kashmir handicrafts, befittingly stocked in the shops and artistically displayed in the showrooms.

Srinagar is the summer capital of Jammu and Kashmir. Essential supplies to Kargil and Leh either originate or pass through the city, during the road open period, generally June to October. A daily bus service plies between Srinagar and Leh at this time. Regular airways flights connect these two stations throughout the year.

Natural Vegetation

Vegetation of the lowland comprises such deciduous species as chinar (*Platanus orientalis*), poplar (*Populus nigra and P. alba*), willow (*Salix sp.*), mulberry (*Morus sp.*), rubinia (R. Pseudo acacia) and walnut (*Jugulans regia*). Chinar with its huge size and thick foliage adorns shrines, gardens, parks and hamlets. Poplar a tall slender tree forms fine avenues along the Valley roads. Its timber goes in the manufacture of fruit boxes. Willow a tree of medium size is widespread in wetlands. It yields firewood and timber for cricket bats. Its dried leaves are used as fodder in winter. Silkworms are reared on mulberry leaves. It is a protected tree in the state. Walnut wood is used in making wood carving articles, a world famous Kashmir handicraft.

The vegetation in the lakes and other water bodies consists of milfoil (*Myriophyllum verticillum*), (*Kashmiri (Ks.) Kend hill*), weed (*Potamogetan sp.*) (*ks. hill*), duckweed (*Lemna minor*) (*ks. mongoli*), bulrush (*Typha sp.*), (*ks. pech*), lotus (*Nelumbiam speciosum*) (*ks. pamposh*), nymphae (*Limnanthemum nymphoids*) (*ks. khor*) and water nut (*Trapa *bispinosa*) (*ks. ghor*). A curse in the inner channels of the Dal is a weed called water fern (*Salvinia natans*) (*ks. bota khor*) which because of its luxuriant growth chokes these waterways. During summer these water bodies provide ample fodder for livestock. Bulrush is used for making mats. Lotus, its fruit and stem, is consumed by humans so is the trapa which grows profusely in the Wular lake. A variety of vegetables is raised on floating gardens. These are the meeting places of land, water and sunshine. The manure used in these strips of land is the dried and decomposed lake weeds. With the help of unobstructed sunshine abundant and quick growth of vegetables takes place. These are carried in punts to the city markets. These floating gardens are confined to the placid waters of the Dal.

The Karewa Uplands

Karewa uplands, called *Wudars* in Kashmiri, composed of ancient alluvium, are distinguishable into two types. The sloping Karewas or the Karewa foothills correspond to the Lower Karewas of the geologists. What they designate as Upper Karewas, are in geography, termed as flat topped Karewas or Karewa tablelands.

Karewa foothills are situated at the periphery of the Valley along the `Pir Panjal range from south-west to north-west. These lacustrine deposits rest on the slopes of this mountain range and conceal its actual topography. Karewa tablelands are largely situated in the middle of the Valley as isolated blocks. At some places, the tablelands are in contact with the Karewa foothills. A profile of the terrain from Srinagar to the Pir Panjal through Nagam, Charari-Sharief and Yusmarg lays bare the relative position of the physiographic units of Kashmir. From Srinagar to Nagam stretches the Veth lowland. The ascent to the Karewa tableland begins at Nagam. It extends up to Charari-Sharief. The ziarat of Sheikh Nur-ud-Din is situated on a part of flat-topped Karewa. Beyond Chari-Sharief to Yusmarg are Karewa foothills under coniferous forests. Above Yusmarg is the Pir Panjal mountainous tract.

At some places Karewas have been completely eroded by stream action. The Lidder below Ganeshbal provides one such example. Here the soft Karewa rocks are replaced by vast expanses of boulders, gravel and sand. Similar conditions exist in the valleys of Vishau and Sindh.

The isolated tablelands are generally dry and barren whereas the sloping Karewas, because of their situation along the Pir Panjal, are served by canals drawn from mountain streams issuing from it. In favourable locations even Karewa tablelands are irrigated by gravity canals. Lately, water to these uplands is carried through lift irrigation. The soft rocks, of which both the Karewas are composed, are subjected to gully and sheet erosion, when this eroded matter finds its way into the master stream.

Although a major portion of Kashmir population is concentrated in the Veth lowland yet the Karewas are not without their share of towns and villages. Availability of water, possibly, is the only obstacle which prevents their occupation by humans. Wherever such facilities exist, human habitations have come up and land used for raising paddy and other crops. Kashmir history reveals how its benevolent rulers executed number of works of public welfare, including canals to carry water to these barren and sterile Karewas. King Lalitaditya (699–736 AD) constructed a canal to carry water of the Lidder for the irrigation of Martand Karewa. Sultan Zain-ul-Abdin (1420–1470 AD) got a canal constructed to carry water of the Madhumati stream to irrigate Zainagir Karewa. Some of the towns situated over these plateaus are Kulgam, Pulwama, Rajpura, Pampore, Tral, Budgam, Beerwah and Tangmarg. The ziarats of Pakharpore and Baba Rishi are also located in the Karewa country. With the increase in population the demand for new housing colonies is bound to grow. Karewa uplands afford open spaces where future townships can be set up. Ompura, near Budgam, is one such example. Hindustan Machine Tools (HMT) and other factories have been established on Zainakut plateau. For further industrialization, Karewas are likely to tackle the problem of space.

The Sloping Karewas

These extend along the Valley-facing slopes of the Pir Panjal from Hirpur in the south-west through Shadimarg, Yusmarg, Chuntmarg, Pushker, Gulmarg, Baba Reshi, Laridura, Sangri to Nichahom, in the north. The Karewa tract between Handwara and Kupwara, because of the paucity of water, is referred to as Kandi belt. The Karewa foothills are composed of clay, silt and sand. In the absence of irrigation these slopes are brought under maize cultivation. Mostly these foothills are under coniferous forests.

Distribution

1. The foothill region of Yusmarg lies between the streams of Romshi and Dudhganga. At Pakharpore, the Romshi is joined by its tributary the Hakriyej. At the confluence, the streams have cut the Karewa beds in a manner that the vertical walls on either side rise to a height of about 130 metres. Standing in the bed of the Romshi, the exposed beds present an ideal section for their study. The layers of bluish clay, brown sand and dark brown clay are easily identified.

Rohmu on Srinagar-Pakherpore road marks the zone of transition between the upper and lower Karewas. The incline commences from Dharamsal and from Tukarpora begin the sloping Karewas. This foothill region is well peopled as is evident from the number of villages in it. The forests of Yus and Nagabal occupy these slopes. In this foothill region is situated the lakelet, Nilanag of Gogjipathri, at an altitude of 2,180 metres. Its area is 6.3 hectares and is 6.5 metres deep. Its origin is attributed to the sinking of the Karewa beds and the consequent damming of the drainage.

2. The sloping Karewa of *Chuntmarg* is located between the Dudhganga and the Sukhnag streams, whereas the Shaliganga flows through its middle. The outstanding feature of this section is presence of Karewa beds in between the spurs of mountains at elevations of more than 3,000 metres. At Ludrmarg (3,180 m) there are two Karewa masses which abound in plant fossils, hence the site is frequented by palaeontologists. Another peculiarity of this sector is the presence of lignite deposits near Raithan in the valley of Shaliganga. Some of the notable Karewa prominences are Kutabal (2,223 m), Mujapathri (2,306 m), Chuntmarg (2,377 m) Hangu (2,173 m), Yarikhah (2,168 m) and Thral Khun (2,131 m). All these Karewa slopes are under coniferous forests.
3. Baba Reshi foothill region lies between the Ferozepore and the Ningle streams. The 13 km long motorable road link from Tangamarg to Gulmarg runs over the sloping Karewas. These deposits have completely covered the underlying glacial moraines in Gulmarg. To the north of Gulmarg, these foothills continue through the ziarat of Baba Reshi to Kachu and Muqam. Well-preserved plant fossils including oak leaves and trapa fruit are found in these deposits in the valley of the Ningle at Dandamuh. The Karewa foothills around Baba Reshi support a thick forest of deodar.
4. With the Pohru stream as the base the Karewa foothills of *Nichahom* are situated between the Mawar and the Talar streams. It lies at a distance of 12 km from Handwara and is noted for its lignite deposits. These comprise a long belt with two well-defined horizons of lignite. The deposits are estimated at 35 million tonnes by Geological Survey of India (GSI). The high percentage of ash content (25 to 40) and moisture (8–12) make it an inferior quality

fuel. The other characteristics include fixed carbon, 15 to 20 per cent, volatile matter, 30 to 35 per cent and calorific value 4,000 to 5,000 BTU (British Thermal Units) per pound. After converting it into briquets, it is burnt in iron stoves for office heating in winter. It is used in the silk factory at Rambag for heating water for filatures.

The Karewa Tablelands

The Karewa tablelands stand at a height of 60 metres above the Veth lowland. At some places these bound the lowland like garden walls but at other places they stand as islands in it. In addition to clay, sand and silt, these consist of marls and loess. Some of the tablelands on the right bank of the master stream are Martand, Salar, Khirram, Tral, Pampore, Burzahom, Zainigir, Hamal, Drugmulla and Gushi. Kulgam Zainapur, Kuyil, Pulwama, Khanpur, Budgam, Arizal, Tangmarg, Kreri and Singhpora are some of the flat-topped Karewas on the left bank of the Veth.

Distribution

1. The Karewa tablelands, it seems, had fascinated Lalitaditya, the 8th century king of Kashmir. He built a sun temple on Martand Karewa. He selected another flat-topped Karewa, Paraspore Wudar, (ancient Parihaspora) as the site for his new capital. This tableland is situated in the centre of the Valley, and from it, Kashmir presents the appearance of a bowl. During his time the confluence of the Veth and the Sindh took place near this plateau. 'No temple', writes Younghusband, 'was ever built on a finer site than Martand and no city was ever set in more lovely surroundings than Parihaspora.'
2. In Zainapur there are two tablelands separated from each other by the Tongri Kol. These are Baed Wudar and Shael Wudar. In the latter, medicinal herbs are cultivated in an area of 80 hectares by the Regional Research Laboratory. Similar drug farms have been set up at Rajmahal tableland (62 hectares) near Pulwama and at Safapore plateau (105 hectares) on the northern shore of Mansbal lake. Such medicinal herbs can be cultivated on other tablelands also.
3. Flat surface and its elevation make Karewa tablelands an ideal site for an aerodrome. The wudars of Damodar and Kuyil have been utilized for this purpose. Damodar Karewa, the site of Srinagar airport, is 10 km long and 3 to 5 km wide. It is only 14 km distant from Tourist Reception Centre, Srinagar. Kuyil wudar is triangular in shape and is bounded by the Veth and the Wankran.

4. Of the several commercial crops cultivated on the Karewa tablelands the most significant is saffron (*Crocus sativa*) grown in Pampore, since ancient times. Saffron is the monopoly produce of Kashmir and in Kashmir its cultivation was monopolized by Pampore. The saffron fields of Pampore tableland shaped into 2.5 m square beds, surrounded by a drainage channel, are observed on either side of the national highway. The corms of this plant yield good produce in well-drained loamy soils, with very low water table and free from trees which, otherwise, deplete the soil of its moisture content. For about eleven months in a year, the saffron fields present a brown and dry appearance. It is from the third week of October to the second week of November, when saffron flowers appear in their purple glory. Saffron comprises the dried reddish brown stigmas of its flower with purple petals. The flowers are to be plucked with great care. It is an exacting and labour intensive operation.

   During the last four decades saffron cultivation has spread to other flat-topped Karewas in Budgam, Payer, Tral, Nagam and Bijbehara. Pulwama district, of which Pampore tehsil forms a part, had the highest hectarage of 3,728 under saffron cultivation. (Shah, 1998). The area involved in other districts is Budgam 439, Srinagar 210, and Anantnag 29 hectares.

5. An isolated hill situated near Magam has an altitude above sea level of 1,838 metres and it rises to a height of 190 metres above surrounding lowland. On the crest of this hill is the shrine of Baba Rafi-ud-Din. Its core is formed of the Panjal trap, which is covered by a thick mantle of Upper Karewa beds. These consist, bottom upwards, of layers of green sand, clay, marl, whitish yellow silt and brown loamy silt. In the marl bed was found a fragment of a well-fossilized tusk. Limb bones of an antelope were collected from the top layer. de Terra calls this feature as Island Mountain.

Natural Vegetation

The sloping Karewas, which lie on the Pir Panjal slopes, bear coniferous forests, where blue pine predominates on lower elevations, and silver fir forms the upper belt. Broad leaved species occupy wetter spaces within these coniferous forests. These include ash (*Fraxinus floribunda,*) walnut (*Jugulans regia*), maple (*Acerpictum*), horse-chestnut (*Aesculus indica*), poplar (P*opulus ciliata)* and birdcherry (*Prunus pedus*). In the open spaces in these Karewas, maize is cultivated. Walnut trees are found scattered in these maize fields.

Apple and other temperate fruit orchards have been established on irrigated tablelands. Most of the trees, including mulberry, which grow in the lowland are found here. The vegetation is sparse on the dry Karewas. Here rubinia (*Kikar*) does well. Almond orchards are found on some dry Karewas.

The Jhelum Gorge

The upper Jhelum which glides sluggishly through a longitudinal valley, in the Kashmir basin, flows in the middle course through an east-west running transverse valley called the Jhelum gorge. It serves as a natural outlet for the passage of the master stream after collecting entire drainage within the Valley. The gorge begins from Kitchhom, where the ridge line, standing high between 2,000 to 2,500 m, is considered to be the ancient divide, which served as spillway of the Karewa lake.

The Pir Panjal range, with a decreasing altitude west of Gulmarg, forms the southern flank of the gorge. Here it stands like a vertical wall with a forest cover of pine and deodar. Like the Chenab in Kishtwar, the Jhelum cuts through the Pir Panjal range at Uri, 41 km downstream of Baramulla. The northern flank is formed by the Kaz Nag range which extends from the Northern range in the vicinity of Chowkibal towards Baramulla town. Wadia considers Kaz Nag range as trans-Jhelum continuation of the Pir Panjal range with a large development of the crystalline core. The former range is designated after its highest peak, 3,695 m, of the same name.

The Jhelum, which in its upper course is a wide, deep and mature river, gets transformed in the gorge, into a youthful, shallow, foaming, mountain torrent which occupies a narrow rock debris-filled valley much below the ground level. The left bank mountain slopes are steep and forested, while the opposite slopes are gentle but bare. Only a part of the gorge has undergone glaciation as is evident from the absence of moraines from Sheri to Rampore. At Rampore there is a huge deposit of sub-angular boulders lying in a matrix of gravelly sand and brown silt. Moraines and erratics are present in fields, hamlets and river bed. These mostly consist of granites derived from the Kaz Nag range. There is a glacio-fluvial fan overlying ground moraines at Naushera. Such composite fans are a conspicuous feature on either side of the river. The area has undergone rejuvenation as is indicated by the presence of river terraces, four to five in number. The gorge lacks level ground. One of the terraces is utilized for the construction of motorable road to Uri. On these terraces are located clustered settlements and cultivated fields.

Hydroelectricity

The swift flow of the river in the gorge is because of the steep gradient of the ground surface. The difference in R.L. of the river between Kitchhom and Uri in a distance of 30 km is 320 metres. This precipitous terrain of the gorge has created a potential for the generation of hydroelectricity. This environmental asset, by now, stands properly harnessed.

The first power house in Jammu and Kashmir, and second in India after Mysore state, was set up at Mohara in 1907. Since its reconstruction in 1962, it generates 9 MW of electricity. It was followed by the Lower Jhelum hydel project which was commissioned in 1978. It has an installed capacity of 105 MW. The latest to come up, in 1997, is the Uri H.E. Project, with an installed capacity of 480 MW, where a barrage across the river diverts the Jhelum into a 11 km long tunnel which in turn carries the entire volume of water to the underground powerhouse. Another 2 km long tunnel carries the tail-end water, back to the river. Here, it is pertinent to mention that in the 176 km length of the Jhelum in the Valley, from Khanabal up to Kitchhom, neither any hydel project nor any gravity canal stands constructed because of the gentle gradient of the lowland that it traverses.

Minerals

Another environmental asset of the Jhelum gorge is the presence in the rocks of Salkhala series, in the slopes of the Kaz Nag range, of non-metallic mineral ores, like gypsum, graphite and ochre. Gypsum of good quality is found in two parallel bands between Ijara and Dhani-Saiydan. Deposits of graphite extend from Braripora through Lachipura nala, Bagna nala to Islamabad nala. At Nurkhaw, Ratsar and Jhuggi are present deposits of ochre. Deposits of good quality slate arc found at Marpathri and Mohrdor and that of white marble at Hashhipura. In the spurs of gorge is found metallic mineral ore of galena. Felspar occurs in Kaz Nag granites.

Communication

In the past the gorge, a low level pass, provided an important line of communication between Kashmir and rest of the world. The road along the right bank has claim to antiquity. It was called the western route. It provided access to west Punjab, Hazara, North-West Frontier Province (NWFP) and Afghanistan. Through it a direct link was established between Kashmir and Kabul, during the Afghan rule in Kashmir (1753–1819 AD). It was a much frequented route, then, for obvious reasons. Another road existed along the left bank which Uri onwards crossed the Haji Pir pass to reach Poonch. On account of its low elevation of 2,590 m, the pass remained open throughout the year. The first 313 km long cart road, linking Srinagar with Kohala, called Jhelum valley road, built along the left bank of the river, was completed in 1890. It opened Kashmir to the outside world.

Uri (1,360 m), the tehsil headquarters is the only urban centre in the gorge. It was, among other places, rocked by an earthquake, of the magnitude of 7.6 on the Richter scale, with its epicentre at Muzaffarabad, on 8 October 2005. This powerful earthquake caused much loss of life and property in this subregion. Most of the mountains in Uri towards west are composed of the Murree series comprising shales and sandstones of purple colour belonging to the Miocene age. To the east, there is an outcrop of older rocks, mainly the Panjal traps disfigured and crushed by folding and faulting. These two series are sharply cut off from each other by the Main Boundary Fault, a tectonic feature of great significance which separates the sub-Himalaya from the Himalaya.

The Uri-Muzaffarabad road has been reopened, lately, for plying a passenger service, called *Karvane-Aman* and a goods service between Kashmir and, so called, Azad Kashmir.

The Kishenganga Valley

Through a deep narrow canyon, formed by branches of the Great Himalaya, flows the Kishenganga river which skirts the outer slopes of the Northern range of Kashmir. It originates from a nook, where the bifurcation of the ridges takes place, to the west of the Zoji la. In the first instance, up to Gurez, the river flows in east-west direction and later on it acquires a north-south course. The inhabited localities are situated on the left bank of the river on this side of the Line of Control. These in succession are Gurez, Keran and Karnah. The complexities of the terrain in the canyon do not permit a direct contact, either land or riverine, between these places. Each is to be approached by a separate pass from the Valley. Gurez is reached from Bandipore through Razdiangin pass, Keran from Kupwara via Sonapind gali and Karnah from Chowkibal through Nestichuen pass.

In Gurez a number of hamlets, in the upper Kishenganga, lie scattered in a linear fashion along the left bank much above the river level. The altitude of Gurez is 2337 metres. Tilel lies some distance upstream of Gurez. A proposed hydel project on the river involves construction of a dam on it to divert its water to the power house through a tunnel with the tail-end water flowing into the Wular lake.

Karnah or Tangdhar in the middle Kishenganga occupies a wide stretch of slope with a gentle gradient. Compared to Gurez and Karnah, Keran is an inhabitation of small proportions.

References

Books

Allami, Abul-Fazl (1871): *The Aini Akbari*, translated into English by H. Blochmann, 1965, reprint Adesh Book Depot, Delhi.

Beal, Samuel (1958 reprint): *Travels of Hiouen Thsang,* Sushil Gupta, Calcutta.

Census of India, 1981 (1983), *District Census Handbooks*, Parts XIII, A & B, Anantnag, Pulwama, Srinagar, Budgam, Baramulla, Kupwara.

de Terra, H. and Paterson T.T. (1939): *Studies in Ice Age of India and Associated Cultures,* Carnegie Institution of Washington, D.C.

Directorate of Economics and Statistics (1995–96): *Digest of Statistics,* Jammu and Kashmir Government.

Drew, Frederic (1875): *The Jummoo and Kashmir Territories,* E. Stanford London.

Kaul, A.K. (1985): *Home Geography (Jammu and Kashmir),* Ambanju Publications, Srinagar/Vinod Publications, Ludhiana.

Kaul, M.N. (1994): 'Late Quaternary Glacial and Climatic History of the Lidder Valley' in *Kashmir Himalayas, in India, Geomorphological Diversity,* R.K. Dishit (ed.), Rawat Publications, Jaipur.

Lawrence, Sir Walter R. (1895): *The Valley of Kashmir,* O.U.P. London, 1967 reprint Kesar Publications, Srinagar.

Parimu, Dr R.K. (1969): *A History of Muslim Rule in Kashmir* (1320–1819), Peoples Publishing House, New Delhi.

Pascoe, Sir Edwin H. (1973): *A Manual of Geology of India and Burma,* Controller of Publications, Government of India, New Delhi.

Pococke, E. (1972 reprint): *India in Greece*, Oriental Publications, Delhi.

Shah, S.A. (1988): *Growth and Expansion of Saffron Cultivation in Kashmir and its Impact on Economy and Society,* Unpublished Ph.D. Thesis, Jamia Millia Islamia, New Delhi.

Spate, O.H.K. (1953): *India and Pakistan,* Methuen, London.

Stein, M.A. (1900): *Kalhana's Rajatarangini, A Chronicle of Kings of Kashmir,* Vol I & II, A Constable and Co., London, 1961 edition, Motilal Banarasi Das, Delhi.

Vigne, G.T. (1842): *Travels in Kashmir: Ladakh and Iskardo,* Henry Colburn, London.

Wadia, D.N. (2004): *Geology of India* (21st Reprint), Tata McGraw Hill Publishing Company, New Delhi.

Annexure – I
Dawn of Tourism in Kashmir

Kashmir, as a world famous tourist resort, has been selling many of its geographical assets to the tourists and the sportspersons. It is endowed with such enviable physical features as lofty mountains with snow-clad peaks and forested slopes, glistening glaciers and sizeable snowfields, foaming torrents and shimmering lakes, gushing springs and placid tarns, diverse fauna and varied flora, and above all a salubrious climate. Wakefield in this connection remarks, 'Nowhere in Asia, nor even perhaps in other quarters of the world, can the paralled be found of such an earthly paradise in itself formed by Nature … there lies spread out a wide expanse of verdant plain, a smiling valley, a veritable jewel in Nature's own setting of frightful precipices'.

Humans here have not lagged behind. Their keen intellect and deft fingers have transferred these natural charms on to different hard and soft mediums like walnut wood and Papier-mache, copper and silver articles and Pashmina and woollen shawls. These handicrafts are equally appealing and alluring. Tourists procure them not only as mementos of their Kashmir visit but also as pieces of Kashmir vistas for keeps. Mulk Raj Anand* in the editorial of *Marg* (1955) comments, 'Few parts of our country can show a continuous tradition of arts and crafts than this valley. They seem to have acquired a peculiar sensitiveness to the nuances of the heavenly landscape … from which they took the motifs for decorating cloth, silver, copperware and wood work … and from their struggle to live they evolved … the living traditions of handicrafts which made the word "cashmere" beloved throughout the world, as the synonym of a quality workmanship.'

The multifaceted geographical personality of Kashmir has made it a tourist resort, par excellence, because of its unique setting, extent and content. It is situated within the Great and the Lesser Himalayas, thus sharing the grandeur of both the ranges. Regarding its extent, Arthur Neve remarks, 'The configuration of the mountains is such that fifty Simlas might be built on comparatively level ground on the Kashmir side of the Pir Panjal range'. It comprises the main longitudinal valley, 180x40 km, and a number of delightful transverse valleys, a mature master stream and its cascading tributaries, lush green meadows both upland and alpine, and rock and snow wilds. Variety is the watchword of tourist itinerary in Kashmir. Whereas there is boisterous Pahalgam with an unending roar of the Lidder, it is silence and solitude in Gulmarg; whereas the sylvan environs of Lolab valley exhibit imposing and massy deodars and walnut trees, it is the projecting tongues of hanging glaciers that greet us in Sonamarg; whereas we have the Dal, a lake displaying cheer and

* Anand, Mulk Raj, *Marg*, Vol. III, No. 2, 1955.

charm, it is serene and still in Mansbal. Kashmir, in fact, consists of series of hill stations, diverse and distinct but set within a single frame.

Kashmir by virtue of its varied topography makes provision for a host of recreational activities for the tourist with number of options to choose from. Sight seeing is carried out in a motor vehicle or in a Shikara, on foot or on horseback. Trekking expeditions are conducted to alpine meadows, glaciers and highland lakes. Water sports facilities like swimming, diving, boating and skiing are available in the Gagribal and Nigeen sections of the Dal lake. Mountain streams, well stocked with trout fish, become the haunts of anglers. For professional and amateur photographers there are innumerable subjects to shoot. Gulmarg, besides being the tourist destination in summer, hosts winter sports. It has the finest ski slopes in the world. Those who arrive in Kashmir, for rest and relaxation, find ample and ideal situations for indulging in such luxury.

Tourism in Kashmir is about 120 years old important economic activity and the contribution of Europeans in laying its sound foundation is praiseworthy. They were instrumental in giving exposure to its scenic splendour by publicizing it. The first to arrive were Bernier (1665), Father Desideri (1714), George Forester (1783), and Moorcroft and Jacquemont (1822). A number of administrators, engineers, doctors, missionaries, educationists, and travellers arrived in Kashmir when it was under Dogra rule. Some of these were in the employment of respective maharajas. This period witnessed the appointment of a British Resident and its staff in the state. With the opening of the Jhelum valley road, in 1890, a steady trickle of foreign visitors entered Kashmir despite the travails of travel, when part of the journey from Kohala to Baramulla had to be undertaken in a horse-driven cart and the rest of it up to Srinagar in a *doonga* boat which had to cross the Wular lake and had to be towed against the current of the river. It is from this point of time that the creation of tourist infrastructure in Kashmir was initiated. The foreigners favoured Gulmarg as a stopover in Kashmir. It shot into prominence and got developed as a European style tourist resort, the aura of which it still exhibits. Construction of houseboats, under the guidance of Martyn T. Kennard, to provide cosy and floating accommodation in Srinagar, was another step in this direction.

These early birds were so enamoured by the natural charms of Kashmir that they wrote articles and books on it. The first to do so was, a Frenchman, Francois Bernier. Some of the other authors, who followed, were Moorcroft and Trebeck, Vigne, Hugel, Drew, Wakefield, Stein, Lawrence, Arthur Neve, Moore, Duke, Miss Morrison, Miss Pirie, Swinburne, Younghusband, Ernest Neve, Biscoe, and Milne (see list of books given in bibliography). Through these works Kashmir got introduced to France and to the English speaking world. Kashmir, also, reached Europe, by the close of 18th century, through its exquisite *Cashmere* shawl which was graced by Napolean when he adorned, with his own hands, the amorous bust of his beloved Georgina with it.

In the history of tourism in Kashmir, 1988 marks the peak year of tourist influx with a record number of 7.22 lakh persons. Out of these, 5.99 lakh were the domestic tourists from various parts of the country when the share of foreigners was 59,000. In addition, 95,000 persons came to Kashmir in connection with the annual pilgrimage to holy Amar Nath. During the eighties of the last century development of the tourism infrastructure, particularly hotel room capacity, received impetus in view of two occurrences. One, was the soaring trend of the tourist arrivals, when it crossed the figure of 5 lakh persons in 1978 against the 1.67 lakh of 1974, which created an urgent need for additional board and lodging facilities. Second, was the easy availability of liberal grants from the government agencies and loans from the commercial banks. Tourist arrivals surged to more than a million in the year 2011–2112.

Bibliography (Annexure – I)

1837 Moorcroft, William and Trebeck, George, *Travels in Hindustan,* 1971 reprint, Sagar Publications, New Delhi.

1842 Vigne, G.T. Already Given (A.G.) on page 79.

1845 Hugel, Baron Charles, *Kashmir and the Panjab,* 1972 reprint, Life and Light Publishers.

1846 Moore, Thomas, *Lalla Rookh,* George C. Harrap, London.

1853 Schonberg, Baron Eric Von, *Travels in India and Kashmir,* two vols., Hurst and Blacket, London.

1863 Torrens, H.D. *Travels in Ladakh, Tartary and Kashmir,* Otley, London.

1875 Drew, Frederic (A.G. on Page 79).

1879 Wakefield, W. *The Happy Valley,* Sampon Low, London.

1895 Lawrence, Sir Walter R. (A.G. on Page 79).

1900 Neve, Arthur, *Picturesque Kashmir,* Sands & Co., London.

1900 Stein, M.A. (A.G. Page 79).

1904 Morrison, Margaret Cotter, *A Lonely Summer in Kashmir,* Duckworth & Co., London.

1906 Pirie, P. *Kashmir, The Land of the Streams and Solitude,* John Lane, The Bodley Head, London.

1907 Swinburne, T.R. *A Holiday in Happy Valley with Pen and Pencil,* Smith Elder & Co., London.

1909 Younghusband, Sir Francis, *Kashmir,* Adan and Charles Black, London.

1914 Bernier, Francois, *Travels in the Mughal Empire,* Archibald Constable, London. (English translation, original in French)

1914 Neve, Ernest F. *Beyond the Pir Panjal,* Church Mission Society, London.

1925 Biscoe, C.E. Tyndale, *Kashmir in Sunlight and Shade,* Seeley Service & Co., London.

1928 Neve, Ernest F. *A Crusader in Kashmir,* Seeley Service & Co, London.

1935 Milne, James, *The Road to Kashmir,* Holder & Stoughton, London.

1971 Doughty, Marion, *Afoot Through Kashmir Valley,* (Reprint) Sagar Publications, New Delhi.

Annexure – II
Visayas or Parganas

In ancient times Kashmir kingdom was divided into two administrative units. The part of the valley to the south of Srinagar was called *Madavarajya* which, with the passage of time, got abbreviated to *Maraz.* The other half to the north of Srinagar was designated as *Kramaraja* or *Kamraz.* A line roughly drawn east to west, passing through the confluence point of Tsunt Kol with the Veth and take off point of Kuta Kol from it, formed the boundary between the two domains or the districts. Here, by inference, it may be stated that by the close of 6th century AD Pandrethan, the old capital, was situated in Maraz and Pravarasenpura, the new capital, was located in Kamraz.

This ancient and basic administrative structure found favour with the later rulers of Kashmir and has been in continuous use up to the present times. During the Mughal rule, as reported by Abu-l-Fazl, in his *Ain-i-Akbari,* the entire city of Srinagar formed part of Maraz. Kamraz comprised the remaining territory to the north of the city. This arrangement continued during the rule of the Dogras. The Valley in 1941 (Table 1.2), consisted of only two districts of Anantnag and Baramulla which were analogous, but for their names, with Maraz and Kamraz. It was at a later date that district Anantnag was split into two districts of Anantnag and Srinagar.

Madavarajya and Kramarajya were further divided into sub-districts called *visayas* in ancient and *parganas* in the medieval times. Below is given a list of these sub-districts with their Sanskrit and Kashmiri names. Against each visaya is given the name of few specimen villages including those which still have the given pargana name as their suffix. The number noted against each village is its 1981 census location code. Urban areas are denoted by letter 'U'. The present tehsil level location of each visaya is also attempted. The spellings of the place names printed in the Census District Directories – 1981 have been reproduced, as far as possible, in original.

(A) Madavarajya or Maraz

	Name		Villages & Towns	Present Tehsil-level Location
	Sanskrit	*Kashmiri*		
1	Phakhuva	Phak	Saidpora Bala (40), Danihama (39) Murrind Darbag (41) Harwan (U-5)	Srinagar
2	Khaduvi	Vihi	Pantachok (7) Zewan (5) Khonamuh (1)	Srinagar
			Khrew (240), Lodhuv (228) Letapora (6), Pampur (U)	Pulwama

Cont'd...

...Cont'd

3	Holada	Vular	Awantipora (3) Rajpora Olar (1) Nowgam Olar (35) Kanipora Olar (36) Reshipora Olar (37)	Pulwama
			Chiva Olar (34) Monghama Olar (30), Narasthan (6) Sotura (4), Tral (U)	Tral
4	Daksinapara	Dachunpor	Kular (18), Salar (22) Lewar (66) Katsu (63)	Pahalgam
			Marhama (2) Wagahama (3)	Bijbehara
5	Vamaparsva	Khovurpor	Hutmurah (25), Akura (6) Pushkriri (2) Nowpura Khovurpora (22)	Anantnag
6	Martanda	Matan	Krangsoo (26), Ranbirpora (27) Bonagund (8), Matan (U)	Anantnag
7	Anyech	Anantnag	Mirungund (170), Sifan (169), Anchi Doru (157)	Anantnag
			Sarsuna Anantnag (15) Batapora Anantnag (277)	Kulgam
8	Kapatesvara	Kuthar	Kot Hair (54), Nowgam Kothar (57) Kriri Kothar (35), Sahibabad (74) Shangas (51) Uttarsoo (50) Achabal (U)	Anantnag
9	Bhrnga	Breng	Nala Sund Brari (123) Danvethpora (129), Sogam (130) Kokernag (U)	Anantnag
10	—	Shahabad Ver	Verinag (34), Nowgam Shahabad (46), Nowpora Shahabad (14) Hillar Shahabad (54), Kriri Shahabad (22) Doru (31).	Doru
11	Devasarsa	Divsar	Qasba Devsar (70), Adigam Dewsar (166), Bona Devsar (71), Tarigam Devsar (82), Zeipora Devsar (65) Nowgam Devsar (52)	Kulgam
			Sangran Devsar (72)	Doru
12	Karala/ Ardhavana	Arwin	Ashthal (181), Gadar (109) Lirow (183), Kakran (170) Arwin (288), Kaimoh (33), Redwana (34), Khudwani (24)	Kulgam
13	Jainapura	Zainpur	Batapora Zainpora (258)	Kulgam
			Zainapora (6)	Shupiyan
14	—	Suparsamun	Hirpora (131), Reshnagri (28), Wachi (2) Sedhove (130) Shupiyan (U)	Shupiyan
15	—	Sukru	Drabhgam (124), Kalampur (127), Bilow Oder Gund (112), Sona Samilo (111)	Pulwama

Cont'd...

...Cont'd

16 —	Savur	Payer (79), Now Nagri (33), Batnoor Showra (63), Banderpora Shora (30), Sinza Showrah (52), Yadri Showrah (53), Odar Showrah (59),	Pulwama
17 —	Chrath	Romu (142), Gusu (146), Ratnipora (15), Goripora (14), Kakapora (213),	Pulwama
		Arigam Chrath (100), Banderpora Chrath (8), Moghulpora Chrath (82), Reshipora Chrath (10)	Pulwama
18 Nagrama	Nagam	Nagam (70), Wagora (32), Gogjipathri (Nilnag) (100), Chrari-Sharief (72)	Chadura
		Arigom (40)	Budgam
19 Iksika	Yech	Karewa Damodar (11), Guda Sathu (20), Ichgam (19), Ichkot (124), Lalgam (23).	Budgam
		Sumer Bogh (9)	Chadura
		Ichehama (152)	Beerwah
		(B) Kramarajya or Kamraz	
20 Dvavimsati	Dunts	Hokalatri (65), Pethakoot (66), Larabal (70), Sangrampora (54)	Beerwah
21 Bahurupa	Biru	Beeru (155), Drang (111) Khag (140), Poshker (146) Sone Pah (50)	Beerwah
22 —	Manchhom	Mulemanchi Hama (26), Rathsun (167), Arıpanthan (162)	Beerwah
23 Parihaspora	Parspor	Dewar Yakhmanpora (38), Gund Khalil (31) Trigam (32), Panji Nara (34)	Sonawari
24 Abhyantara kotta	Andrkoth	Rakh Asham (21) Sumbal (25), Markundal (17), Hajin (70)	Sonawari
25 Bhangila	Bangil	Chandi Lura (18), Mula Bangil (78), Osan Bangil (42)	Tangmarg
		Sherpora Bangil (24), Waripora Bangil (19)	Baramulla
26 Pattana	Patan	Pattan (57), Palhalan (60), Taper Waripora (66)	Barımulla
27 Tailagrama	Tilgam	Frastahar Tilagam (76), Tilagam (40), Sherpora Tilagam (100)	Baramulla
28 Krodhana	Kruhin	Kanispora (169), Hewan (147), Sheri Narwav (148), Baramulla (U)	Baramulla
29 Samala	Hamal	Wangam (46), Nowgam (102) Hajan (76), Kalam Chakla (110)	Handwara

Cont'd...

...Cont'd

30 —	Machpur	Bada Kot Machipora (124), Krim Har (133), Nicha Hama (148), Badr Kol (127), Rajpora (143), Handwara (U)	Handwara
31 Uttara	Uttara	Gushi (81), Haihama (73), Panzgom (107), Kupwara (U)	Kupwara
32 Laulaha	Lolab	Sogam (30), Darapur (31) Lalpur (32), Dever Inderbugh (40), Kroshan (27)	Kupwara
33 Zainagiri	Zainagir	Sagipora (1) Zalura (2), Wadura (8) Bumai (11), Sopore (U)	Sopore
34 Khuyasrama	Khuyhom	Mantrigam (32) Ahim Sharief (38) Konan Baba Gund (45) Gamroo (47), Sonarwani (55) Nadihal (56) Bandipore (U)	Bandipore
35 Lahara	Lar	Kangan (22) Wangat (28) Manigam (43) Tulmulla (107) Qasba Lar (117) Chunt Valiwar (119) Ganderbal (U)	Ganderbal

5

The Himalayan Kashmir (II)

Drainage

The Jhelum

The main drainage artery of Kashmir is the Jhelum. Its source is the spring of Verinag situated in south Kashmir. The Verinag stream joins the Sandren, one of the three tributary streams that drain the south-eastern part of the mountain girdle. The other two are Brenghi and Arpath. All the three streams combine at Khanabal. This place onwards the Jhelum becomes a deep and leveed river up to Baramulla. Below Khanabal it is joined by the Lidder on its right bank.

Sangam marks the confluence of the Jhelum with the combined streams of the Vishau and Rembiar. It becomes a river of ample volume after this merger. A series of tributaries flowing down the Himalayan and the Pir Panjal slopes join it on its either bank. It then passes through Srinagar. The Sindh joins it at Shadipore. The Jhelum enters the Wular lake on its south at Banyari and leaves it at its north-west corner and flows through Sopore and Baramulla. The right bank tributary below Sopore is the Pohru. Within the Valley, it is a meandering and a mature river. Khanabal to Kitchom it covers a distance of 176 km.

From Kitchom begins the gorge where the river changes into a youthful torrent. At Domel it is first joined by the Kishenganga and then some distance downstream by the Kunhar, on its right bank. It turns south at Kohala and forms the western boundary of the state. Mangala Multipurpose Project is constructed on it at Mirpur. This station onwards, it becomes one of the five rivers of the Punjab. From its source to its confluence with the Chenab, at Trimmu, total length of the river is 720 km.

The Name

This master stream of Kashmir is called the Veth. 'This modern designation', according to Stein, 'is direct phonetic derivation of the ancient,

Sanskrit, *Vitasta,* which we meet among the river names of the *Rigveda'*. The immediate Prakrit form *Vidasta* appears to be adapted by the Greeks and the Romans. Ptolemy calls it *Bidaspes.* The Jhelum is the name given to it at a later date. Alberuni, in his Kitab-ul-Hind writes '... the river Biyatta known as Jailam, from the city of this name on the western bank'. Pir Ghulam Hassan Khuyhami mentions that the Sanskrit name of the river is *Vitasta* and it is called *Behat* in Persian. In this context the following statement of Lawrence is pertinent. 'The Hydaspes of the ancients, the Vedesta of the Hindus, is known to Kashmiris as the Veth, when it leaves Kashmir at Baramulla it is called the *Koshur Darya* and after joining the Kishenganga it is spoken as the Jhelum river.' In this volume the Veth corresponds to the Upper Jhelum and the *Koshur Darya* to the Middle Jhelum as termed by de Terra (de Terra and Paterson, 1939).

Birthday Festival

The legend has it that after the desiccation of lake *Satisara,* Kasyapa prayed to Siva for blessing Kashmir with a river. The latter struck the ground with his trident when water gushed forth, in the form of a river, from the fissure called *Nilakunda* or *Nilanaga.* The spring on account of its situation in the 'pargana' of Ver came to be called, at a later date, as Verinag.

The people of the Valley celebrated the birthday of the river on *Vethatruvah,* the thirteenth day of the bright fortnight of Bhadoon (August). It was an expression of gratitude for the numerous favours bestowed upon them by it. Besides being a significant element of their environment it fulfilled all their needs of water – drinking, bathing and washing. It functioned as a means of recreation when they partook in outings by means of boat rides. Above all, it served as the main highway of trade and travel.

On this night, among other things, burning earthenware lamps on dry grass floats, and flowers were offered to the Veth. The public involvement and enthusiasm was so intense that even, the benevolent ruler of Kashmir, Sultan Zain-ul-Abdein, participated in this festivity. The festival was observed even during the rule of the Mughal emperor Jehangir (1605–1626 AD) who presents its first hand account in his Tuzuk. It reads, 'On the night of Thursday, the 13th, the Kashmiris had lined with lamps both sides of the Bihat. It is an ancient custom ... undoubtedly lamp lighting was good. I sat in a boat and went round to see it'.

The Upper Jhelum

The Veth occupies a longitudinal furrow in the Valley floor which runs in south-east to north-west direction from Verinag to Banyari, on the

Wular lake. This peculiarity the Upper Jhelum shares with other rivers in the western Himalayas like the Upper Indus in Ladakh and the Chenab in Jammu. It occupies the deepest part of the Valley floor hence all streams, draining the inner slopes of the mountain girdle, pour their volumes of water into it. It attains the role of a master stream. 'In the middle', mentions Nilamatpurana, 'flows making as it were the parting of the hair – the Vitasta ... visibly born of the Himalayas'.

It has been the binding force which united and gave coherence to Kashmir. Much of the Valley could be reached through this master stream – its tributaries and canal linked lakes – with the help of flat bottomed wooden boats of various shapes and sizes. Throughout the chequered history of Kashmir, the Veth has been witness to the rise and fall of many ruling dynasties.

Physical Attributes

The total length of the Veth from Khanabal to Baramulla is 164 km (Table 5.1) and its catchment area within the Valley is 10,100 sq km. The river is navigable from Khanabal to Khadinyar. For this portion of its length it is a mature and graded river which flows sluggishly in a meandering course through the soft Pleistocene beds. Graded nature of the river is indicated by its almost imperceptible gradient. The fall in the gradient from Khanabal to Srinagar is 9 cm in a km, when it is 7 cm in a km in the stretch of the river from Srinagar to Banyari. The river, therefore, flows more slowly below Srinagar than above it.

The river meanders heavily in Khanabal-Banyari section because of the fact that its thalweg length is 130 km against the road length of 100 km. The prominent meanders are observed at Sangam, Lethapora, Pampore, Shivpora and Panznor. The Veth a leveed river is also alluvial in character. It flows in a single channel confined within the embankments. The river divides the Valley floor into two unequal parts. Along its right bank it glides past mountain spurs and Karewa precipices. There is a wide plain along its left bank. The river is wide above and below Srinagar. At Bijbehara it is 91 m wide and has a depth of 3 to 3.6 metres. It narrows down as it passes through Srinagar where its width is 60 to 75 m and a depth of 4.2 to 6.2 metres. The narrow width together with obstructions created by the piers of bridges makes the city vulnerable to floods. A 0.6 metre high weir at Chattabal raises the level of the river in the city during the lean periods of its flow. On the west of the weir is a lock system which facilitates boat traffic on it. At Shadipore is the confluence of the Veth with its right bank tributary of the Sindh. Between Srinagar and Shadipore the river has a width of 121 m. At Sumbal, the Veth is the widest (213 m). Here, push back of the Wular lake slackens its speed when the river water appears to flow backwards. The sediment in it undergoes a churning movement with bottom particles rising to the top and vice versa.

Table 5.1
Jhelum Thalweg in Kashmir*

Distance in km	Station	R.L. in Metres
(A) Upper Jhelum or the Veth		
0	Khanabal	1586.98
20	Sangam	1584.80
35.5	Awantipora	1584.69
71.5	Padshahi Bagh	1580.36
76.5	Munshi Bagh	1580.14
86.5	Gagarzu	1578.86
103.2	Shadipur	1577.78
113.2	Asham	1577.06
130.0	Banyari	1575.35
149.5	Sopore	1573.88
164.2	Baramulla	1572.15
(B) Middle Jhelum or the Gorge		
176.0	Kitchhom	1557.52
206.0	Uri	1237.0

* From the book, *Flood Control, Drainage and Reclamation in Kashmir Valley* by H.L. Uppal, CWPC, New Delhi, 1956.

Banyari, on the southern shore of the Wular lake is the entry point of the Veth into it. It deposits its entire load of sediment in the lake and builds a lacustrine delta in it. The river water as it enters the lake is of coffee colour and when it leaves the Wular it is sage green. The Upper Jhelum from Verinag to Wular completes its first life cycle in the Valley. The river flows in the mountain stage from its source to Khanabal, through plain stage up to Banyari. It forms a lacustrine delta in the Wular and merges with it.

Part of the river from Sopore to Khadinyar is called outfall channel. Here the river is joined by the Pohru and a number of hill torrents. Huge deposits of rock waste are poured into the river in this section. The raised bed of the river impedes the free flow of river water. The outfall channel, consequently, has been an area of concern in the hydrology of Kashmir. The river ceases to be navigable below Khadinyar with the presence of first rapid in its bed.

The Tributaries

The tributaries of the Veth can conveniently be grouped into three clusters, depending upon the part of the mountain girdle drained by them. These tributary clusters are the Himalayan, the Pir Panjal and the north-western. The Himalayan tributaries join the master stream on the right bank, the Pir Panjal tributaries on the left bank and the north-western drainage below Sopore on the right bank.

The Himalayan Tributaries

The Sandren

This is the southernmost of the Himalayan tributaries which has its source in the tarn of Sarbal, below the Kaukut peak. For the first part of its course, it occupies a narrow valley which widens near the Verinag spring, water of which enters it at Bunagund. The Sandren in winter is reduced to a trickle. It is the water of the Verinag spring which feeds the Veth throughout the year. The total length of the Sandren, up to Hainz Danter, is 53 km.

The Brengi

The Eastern range from the Sunderkanthi peak in the south to the Margan pass is drained by several mountain torrents, the chief being the Ahlan, the Raziparyin and the Nowbugh, each occupying a separate valley. These combine together at Vailo to give rise to the Brenghi stream. It flows through a wide boulder covered bed carrying a small volume of water. To it is added the water of a number of springs situated in its valley including that of Kokernag.

The Arpath

It rises from the Panchalthan part of the Eastern range and drains the Kuthar area. It flows through the town of Anantnag. Into it enters the water of the copious springs of Anantnag and Achabal. The Arpath joins the Brenghi at Mir Danter and the combined stream unites with the Sandren at Hainz Danter near Khanabal.

The Lidder

This stream drains the high alpine region of the eastern Kashmir dotted with glaciers, snowfields and tarns. From the Sheshnag tarn flows out the east Lidder which passes through Chandenwari to Pahalgam. It flows down the steep bed, with a roar, in rapids, losing an elevation of 1,830 m in a distance of 21 km. The west Lidder rises from the snout of the Kolahoi glacier and flowing through Lidderwat and Aru, joins the east Lidder at Pahalgam. In 35 km length of the west Lidder, the fall in the stream bed is 1,280 metres. The west Lidder drains a larger area than the east Lidder. Pahalgam onwards, the valley of Lidder narrows down. The rapids in the stream are distinct and frequent. Below Ganeshbal, it flows through a wide valley with the bed filled with boulders of all sizes. Near Okur, the stream splits into branches which join the Veth at Gur and Odur.The total length of the Lidder is 66 km and it has a catchment area of 1,160 sq km which remains snowbound for about nine months in a year.

Lidder Thalweg*

Km	*Station*	*Altitude (metres)*
0	Sheshnag	3575
16	Chanhaij	2249
21	Pahalgam	2195
30	Batakut	1951
37	Ganeshbal	1869
66	Gur	1595

*From Uppal – 1956

The thalweg of the Lidder stream shows a very steep slope from the source to Chanhaij where the fall in elevation is 1,326 m in 16 km. For the next 5 km the stream bed has a gentle slope. From Pahalgam to Ganeshbal it is steep when Ganeshal onwards it is again gentle.

Sangam

Sangam, which means confluence, is the meeting place of the Veth, draining the Himalayan slopes of the south-eastern Kashmir and the combined streams of the Vishau and the Rembiar, coming from the Pir Panjal slopes of south-western Kashmir. Both the water courses at the confluence carry almost equal volumes of water. The gauge station here records the water level of the river.

The Arpal

Downstream of Sangam, the first right bank tributary is Arpal which issues from Hajnar in the valley formed by the Wasterwan and the Kamlawan spurs. Water of the Arpal spring joins it and is named after it.

The Arpal joins the Veth at Chraligund, on the national highway, south of Awantipore. The stream up to national highway flows in a direction, almost opposite to that of the master stream, but after passing below the bridge it flows in same direction as the Veth, just before its confluence with it. Such stream behaviour, in Kashmir, has relevance to its Late Tertiary drainage (Annexure – I).

The Marsar Stream

With its source in high altitude lake of Marsar, in the Kolahoi region, the Marsar stream flows west through a narrow defile and passes through world famous wildlife sanctuary of Dachigam. Part of the water of this stream is diverted into the Harwan reservoir. Rest of it flows as Arra stream. Lower down it forms the Telbal nala and joins the Dal. The Marsar stream leaves the Dal through the lock system at Dalgate and assumes the name of Tsunt Kol, which joins the master stream at Gowkadal. Opposite to this confluence, near Shergarhi, leaves the outflow channel of the Kuta Kol.

The Veth in Srinagar

The total length of the Veth in Srinagar between Munshi Bagh and Chattabal is 12.0 km. It flows here at the rate of 2.4 km per hour. The river undergoes two right angled bends, one near Lal Ded hospital and the other at Zainakadal. In the first instance it flows in southeast to north-west direction up to the first bend, wherefrom it moves from south to north. After Zainakadal it turns north west. The river is approached through numerous landing places called *ghats* or *yarbals,* comprising steps made of hewn Triassic limestone blocks which descend to the water's edge and even below it. Boats, both residential and cargo, line the river banks in the city. In addition to houses, the water front is dotted by temples, *Khanqahs* and mosques.

The Dal Lake

All the big lakes of Kashmir are situated in or below Srinagar along the right bank of the Veth. The Dal, lake charming of Kashmir, is located in the eastern part of Srinagar. The area of this large lake has now shrunk, from 24 sq km before 1947, to 19.6 sq km. A substantial area of the lake in the west and the north-east is marshy and covered by floating gardens.

A causeway was built across the Dal by Mahesh Shanker Das Chaudhary, adviser to Mughal governor Saif Khan in 1666, to link Rainawari quarter of Srinagar with Nishat and Ishabor. It divided the lake into two unequal parts. To allow intra-lake movement of boats, the traditional, seven bridges were built on this causeway. At a later date another causeway was built to link Rainawari with Hazratbal and Naseem Bagh. Today, the two major sections of the lake are the Bod (big) Dal in the north and Lokut (small) Dal in the south. Each portion has an island in the middle. The depth of the Bod Dal is 4 to 5 m and that of the small Dal 2.6 to 3 m. Telbal nala carries lot of silt into the Bod Dal and makes its water turbid. The other minor, yet striking, sections of the lake are Gagribal and Nigeen, where most of the house boats are moored. The bathing boats, confined to these lakelets, provide facilities for swimming and water skiing. Of all the parts of the Dal, the Nigeen is the deepest with a depth of 5.2 to 5.5 m.

The colourful and cosy shikaras or water taxis, with amusing names, gliding gracefully on the lake surface, take the occupants for joy-rides. Hundreds of small boats carry lake produce to city markets. These and other tourism related activities provide means of livelihood to a large proportion of Kashmir population, living in and around Dal.

The surface of the Dal lake in the west, in summer, is covered by large, round, velvety green leaves of the lotus plants. Its pink flowers are carried aloft on their slender stems.

The lock system at Dalgate regulates boat traffic between the Dal and the Tsunt Kol as the water level in the lake stands at a higher level than that of the stream.

This elegant gift of nature did not escape the attention of the humans. Tirthas and temples were built round it in ancient times. The Mughals embellished its shores by laying-out terraced gardens. They also built an observatory on a spur of the Zabarwan hill called Pari Mahal. On the western shore of the Bod Dal stands the imposing and venerable dargah (shrine) of Hazratbal which is a repository of the holy relic of the Prophet. A boulevard round the lake from Dalgate to Brein and a palace on the southern shore of the Gagribal lake was built by the last Dogra ruler, Hari Singh.

The environmentalists are deeply distressed regarding the future of this much adored gem of a lake. Its area is fast shrinking due to encroachments where water is being replaced by land. The quality of its water is deteriorating due to the entry into it of pollutants including chemical fertilizers and pesticides from the surrounding cropland and orchards. The major pollutant is the untreated human excreta which empties into it from house boats, floating on it and houses and hotels built in it.

Given below is the break up of the area, in sq km, of the Dal lake computed by Environmental Engineering Department of J &K Government.

(A)	Present (1985) Area	:	19.6
(i)	Open Water Area	:	11.7
(ii)	Floating Gardens	:	3.9
(iii)	Marshes	:	2.6
(iv)	Land	:	1.4

The Anchar Lake

This lake with an area of 19.4 sq km and a depth of 2.5 metres is situated to the north of Srinagar. As the Sindh stream debouches into it with a heavy load of sediment it is fast silting up and appears more like a marsh than a lake. In the delta of the Sindh, formed along the northern shore of the lake, the land obtained has been brought under paddy cultivation. Wicker willow imported from England by Mr Abbey, in 1918, grows on the mud flats of the lake. It provides raw material for a famed Kashmir handicraft of basket making. The lake produce includes fodder for cattle, weeds for ducks and lotus stems for humans. Horses are found feeding on the succulent marsh grass in shallow parts of the lake. It is connected with the Dal lake through nala Amir Khan. Its open water area is 700 hectares.

The Sindh

This local stream of Kashmir, which rises and loses its identity within the Valley, is by virtue of its name and its situation along Srinagar-Leh road, often, mistaken for the mighty Indus or the Sindh, flowing through Ladakh.

This longest tributary of the Veth drains the highest part of Kashmir Himalaya. Below Sonamarg, it cuts through the Northern range giving rise to Gagangir gorge. In this section the drop in water level is 152 metres in a road distance of 4 km because of which it flows in several large rapids. It flows as a foaming torrent up to Kangan where it is joined by the Wangat stream. At Fatehpore it gets divided into several branches which enter the Anchar lake and other adjacent marshes. It leaves the lake in a single channel to join the Veth. The stream is navigable from Ganderbal to Shadipore. Building materials like sand and gravel collected from the stream bed are valued for their quality. Drift wood is also collected at Ganderbal. Haran, a large willow plantation in the wetlands of the Sindh delta, with an area of 1,268 hectares, is managed by the State Forest Department.

The Sindh Thalweg*

Distance in km	*Station*	*Altitude (metres)*
0	Source	—
4.5	Panjtarni	3,662
8.5	Sangam	3,569
16.0	Bazkhoran	2,911
18.5	Baltal	2,880
32.0	Sonamarg	2,668
45.0	Gagangir	2,306
55.5	Gund	2,097
73.0	Wusan	1,729
88.0	Dudarhom	1,584
104.0	Shadipore	1,577

* From Uppal, 1956

This 104 km long stream exhibits a fall in gradient of 2,085 m from Panjtarni to its confluence with the Veth. It has steep gradient of 1,365 m up to Gagangir, below which the slope is relatively gentle, with a drop in level of 729 m.

The Mansbal Lake

This small but enchanting lake is 3.8 km long and three quarters of a kilometre wide with an area of 280 hectares. This is the deepest lake in the Valley floor and has a maximum depth of 14.3 metres. Its bed is supposed to be deeper than the bed of the Jhelum gorge at Kitchom. The origin of the lake is attributed to the subsidence of tne underlying strata. The lake is fed by a large number of springs, both cold and warm. In winter when snow collects on the water of the lake some blanks are observed in this otherwise white and frosty surface which indicate the sites of the warm water springs. It is surrounded by the Karewa tableland on the north, limestone prominences in the east and an isolated hill, Ahateng, in the south. It is connected with the Veth at Sumbal by a short canal which leaves the lake on the west.

Sonawari

The reclamation of land, constructing embankments, dewatering the area reclaimed and providing it, subsequently, with irrigation facilities has converted the low lying area extending from Sumbal to Banyari, from *Saenwaer* (deep bowl) into *Sonawaer* (a bowl of gold), during the sixties of the last century. The above-mentioned area was frequently subjected to floods in the river and the only means of livelihood left were fishing and collection of water nut in the Wular lake.

Sonawari block, with its headquarters at Sumbal, comprises 87 villages, spread over an area of 3,000 hectares of land and supporting a population of more than a lakh persons. The programme of national reconstruction initiated with the launching of Five-Year Plans, involved the construction of 1,328 km long embankments to a height of RL 1,580. Pump sets were installed for dewatering purposes and canals built for irrigation. These measures brought about a phenomenal transformation in the occupational pattern of the affected population, as in the reclaimed area, cultivation of paddy was introduced together with planting of mulberry trees and laying of orchards. This was in addition to their traditional vocations. Co-operative societies were established for the marketing of the produce.

The Wular Lake

It has the distinction of being the largest fresh water lake of India. It measures 20 km by 8 km, under normal conditions, and has an area of 168 sq km at R.L. 1,578.8 metres. Its average depth is 4.7 m. It is shallow on the south but in the north it has a depth of 9.1 metres. The boundaries of the lake are irregular on the south and the west where it is thrown into numerous bays and inlets, marshy and peaty patches. The mud floats are overgrown with willow trees and marsh grass. In winter and early spring, the lake surface is clear but in summer it is covered with the floating leaves of horned water nut.

The lake in the east and the north is bounded by elevated and bare basaltic crags. The snowy peaks of the Harmukh massif, in the north-east, are often found mirrored in it. Absence of level ground in the east necessitated cutting of number of projecting spurs in the construction of Srinagar-Bandipore road which, for the most part, occupies high ground. In the north the mountain range stands receded, leaving a wide stretch of level ground. On the north-west, where the river emerges from the lake, is the isolated hill of Baba Shakur-ud-Din. Watlab gap allows road communication between Bandipore on the Wular with Sopore on the Veth.

The Wular serves as a settling tank for all the silt, the product of the processes of degradation going on within the Valley. New patches of land appear as a result of the formation of a lacustrine delta, leading to the shrinking of its area. The island, called Zaina Lank, which once stood in the middle of the lake, now lies close to the eastern silted shore.

The ancient name of the lake was *Mahapadmasaras.* The present name Wular is derived from its another Sanskrit name *Ullolasaras,*

Figure 5.1

Drainage: Kashmir Region

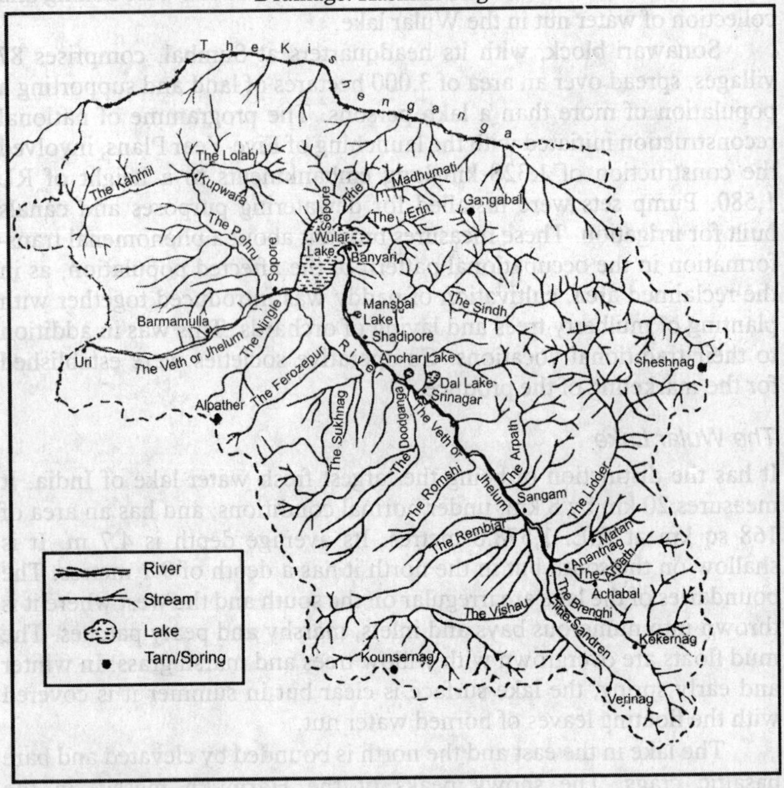

which is interpreted – as has been done by Dr Buhler – as the lake with high going waves.

This vast sheet of water, which generally appears calm, is subjected to squalls which moving down the mountain slopes, in the afternoons, disturb its surface resulting in high rising waves. Cruise in a flat bottomed boat on such occasions becomes perilous. To avoid fatal accidents boats cross it, invariably, before noon.

A characteristic product of the lake is *singhara* or the trapa. The nut when unripe is greenish-yellow and soft, but when ripe its shell hardens and turns black. The fish present include a local carp, mirror carp and, occasionally, mahseer. In summer some catch is sun-dried. From the lake are collected marsh grass, other types of fodder, reeds and willow twigs. Large willow plantations, on its mud flats and wetlands in the west are raised by the State Forest Department. These are designated as the Ningli forests and are spread over an area of 2,882 hectares.

The Erin

This stream has its source in a large and deep tarn of the Sarbal, which lies 1,200 m below the eastern peak of the Harmukh. Water from another highland lake, the Shirasar, also joins it. After flowing for a distance of 29 km it enters the Wular lake at Nadihel. It bounds Bandipore town on the south.

The Madhumati

The high altitude lakes, on the north-western slopes of the Harmukh, the Shalinisar and the Lolgulsar constitute the sources of this stream. This 35 km long stream enters the Wular at Nus ghat where it forms a lacustrine delta. The Zainagir canal is drawn from this stream at Sonarwani. The motorable road to Gurez starts from this place.

The Pir Panjal Tributaries

The Vishau

It rises from the tarn of Kounsernag and also collects the drainage of the long stretch of the Pir Panjal on either side of the Sedau pass. The stream passes through a narrow gorge which for the most part is forested. Two mountain torrents, the Zaijnar and the Harseni join the Vishau below Kongawattan. Steep gradient of the area makes it a fast flowing roaring stream. At Ahrabal, the stream tumbles down in the form of a waterfall. The faulted valley consists of the Panjal volcanics and has a width of 12 m. The water here falls through a height of 21 m (Mehta, 1963). Downstream of Ahrabal the Vishau undergoes a right-angled bend to flow in west-east direction. Canals drawn from it are the Sonaman Kol, Tongri and Mau Kol. The Sonaman lays claim to great antiquity.

At Kulgam the wide stream bed is covered with big and small boulders with water flowing through several channels. Kaimuh onwards it is fringed by embankments and is navigable for 12 km up to its union with the master stream. The Nandi canal is taken off from it at Kaimuh. The Vishau has a total length of 70 km.

The Vishau Thalweg*

Distance (km)	*Station*	*Altitude (metres)*
0	Kounsernag	3,452
20	Ahrabal	2,421
42	Kulgam	1,748
54	Palapur	1,609
70	Sangam	1,595

* From Uppal, 1956

The total reduction in altitude of the Vishau from its source to Sangam is 1,857 metres, out of which the drop in the first 20 km from source to Ahrabal is 1,031 m. This accounts for its fast flow in this section of its course.

The Rembiar

This stream has its source in the snowfields near the Pir Panjal pass. It is joined by a number of rills flowing down the steep slopes of this watershed range, including those issuing from the tarns of Chandansar and Nandansar. At Hirpur the stream has cut deep canyons through the sloping Karewas which afford excellent study-sites of this formation. The stream at Shupiyan is about a km in width and here the incidence of boulders increases to the maximum. At Chogam, Soengul and Nathu-payin canals have been drawn from it. Beyond Shrimal the stream narrows down between high banks up to Naiyun. It is a stream of small volume compared to the Vishau with which it unites at Naiyun. The combined deep stream (ancient Gambhira) then flows for 2 km to merge with the Veth at Sangam.

The Romshi

The source of this stream lies below the peak of Romshi Thong. It is joined by the Birnai at Aglar and the Hakriyej at Pakharpore. It is a stream of small volume compared to the Vishau or the Rembiar. On entering the Veth lowland it acquires a deep meandering course through narrow alluvial banks. It joins the Veth at Kakapore. The two important canals drawn from it are the Mamshi and Khamshi which irrigate the tablelands of Pakharpore and Khampore respectively.

The Flood-Spill Channel

This inundation canal takes off from the Veth on its left bank near Jawahar Nagar. It was built under the guidance of Major J. de Lotbiniere in 1904. This 173 metre wide flood-spill channel was constructed to protect Srinagar city against the fury of floods in the Veth. It enters the Batamolo wetland when a branch of it joins the river at Parimpore. The main channel passes through the wetlands of Hokarsar, Mirgund, Nowgam and Haigam and finally joins the Wular at Haritar. It has a total length of 48 km.

The Dudhganga

It drains part of the Pir Panjal range below the Tratakuti peak. Near Badipore it is joined by the Nilanag rill. It receives the important tributary of Shaliganga near Wathore. The Dudhganga enters Srinagar at Rawalpore and it used to join the Veth at Chattabal. Its course got disturbed, in the city, with the construction of the flood spill channel.

The Sukhnag

It rises from that part of the watershed range which lies between the peaks of Nurpur Ka Neza and Shin Mahinyuv. The area is studded with a number of tarns which feed the stream. The torrents flowing down from Tosmaidan also merge with it. It passes through a narrow gorge up to Rengzabal and cascades down in rapids. At Guripore, near Beerwah, it passes through another small rocky gorge with vertical walls. Beerwah onwards it flows through soft-rock beds. The Sumbal canal is drawn from it at chak Kawoosa. The Sukhnag combines with the Ferozepore stream at Trikulabal.

The Ferozepore

Between the peaks of Shin Mahinyuv and Nilakant ki Gali the Pir Panjal is drained by the Ferozepore stream. It also receives the water of Kantarnag. From its source to Gowran the direction of flow of the stream is south-west to north but near Drang it runs from west to east. It debouches into the plain at Tangamarg, where an irrigation canal is drawn from it. Part of the water of the Sukhnag and the Ferozepore enters into the wetlands of Hokarsar and Mirgund. The combined stream beyond Trikulabal empties into the Wular.

The Ningle

It originates from the western slopes of the Apharwat ridge and leaves the rocky gorge at Dandamuh. It joins the Veth on the left bank near the village Ningle and carries with it a heavy load of coarse sand and gravel, and deposits it in the outfall channel. The catchment area of the Ningle stream is 130 sq km and a total length of 44 km. There is a large willow plantation in the lower course of this stream.

North-Western Drainage

The Pohru

The streams of Lolab and Kahmil, with a length of 27 and 28 km respectively, join together at Kupwara to give rise to the Pohru stream. It is the major tributary of the Veth in its outfall channel. The Pohru basin is composed of the Karewa series. The stream and its tributaries flow in this Karewa country in meandering courses and carry with them large quantities of sediment which in colour varies from light yellow to dark brown, depending upon the type of Karewa eroded.

The Talar, Mawar and Hamal are its main tributaries which join it on the right bank. Two rivulets running on either side of the Karewa foothills of Nichahom join together to form the Talar which unites with the Pohru at Wadipora. The longest of its tributaries is the Mawar which merges with Pohru at Dukalabal. The Hamal enters the Pohru at Suil. Downstream of Suil, the Pohru moves in north-south direction. Its waters mingle with that of the Veth at Doabgah, after traversing a distance of 49 km. The stream is navigable for 30 km from Awatkula to Doabgah.

The Pohru brings with it a heavy load of clay, coarse sand and gravel which it deposits in the bed of the main river in the shape of a sediment bar. It is in the form of a ridge which slopes either ways. As the Pohru runs in a direction opposite to the direction of flow of the Veth, the sediment bar extends in the direction of, and as far as, the Wular lake. Its presence obstructs the river flow in the outfall channel. The direction of flow of the Pohru opposite to that of the Veth serves as an evidence in determining the Late Tertiary drainage of Kashmir.

Water Discharge of the Veth

The river records the maximum discharge, at Baramullah, of 19,496 cusecs in May and the minimum volume of 2,290 cusecs in January (Figure 5.2, Table 5.2). In January, the precipitation received in the Valley is largely in the form of snow and the frosts are common. Most of the tributaries carry very little water. This results in the least volume of water; 2.0 per cent of its total annual flow. In February, there is a marginal increase in the river discharge as the precipitation in this month, at times, takes the form of sleet. It is 3.2 per cent of the total.

Table 5.2

Water Discharge of the Veth (Upper Jhelum) at Baramulla
(From Uppal – 1956)

Month	*Average Water Discharge (cusecs)*	*Percentage of the Total*
January	2,290	2.0
February	3,669	3.2
March	9,752	8.6
April	17,971	15.8
May	19,496	17.2
June	17,246	15.3
July	12,970	11.5
August	10,313	9.2
September	4,406	3.9
October	4,105	3.6
November	5,487	4.8
December	5,658	4.9
Total	113,313	100

Kashmir experiences the highest rainfall in March. With the increase of mean monthly temperature of its second fortnight, thaw sets in at lower elevations. Both these factors increase river discharge, almost, threefold compared to that of February. Kashmir continues to receive frontal rainfall during April and May. The increased air temperature leads to the melting of snow in the higher reaches.The river level continues to rise through these months till it attains in May, the maximum value of 17.2 per cent of the total annual discharge.

Figure 5.2

Kashmir Region: The Jhelum Thalweg and Water Discharge

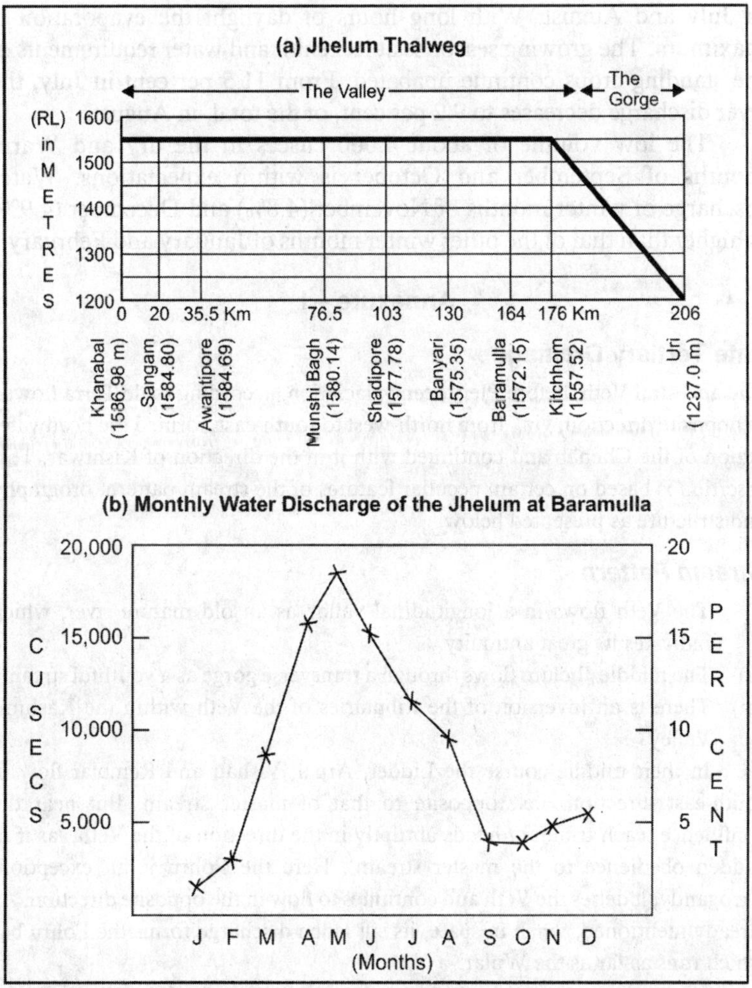

June, with a river volume of 17,246 cusecs, marks a decrease in water discharge. It is a month of low rainfall. Much of it is contributed by local storms. With rise of temperature April onwards, the water requirements of the cropland, particularly under rice cultivation, increase manifold. The irrigation canals run to their full capacity by June, thereby increasing the water take-off from the source streams. Consequently, much less water finds its way into the master stream. This is despite the fact that the higher June temperature causes melting of more snow in the mountain girdle. June claims a share of 15.3 per cent against the 17.2 per cent in May.

The river level (RL) continues to fall even during monsoon months of July and August. With long hours of daylight the evaporation is maximum. The growing season is at its zenith and water requirements of the standing crops continue unabated. From 11.5 per cent in July, the river discharge decreases to 9.2 per cent, of the total, in August.

The low volume of about 4,000 cusecs in the dry and Warm months of September and October is within expectations. Water discharge of winter months of November (4.8%) and December (4.9%) is higher than that of the other winter months of January and February.

Annexure – I

Late Tertiary Drainage

The ancestral Veth, before Pleistocene glaciation, according to de Terra flowed in opposite direction, viz., from north-west to south-east, formed the headwater region of the Chenab and continued with it in the direction of Kishtwar. This assertion is based on certain peculiar features of the stream pattern, orography and structure as presented below.

Stream Pattern

(i) The Veth flows in a longitudinal valley as an old mature river, which indicates its great antiquity.

(ii) The middle Jhelum flows through a transverse gorge as a youthful stream.

(iii) There is an inversion of the tributaries of the Veth within the Kashmir Valley.

In their middle course the Lidder, Arpal, Vishau and Rembiar flow in south-east direction, i.e., opposite to that of master stream. But near the confluence, each tributary bends abruptly in the direction of the Veth, 'as if in sudden obedience to the master stream'. Here the Pohru is an exception. Arrogantly, it defies the Veth and continues to flow in the opposite direction. As already mentioned, when in spate, its silt laden discharge forms the Pohru bar which runs as far as the Wular.

Orography

(i) In the orography of Kashmir, a relative stability of its north-western corner (the Lolab valley and the synclinal drainage of the Pohru) is noticed. As part of the great Himalaya it had attained its present elevation during the Late Tertiary epoch.

(ii) The low elevation of the Pir Panjal in the pre-glacial period and its subsequent rise to the present altitude during the Quaternary Ice Age.

(iii) The Pir Panjal, at present, is the watershed between the Chenab and the Jhelum.

Structure

The particular attribute of the structure of Kashmir is its synclinal origin and its possible continuation with the Upper Chenab and their alignment in the same straight line.

The Inference

With this premise, de Terra presents the following perspective regarding the Late Tertiary drainage of Kashmir.

The river in Kashmir, the ancestral Veth, flowed from north-west (Lolab) to south-east (Verinag) and joined the ancestral Chenab forming its headwater region. In due course of time, the Valley bottom sank in relation to the Pir Panjal range, on account of faulting. Consequently, the ancient Chenab got beheaded of its headwater course and flowed south.

At the same time the ancestral Jhelum, from the west (present Muzaffarabad), was croding the soft Murree series. Its headward erosion continued into the watershed formed by the Pir Panjal. At one stage, ancestral Jhelum cut through the watershed and captured the Kashmir longitudinal drainage (the ancestral Veth). This has been a clear-cut case of river piracy. The Veth, thenceforth, flowed in the present direction (south-east to north-west) and left Kashmir along the course of the ancestral Jhelum.

Annexure – II

Suyya's Engineering Works

In the beginning of Avantivarman's reign (AD 855–883), famine conditions prevailed in Kashmir caused by the submergence of large acreage of cropland due to the abnormal rise in the river level. Avantivarman's engineer-minister, Suyya executed several engineering works for the improvement of Kashmir drainage.

Reclamation of Arable Land

This demanded a substantial reduction in the water level of the Veth. The problem spot identified, in this connection, was Dyargul, some distance downstream of Baramulla. The topography of the area is such that the ridges stand quite close to the river and some spurs project into it. Consequently, rock waste sliding down the mountain slopes finds its way into the river. The massive deposition of rocks and other eroded material also brought down by the river had clogged its channel and thereby raised its level. This huge obstruction needed to be removed.

As a first step, he got a stone coffer dam built across the river above Dyargul. Simultaneously, stone walls were constructed on either bank to prevent further rock slides. The river was blocked completely for seven days and during this period the entire rock debris from the river bed was got removed. When the coffer dam was dismantled the great force of the blocked rushing waters flushed the river bed clean of entire residual rock deposits. Soon after, there was a considerable fall in the river level and the submerged cropland was thus reclaimed and brought under cultivation. On the reclaimed land, along the Veth, below the Wular, he founded the town of Suyyapore, the present Sopore.

Taming of the Veth

The earlier confluence of the Veth and the Sindh lay between Paraspore and Trigam. After this confluence the river had adopted a vagrant and irregular passage through a number of marshes created by it. Here the works planned, included the construction of 67 km long stone embankments for diverting the river into a shortest and regular channel which opened directly into the Wular. Some villages, subjected to recurrent floods, in this section, were protected by the construction of circular (Kundala) dykes round them. Two such existing villages are Wustakundal and Markundal. As a result of these works the Veth-Sindh confluence shifted to Shadipore. The river remained confined to the designated channel, the habitations on either bank became free from inundations and even some marshes got drained. More land became available for cultivation which led to increased food production.

Irrigation

Suyya did not stop here. He got the soil of a particular locality tested for its permeability and fixed its water requirements accordingly. Irrigation canals, drawn from mountain streams, carried water to arable land. This ushered in, so-to-say, a green revolution in Kashmir.

Suyya's efforts culminated in the reclamation of land, flood control, diverting the river into a well-defined passage, development of fisheries and recreation, which in modern times form the constituents of a multipurpose project. These engineering works heralded a period of peace and prosperity in Kashmir. Here is an apt applause from a present day engineer, H.L. Uppal, to the engineer of the past, 'Tribute, however, must be paid to the great genius and engineering skill of Suyya'. To the grateful people of the time, Suyya became an *Annapati,* the Lord of food, the *Batae Khodai.*

Annexure – III

Floods

Floods, fires and famines have been the recurring ravages of the people of Kashmir. Floods, by and large, take place in the summer months of July to September.

The Veth is the only drainage artery of the streams and lakes of Kashmir. Like all leveed rivers the water flow in the stream is confined within the embankments. It has a safe discharge capacity of 50,000 cusecs below Sangam which is reduced to 35,000 to 40,000 cusecs in Srinagar (Uppal, 1956). Several days of incessant rain in south Kashmir, its source area, increases the volume of water to 80,000 to 100,000 cusecs. This leads to devastating floods downstream for the simple reason that the volume of water that enters the river, on such occasions, is double of its carrying capacity. Consequently, the excess water either overflows the dykes or causes breaches in it. The two localities vulnerable to such breaches are Masyari and Kandzal. In either case, flood waters submerge vast expanses of the Veth lowland. But the topography of the area is such that entire volume of flood water flows back into the river above Srinagar, thus rendering the city a prey to their fury. The preventive measures for safeguarding the city are, one, the Flood Spill Channel with a carrying capacity of 18,000 cusecs and two, raising the height of the embankments on either bank of the river.

Flood control schemes have been in place since very early times. The first recorded are Suyya's drainage operations. In the beginning of the last century the steps for the clearance of outfall channel were recommended by two foreign engineers, Major Lotbiniere and Mr Field, in the employ of Maharaja Pratap Singh. An electricity-driven (from Mohra Powerhouse) dredge was launched at Baramulla. The dredging operations were carried out for 4 years which resulted in the reclamation of 15,250 hectares of land.

With the flood situation assuming alarming proportions in the post-Independence period, the state engineers in consultation with Central Water Power Commission (CWPC) devised a flood control master plan in 1958. A separate Flood Control Department was established in 1959. The objective mooted upon was to provide quick passage to the flood waters in the Valley. During the Fifth Five-Year Plan, two diesel operated dredges – 'Suyya' and 'Budshah' were acquired by the state for the clearance of the outfall channel bed at Sopore and downstream. Each of these is capable of dredging to a depth of 7.5 metres below the surface of water, excavating mud, sand and shingle, and pumping away these materials through a pipeline 1,000 metres in length. Other measures, incorporated in the plan, are being implemented to secure the Valley against the flood ravages.

The river bed, above and below Srinagar, has been rising due to deposition of the products of erosion brought down by tributary streams particularly from bare and exposed Karewas. The Veth being a sluggish river is unable to carry its entire load of sediment. This grave problem has to be taken care of, through afforestation and other soil conservation schemes.

References

Books

de Terra, H. and Paterson, T.T. (1939): *Studies in the Ice Age in India and Associated Cultures,* Carnegie Institution of Washington, Washington, D.C.

Douie, Sir James, (1963 reprint): *The Panjab, North-west Frontier and Kashmir,* Seema Publications, Delhi.

Drew, Frederic (1875): *The Jummoo and Kashmir Territories,* E. Stanford, London.

Kumari, Dr Ved (1968): *The Nilamatapurana,* J & K Academy of Art, Culture and Languages, Jammu.

Lawrence, Sir Walter R. (1895): *The Valley of Kashmir,* O.U.P. London, 1967 reprint, Kesar Publications, Srinagar.

Mehta, R.L. (1963): *Elements of Geology,* Hari Chand Mehta, Jammu.

Sachau, Dr Edward C. (1964 reprint), *Alberunis India,* S. Chand & Co., New Delhi.

Stein, M.A. (1900): *Kalhana's Rajatarangini, A Chronicle of Kings of Kashmir,* Vols. I & II, Archibald Constable, London, 1961 reprint, Motilal Banarsidas, Delhi.

Tuzuki – Jehangiri, translated by Alexander Rogers (1909), The Royal Asiatic Society, London, 1986-reprint, Munshiram Manohar Lal, Delhi.

Uppal, H. L. (1956): *Flood Control, Drainage and Reclamation in Kashmir,* Central Water and Power Commission, New Delhi.

Papers and Articles

Kaul, V.K. and Zutshi D.P.: A Study of Aquatic and Marshland Vegetation of Srinagar, *National Institute of Science of India,* September, 1967.

Zutshi, D.P., et. al.: Comparative Limonology of Nine Lakes of Jammu and Kashmir, *Hydrobiologia,* Hague, Netherlands, 1980.

6

The Trans-Himalayan Ladakh

Physical Features and Drainage

The Name

An intricate series of towering ridges of such mighty mountain systems of the world as the Himalaya and the Karakoram bound Ladakh region in the south and the north. In their intervening space extend two more mountain ranges of the Zanskar and the Ladakh. Within this frame, cris-cross a number of big and small rivers through deep and narrow valleys. Plains and plateaus there are many but situated at staggering elevations. Its dry and cold climate has given rise to a cold desert environment. In spite of all these environmental constraints human groups, though in small numbers, have inhabited Ladakh from very early times. For leading some semblance of civilized life, among other prerequisites, communication was most essential, particularly for levelling of the surpluses of essential commodities of one area to make good the shortfalls of the other so basic for survival.

How could this bc possible in tlie given situation? Through passes in mountain ranges. For intra-regional movement access from Leh is provided by the Fotu la and the Namki la to Kargil, by the Khardung la to Nubra valley, by the Chang la to Chusul, by the Namshang la to Rupshu and by the Penzi la from Kargil to Padam. An intra-regional exchange of subsistence goods, including food grains and salt, was carried out by petty as well as professional traders. These articles of trade were carried by humans and animals over mountain tracks leading invariably to a pass. It was not uncommon to find a Champa from Rupshu bartering common salt, that he had collected from the Tso Kar, with grim with a peasant from Thiksey in the Indus lowland. Through these short and long trade circuits the available products were transported to every part of the region which paved way for Ladakh's economic independence and social cohesion (Janet Rizvi, 1966).

The inter-regional routes crossed the Umasi la to Kitshtwar, Zoji la to Kashmir, Karakoram pass to Chinese Central Asia, and Shingo la to Lahaul. These routes caused material gains through trade with surrounding regions. The Indus route provided communication with Tibet which bestowed spiritual solace through the perpetuation of the religion. All this indicates that whichever direction one has to go whether inside or outside Ladakh a pass has to be crossed.

The preponderance of the passes in Ladakh can best be illustrated by the 11-day trek from Lamayuru to Padam. It involves a traverse through the following six passes of varying elevations. These, in succession, are Prinkit la (3,400 m), Sirsir la (4,990 m), Boumtse la (4,400 m), Shingi la (5,060 m), Nerak la (4,350 m) and Namatse la (4,350 m) (Kapadia, 1999).

It is, thus, evident that here is a place which abounds in passes. The name Ladakh is derived form a Tibetian term *La-tags* where *la* stands for a pass and *tags* for a country. Ladakh, therefore, means a country of passes.

Layout

Ladakh region, as already stated, occupies the third and the uppermost step of the terrace – the form assigned to the topography of Jammu and Kashmir. Consequently, one prominent feature of this region is high altitude of all types of its landforms: mountains, plateaus or plains. Contrasting with towering mountain ranges are deep river gorges, and matching with elevated plateaus are high passes. Two highest motorable roads of the world here cross the passes which stand at dizzying heights of above 5,300 m. Ladakh has the distinction of being one of the highest inhabited regions of the world, where inhabited areas range in elevation from 2,750 m in Kargil to 4,572 m in Karzok. Lofty and rugged, rocky and desolate, best describe its terrain. Ruggedness of its terrain goes hand in hand with the vastness of its area. Like deserts, whether hot or cold, the region is characterized by barren landscape, vast empty spaces, stony silence and a sparse population.

A small area in the central Ladakh is composed of sedimentary rocks (the Mesozoic and the Tertiary) when most of the region consists of igneous and metamorphic rocks like granites, gneisses and schists. Rate of disintegration of these rocks is dissimilar. Mechanical weathering of the rocks is quite intense but the region lacks in erosion due to running water. Weathered rock-waste lies either *in situ* as scree or at the foot of the slope as talus. The prolonged frost action chisels the mountain peaks into pinnacles and pyramidal shapes. The sand-laden fierce winds have sculptured softer rocks into bizarre pillars.

Precipitation in this highland region is scanty as it lies in the rain shadow of the Great Himalaya. It is too meagre to favour tree growth. The mountain slopes are bare and barren. All these processes and phenomena, acting in unison, have created a landscape of strange patterns and colours. Those who see it for the first time, in amazement, call it moonland. The widespread rock waste, low temperature, scanty rainfall and absence of natural vegetation make it a highland cold desert.

Wherever water became available, villages have come up, mostly on alluvial fans. No crop, whether tree or plant, can be raised without irrigation. At this high altitude, low temperature and short growing season, favour the growth and ripening of a hardy variety of barley called 'grim'. The principal tree crops are willow, poplar and apricot. There is a sprinkling of apple, walnut and mulberry trees also.

Rows of trees along the water courses, and growing crops in the fields create a green patch close to the cluster of flat roofed, white-washed dwellings. Such a settlement stands in sharp contrast to dull and drab rocky precipices in the background. This setting makes it appear as an oasis in a desert. This together with stacks of dry fodder piled on the rooftop depicts a sedentary lifestyle with emphasis on crop cultivation and rearing of animals. In the high plateaus of Changthang, on the other hand, migratory livestock rearing is the dominant activity.

An outstanding feature of the topography of Ladakh region is the Indus furrow, which is walled in the south by the Zanskar range and in the north by the Ladakh range. To the south of Zanskar range the region is bounded by the Great Himalaya. In between these two southern ranges lie the valleys of Dras, Suru and Zanskar. Dras is exclusively a Himalayan valley and Zanskar valley is confined to the Zanskar range. The Suru valley is located between the Great Himalaya and the Zanskar range. The Karakoram runs to the north of the Ladakh range. These enclose the Shyok-Nubra valley. Huge valley glaciers occupy the heights of the Karakoram range. The largest of these is the Siachen. All the mountain ranges, detailed above, run almost parallel to one another.

In the east and the south-east of the region are the high plateaus of Changthang which are dotted with salt water lakes. These salt water lakes yield sufficient evidence of progressive desiccation of the region. Vast and depressing, high and wind-swept plains of Aksaichin, Lingzhitang and Depsang occupy north-eastern part of Ladakh.

This is the presentation of the relief of Ladakh at macro-level, which illustrates how different it is from the other two regions of

Kashmir and Jammu. At micro-level it exhibits immense diversity in landscape, climate and human response thereof. Enough areal differentiation is noticed between Rupshu and Nubra, and the two adjacent valleys of the Suru and the Zanskar.

Ladakh, the largest district in the country was bifurcated into the districts of Leh (82,665 sq km) and Kargil (14,036 sq km) in July 1979.

Physiographic Divisions

The Indus Furrow

The Indus enters India, in Ladakh, at Demchok and flows parallel to the strike of the Himalayas up to its syntaxial bend in Gilgit. First two-thirds of this longitudinal valley of the Indus lies in Ladakh which shall be referred to as Upper Indus. The Indus furrow, a conspicuous feature of the physiography of Ladakh, constitutes the deepest part of this inter-montane tract. The Upper Indus is crossed by Manali-Leh road at Upshi and by Srinagar-Leh road at Khaltse. These two road-crossing spots divide upper Indus into three well-defined but dissimilar sections – the South-Eastern, the Middle and the North-Western. (Figure 6.1)

The South-Eastern Section

From Demchok to Upshi the Indus covers a distance of 300 km (Kapadia, 1999) most of which lies in the Rupshu plateau along its eastern edge. It has carved a deep narrow valley in this section which at places like Rong takes the form of a gorge. Its catchment area is small as it lies wedged between the inland drainage basins of the Pangong Tso in the east and the Tso Moriri in the south. The ground, with few exceptions, is detritus covered and surrounded by bare mountain slopes.

Demchok, situated on the Indus is a border post. The road beyond it, towards south-east leads to Lake Mansarovar and Mt. Kailash in Tibet. A short tributary, the Hanle, after cutting a gorge, joins the Indus on the left bank. The Indus meanders through alluvial flats which range in width from one km at Mahe to more than 6 km at Dungti bend. The river undergoes several minor and major bends. At first major bend it flows from south-east to north-east but near Nyoma second bend sets it in the usual south-east to north-west direction. The foothills on either side comprise sedimentary rocks of Eocene period mostly Nummulitic limestones and shales. These limestone hills stand in sharp contrast to the craggy granite mountains on either side behind them. The surrounding slopes are treeless but on alluvial flats close to the river, grass grows in adequate quantities to afford excellent pastures where, in most cases, Changpas with their livestock camp in winter. Being a dry area, snow does not fall in many places in this part of the river valley,

Figure 6.1
Jammu and Kashmir: Drainage
Details of Ladakh Region Including
The Three Sections of Indus Furrow

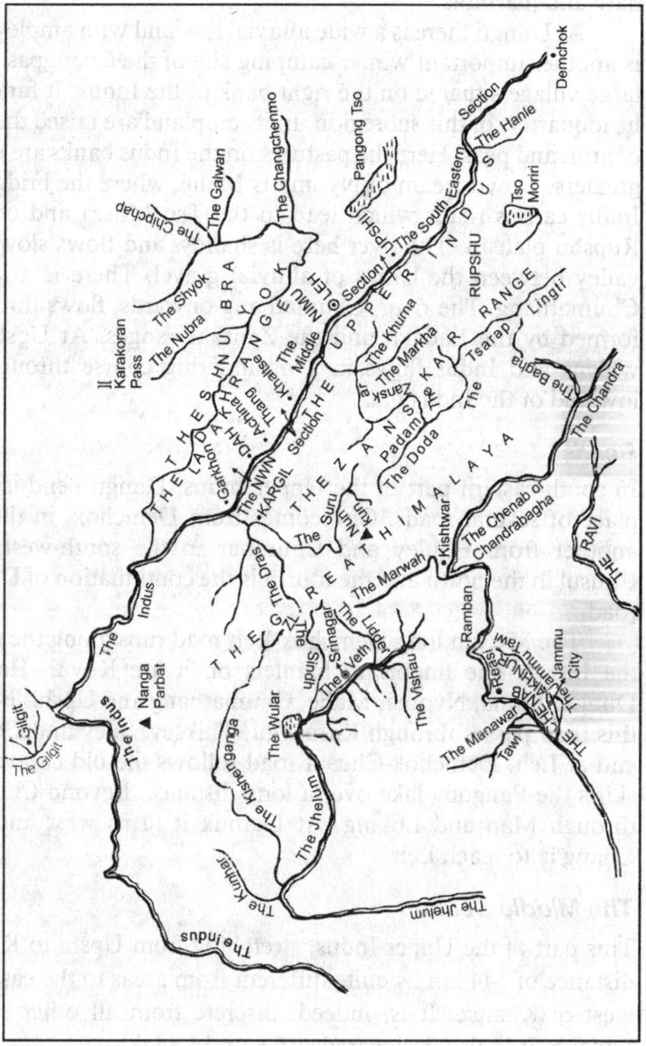

and where it falls it does not stay on the ground for long. These pastures without a snow cover permit good grazing. One such winter camping site is at Dora. Availability here of herbages and water has resulted in the presence of wildlife which consists of Kyang (wild ass), Tibetian hare and marmots.

At Dungti there is a wide alluvial lowland with ample pasturage. It is another important winter camping site of the Changpas. Nyoma is a large village situated on the right bank of the Indus. It functions as the headquarters of this subregion. In its cropland are raised the usual crops of grim and peas. Here the pastures on the Indus banks are used by local graziers. Downstream of Nyoma is Mahe, where the bridge across the Indus carries roads which lead to the Tso Moriri and other lakes of Rupshu plateau. The river here is shallow and flows slowly in a wide valley between the banks of alluvial gravel. There is a hot spring at Chumathang. The river, Chumathang onwards, flows through a gorge formed by the Ladakh and the Zanskar ranges. At Upshi the valley widens and Indus flows in a meandering course through the Indus lowland or the Indus flat.

Roads

In south-eastern part of the Upper Indus, Dungti bend is the meeting place of several roads. One comes from Demchok, in the south-east, another from Hanley and Chumnar in the south-west, third from Chusul in the north and the fourth is the continuation of Demchok-Leh road.

The 356 km long Demchok-Leh road runs along the right bank of the Indus. The important hamlets on it are Koyul, Hanle, Rongo, Dungti, Loma, Nyoma, Mahe, Chumathang and Upshi. Beyond Upshi this road passes through Karu, Igu, Thiksey, Shey and Choglamsar to end at Leh. Demchok-Chusul road follows the old caravan route and skirts the Pangong lake over a long distance. Beyond Chusul it passes through Man and Luking. At Darbuk it turns west and crosses the Chang la to reach Leh.

The Middle Section

This part of the Upper Indus, stretching from Upshi to Khaltse over a distance of 144 km, is quite different from areas to the east of Upshi or west of Khaltse. It is, indeed, discrete from all other subregions of Ladakh. It is also designated as Central Ladakh.

Core Area

Leh, the regional capital, located in this section, lay on the cross-roads of the caravan routes of Central Asia, Tibet and India and thereby served as a significant entrepot in the past. Before 1947, in its bazaars were seen traders, of different nationalities, different ethnicity, speaking different languages, busy in transacting business deals and exchanging merchandise. As a hub of trade it provided its people alternate avenues of livelihood particularly in service sector. This important resource base paved way for the emergence of the Central Ladakh as a core area which furnished the region a stage for the enactment of its history and a nursery for the nurture of its culture. The revenue yielding lucrative trade in Pashmina wool tempted many regimes, like the Mughals, the British and the Dogras, to meddle in the affairs of Ladakh kingdom. Janet Rizvi calls Central Ladakh as the geographical backbone, historical and cultural heartland of Ladakh. Among its cultural features the most noteworthy are the Buddhist monasteries, or gompas located on either bank of the Indus. These meticulously maintained gompas have become chief centres of tourist attraction. The annual Hemis gompa fair, held in June, is mostly thronged by foreigners.

Structure

The receding lines of the Ladakh and the Zanskar ranges have given rise to, comparatively, an open country with a sunny prospect. This physical attribute not only aids in the timely ripening of the cereals and fruit but also in the melting of snow, in the mountain recesses, to release water into the side streams.

Between the inner granite ridges of Ladakh range and low foothills edging the Indus is a high plain, dissected by cross-valleys and ravines which originating from the mountains descend towards the river. This high plain in this way is divided into wide strips of land, which at a number of places are irrigated and occupied by villages. A succession of such villages is found in the main valley of Indus. Some of these between Leh and Khalatse are Bazgo, Tarutse, Yangthang, Himis Shupka and Temisgam. Another set, at a lower level and in some cases close to the river, comprises Spituk, Nimu, Saspol, Nurla, and Khaltse. Khaltse at an elevation of 2,591 m is a large village with a long strip of cultivable land. Besides grim, fruits like apple, apricot and walnut grow here. Spituk by virtue of its proximity to the river is served by it for its water requirements. From Leh to Upshi some right bank, human habitations are at Choglamsar, Shey, Thiksey and Karu. In this part villages situated in the foothill tract of Zanskar range are Stok, Matho and Sabo. The Hemis Gompa lies in one of the side valleys on this side. Chushot, Stakna and Marchelang have a riverine location.

Arable Land

Alluvial fans, a physiographic feature of common occurrence in the Ladakh region, provide most of its cropland. It is formed when a side stream debouches into the main valley. The thin layer of soil over this inclined fan is liable to erosion by running water. A heavy downpour or the gushing water of an irrigation channel can prove disastrous. In either case, the alluvial fan is divested of its precious soil cover, thereby playing havoc with its scarce arable land and its fragile environment.

A notable feature of this middle section of Indus furrow is that the cropland, in addition to alluvial fans, is contributed by the Indus plain situated along the river, formed and watered by it. To the south-east of Leh and for a distance of 30 km the Indus flows along a fault which brings it against the soft Eocene rocks. Along either bank of the river stretches the alluvial plain, composed of clayey soils, which constitutes the fertile cropland. It is extensive and level around Chushot, where wheat is cultivated and tractors are used in farming. This lowland for raising crops is served by the canals drawn from the Indus. The Chushot *mayur* (canal) which takes off from the river at Stakna irrigates the cropland in Chushot, Gongma, Shama, Yokma and Balan. The Thiksey mayur carries water for irrigation to Thiksey and Ranbirpora. A major irrigation scheme, Igu-Phey project, involved the construction of a 25 km long canal to irrigate about 200 hectares of the Indus alluvial plain.

Standing in this lowland in Thiksey, in the month of August and restricting the gaze on the farm land, with lush green fields of 'grim' or wheat, willow trees in full leaf and water rushing through rills the perceivable scene is in no way different from one witnessed in Kashmir. The entire upper Indus valley, but for this alluvial flat, is a broken and barren expanse where dry, bare, detritus covered slopes are a common sight.

High altitude restricts the growing season in Central Ladakh to less than five months, May to September, which permits cultivation of only one crop in a year. Such an area extending from Nimu to Changthang, is known locally, as *sham* when the two crop area from Kharbu to Nimu is called *stot.*

The usual vegetables previously grown were raddish, turnip and potato. Use of green houses and polythene mulching technology has helped in increasing the number of vegetables including the exotic tomato and cauliflower. The constant demand for their supply to the army has acted as an incentive. The role of the Field Research Laboratory (FRL) and some NGOs, in this connection, has been rewarding.

Apricot *(Prunus armenica)* is the most suitable fruit tree for the Ladakh environment as it can withstand a very low temperature of –30°C. Attempts are afoot for its quality improvement. Apricot has not found foothold in the Indus flat as the area is exposed to fierce chilly winds.

Livestock forms the bedrock of farm economy in Ladakh. Yak, the type animal of this highland cold desert, is a beast of burden. Dzo, a cross between the yak and the cow is used in ploughing. Efforts are on for the quality improvement of the livestock. Cross-bred Jersey cows and Merino sheep already stand introduced. Russian Merino sheep farms have been established at Matho, Upshi and Loma, and so is the Angora goat farm at Stakna. Ponies and donkeys, which functioned as carriers of merchandise during the carvan days of the past, continue to be in demand for army related duties. Most of the milk, obtained locally, is converted into butter.

Each farmer reserves a portion of the farmland for raising fodder crops. The common fodder is *ole*, alfa alfa or Lucerne. A number of fodder farms have been set up by the government. Ladakh region falls within the ambit of Desert Development Programme which entails the construction of minor irrigation schemes and check dams, afforestation and fodder production.

Hydroelectric Power

A 4 MW Stakna hydel project on the Indus supplies electricity to Leh town for about eight months in a year. The Igu-Phey irrigation project has a power component too. It is to supply water to 3 MW Igu-Marchelang hydroelectric project. A 45 MW Nimu-Bazgo hydro-electric project is under construction on the Indus. Lately emphasis has been laid on the installation of mini hydel projects in various parts of the region. A wind mill lifts water from the river at Choglamsar. The non-conventional sources of energy available in abundance in Ladakh are solar, wind and water. It also possesses geo-thermal energy source in Pugga valley.

Human Response

The judicious response of the humans to their harsh, inhospitable and fragile physical environment of Ladakh was nourished and sustained by a distinct culture with its unique peculiarities rooted in Tibetian version of Buddhism. Contentment and self-abnegation, polyandry and non-fragmentation of family's landholdings, maintenance of symbiotic relationship with the gompas, among other factors in the past, enabled them to live in harmony with their natural environment without subjecting it to undue stress. Here is an illustration. In Ladakh the higher reaches of the mountain ranges receive winter precipitation in the form of snow. The meltwater of the glaciers and snowfields flowing down the side valleys is the source of much needed water for the growth of cultivated plants and for the consumption of humans and animals. The main rivers of Ladakh region flow much below their high banks, whereas the terraced fields lie at a still higher level. Water of the rivers, except that of Indus near Leh, could not be used for the irrigation of cropland. Water courses from the side streams, situated far above and away from the human habitations have been carefully planned and diligently executed to bring an assured and steady supply of water to the villages. Its passage in channels along the contours retards its speed and this slow moving water reaches the cropland without causing any damage to the thin but rare soil cover. This ideal, safe and effective water management is an outcome of native ingenuity.

Leh

Leh, literally meaning a plateau, is so named because of its situation at a height of about 300 metres above river level. It occupies a large alluvial fan on the right bank of the Indus. Here two spurs descending from the Ladakh range, and widening as they proceed riverwards, enclose a triangular space with each side of 8 km length. Base of the triangle is formed by the river between Spituk and Choglamsar. At the apex of the triangle lies the old township with the nine-storey high palace of Sengge Namgyal, built in Tibetian style of architecture, standing in the background. In the east is a barren ridge which overlooks a large level stretch of land, called polo ground, the venue of cultural, sports and political activities. A terraced expanse of arable land watered by a channel drawn from a side stream and dotted with hamlets, lies on the west. The town has a southern aspect and the ground slopes gently towards the river in steps. On the middle step are the new quarters of the town. Choglamsar, on the river bank, forms the lowest step. Towards south, across the river is observed the snow-clad peak of Stok Kangri (6,150 m) in the Zanskar range. (A mountain range with snow covered peaks is called *Kangri* in Ladakhi, *Sar* in Balti, and *Muztag* in Yarkandi).

The present accessibility of Leh is because of the two motorable roads and the airways. The 434 km long, Srinagar Leh road, built in 1960, traverses the passes of Zoji la (3,505 m) in the Great Himalaya, Namki la (3,719 m) and Fotu la (4,094 m) in the Zanskar range. The other is the Manali-Leh road, motorable since 1978, with a length of 473 km. It crosses the passes of Bara lacha la (4,892 m) in the Great Himalaya, in Himachal Pradesh, Lunglacha la (5,059 m) and Taglang la (5,325 m) in the Zanskar range in Ladakh region. The Taglang la is the second highest motorable pass after Khardung la. A comparison between these two roads, leading to Leh, is interesting. Both the roads in the first instance cross a pass in the Great Himalaya – Bara lacha la and Zoji la. Then these cross two passes in the Zanskar range. Out of these two, the second, Taglang la and Fotu la, is of higher altitude than the first. The passes in the Great Himalaya remain snowbound for more than six months in a year when the vehicular traffic on both the highways remains suspended. The 'road-open' period of Srinagar-Leh and Manali-Leh highways is five, and four and a half months respectively. A year-round air link with Srinagar, Jammu, Chandigarh and Delhi is maintained through regular scheduled flights. Winter stocks of food, fuel, fodder, feed, medicines and other essential commodities are built up during this brief road-open period. It is a hectic time for the trading community involved in handling of the imports, their storage, distribution and sale. Pashmina wool and apricots, as always, are the only exports. This is the time for the arrival of the tourists.

Ladakh was opened to tourists since 1974. Today tourism is a big business. Leh, by now, has a well established tourism infrastructure in place. All managerial tasks are discharged by the locals. In addition to sight seeing and visits to the gompas, the tourists indulge in trekking and river rafting. Ladakh, therefore, is an adventure and cultural tourism destination.

Leh performs administrative functions as the headquarters of the district of the same name. It is also, since 1995, the seat of the Hill Development Council.

The North-Western Section

Low Altitude Belt

Downstream of Khaltse is the low altitude belt of the Upper Indus which includes the large villages, among others, of Domkhar, Skurbuchan and Achinathang. Level of the Indus here is 2,743 metres above sea level and Achinathang is situated 60 metres above the river. The strip of arable land in this village is long but narrow, when it is wide and long in Skurbuchan. Low elevation and less strenuous life have left their stamp on the physique of its inhabitants, who are taller and well built compared to the residents of Leh. Villages in this part of Indus furrow exhibit affluence.

The Brog-Yul

West of Achinathang the Indus valley acquires the form of a narrow gorge with a width of 14 to 20 metres, where the granite ridges stand wall like. In the thick detritus covered rocky surface of the area, along the right bank of the river, construction of a path in the past was neglected which made this area inaccessible. It is inhabited by the Dards who chose to settle down in this rocky tract after their migration from Gilgit. They are considered to be the pure survivors of Indo-Aryan race.

This small group of few thousand people with typical Aryan features are called Drogpas or Brogpas and the area they inhabit is Brog-Yul (the mountainous country). Garkhon, Da, Bema, Darchik, Upper Hanu and lower Hanu are the Brogpa villages. Garkhon, at the western extreme of Brog-Yul is 68 km distant from Khaltse. It is the largest, the lowest (2,133 m) and warmest of these villages. To its east lies Da at a distance of 6.5 km. This secluded tract secured the Brogpa lifestyle against extraneous influences. It appears Brogpas had imposed voluntary isolation on themselves, in view of such considerations, as the preservation of the purity of their race and dread of pollution by contact with outsiders. In this way they lived a peaceful, uninterfered and self-dependent life within the natural granite fortification, and consequently preserved their racial purity and cultural identity. Some of them have adopted Buddhism but these Buddhist Dards continue to worship their *Lhas* (deities). They abhor the cow and its milk. Goat to them is the sign of fertility and therefore use its milk and meat. In their appearance and customs they stand in sharp contrast to the Dards of Dras or the people of Tibetian race inhabiting Leh. It is only recently that some Drogpa villages have been linked by roads with Leh and Kargil and opened to outsiders.

The spurs descending from the Ladakh range in this part are rugged and desolate. Cultivable land, though scarce, is fully utilized for raising grim, fruit and vegetables. Low elevation and southern aspect favour cultivation. Brogpas also partake in pastoral activities. They rear sheep and goats in highland pastures. Shepherds from Garkhon move with their flocks to Banju heights. From upper Hannu the path leads to Chorbat pass (5,090 m) in the Ladakh range.

South of the Indus

To the south of the Zanskar range stands the more imposing and towering mountain chain of the Great Himalaya. It forms the southern limit of Ladakh region.

The Great Himalaya

From Bara lacha la, the Great Himalaya continues in north-west direction through the Nun-kun massif, Dras, Burzil pass to Nanga Parbat. Its summit lies above the snow line and hence bears a perpetual snow cover. When viewed from afar (say Khillanmarg or Gulmarg) the peaks appear like waves in a sea of snowy wilderness. Snowfields and glaciers in it constitute the main sources of water in the valleys of Dras and Suru.

The Kargil war of 1999 was, mostly, fought on the Himalayan heights of Mashkoh, Tiger Hill, Marpola, Tololing, Bimbat, Kaksar and Batalik. Only a small area in this war lay across the Indus at Chorbat pass in Ladakh range and at Turtuk, south of the Shyok river.

The Zoji la

Zoji la is the gateway of Ladakh from Kashmir side. The ascent to the pass is quite steep but the slope towards north is gentle. The change in gradient in the latter slope, though small in the beginning, causes the flow of water northwards to join the Indus. The pass is almost a level feature, about 400 metres wide, guarded on either side by a series of lofty ridges, treeless and barren. There is a sudden and shocking changeover from lush green and bland landscape of Kashmir to the bare and rocky wilderness of the pass. That mountains act as a climatic divide, is best illustrated by this transformation in natural environment from Kashmir to Ladakh after crossing Zoji la.

The Dras Valley

The Dras stream flows through a long narrow valley lined by mountains attaining an altitude of 4,900 to 5,100 metres. It has its source in Machoi glacier situated in the north-east of Zoji la. Ridges and spurs that branch out of the main range too, are very high. In the floor of this 120 km long valley the Dras stream occupies the eastern part along the foot of the ridge that forms its right bank. The stream flows some metres below the ground level and its course, at a number of places, is identified by the presence of rows of willow and poplar trees. It becomes a stream of large volume after it is joined by the Gumri nala and Mashkoh nala. By the time it reaches Dras village, it becomes a gushing and deep stream which carries a sediment of grey colour. Some of the villages in the Dras valley are Matyan, Pandras, Tashganı, and Kharbu. A number of willow and poplar plantations at Bhimbet, have imparted greenery to the area. The Srinagar-Leh highway crosses the Dras river at Tashgam and runs, thenceforth, along its right bank. Kharbu delimits the, comparatively, warm zone where two crops in a year are raised. Mountain ranges bounding Dras valley continue to be tall and bare with scree covered slopes and heaps of talus. It is precursor of the relief of Ladakh region which may vary in degree but not in kind. The Dras joins the Suru near Kargil.

Dras

The narrow Dras valley widens at Dras village (3,066 m) to cause a space about 5 km long and 2 to 3 km wide. The 5,100 to 5,400 m high serrated ridges have peaks chiselled into horns. Mountains on the north are granite crags, naked but graceful. In the north-west is a peak resembling Matterhorn (a type peak in the Alps), with patches of snow but without a banner cloud. To the south stand limestone mountains, badly mutilated by frost action. These stratified rocks are hewn into strange shapes. The surface of the Dras opening is undulating. The plateau-like features are actually moraine heaps which consist of angular stones and rock meal. These dome shaped uplands, covered with a layer of alluvium, are barren like the surrounding mountain slopes. The area abounds in springs. Source of the piped water supply is a spring on way to Goshan. Springs in the locality serve as the main sources of water in winter when the piped water supply ceases to function due to constant below freezing temperatures. There is a glacier in the south-east corner of Dras village which is not visible from the habitation. A rill flows down from it.

The Dras stream enters the locality through a narrow gorge. It is wide here as is indicated by the span of suspension bridge over it. In terms of volume and speed it is comparable with the Sindh at Gagangir in Kashmir. The stretches of level land where water for irrigation is available are under plough and the crops raised are grim, peas and turnips. Fodder, too, is cultivated in the arable land. Willow and poplar plantations are found along the Dras river and other water channels. Both of these trees are valued for timber. This holds true for the entire Ladakh region where timber and fuel wood is rather scarce.

In summer the brown and buff hues on mountain sides are interspersed with green patches of wild fodder. It grows where there is soil with meltwater permeating through it. The livestock from the village is driven to these mountain pastures for grazing. This practice of gathering livestock, in village commons in the morning and leading them to these mountain pastures for grazing has been observed in Pandras also. In the livestock the sheep outnumber other animals. In this highland region of short growing season animal rearing has an edge over agriculture.

An alternate road from Dras to Kargil will cross the Umba la to reach Sankho in the Suru valley. The latter station is 40 km distant from Kargil.

The Suru Valley

The Suru valley lies wedged between the Great Himalaya in the west and the Zanskar range in the east. The ridge of the Zanskar range on which the Penzi la is situated serves as the watershed between the drainage of the Suru and the Zanskar streams. The Zanskar originates from its south-eastern and the Suru from its north-western slopes. Ringdom gompa is situated on a hill top to the south of the Penzi la. It overlooks a vast marshy plain, of the same name, which has an altitude of 3,800 metres.

A rivulet, called Ringdom Sankpo, rising from the Penzi la is fed by the meltwaters of the glaciers Lalung, Chilung and Dalung situated on its west. It skirts the Ringdom plain on its east and north. The stream from Ringdom gompa to Parakchik, called Karcha nala, flows in east-west direction for a distance of 40 km. The twin peaks of the Nun and Kun lie to the south of this nala.

From Parakchik to Panikhar the river takes a U-turn, flowing south in the first instance and then Tongol onwards it turns north. At Panikhar the river is joined by Botkol stream which has its source in the Botkol glacier. The glacier extends up to the Botkol pass which leads into Kishtwar. This route was followed by General Zorawar Singh for his Ladakh campaigns. Throughout its course, the river is joined by a number of torrents, on its right and left banks, which drain the Zanskar and the Himalayan slopes respectively. Here, both the ranges abound in glaciers. It is joined by a large left bank tributary the Chalong nala at Namsuru. The river, this place onwards, acquires the name Suru. The other large tributaries are the Shansi nala and the Umba nala which join the Suru, on the left bank at Tesul and Sankho respectively. A right bank tributary, the Phu Lungpha, merges with the Suru at Lumpur. The Suru continues to flow first, towards north and then in the north-east direction, up to Kargil, covering a total distance of 140 km. It joins the Indus at Marol.

The Verdant Landscape

The Suru valley has an average elevation of 3,000 m. On account of its lower altitude, compared to Dras and Leh, its summers are long and even hot. High temperatures favour melting of snow on the mountains, thereby making water available in abundance for the growth of all kinds of crops food, fodder and trees. Stretches of alluvial flats and sloping uplands, cut into terraced fields, provide sufficient land for cultivation. A long warm summer results in the ripening of two crops during the growing season. All these factors lead to a thriving agriculture with a surplus of food grains. Crops raised are wheat, grim, peas and vegetables. Fruit trees include apricot and mulberry. Apricot grows in plenty and dried fruit is an important item of export. Extensive groves of willow and poplar, along the water courses, with large girths and heights, dot the valley. In the main valley and several side valleys the trees along with bushes and shrubs, with luxuriant growth of foliage, together with the growing crops, assign the landscape against the background of bare rocky slopes, a pleasing lushness, an uncommon site in Ladakh region. Downstream of Panikhar the Suru valley is quite picturesque. Most of the villages of Kargil district are situated in this part of the Suru valley.

Kargil

Kargil town (2,750 m) is situated on the left bank of the Suru river. Part of it occupies the level space along the river while the rest of it is spread over the hill slopes. The predominant strata consists of moraines with angular blocks of granite, remnants of the Pleistocene glaciation. The dressed white hued granite is used in the construction of buildings. At a number of places stream deposits, rounded pebbles in a matrix of clay, are found in the vicinity of moraines. These lacustrine deposits also contain wind-blown loess. In the east, the hills consist of clay and sandstone. Presence of pervious and impervious rocks have caused reservoirs of ground water which have been successfully tapped with the help of hand pumps. In addition to being the headquarters of the district of the same name, Kargil town is the seat of Hill Development Council.

Irrigation and Power

At Pashkyum, 8 km beyond Kargil, is an alluvial tract irrigated by the water of the Wakha Cho. This rivulet rises from the Zanskar range in the vicinity of Wakha la. It passes through Mulbek, Shergol and Pashkyum and joins the Suru on the right bank near Kargil. The nearby barren alluvial terraces of Khurbathang plateau remained unutilized for want of irrigation. A major irrigation scheme, on the scale of Igu-Phey project of Leh, called Khurbathang irrigation project has since been completed. Here a 16 km long canal has been constructed to carry water from the Wakha Cho to this upland covered with alluvial gravel. More than a thousand hectares of this land have been brought under plough. Preference is given to the cultivation of commercial crops like apricot and vegetables. On the right bank of the Suru, opposite to Kargil town, is the Iqbal hydel project which was commissioned in 1995. It produces 3.75 MW of electricity.

Roads

Kargil lay on the caravan routes of the past leading to Leh, Skardu and Srinagar. Being surplus in food grains it was the most frequented destination of native traders who, in earlier times, transported the same to other deficit areas of Ladakh. This practice paved way for the region's self-sufficiency in food.

It lies at a distance of 204 km from Srinagar and is the main staging point between it and Leh. From Kargil the highway passing through Pashkyum and Mulbek winds uphill to cross Namki la. The road with a gentle gradient descends to Bodh Kharbo. It again ascends to another pass, in the Zanskar range, called Fotu la. It is the highest of the three passes in this highway. Fotu la onwards the road passes by Lamayuru to reach Khaltse. It, in this section, undergoes repeated bends while negotiating a fall of 1,200 m in a distance of 40 km.

A torrent draining the Fotu la ridge, flowing past Lamayuru, joins the Wanla stream which in turn enters the Indus near Khaltse. In the vicinity of Lamayuru are observed cream and buff coloured, wind eroded, queer looking, several hundred metres thick rock formations of alluvial and lacustrine origin. It appears that these formations were, once, deposited in this water filled valley.

A 234 km long road built through the Suru valley crosses Penzi la to link Kargil with Padam in the Zanskar valley. Kargil serves as a centre for the distribution of essential commodities, imported during the road-open period, to the inhabitants of both these valleys. In the pastures of Ringdom ridge arrive the Bakerwals from Jammu region with their flocks, in summer, to feed them on its nutritious grasses.

The grandeur of the twin peaks of Nun and Kun has made the Suru valley another centre of tourist attraction in Ladakh region. They arrive here for trekking and mountaineering. Panikher is the base camp for such adventure tourism pursuits. Kargil also functions as the starting point for trekking expeditions into the Zanskar valley.

Kargil gave its name to the war fought in the region during May-July 1999. It shot into prominence and was projected on the world scene by the coverage of the war by the electronic media. As a sequel to this intense exposure, tourists are arriving in Kargil area to obtain the first hand experience of the recaptured strategic posts including Tololing and Tiger Hill.

The Zanskar Range

This mountain range after branching out from the Great Himalaya, near Kangra, runs parallel to it on its north. Wadia considers the Zanskar range as the principal continuation of the Great Himalayan chain because of the prominent development in it of the crystalline core. It overlooks the Indus furrow and high plateau of Rupshu on its north and the Suru valley in the south. It forms the boundary of Ladakh with

Himachal Pradesh in Lahaul, Spiti and Kangra. The average altitude of the range is 5,940 metres. It is inconsistent in its direction and altitude. This together with its ramifications have resulted in its complex topography consisting of a maze of ridges, cliffs, valleys and gorges. Like other mountain ranges of Ladakh this range also comprises brown and bare ridges, protruding cliffs covered with weathered rock waste. The mountains are subject to intense frost action and subaerial denudation.

Its intricate topography has made access to the Zanskar valley arduous and restricted. It can be reached from Kargil in summer, by road, for a brief period of 3 to 4 months, when the Penzi la is open. Pony tracks lead into it from Lamayuru and Rupshu. Throughout the long winter it gets cut off from rest of the region. Contact with Leh, however, is possible when the water of the Zanskar river freezes hard (the chaddar) to permit trekking over it. The Zanskar range is a significant relief feature of the Ladakh region as either of the roads, from Srinagar and Manali, cross it through two passes each.

The Zanskar Valley

Two streams, the Doda or Stod and the Tsarap Lingti or Lungnak, coming from opposite directions meet in a broad plain, to form the Zanskar river. The Doda or the Stod rises from the glaciers of the Durung Drung near Penzi la. It flows in the south-east direction in a broad open valley. Abran hamlet onwards the surface slope is gentle. The Tsarap Cho on the other hand commences in the south-east of Rupshu. It is joined at the extreme end of the Lingti plain by the streams Yunam, Sarchu and Lingti. The combined river is called the Tsarap Lingti. The Phutgal gompa, situated in the valley of the Tsarap Lingti, is reverent as well as spectacular. It flows through narrow gorges in a circuitous course. To it, joins the Kargiak stream which drains the slopes of the Shingo la. The main stream after this confluence is named the Lungnak. It combines with the Doda or Stod stream near Padam. The two streams coming from opposite directions form almost a straight line along the point of merger. The river so formed is the Zanskar.

At the meeting place of the two streams is a wide plain, triangular in shape, with a base length of 11 km which forms the central part of the Zanskar valley. After Padam, the Zanskar meanders through a vast area where it is joined by a number of big and small tributaries. It flows towards east for some distance and then at Rinam takes a detour towards north-east. At Neche it is joined by the Zingcham Topko. At and ahead of Lamaguru its right bank tributaries are the Markha and the Khurna. The Markha also has cut a gorge through the Zanskar range. The Zanskar river, after Markha confluence, passes through an awful gorge carved through the Zanskar range. The walls of the gorge which are hardly 5.5 m apart, are constituted of sheer rock rising to a height of 500 m above river bed. Finally, the Zanskar, with a volume generally in excess than that of the Indus, joins it at Nimu. The *Chaddar* trek on frozen Zanskar river from Nimu to Padam is 150 km long and is undertaken from January to early March.

Climate

Girdled by soaring mountains, Zanskar valley receives heavy snowfall for almost half the year, which followed by hard frosts, cause the severity of its climate. The inhabitants are compelled to stay indoors for half the year and so are the cattle and other livestock. The growing season is short and lasts from May to September. Sods are thrown on the cropland to help in the melting of the snow, in case it continues to stay on the ground, at the sowing time. A large number of glaciers, though small in size, occupy the mountain recesses which feed numerous water courses. Abundance of water have endowed the area with ample pasturage. Milk and butter are available in bulk. Alluvial fans and terraces are under plough and the crops cultivated are the usual: grim, vegetables and fodder. Human habitations lie scattered in the side valleys of the Stod and the Lungnak as well as in the main valley of the Zanskar.

Road Link

A 234 km long road link, between Kargil and Padam, was established in 1989. Starting from Kargil it passes through Buru, Trespone, Sankho, Panikhar and Parakchik in the Suru valley. It rises to the Ringdom ridge and goes across the Penzi la (4,400 m) to enter Zanskar valley. Penzi la, the gateway to Zanskar, remains open from mid-June to Mid-October. People of this subregion maintain contact with Kishtwar through the Umasi la and Lahaul through Shingo la.

Padam

Padam, 3,505 m, the sub-divisional headquarters, has a superb location. It is situated at the meeting place of three valleys surrounded by high mountains. It is spread over a heap of moraines about 25 metres high, comprising blocks of gneiss. The plain around Padam is level but littered with detritus. In summer it gets inundated due to the accumulation of snowmelt. Karsha is situated opposite Padam, across the river. The total area of Zanskar subregion is 7,000 sq km.

The physical environment of this place offers ideal situations conducive to adventure tourism and river rafting. Zanskar is considered to be trekkers paradise. Trekking routes to various destinations are overcrowded and the trekkers are by and large foreigners. A part of the river in the gorge in summer provides an excellent site for white water rafting. Some visitors arrive in winter to participate in Chaddar trek.

North of the Indus

To the north of the Ladakh range stands the massive mountain chain of the Karakoram.

The Ladakh Range

The altitude of this northern rampart of the Indus furrow varies from 5,486 to 5,790 m when some of its peaks rise to 6,200 metres. With a length of more than 300 km, it forms the backdrop of Leh town and all the villages situated along the right bank of the Upper Indus. It acts as a watershed between the Indus and its large right bank tributary, the Shyok. Composed of granites the range is craggy and bare. The passes in it, lead into the tract which lies between it and the Karakoram. A metalled road from Leh winds uphill and crosses the Khardung la (5,578 m) to enter the Nubra valley. It has acquired eminence for being the highest motorable pass in the world. The other side of the range is snowbound and the road is wet and slippery. It is extremely cold here as icy winds blow constantly and snow falls even at the height of summer. A steep descent of 500 m leads to Khardung village situated on a denuded alluvial plateau. Another road leaves Leh to enter a side valley at Karu, 32 km upstream, which runs across the Chang la (5,475 m) to reach the Pangong Tso.

The Pangong Range

To the west of the Pangong Tso and some distance away from it stands the Pangong range with a length of about 100 km. It runs parallel to the Ladakh range and is separated from it by the Tankse stream. The Pangong range is loftier than the Lakakh range and its highest peak has an altitude of 6,725 m. The space between this mountain range and the lake is filled with granite detritus. This range carries hanging glaciers at lower elevations and snowfields in the upper reaches.

The Karakoram

A number of mountain chains originate from the Pamir knot in Central Asia. Two of these which extend into Indian subcontinent are the Himalaya and the Karakoram. The Karakoram (meaning black gravel) occupies northernmost part of the Jammu and Kashmir from west to east. Its length compared to the Himalaya is less but what it lacks in length is compensated by its high elevation. There are 33 peaks above 7,300 m in it. K2 or Mt. Godwin Austen (8,621 m) is the second highest peak of the world after Mt. Everest. Its eastern termination, the Sasser Kangri II (7,672 m) is its highest peak in Ladakh. The largest glaciers in the world, outside the sub-polar region, are located in this mountain chain. These are Siachen, Baltoro, Hispar, Remo, Baifo and Bradlu. The two passes in the Karakoram, which provide access into Chinese Central Asia and province of Xingjiang, are the Karakoram (5,575 m) in the east and Khunjerab (4,590 m) in the west. In age, this range is considered to be older than the Himalayas, being formed during the Hercynian orogeny. Our study of this range is restricted to the eastern part.

Siachen means place of roses as wild roses grow aplenty near its snout and in the lower valleys. Of all the glaciers of the Karakoram, Siachen is the longest with a geographical length of 76 km and a width of 2 km. It occupies a vast depression on the slopes of the Karakoram range and has all the attributes of a valley glacier. With a north-west to south-east delineation, its snout faces the Nubra valley. Its elevation varies between 3,350 and 5,840 m.

Siachen glacier since 1984 has become the highest battlefield in the world where the Indian and Pakistani armed forces stand entrenched. Several thousand Indian troops defend it along the Saltoro ridge and thereby, control the access to the glacier. Other pickets are situated far away. It takes 28 days to trek over a distance of 128 km to reach the farthest picket. Casualties, in addition to army operations, are caused by unkind weather, with the temperature falling to –66°C, avalanches and crevasses. Frostbites and snow-blindness result in disabilities. Men and materials are ferried by helicopters to the pickets.

The Shyok-Nubra Valley

The Shyok river rises from the Remo glacier and flows south in the beginning. Its disastrous floods, in the past, resulted in much loss of life in the villages situated downstream. The river, consequently, came to be called the river of death or Shyok. In its more southward course it is joined on the left bank by the three streams, coming from the east, namely Chip Chap, Galwan and Chang Chenmo. The Chip Chap drains a glacier in the Depsang high plain, in north-eastern Ladakh. It flows along the western slope of the Sasser la to join the Shyok near its confluence with the Galwan. Its course is marked by rapids and waterfalls. The Galwan also begins from the Depsang plain. The Chang Chenmo has its source in a glacier occupying the western slopes of the Lanak la in eastern Ladakh. It flows through a deep gorge.

The Pangong range obstructs the further southward flow of the Shyok and the river gets diverted, in the first instance, towards west and then in the north-west direction, Shyok village onwards. Its volume in summer increases due to the melting of glaciers which makes it difficult to cross. Floods, too, are common in this season.

At Khalsar, the Shyok is joined on its right bank by the Nubra. Several rivulets issuing from the snout of the Siachen glacier combine together to form the Nubra. It also receives the meltwater from the western slopes of the Sasser Kangri II massif. This high and huge mountain mass occupies middle portion of the Shyok U-turn and serves as a watershed between these two rivers. It can be reached from either side, from the Shyok in the east and the Nubra from the west. The Nubra is also a river of large volume. It is deep, flows fast and is difficult to cross in summer.

The Shyok after its confluence with the Nubra becomes a vast and an unrestrained river. It meanders through a wide sandy plain with shifting channels. In summer when in spate it inundates the surrounding plain and converts it into a marsh. The Shyok and the Indus run parallel to each other, 70 km apart, separated by the Ladakh range which it cuts to join the Indus some distance upstream of Skardu.

The entire area above and below the confluence of the Shyok with the Nubra, for administrative purposes, is designated as Nubra. The headquarters of the Nubra subdistrict is located at Deskit. Nubra plain is formed of sand and shingle, which make it unfit for cultivation on account of porous soils and rock waste cover. Cultivable land is provided by the alluvial fans in the surrounding mountains. These ridges rise vertically and have added to the grandeur of the valley. The rocky precipices are so steep that snow does not stay on them. These, too, are bare. The aspect of the Nubra valley is sunny and open. Altitude of the places like Hunder (3,048 m) and Panamik (3,231 m) is less than that of Leh. It, therefore, enjoys a warmer climate. This helps in the profuse growth of cereals like wheat and grim and fruit like apricot, apples and walnuts. The river plain abounds in pastures and the mountains have a thick cover of herbages. Animal rearing is a major activity. Vast stretches of land in the valley floor, unfit for cultivation, favour a luxuriant growth of a wild bush called seabuckthorn which serves as a fuel. Nubra subregion because of this bush is self-sufficient in fuel wood. Willow and poplar groves line the water courses. Alfa alfa farms have been set up here. Flowers, including roses, grow in wild profusion. This peculiarity of area justifies its name – Nubra which means a valley of flowers. The area towards Hunder is marked by shifting sand dunes. Here are found double humped Bactrian camels, the reminders of the past carvan trading ventures.

The old caravan route to Yarkand, Central Asia, through the Sasser la (5,395 m) and the Karakoram pass, traversed the Nubra valley where Panamik was the last village on it. The valley again shot into limelight since 1985, because of the 158 km road link from Leh to Sasoma on way to Siachen glacier.

The South-Eastern High Plateaus

Changthang

An intermontane, high plateau tract, called Changthang, with altitude varying between 3960 and 4,570 m, constitutes southern and eastern Ladakh. In addition to high elevation this subregion is characterized by inland drainage. Here, the land surface does not slope in one particular direction to allow the water to flow away in the form of a rill or a rivulet to join a stream. On the contrary, it is shaped into a number of vast basins where the meltwater collects in the middle. This fresh water reserve without any outlet and with a drier climate, in due course of time, gets converted into a salt water lake.

Most of the area of this upland is barren and only a small percentage of it, about 15 to 20, is under pastures. These have been put to economic use by its inhabitants, the *Changpas* or *Champas* by rearing animals like sheep, goats, horses, yaks and Pashmina goats. The climatic attributes of Changthang are extreme aridity, scant snowfall, hot days and very cold nights during which water freezes even in July and August. These migratory Changpas live in tents, made out of black yak hair cloth, called *rabos.* There is an opening at the top of the tent for the escape of smoke and fumes. Lately, some of these tents have been lighted by solar lanterns. The Changpas, only several thousand in number, practise transhumance from May to September, over widely scattered pastures. While tending their live stock, over the length and breath of the desolate and dreary Changthang, they are exposed to harsh and hostile environmental conditions. The life they lead is arduous, exacting and devoid of comforts. Yet they have the nerve to face it with a smile.

Access to Changthang from Leh is obtained through two important routes. One, over the Chang la, on its south east, reaches the Pangong basin. The other, over the Namshang la, on its south proceeds to Rupshu.

The Pangong Basin

There is a long narrow basin of inland drainage extending from the south-west of Tankse to the valley of the Shyok which is partly occupied by the Pangong tso. This L-shaped lake measures 130 by 6 km and lies at an altitude of 4,270 m. It is situated on the border with Tibet. Only 40 km of its length falls in India. The lake on the eastern side is bounded by high mountains, with scree-covered slopes. A few small streams, including the Chusul and Lunik, pour their meltwater into it. The lake is without an outlet. Its water is brackish and contains salts like the chlorides of sodium and potassium and magnesium sulphate. The maximum depth of the lake is 43 metres.

To the south of Pangong lake lies Chusul at an elevation of 4,360 m. It is a place of historical and strategic importance. It lay on the old trade route from Rudok in Tibet to Central Asia. In the forties of the 19th century it served as the launching pad for the Tibetian campaigns of Dogra general, Zorawar Singh. It became a theatre of war during the Chinese Aggression of 1962.

To the west of the lake are the summer dwellings of the Pangong Champas. In winter they shift to different favourable locations. A number of hamlets like Mirak, Man, Spanmick and Lukung are located in the west of the lake. In the available cropland grim and peas are cultivated. In the Pangong basin the extent of the area in which pastoral activities can be carried out is small, compared to Rupshu.

Lake Structure

Frederic Drew had observed beaches on the southern mountain sides at a height of 12 to 15 m above the lake level. He also identified margin marks, formed by the action of the waves, at a height of 30 metres. On the basis of this evidence he concluded that the lake water in the past stood at a higher, compared to the present, level. Earlier, the outlet of the lake was traced in the extension of the lake basin towards the Shyok by Godwin Austen. He studied the area in detail and inferred that the increase in the lake level was due to the damming of the old outlet by a series of alluvial fans.

The lake level due to this blockade rose to a height of 30 m but not for much time as the margin marks are not so well-defined. Probably, the dam got breached and the level of the lake fell to 13 to 15 m height. This was followed by a change of climate, a more drier period than before. Consequently, the rate of evaporation exceeded the amount of water that entered the lake. The fall of level was gradual and with each fall a beach was formed. It is at this stage that the lake water became brackish. The lake got reduced to the present level, which is likely to continue so long as the water added to the lake equals the water lost due to evaporation.

The Rupshu Plateau

Rupshu, the highest part of Changthang, is bounded on the east and the west by the Ladakh and the Zanskar ranges, respectively, when its northern and southern limits are formed by the Taglang la and Chumnar. It has an area of 10,360 sq km. The mountains, as elsewhere in Ladakh, are bare and slopes scree covered. Vegetation comprises patches of pasture present near a spring, along the wet banks of a stream or where snowmelt spreads on the ground. The grass is short but nutritious. It is these sparse greens which feed about 2 lakh animals of Changpas during summer months. In their transhumance they follow an age-old pattern of shifting from one particular grazing area to the other.

The Champas are essentially a pastoral community. Each family owns a large flock of Pashmina goats in addition to other livestock. These goats are small in size and have long hair. Pashmina wool is an undergrowth at the hair roots which appears as a protection against the severe cold of their habitat. Besides these goats, where it develops excessively, this wool, in small quantities, grows on accompanying dogs and Yaks. It is in much demand and fetches a good price, as it is the raw material on which the shawl industry of Kashmir is based. During summer these nomadic graziers make several moves over the vast Rupshu plateau. But in winter they stay at one favourable spot and feed their livestock on the fodder available at the camping site or on dried fodder. Some of the prominent camping stations are Hanley, Dora, Debring, Mahe, Dungti and Thugji, on or close to the Indus.

The climate of Rupshu is quite arid. In summer it exhibits extremes of temperature between day and night. At noon when the sun rays are powerful it is very hot. But as the day advances, fall of temperature takes place. It is cold in the afternoon, which continues to intensify due to strong and piercing winds. Water freezes at night excepting when the sky is overcast. The rigours of winter cold are simply horrible. Regarding the life spent in such inimical surroundings by the Changpas, Drew remarks, '... But the Champas weather it in their tents. The hardiness of these people, the way in which they enjoy rather than endure their climate is an instance somewhat remarkable of the power of adaptation that the human race possesses'.

Lakes of Rupshu

The Tso Moriri

The Tso Moriri, a large salt water lake, situated at a height of 4,542 m, occupies a vast glacial depression. It serves as an inland drainage basin for the snowmelt that flows into it from various directions. The lake is 25 km long and has a varying width of 5 to 8 km. The water, though bluish in colour, is brackish and fit for the use of animals only. It has a maximum depth of 30 m on the eastern side and is without an outlet. The lake is surrounded by high mountains and the highest peaks on the eastern side are Lungser Kangri (6,666 m) and Chhamser Kangri (6,622 m). Like other lakes of the region it freezes in winter. An island in the lake is situated towards the western shore which stands some metres above the water level. It is a haven for birds, particularly Nagpas, a variety of wild geese, who nest on it.

The lake is supposed to have been formed in the following manner. To the south of the hollow, occupied by the Tso Moriri and in continuation of it, is a valley into which flowed the Phirsa stream. In this valley the stream had, at a certain stage, spread a large fan-shaped delta across its breadth. Consequently, this hollow got filled with meltwater and became a lake. From the presence of high level beach marks it is evident that the lake water, earlier, stood 12 m above the present lake level. The fall in the lake level was due to warm and dry climate. This also resulted in the concentration of soluble salts and its conversion into a salt water lake. At present, the rate of evaporation and rate of water supply to it, balance each other.

Karzok is situated on the western shores of Tso Moriri. Most of its inhabitants are graziers. The few people left, cultivate several acres of cropland for raising grim. The fields are watered by Karzok rivulet. In view of its high altitude the ripening of the crop every year is not certain. Karzok has a claim to be the highest, permanent agricultural settlement in the world.

The Tso Kyaghar

It is a small salt water lake situated to the north of Tso Moriri. An isolated hollow, about 45 m below an alluvial plateau, is occupied by it. The lake is bounded on all sides by low hills composed of gneiss rocks. The colour of its water is green and is brackish in taste.

The Salt Lake Valley

It consists of a large basin of inland drainage in the Rupshu plateau and is situated to the north-west of the Tso Moriri at an elevation of 4,540 metres. It has a north-south extent of 20 km and a width of 8 km. The hills that surround the valley are relatively low and scree covered. The materials that cover the valley floor vary in composition from sand and gravel to white laminated clay and carbonates of sodium. This valley contains two lakes – a small fresh water lake and a large salt water lake.

The Startsapuk Lake

This fresh water lake has an area of 2.5 sq km and a depth of 3 m in the middle. This lake receives its water supply from the springs found in the valley. It lies more than a metre above the salt water lake of Tso Kar. Water from the Startsapuk lake flows into the Tso Kar and forms its main source of water.

The Tso Kar

This salt water lake covers an area of 17 sq km and has a depth of 9 m on the eastern shore. But along the southern bank, it is quite shallow. It is here that water of the lake gets evaporated to deposit common salt (sodium chloride). The lake water has a bitter taste because of the presence of magnesium salts in it. The Changpas used to collect this salt and bartered it for food grains. It was supplied to the entire Ladakh region.

It is assumed that the Startsapuk lake and Tso kar, with a total area of about 20 sq km, are the remnants of a large salt lake which filled the entire salt lake valley and covered an area of 150 to 170 sq km. On the bank of the Tso kar is the uninhabited village of Thugji, which functions as the winter camping station of the Champas.

The Pugga Valley

To the east of the salt lake valley lies Pugga valley at a distance of 22 km across the Polokangka la (5,030 m). It is known for its geothermal springs and deposits of borax and sulphur.

Wetlands

The wetlands of Ladakh region are located close to the lakes of Tso Moriri, Tso kar and Pangong Tso while there are marshes at Chusul and Hanley.

Roads

The Manali-Leh road traverses the Rupshu plateau in the west, where most of the area, is uninhabited and desolate. After crossing the Bara lach la, in Himachal Pradesh, the road passes through the valley of Yunam. Sarchu, within Ladakh, lies at a distance of 30 km from the above noted pass. First pass in the Zanskar range crossed by this road is

Lunglacha la. Pang across the pass is a wind-eroded area where the sand-laden winds have carved rocks into grotesque shapes. More plain constitutes 200 sq km of undulating wilderness at an elevation of 4,700 metres. Second pass in the Zanskar range crossed by this road is Taglang la. At the foot of this pass is Debring, another camping station of the Changpas. The road then passes along the Gya stream. Outside Rupshu this road passes through Rumtse, Miru, Gya and Upshi. At Upshi it crosses the Indus, from its left to the right bank, to join the Demchok-Leh road.

The North-Eastern High Plains

In the north-east of Ladakh are high, bleak, wind-swept and frost-bitten plains of Aksaichin, Lingzhitang (4,880 m) and Depsang (5,170 m). Aksaichin is situated on the northern glacis of the Karakoram, while Lingzhitang lies to its south and Depsang to its south-west.

These plains, at an elevation of 4800 to 5,200 m, are said to be of lacustrine origin as these were formed when salt lake basins, without any outlet, got silted and desiccated. Wadia opines that these extensive plains or depressed tracts among the mountains are too wide to be called valleys. About Depsang, Younghusband remarked, 'Of all parts of the world this is the most God forsaken dreadful in any way. The plain consists of an open expanse of gravel bounded by rounded dull barren hills. Across it incessantly sweep winds of piercing cold'.

Climate of these high plains is one of daily extremes. Excessive aridity is one of their significant traits. Temperature keeps on increasing up to two hours after noon. Direct rays of the sun and the radiated heat from the ground make conditions quite oppressive. By the time the sun sets, a keen harsh wind begins to blow. It dies down by nightfall and during night frost takes place. In this wild and bleak environment, the ground for most of the time remains frozen. The area is lashed by high velocity winds and blizzards. All these factors make this area unfit for human occupation. The area has been traversed mainly by explorers, surveyors and administrators and their entourages. This subregion constituted the vacant land of Ladakh. This is the expanse where not a blade of grass grows and was, therefore, left unguarded. China took advantage of this situation and encroached upon this empty space. Aksaichin and other adjoining areas are under its illegal occupation since 1956. Roads have been built over this high plain to link hostile Tibet with the turbulent Chinese border province of Xingjiang.

The Indus Drainage Basin

The Indus along with its tributaries forms one of the three northern drainage system of Indian subcontinent. It is one of the prominent rivers of the world with a total length of 2,880 km which it now shares with Tibet, India and Pakistan. The total catchment of the river is 11,65,000 sq km out of which 3,21,290 sq km lie in India. The Indus has played a vital role in the history and civilization of undivided India. In fact, it has given name to this subcontinent. [Indus>Indies>India; Sindhu> Hindu> Hindustan].

The Indus has its source in the Mansarovar lake, in Tibet, at an altitude of 5,180 metres. It flows from Demchok for about 800 km in the south-east to north-west direction up to Bunji where it undergoes a hairpin bend round Nanga Parbat massif. At its syntaxial bend it is joined, on the right bank, by the Gilgit river. Bunji onwards it keeps on changing its direction and finally flows out of Jammu and Kashmir, Chilas onwards, towards west. Within the state it flows through a narrow valley in the districts of Ladakh, Baltistan and Gilgit.

The first left bank large tributary of the Indus is the Zanskar. Equally large in volume is the second left bank tributary of the Suru. The combined Shyok-Nubra is a river of large volume. It joins the Indus on the right bank. The other rivers of Jammu and Kashmir which form part of Indus drainage system are the Jehlum, Chenab and Ravi. These combine together with other rivers of the Punjab to form the Panchnad which ultimately debouches into the Indus. (Figure 6.1)

A total of six rivers, the Indus to the Sutlej, flow from India to Pakistan. For sharing the water of these rivers, after Partition, Indus Water Treaty was signed by these two countries in the sixties of last century. According to this treaty the three west flowing rivers – Indus, Jhelum and Chenab are awarded to Pakistan. India can utilize the water of these three rivers within its territories for the construction of run-of-the-river hydel projects. Storage of water in any form is not permitted except in those schemes which were in operation prior to the implementation of this treaty. The three east flowing rivers – Ravi, Beas and Sutlej – are awarded to India.

References

Books

Ahluwalia, Maj. H.P.S. (1987): *Ladakh Nubra the Forbidden Valley,* Himalayan Books, New Delhi.

Daruwalla, Keki N. (2006): *Riding the Himalayas,* Niyogi Books, New Delhi.

Department of Economics and Statistics, 2006–07, *Digest of Statistics,* Government of Jammu and Kashmir.

Drew, Frederic (1875): *The Jumoo and Kashmir Territories,* E. Stanford, London.

Jina, Prem Singh (2000): *Ladakh, Past and Present,* Gyan Publishing Co., New Delhi.

Kapadia, Harish (1999): *Across Peaks and Passes in Ladakh, Zanskar and Eastern Karakoram,* Indus Publishing Co., New Delhi.

Kaul, A.K. (1986): *Why and How of Geography Teaching,* Ambanju Publications, Srinagar/Vinod Publications, Ludhiana.

——. (1987): *Home Geography (Jammu and Kashmir)* Ambanju Publications, Srinagar/Vinod Publications, Ludhiana.

Kaul, Shridar and Kaul H.N. (1992): *Ladakh Through the Ages towards New Identity,* Indus Publishing Co., New Delhi.

Negi, S.S. (1998): *Cold Deserts of India,* Indus Publishing Co., New Delhi.

Pascoe, Sir Edwin (1973): *A Manual of Geology of India and Burma,* Controller of Publications, Government of India, New Delhi.

Rizvi, Janet (1966): *Ladakh, Crossroads of High Asia,* Oxford University Press, Delhi.

Verma, Maj. Gen. Ashok Kalyan (2002): *Kargil Blood on Snow,* Manohar Publishers, Delhi.

Wadia, D.N. (21st Reprint, 2004): *Geology of India,* Tata McGraw-Hill, New Delhi.

Papers and Articles

Balpreet, 'Breathless in Leh', *The Hindustan Times,* Chandigarh, 27 July 2007.

Cheema, Sujata Aishwarya, 'Lake Placid', *The Hindustan Times,* 24 January 2004.

Dolma, Yangchan, 'Awesome Ladakh', *The Hindustan Times,* 16 May 2004.

Jora, Nawang Rigzin, J&K need Balanced, Equitable Development', *The Daily Excelsior,* Jammu, 1 September 2006.

Singh, Rahul, 'Battleground Siachen', *The Hindustan Times,* 12 April 2009.

Wangchuk, P.P., 'Gates of Heaven', *The Hindustan Times,* 23 July 2004.

Annexure – I
Human-Environment Interaction

For the assessment of the relationship between humans and environment, cognizance has to be taken of requisite geographical postulates. These are: Geographer's space is concrete. It is varied. No two areas are alike. It is also variable. Changes are brought about by nature as well as by humans. Nature works without humans, whereas humans work with nature. Further, humans are rational and creative beings. Unlike other animals, human response to the stimuli of nature is not only confined to instincts but is also defined by the culture, inherited from the social groups. Culture, among other things, includes beliefs, customs and technology. Humans have created a cultural environment with nature as the base. 'The sphere of human-environment interaction is viewed as a triangle of forces—nature, technology and human institutions. Nature provides the base, technology bends the natural processes and human institutions regulate human-environment interaction.'

In chapters, third to sixth, on physical features and drainage, such components of the environment, as location, relief, rocks, minerals, water bodies and vegetation of each region, stand thoroughly explained. At the end of this presentation, it is worthwhile to find out to what extent the varied geographical conditions have bestowed each region with environmental assets, which in this discussion shall be restricted to forests and arable land. It is also essential to know how humans in each region have modified their environmental constraints to serve their needs. This shall be illustrated with the available facilities of irrigation.

Environment

Area under Forests

In Jammu region the area under forests is 45.8 per cent (Table 6.1) of the total geographical area. It is 50.9 per cent of the total geographical area in Kashmir region. In relative terms both these regions are favourably placed with regard to this natural resource. A highland cold desert and forests sound discordant. Nature has not been kind to Ladakh in this respect. But the humans here are worthy of admiration for their venture which will appear in the concerned section.

Table 6.1

Jammu and Kashmir: Regionwise Area Under Forests

S. No.	*Subject*	*Regions*		
		Jammu	*Kashmir*	*Ladakh*
1.	Total Geographical Area (sq km)	26,293	15,948	96,701
2.	Area Under Forests (sq. km.)	12,066	8,128	36
3.	Percentage of Forested Area	45.8	50.9	0.037

Arable Land

Area according to village papers is the reporting area for which data on land use classification are available. The net sown area in Jammu region (Table 6.2) is 21.8 per cent of the total area according to village papers. In other words only about one-fifth of the total area is fit for cultivation. The remaining four-fifths is under non-agricultural use like barren and unculturable land, permanent pastures, and other grazing lands, land under miscellaneous tree crops, culturable waste, fallow lands and current fallows. This net sown area is small, indeed. A subtropical climate favours year-round farming in many parts of Jammu. Consequently, the total sown area swells to 38.7 per cent. The net sown area in Kashmir is 58.9 per cent of the total area according to village papers. These figures indicate that more than half of the total area is available for cultivation. A small area under *Rabi* crops increases the total sown area to 73.2 per cent. In the words of de Terra, 'Over its entire width of 40 km, the Valley is cultivated and by its fertility it has, through the ages, given bread and culture to its people'.

In spite of the largest geographical area of Ladakh, its area according to village papers is only 64 thousand hectares which stands in no comparison with the similar area of Kashmir (556) and Jammu (1,794). The net sown area of this highland region is 31.2 per cent. It follows that less than one-third of the total area is under cultivation. In some places of lower elevation, a second crop set is raised in *Kharif* sowing. It pushes up the total sown area to 32.8 per cent.

Table 6.2

Jammu and Kashmir: Regionwise Area – Sown and Irrigated
(000' Hectares)

S. No.	*Subject*	*Regions*		
		Jammu	*Kashmir*	*Ladakh*
1.	Total Area According to Village Papers	1,794	556	64
2.	Net Area Sown	392	328	20
3.	Percentage of Net Area sown (2/1)	21.8	58.9	31.2
4.	Total Area Sown	696	408	21
5.	Percentage of Total Area Sown (4/1)	38.7	73.2	32.8
6.	Net Area Under Irrigation	97	191	20
7.	Percentage of Irrigated Area (6/2)	24.7	58.2	100

Note: Data for Tables 6.1 and 6.2 from *Digest of Statistics (2006–07)*, DOES, Government of Jammu and Kashmir, Table Nos. 4.01, 6.01, & 7.00

Humans

Forest Area in Ladakh

As per the *Digest of Statistics (2006–2007)* the area under forests in Ladakh is 36 sq km, most of which is located in Leh district. In the absence of natural tree growth because of scanty rainfall, the creation of willow and poplar plantations, with the help of irrigation, is the outcome of dedication and consistent endeavour of several generations of forest workers. This stupendous effort on the part of the humans of the region deserves acclaim.

Irrigation

Irrigation is one of the vital inputs of productive agriculture. The climatic diversity of the state induces the urgency of irrigation in each of its three regions.

The net irrigated area in Jammu region is 24.7 per cent. (Table 6.2). This indicates that 75.3 per cent of net area sown is still dependent on rainfall for its water requirements. Major share of this irrigated area, amounting to 80 per cent, is claimed by the districts of Jammu (58.2) and Kathua (21.8). The areas served, include Outer Plain and some parts of Kandi. The irrigated area in the remaining four districts ranges between 3.6 and 6.6 per cent. That only a quarter of the total sown area in Jammu is irrigated is vindicated by its terrain. Most of these irrigation works are of recent origin.

In Kashmir region 53.2 per cent of the sown area is irrigated. For a satisfactory farming of rice, the single crop in the Valley, irrigation was a climatic compulsion. The high percentage of cropped area under irrigation is attributed to its historical heritage and geographical endowments. Kashmir was always a single kingdom with a central authority to rule it. Irrigation was a major concern of most of its rulers. Some of the canals here are of great antiquity. The presence of soft rocks, clays and loams, and the location of the tributary streams at a higher elevation than the cropland helped in the distribution of water through a network of gravity canals.

Of the net sown area, cent per cent is the irrigated area of Ladakh. No irrigation, no crop. Contrary to the conditions obtainable in Kashmir, the cropland in Ladakh is situated at a higher level than the rivers. Water for irrigation is to be brought down the mountain slopes from a distant glacier fed, side streams. In view of the fragile environment of the region, a slow and steady flow of water is expected to reach the sloping farmland. The planning and execution of these water courses is another example of creative endeavour of the humans of this region.

7

Weather and Climate

A Systematic Study

Weather and climate after relief is the most dominant element of our physical environment. Its impact on soils, vegetation, water resources, agriculture, animal life, human health and comfort is profound and persistent. Further, its outcomes like running water, moving ice, frost action, winds and waves, as tools of earth sculpture, play a vital role in shaping the personality of a given area.

Weather and climate of a state, or a country, is marked by great diversity. The branch of geography which deals with the description and explanation of weather and climate, as it differs from place to place, and its relation to human activities is called climatology. It is closely linked with meteorology which is defined as physics of the atmosphere or scientific study of physical processes which are constantly at work in the atmosphere. Data for climatology is provided by the meteorological observatories stationed in different parts of the world.

It is essential, in the first instance, to distinguish between weather and climate. Weather is day-to-day, even hour-to-hour, state of the atmosphere. It involves the daily observation of such meteorological phenomena as air temperature, atmospheric pressure, wind direction and speed, humidity, evaporation, precipitation, sunshine and cloudiness. These are referred to as atmospheric variables or elements of weather. Climate, on the other hand, is a generalization or integration of weather conditions spread over a long period of time, usually 31 years as suggested by World Meteorological Organization (WMO). Weather is an everyday experience; climate an abstract concept (Stringer, 1971). Relationship between these two terms has been aptly summed up in the following words by Heintzalman and Highsmith (1965), 'Weather is like the pages of a book, each one a new varied experience; climate is the sum total, the volume'. Weather data comprises actual and daily observations with the help of the scientific instruments recorded at a particular place. Climatic data consists of computed mean values of recorded weather data. Whereas weather affects our day-to-day activities, like clothing, mode of transportation, farming, etc., climate decides natural vegetation, cropping pattern, land use, water potential and housing. 'Psychologically each climate tends to have its own mentality, innate in its inhabitants ...' (Miller, 1972).

Elements of weather get modified by such factors as latitude, altitude, direction of mountains, distance from sea and ocean currents. The resultant weather and climate due to interaction of the elements and factors constitutes climatic control (Menon, 1993). The diversity in the distribution of plants and animals is due to the variations in the climate. Natural vegetation is a visible indicator of climatic conditions.

The Atmosphere

Our earth is a unique planet in the solar system. It consists of a solid part called the lithosphere, a liquid part the hydrosphere and a gaseous envelope, the atmosphere. Of these three physical realms the atmosphere is the most dynamic. It is rightly designated as restless atmosphere. Gravitational pull of the earth is strong enough to prevent its escape. The earth is situated at a distance from the sun where it is neither excessively hot like the dwarf planets nor horribly cold like the giant planets. Temperature variations on it are such as to allow water to exist in solid, liquid and gaseous states. It is, so far, the only planet where life, as it is, exists. The atmosphere has played a vital role in the evolution and maintenance of life on it. This has been possible, among other things, by the presence of water, oxygen and atmosphere which fuelled by the solar energy causes weather. The atmosphere and the weather in it constitute the life support system.

Earth in Space

The earth rotating about its axis revolves round the sun in an elliptical orbit. The axis is inclined at an angle of 23.5° to the ecliptic. These planetary attributes are fixed and play a decisive role in the formation of weather and climate. Rotation causes formation of days and nights, which are of varying duration due to the inclination of its axis. Rotation, revolution, inclination of the axis and its parallelism result in considerable variations in the angles of incidence of the rays of the sun and thereby to the phenomenon of seasons. Days are long on summer solstices, short on winter solstices and of equal duration on equinoxes.

Heat Balance

In the light of above explained causes, our planet gets heated differently and on it are found areas of heat surplus as well as that of heat deficit. The highest latitudes where the sun's rays are vertical are 23.5° north (Tropic of Cancer) and 23.5° south (Tropic of Capricorn). This makes the areas between the equator and the tropics a zone of heat surplus. The thermal equator shifts north or south in accordance with the apparent movement of the sun. Polar circles (Arctic and Antarctic) lie 23.5° south and north, respectively, of each pole. Despite long duration of periods of daylight, the low angle of incidence of the sun's rays together with great depth of the atmosphere through which these rays have to pass, make the polar circles zones of heat deficit. These latitudinal thermal inequalities are levelled by the transfer of heat from the tropics to the polar circles, mostly through winds and weather systems and partly by ocean currents.

Structure

The atmosphere, in its vertical extent, is divided into four zones – the troposphere, the stratosphere, the ionosphere and the exosphere. The troposphere, which means a sphere of change or turbulence, is the lowest layer which extends to a height of 18 km along the equator and 8 km along the poles. Water vapour, clouds, winds, storms and dust particles are associated with this zone. Weather phenomena, by and large, are restricted to troposphere. This layer is marked by thermal convection and more the thermal convection the greater the height of the troposphere. Normal lapse rate, or the fall of temperature with the increase of altitude is uniform in it. Temperature falls at the rate of 6.4° C per 1,000 metres or 3.5° F per 1,000 feet of ascent.

The next layer above the troposphere is stratosphere. The plane of separation between the two is called tropopause. In the lower part of the stratosphere the temperature remains fairly constant and air movement is almost horizontal. In the upper part of this layer there is an abundance of ozone which acts as a shield against the harmful ultraviolet radiation and allows only desirable amounts to reach the surface of the earth.

Composition

The atmosphere, or air, is a mixture of gases. The principal gases present are nitrogen (78%) and oxygen (21%). The other gas present, of the amount of 0.04 per cent, is carbon dioxide. Oxygen is indispensable for life and also supports combustion. Nitrogen dilutes the latter function of oxygen. Nitrogen and carbon dioxide are essential for plants. Traces of other gases in the air are argon, neon, xenon, krypton, helium, hydrogen, ozone, methane, sulphur dioxide and oxides of nitrogen. Air also contains water vapour and suspended particles. Carbon dioxide, from the point of view of weather, is the most important gas and its amount varies in space and time.

Changing state of water gives rise to a variety of weather phenomena as large quantities of heat are absorbed or released when its change of state takes place. Water vapour is added to the atmosphere by evaporation which takes place at all temperatures. The air as a result of evaporation gets cooled. Condensation of water vapour leads to liberation of latent heat when large quantities of heat energy is released into the atmosphere which, in turn, energizes a number of weather occurrences. Water vapour after condensation is returned to the earth through various forms of precipitation. Water vapour is lighter than air which makes moist air more buoyant than dry air. Atmosphere is said to be unstable when the air near the surface is warm and moist compared to cool air above.

Suspended matter comprising dust, fine sand, carbon particles, volcanic ash, pollen and specks of salt are constantly added to air. Some of these particulates serve as condensation nuclei for water vapour. Dust particles and gas molecules scatter sunlight. Tiny droplets of water and minute crystals of ice, due to their varying shapes cause reflection, refraction and dispersion of light. The resultant phenomena are blue colour of the sky, rainbow, reddish tint at sunrise and sunset and the halos round the sun and the moon.

In the following pages of this chapter a systematic study of such background topics as solar radiation, elements and factors of weather with reference to Jammu and Kashmir shall be taken up. Included in it, also, is the rationale of the classification of seasons. A detailed discussion of the weather and climate of its three regions shall be presented in the following chapters.

Solar Radiation

The sun is the main source of energy which fuels processes of change on the earth's surface and in atmosphere. A continuous flow of solar radiation is poured into space, of which a very small fraction is intercepted by the earth. This radiant energy that strikes the earth is called incoming solar radiation or, in brief, insolation. It travels in the form of invisible waves of short wavelengths. While passing through the space these waves have no warmth but on colliding with the surface of the earth insolation is absorbed and converted into heat. At this stage earth's surface behaves like a radiating body when energy is sent back in the form of invisible waves of long wavelengths. This is referred to as terrestrial radiation. These long waves are readily absorbed by the atmosphere. The air, therefore, is not heated directly by the incoming short wave radiation but by the re-radiated long waves. Earth's atmosphere permits a free entry of most of the insolation but does not allow the terrestrial radiation to pass through it as easily. Terrestrial radiation is partly absorbed by water vapour, ozone, carbon dioxide, methane and nitrous oxides present in the air. Consequently, a green house effect is created. The atmosphere serves as a blanket and maintains the earth, as a whole, at an average temperature of 13°C.

Heating and cooling of the atmosphere is determined by the balance between the radiant energy of different wavelengths received and reflected by the earth. On a clear day the insolation far exceeds the outgoing radiation, resulting in net gain. Temperature of air rises and attains maximum value, on land, two hours after noon. During a clear night, on the other hand, outgoing radiation continues whereas insolation is absent. There is a net loss and the temperature of the air falls. The minimum temperature is recorded few hours before dawn. All the three processes of heat transfer – conduction, convection and radiation are involved in the heating of the atmosphere. It is through radiation that the solar energy is received on the earth. Layers of the air in contact with the earth get heated by conduction. Air also gets heated by convection which has both horizontal and vertical components.

Global Warming

Among other things, two chief functions of the atmosphere are to shield the earth against injurious ultraviolet rays accompanying solar radiation and to trap heat to maintain the planet at a suitable temperature. There has been a considerable increase in the amount of green house gases like carbon dioxide, methane, tropospheric ozone and nitrous oxides during the last fifty years due to such human activities as burning of fossil fuels, clearing of forests, raising of livestock, etc. To this list of green house gases can be added the industrial chemicals called chlorofluorocarbons which trap heat in the lower atmosphere and deplete the ozone layer in the stratosphere. Carbon dioxide added to the atmosphere continues to remain in it for more than a hundred years (Stern, 2007). The large quantities of green house gases entrap proportional amounts of heat in the troposphere. The increase in atmospheric carbon dioxide from 288 parts per million (ppm) before industrialization, to 388 ppm now, is the main cause of global warming.

'Global warming is visible, is measurable and we project will get worse', asserts R.K. Pichauri.

Global warming, in turn, has led to climatic change which is manifest in rising temperatures, melting of ice caps and glaciers, increase in sea level, heavy rainfall around the world and extremes of weather. Global mean temperature of 13°C had increased to 14°C and then to 14.52°C in 1998 and was estimated to increase to 14.54°C in 2007. Extinction of both, animal and plant species, to the tune of 20 to 30 per cent, is likely to take place if temperature increases by 1.5 to 2.5°C. This does not bode well even for human life and activities. 'Go Green', is the recommended action plan for countering this unprecedented increase of green house gases in the atmosphere.

Insolation

The amount of insolation and consequent air temperature is determined by a number of causes, astronomical and meteorological.

Inclination of the Rays of the Sun

The angle at which rays of the sun are incident on the earth's surface is a function of latitude. The midday sun is vertically overhead only within the tropics. The rays become oblique as we move away from the tropics towards the poles. It is a well-known fact that vertical and oblique rays have different heating powers. By virtue of its location, between the latitudes of 33° and 37° N, Jammu and Kashmir lies in the subtropics. Table 7.1 gives the latitude of each representative station and the angle of incidence of the rays of sun at noon on different occasions in the year.

Table 7.1

Jammu and Kashmir: Angle of Incidence of the Rays of Midday Sun at the Three Representative Stations

S. No.	*Station*	*Latitude*	*Summer Solstice (June, 21)*	*Equinoxes (March, 21, September, 22)*	*Winter Solstice (December, 22)*
1.	Jammu City	32° 40' N	80° 50'	57° 20'	33° 50'
2.	Srinagar	34° 05' N	79 25'	55° 55'	32° 25'
3.	Leh	34° 09' N	79 21'	55° 51'	32° 21'

Table 7.1 reveals that the inclination of sunrays, at noon, is less than 90° at all the stations even at the time of summer solstice. This is expected of places located in the sub-tropics. Angle of incidence is maximum in Jammu city and minimum in Leh. It indicates a decrease

in the angle of inclination with the increase in latitude. This makes the state, compared to tropics, an area of low insolation intensity. The values of the angles of incidence, in each region, show a marked decrease as the year marches from summer solstice, through autumn equinox to winter solstice.

Duration of the Day

The second astronomical factor which determines the amount of insolation, after altitude of the sun, is the duration of day – the length of time between sunrise and sunset. On the world scale, the duration of the day at the equator is 12 hours and it increases progressively to 13hr 56 min at 30°; to 14 hr 51 min at 40°; 24 hours at 66° 30' latitudes; and 6 months at the poles (90°), (Critchfield, 1965). The length of the day varies from season to season. The duration of the day on summer solstice is 14h 10 min in Jammu city, 14h 26 min in Srinagar and 14h 29 min in Leh. The obliquity of sun's rays in these stations is compensated by the long duration of day in summer which results in greater insolation. The effect is reversed in winter. The maximum and minimum temperatures are experienced soon after summer and winter solstices respectively. Daylight of more than fourteen hours together with the highest altitude of the sun, during summer, helps in the growth and ripening of the crops particularly in Kashmir and Ladakh as life processes of the plants are solely dependent on daylight.

Sunshine and Cloudiness

In between the invisible bands of ultraviolet and infrared rays in the solar radiation lies the visible region called sunlight or sunshine. This is the most effective agent for heating the earth because longer the hours of sunshine the greater is the total possible insolation. Amount of sunshine is partly determined by the length of the day and partly by the presence or absence of cloud cover. The former is the function of latitude and the latter a meteorological phenomenon. A clear sky during the day guarantees great amounts of insolation and hence a high day temperature. Conversely, a clear sky at night permits a free flow of terrestrial radiation resulting in a sharp fall in night temperature. An overcast sky at night impedes dissipation of outgoing radiation. In summer, particularly in the months of July–August, with high humidity, cloudy nights increase mugginess leading to discomfort. In winter a cloudy night at a place like Srinagar means a frost free morning.

Regarding sunshine no quantitative inference can be drawn for Jammu city and Leh for want of required data. However, Leh a cold highland desert experiences clear skies for a greater part of the year. Most of the Jammu region shares sunshine characteristics of tropical monsoon climate.

With the installation of the sunshine recorder in Meteorological Centre, Srinagar, sunshine data was first available in 1977. Table 7.2 gives the total monthly hours of sunshine. Maximum amount of 250 hours of the same was received in June and minimum of 96.2 hours in December.

Percentage relationship between available hours of monthly sunshine and duration in hours of the daylight (Table 7.2) indicates that the sunniest month of the year in Srinagar is October, followed by November and February. For five months the percentage of sunshine is less than 50. A comparison between February and September in terms of percentage of monthly sunshine is of interest, whereas in both the hours of sunshine is nearly same, the sunshine percentage is dissimilar. Why? Srinagar receives average annual sunshine of 6 hrs 15 min against the average annual daylight of 12 hrs 9 min. It works out to 51 per cent. Srinagar, it follows, is not very favourably placed in terms of sunshine.

Table 7.2

Srinagar: Percentage of Monthly Duration of Sunshine and Daylight

Particulars	*J*	*F*	*M*	*A*	*M*	*J*	*J*	*A*	*S*	*O*	*N*	*D*	*Annual Average*
Monthly Duration of Sunshine (Hrs, min)	3–33	6–40	6–56	4–00	6–52	8–20	7–46	6–18	6–49	7–46	6–57	3–06	6–15
Monthly Duration of daylight (Hrs, min)	10–07	10–56	12–02	13–06	13–58	14–23	14–10	13–23	12–12	11–18	10–23	9–47	12–09
Percentage	31	61	55	31	48	58	52	47	54	67	64	32	51

Transparency of the Atmosphere

Clouds, dust particles, water vapour and certain gases play a vital role in absorbing, reflecting and scattering insolation. Slow pace of industrialization, absence of heavy industries using coal as fuel accounts for relative purity of air in Jammu and Kashmir. But the rapid development of road transport and the use of diesel and petrol in it, contributes its share of exhaust fumes and consequent pollutants to the air. Dust storms are of common occurrence in Jammu during dry hot summer. Large quantities of wind blown loess finds its way into the Valley. On such occasions the dust particles deplete the insolation by scattering it. The melting of snow in Kashmir mountains, in spring, is delayed, at times, by the loess hanging in the atmosphere, referred to as *zand* by the locals. As the air at higher altitudes is rarefied and clear, Ladakh region receives more effective insolation. This is, also, aided by the absence of water vapour and dust particles in its air.

Air Temperature

Air temperature is an important manifestation of solar energy. Among the elements of weather and climate, temperature is an independent variable. Changes in temperature cause variations in distribution of atmospheric pressure, wind direction, humidity, condensation, cloud formation and their movement. Temperature, in brief, controls all other elements both directly and indirectly. It is of great significance to living beings and affects their distribution. A number of factors influence the horizontal distribution of temperature on the surface of the earth. These are:

Latitude

As mentioned earlier, by virtue of its latitudinal location the entire state of Jammu and Kashmir lies in the subtropics. But the actual ground position presents an entirely a different picture. Subtropical climatic conditions are restricted to the southern half of the Jammu region. Prevalence of bamboo, the associated vegetation, sets its limit. Climatic data of Jammu city represents this sub-tropical climate. The remaining parts of the state like the highland belt of Jammu region, Kashmir and Ladakh experience different temperature conditions ranging from temperate to cold. Climate of these places can be denoted as modified subtropical and the modifying factor is altitude.

Altitude

In this hilly and mountainous state the altitude of places increases from south to north as is evident from the height above sea level, in metres, of Ranbir Singh Pura (The outer Plain) 300; Jammu city (The Siwaliks) 367; Batote (The Jammu Mountains) 1,540; Banihal (The Pir Panjal) 1,630; Srinagar (The Valley) 1,587; Dras (The Great Himalaya) 3,066, Leh (The Ladakh Range) 3,514; Karzok (The Rupshu Plateau) 4,572; and Sasser Kangri II (The Siachen Glacier) 7,672. The impact of altitude on temperature can be comprehended in view of the 'normal lapse rate'. High altitude areas are at lower temperature compared to places at lower altitude even on the same latitude.

Moreover, atmospheric pressure decreases with increase in altitude when air at higher elevations becomes rarefied. This rarefied atmosphere combined with absence of cloud cover and water vapour, as in case of Leh, inhibits green house effect. Consequently, in such highland areas free insolation during the day is followed by rapid radiation at night, marking a steep variation in its diurnal temperatures.

Climatic Zones

Temperature has been used to grade climatic zones on a scale of five: (a) *tropical* with annual and monthly averages above 20°C, (b) *sub-tropical* with four to eleven months above 20° and the balance between 10° and 20°C, (c) *temperate* with four to twelve months at 10° to 20°C and the rest cooler, (d) *cold* with one to four months at 10° to 20°C and the rest cooler, (e) *polar* with twelve months below 10°C. In places with modified subtropical climate a variation of + one month is acceptable. On the basis of this criteria let us evaluate the climate of Jammu city, Srinagar and Leh.

In Jammu city (Table 8.1) the average monthly temperature of above 20°C is registered in seven months while for the remaining five months it is between 10° and 20°C. So the climate of Jammu city is sub-tropical.

Figure 7.1

Jammu and Kashmir: Temperature Based Climatic Zones

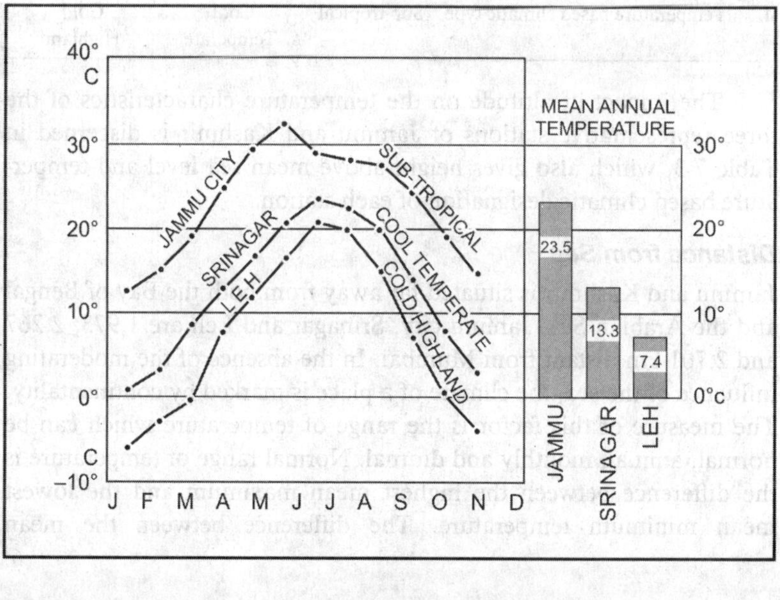

With the monthly mean temperature of 10°C to 20°C for three months the climate of Srinagar is temperate (Table 9.1). Is it warm or cool temperate? It can be warm when there is no month below 6.6°C (Miller), otherwise cool. In case of Srinagar, there are three months, January, February and December with an average monthly temperature of less than 6.6°C. Srinagar climate, therefore, is cool temperate. The main feature of the cool temperate climate, is a real cold season which retards or inhibits plant growth and places a check on farming activities. Plant growth among other factors, depends on soil temperature. According to Critchfield, most plants cease growth when soil temperature drops below 42°F or 5.5°C.

Average monthly temperature of Leh (Table 10.1) is between 10° and 20°C for 3 months and for seven months below 10°C. Leh climate, consequently, is cold highland but not polar or arctic.

Table 7.3

Jammu and Kashmir: Temperature Based Climatic Zones

Sr. No.	*Particulars*	*Jammu City*	*Srinagar*	*Leh*
1.	Altitude (metres)	367	1,587	3,514
2.	Mean annual temperature (°C)	23.5	13.3	7.4
3.	Hottest month	June	July	July
4.	Temperature based climatic type	Sub-tropical	Cool Temperate	Cold Highland

The impact of altitude on the temperature characteristics of the three representative stations of Jammu and Kashmir is discerned in Table 7.3, which also gives height above mean sea level and temperature based climatic designation of each station.

Distance from Sea

Jammu and Kashmir is situated far away from both the Bay of Bengal and the Arabian Sea. Jammu city, Srinagar and Leh are 1,973; 2,267 and 2,701 km distant from Mumbai. In the absence of the moderating influence of the sea, the climate of a place is marked by continentality. The measure of this factor is the range of temperature which can be normal, annual, monthly and diurnal. Normal range of temperature is the difference between the highest mean maximum and the lowest mean minimum temperature. The difference between the mean monthly temperature of the hottest month and the mean monthly temperature of the coldest is the annual range. Monthly range of temperature is calculated by subtracting the mean minimum temperature of a particular month from the mean maximum of the same month. The difference between the maximum and minimum temperature of a specific day is the diurnal range. Annual range of temperature of the three stations of Jammu and Kashmir is given in Table 7.4. It is highest in Leh and lowest in Jammu city. It reveals that all the three stations of Jammu and Kashmir have a continental type of climate wherein the climate of Leh is more continental than that of Srinagar and climate of Srinagar more continental compared to that of Jammu city.

Table 7.4

Jammu and Kashmir: Annual Range of Temperature

Sr. No.	*Particulars*	*Jammu City*	*Srinagar*	*Leh*
1.	Distance from Mumbai (km)	1,973	2,267	2,701
2.	Mean temperature of the hottest month (°C)	32.9	24.1	21.5
3.	Mean temperature of the coldest month (°C)	13.2	1.5	–6.8
4.	Annual range of temperature (°C)	19.7	22.6	28.3

Nature of the Surface

Another factor that affects temperature is the nature of the land surface which depicts a great variety. In the northern hemisphere, slopes with a southern aspect have a sunny prospect. Snow does not stay on such slopes for long. These are, generally, bereft of vegetation. On the contrary snow melts gradually on north-facing slopes and provides soil with moisture to sustain plant growth. The saplings after getting the foothold in the soil throw out foliage which in turn shelter the ground beneath and help it to retain moisture. Bare and rocky surfaces reflect and scatter heat whereas, covered and wet surfaces absorb it. Constituents of the land surface are differently effected by the sun. Sand heats up and cools quickly. Clay, on the other hand, absorbs heat. Temperature of ice and snow cannot rise above O°C even on the hottest day.

Climate of an area is considerably altered where houses and factories are constructed in place of farms and forests. Cities of today have become jungles of concrete where thousands of tonnes of concrete, stones, bricks and iron go into the construction of high rise buildings, where soft and loose soil is replaced by waterproof asphalt covered roads and building blocks. In such environs the heat reflected and scattered creates, almost, desert like conditions.

Atmospheric Pressure and Winds

Climatological significance of atmospheric pressure lies in its control of winds. Wind is air in horizontal motion. It is caused by variations in air pressure. The pressure difference is the result of unequal heating of the earth's surface. Free movement of the air equalizes pressure variations. Winds blow from areas of high pressure to areas of low pressure. Wind speed depends on pressure gradient.

As air has weight, it exerts pressure upon the earth on which it rests. The lower layers of the atmosphere are denser as these are compressed by the layers above. Air pressure is maximum at sea level but decreases with the increase in elevation. It changes from place to place and at the same place from time to time (Table 9.3). Table 7.5 gives the standard pressure and height relationship.

Table 7.5

Pressure-Height Relationship*

Height		*Pressure*	*Height*		*Pressure*	*Height*		*Pressure*
(Feet)	*(Metres)*	*(mb)*	*(Feet)*	*(Metres)*	*(mb)*	*(Feet)*	*(Metres)*	*(mb)*
Sea Level		1,013.25	5,000	1,524.0	843	10,000	3,048.0	696
2,000	609.6	942	6,000	1,828.8	812	15,000	4,572.0	672
4,000	1,219.2	875	8,000	2,438.4	753	20,000	6,096.0	466

* After Critchfield — mb: millibar

The table reveals that there is a close link between altitude and atmospheric pressure and higher the altitude lower is the pressure. Consequently, the air at higher elevations becomes rarefied. The rarefied air at a height of 3,000 metres contains small amounts of oxygen so more air has to be inhaled, in order to get the required amount of this life sustaining gas. This leads to faster breathing and other forms of sicknesses. Survival above 6,000 m is difficult without inhaling oxygen from an external source.

The mean annual station-level pressure in Jammu city is 975 mb or hPa (hecta Pascal). It is 840.5 hPa in Srinagar and 686.4 mb in Leh. Leh with the highest altitude has the lowest atmospheric pressure. It is higher in Srinagar and highest in Jammu compared to Leh. Line graphs depicting station-level pressure of Jammu city, Srinagar and Leh are presented in Figure 7.2

Figure 7.2

Jammu and Kashmir: Station-Level Pressure (mb or hPa)

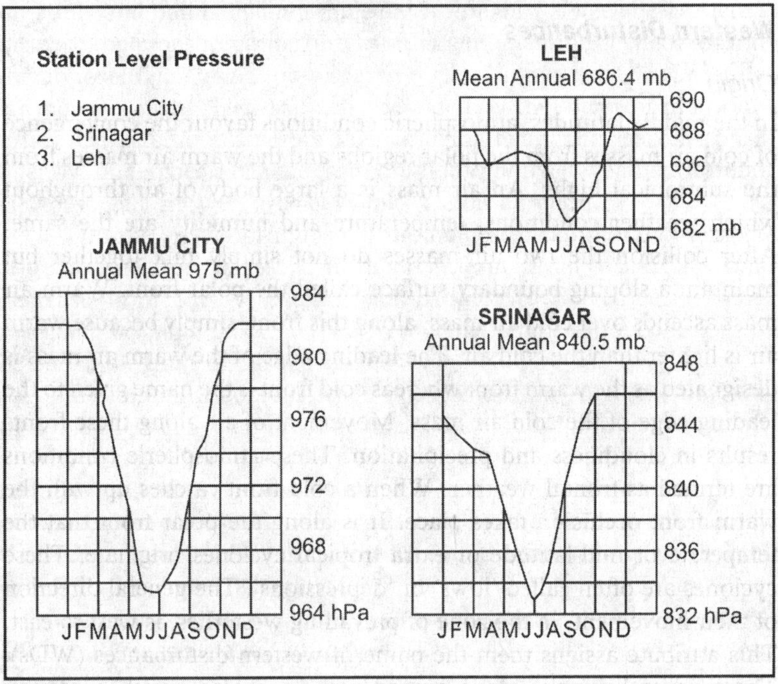

Wind Systems

A hypothetical arrangement of pressure belts and planetary wind systems has been identified on thc globc. Ncar thc cquator is an area of low pressure called equatorial low or Doldrums. Air from the northern and the southern hemispheres converges in this low, giving rise to inter-tropical convergence zone (ITCZ). At about 30°N and 30°S is an area of high pressure known as sub-tropical high or Horse Latitudes. Near the polar circles is the sub-polar low pressure belt. The region of high pressure near the poles is labelled as polar high. There is a south and northward shift of these pressure belts with the movement of the thermal equator. Trade winds blow from sub-tropical high towards the equatorial trough. Winds blowing from the sub-tropical high towards sub-polar low constitute the westerlies. With the shift of the thermal equator towards the Tropic of Capricorn, the westerlies move southwards and cause rainfall in the Mediterranean region. At this time Jammu and Kashmir comes under their influence. This is the cause of its winter precipitation. During summer, when the thermal equator shifts towards the Tropic of Cancer, this arrangement gets disturbed when the Indian subcontinent is visited by onshore monsoons.

Western Disturbances

Origin

In the middle latitudes, atmospheric conditions favour the convergence of cold air masses from the polar regions and the warm air masses from the subtropical highs. An air mass is a large body of air throughout which weather conditions, temperature and humidity are the same. After collision the two air masses do not simply mix together but maintain a sloping boundary surface called the polar front. Warm air mass ascends over cold air mass, along this front, simply because warm air is lighter than the cold air. The leading edge of the warm air mass is designated as the warm front whereas cold front is the name given to the leading edge of the cold air mass. Movement of air along these fronts results in cloudiness and precipitation. These atmospheric conditions are termed as frontal weather. When a cold front catches up with the warm front occlusion takes place. It is along the polar front that the temperate or mid-latitude or extra tropical cyclones originate. These cyclones are often called 'lows' or 'depressions'. The general direction of their movement, in the zone of prevailing westerlies, is west to east. This attribute assigns them the name of western disturbances (WDs). These generally move along curved paths and also travel in groups. Western disturbances originate from eastern Mediterranean sea and pick up moisture from the Caspian sea and the Persian gulf, depending upon the direction of their movement. When these mid-latitude cyclones pass over the rugged terrain of Iran, Afghanistan and Pakistan they undergo a change in their moisture content and reach north-western India in an occluded form. In that case they give little or no rainfall. But on most occasions they arrive with, both, a warm front and a cold front and the precipitation received is plentiful. The arrival of the western disturbances in India is facilitated by that branch of the jet stream which re-establishes itself to the south of the Himalayas in winter.

Associated Weather

As the depression advances a definite sequence of temperature change, cloud type and kind of precipitation is observed with each passing front, warm or cold. Arrival of the depression is heralded by the appearance of cirrus clouds. Temperature increases but pressure falls with the advent of the warm front. Clouds thicken into stratus type, sky becomes overcast and rainfall follows. It is moderate but widespread and may change into sleet and snow. After passing of the warm front the pressure increases and temperature begins to fall. With the arrival of the cold front cumulus clouds replace the stratus and the dominant cloud is the cumulonimbus. Heavy showers of rain are received accompanied by lightning and thunder. It is soon followed by clear weather and blue sky. A stage reaches when the cold front overtakes the warm front which results in occlusion after which the cyclone dies away.

Frequency

A total of twenty-eight western disturbances in a year arrive in Jammu and Kashmir during winter and spring, from January to May and November to December. Precipitation in the lowlands takes the form of rainfall and in highlands it falls as snow. The reserves of snow in the Pir Panjal, the Great Himalaya, the Zanskar, the Ladakh and the Karakoram get replenished due to this frontal precipitation. It is the main source of water in all the three regions of the state. Spring rainfall in Kashmir helps in thawing and softens the soil for its easy ploughing. The rabi crops in Jammu region, including wheat, in unirrigated areas depends entirely on this frontal rainfall.

Heavy snowfall in highlands like Dras, Sonamarg, Tilel, Gurez, Keran, Chowkibal and Machil followed by avalanches and landslides, at times, cause a heavy loss of life and property as was witnessed during the winters of 2004–2005 and 2011–2012. Snowstorms and blizzards, with poor visibility, are also experienced in highlands.

Monsoons

Monsoon wind system is a seasonal wind characterized by a complete reversal of direction from one season to another. The winds blow from sea to land in summer and cause rainfall. In winter they move from land to sea. The main sphere of influence of monsoon winds is south and south-east Asia. India has a well-developed and an ideal monsoon regime because of its nearness to the equator, presence of a lofty mountain barrier in the north and the Indian ocean skirting it in the south.

Mechanism

Monsoon is a complex phenomenon and its mechanism is still far from clear. An earlier view is based on the principle of differential heating of land and water and the consequent thermal contrast leading to pressure variation. During summer months land gets heated more quickly than water. An area of low pressure develops overland, when the pressure is high over the sea. Winds blow from high pressure area over the sea to land where the pressure is low. In winter the location of the pressure systems gets reversed and winds blow from land to sea. This causal behaviour of monsoons categorizes it as sea and land breeze on a gigantic scale.

The later investigations, including the Monsoon Expedition (MONEX, 1973), revealed that in addition to the above-mentioned pressure systems and surface winds, upper air winds and their circulation play a vital role in the monsoon mechanism. It is also aided by the presence of snow covered Tibetian plateau and the Himalaya. The upper air wind circulation involved is the jet stream, which normally travels between the latitudes of 20° to 40° north at an altitude of 7 to 11 km. The Tibetian plateau and the high Himalaya, acting as a barrier, bifurcates it into the northern and the southern branches. During summer, with high and low pressure systems in place over sea and land what accentuates the onrush of monsoon winds, at this stage, is the dislocation of the southern branch of the jet stream which, by the middle of June, shifts to the north of the Himalayas. Both these factors create conditions conducive to the attraction of the trade winds from the southern hemisphere. The south-east trades are sucked in which, after crossing the equator, undergo a change in direction. Due to the shift of the thermal equator towards the Tropic of Cancer these planetary winds assume the form of equatorial Westerlies. This becomes the summer or the south-west or the onshore monsoon. Tropical continental air of the subcontinent is replaced by equatorial maritime winds which give widespread and abundant rainfall. The surface low pressure system is joined by a series of tropical cyclones which determine the distribution pattern of monsoon rainfall.

Monsoon mechanism, of late, has also been linked with an occasional phenomenon of 'El Nino' which comes about the coast of Peru where a warm ocean current temporarily replaces the cold Humboldt current. Its occurrence is a harbinger of weak monsoon as it causes drought in Asia.

With the fall in temperature in north-west India, October–November onwards, a high pressure system is in place here. Winds blow from this high pressure area towards sea where there exists a low pressure system. The direction of these winds is north-east to south-west. These winds are dry except when they pass over a stretch of sea and pick up moisture. Areas of winter monsoon rainfall are Tamil Nadu and eastern Sri Lanka. By this time the southern branch of the jet stream resumes its earlier position. Its presence favours the arrival of extra tropical depressions.

Regime

Indian meteorologists have come up with a schedule for the arrival and retreat of south-west monsoon. Their date of arrival in Keraḷa is first of June and by 15 July the entire subcontinent is covered by them. Retreat of summer monsoon from north-west India takes place by 15 September.

The south-west monsoon gets bifurcated into the Bay of Bengal branch and Arabian Sea branch. Deflected by the Arakan Yoma, of Myanmar, the Bay of Bengal branch runs almost parallel to the Himalayas. The Arabian Sea branch moves along the western parts of the country as far as Rajasthan. The two branches combine together and proceed towards north-west. The onset of monsoon at a place is heralded by dark clouds accompanied by lightning and thunder and a heavy shower of rain. This phenomenon is called the 'burst of monsoon'.

Summer monsoon brings abundant rainfall to the Indian subcontinent which receives 75 to 90 per cent of it from June to September. But this rain does not fall continuously. It is erratic as, in it, wet spells alternate with dry periods. Much of this rain is the result of tropical cyclones.

An extension of the seasonal low into the Indo-Gangetic plain is called monsoon trough. It is a low pressure area strong enough to pull monsoons in its direction. The tropical depressions which originate at the head of the Bay of Bengal move in the west-north westerly direction along the axis of this monsoon trough. The trough oscillates to the north and to the south. Indian plains receive fair amounts of rainfall when the monsoon trough is stationed over Indo-Gangetic plain. In case it shifts north, close to the Himalayas, the dry spell in the plains become longer. A copious rainfall takes place in the highland region where lie the catchment areas of the Himalayan rivers. The rivers overflow with excess water causing devastating floods in their middle courses. Thus, the track of tropical cyclones is determined entirely by the monsoon trough. Sometimes in late August or early September the tropical depressions recurve on reaching Rajasthan and move in northerly or north-westerly direction towards Jammu and Kashmir causing widespread heavy rainfall leading to floods in its rivers (A. Krishnan and Bhatia, 1960). In case they do not recurve, such depressions give heavy rainfall over western India. The amount of monsoon rainfall received depends on the direction, intensity and number of tropical cyclones together with orography.

During the period of onshore monsoon the amount of rainfall received at different places is not uniform for two reasons. First, the rainy season in the south lasts for four months, June to September but in the north it is restricted to July to September. Second, as the distance from sea increases the moisture content of these onshore winds decreases with their passage inland. When the total rainfall of Kolkata is 120 cm, it is only 56 cm at Delhi. With the arrival of rains, temperature falls but humidity increases which gives respite to humans as well as animals from the scorching heat of the dry summer. Plant growth gets accelerated and the landscape is transformed from brown to green.

Attributes

Monsoon is fickle. It is known for its vagaries. It may arrive late or retreat early. Rainfall may be too little or too heavy. It is not unusual to find famine conditions at two places, simultaneously, in one due to floods and in the other due to drought. The breaks between the spells of rainfall may be too long to cause crop failure. There has been perceptible increase in the area under irrigation, due to socio-economic development plans, yet a substantial portion of our cropland, to the extent of about sixty per cent, still relies upon rainfall. The dependence of economic health of India on the monsoon continues to be total as is evident from the failure of monsoon in 2009 and consequent worst drought since 1972.

The subtropical areas of Jammu region form part of the monsoon regime. A well-defined rainy season is experienced here from July to September. Monsoon rains are widespread and heavy up to the outer slopes of the Pir Panjal range. Many scholars are sceptical about the extension of monsoon influence to Kashmir and Ladakh on account of the intervening lofty mountain barriers. But an appraisal of the rainfall data of Srinagar and Leh, in the regional section, testifies to the arrival of the south-west monsoon into these regions, though with less intensity.

Jet Streams

In the zone between the upper troposphere and lower stratosphere, in mid-latitudes, high speed winds blow from the west to the east. These winds called jet streams encircle the globe with a width that varies from 40 to 160 km. These have a depth of 2 to 3 km. The wind speed in summer is 50 km but it changes to 120 km in winter. This upper air wind circulation needs to be differentiated from the surface winds. Jet streams play a vital role in causing weather. Lately, these winds have been found to contribute their share in the monsoon mechanism. These also facilitate the arrival of western disturbances into the north and north-western India.

Cold Waves

In winter an anticyclone gets established in the middle of Asia at 45°N and 110°E. It is called the Siberian high. In January, there is maximum accumulation in it of cold continental air. Winds from this anticyclone find their entry into north-western India, including Jammu and Kashmir, despite the barrier effect of the Himalayas. This cold air results in considerable fall of temperature at the places of their visit. In Ladakh winds of sub-zero temperature are experienced. But while moving down the Himalayan slopes there is a slight increase in their temperature. Consequently, these winds are less cold as they reach Kashmir. According to India Meteorological Department (IMD) criterion, a cold wave prevails when the fall in night temperature is 6°C below normal. It is a severe cold wave, when the decrease in temperature is 8°C or more. Generally, Ladakh region is subjected to severe cold waves when Kashmir experiences cold waves. With the arrival of the western disturbances, cold wave conditions are broken and normal weather is restored.

Atmospheric Moisture

Water present on the earth's surface in oceans, lakes, rivers, wetlands, glaciers, ice fields and even in falling rain and snow is converted, constantly, into the gaseous state as a result of the process of evaporation. Evaporation changes visible water into invisible water vapour which becomes an essential constituent of air. Water vapour is the most important gas so far as weather is concerned. It is added to the atmosphere by life forms through respiration and by plants through evapotranspiration. It is restricted to the lower layers of the troposphere. In its cool upper layers it condenses to form clouds. Rain bearing clouds are carried thousands of kilometres inland and the precipitation that follows fills the ice fields, lakes, streams and reservoirs. It returns to the sea through rivers. In this way an uninterrupted exchange of water between the oceans, the atmosphere and the land takes place. This is called hydrologic cycle. Atmospheric moisture is manifest in such weather phenomena as humidity, different forms of condensation and precipitation.

Humidity

Air can be dry or humid depending upon its water vapour content. Humidity connotes the state of atmosphere with respect to presence of water vapour in it. Water holding capacity of air varies with the variations in temperature. It increases with the increase in temperature and decreases with its fall. The three indices of humidity are absolute, specific and relative. The index in common use is relative humidity.

Relative humidity is the ratio between the amount of water vapour actually present in a given volume of air and the amount of water vapour required to saturate it. It is expressed in percentage. It is 100 per cent in saturated air. The critical temperature at which air gets saturated is called dew point. At this temperature water vapour begins to change into water. In case the relative humidity is 50 per cent the air is unsaturated and its moisture holding content is half of its moisture holding capacity at that temperature. Low value of relative humidity indicates a relatively dry air. The average annual relative humidity of Jammu city, Srinagar and Leh is 53.7, 69.7 and 40 per cent respectively. It is inferred that the climate of Srinagar is more humid than that of Jammu city and Leh and the climate of Leh is relatively dry.

Sensible Temperature

Humidity plays a significant role in human health, comfort and work efficiency. Human comfort or discomfort is not caused only by temperature but by temperature associated with humidity. Sensible temperature is the term used for this purpose. It does not refer only to thermometer reading but to the heat or cold one actually feels. High temperature and high humidity produce high sensible temperature leading to much discomfort. It is on this account that we feel unease on hot muggy days of July–August.

Body of a healthy human being is maintained at a constant temperature of 37°C (98.4°F) and its defence mechanism prevents either too much absorption or too much loss of heat. Heat produced in the body as a result of metabolism must balance the heat loss so as to maintain equilibrium. On a hot dry day the body perspires excessively and its quick evaporation from the skin and the respiratory tract causes cooling. On the contrary, on a hot humid day the surrounding saturated air hinders evaporation and one feels uncomfortable. Comfort sensations are basically concerned with the process of heat loss from the body. The stress is reduced to minimum by creating a micro-environment through artificial cooling through air-conditioners, fans, coolers, etc. (Menon, 1993). The extreme weather conditions as too hot, too cold, too humid and too dry are detestable. An ideal climate is defined as sunny, warm, dry and free from wind. Satisfactory working conditions are when the temperature ranges between 15.5° and 24.5°C and relative humidity is between 40 to 70 per cent. The feeling of comfort being highly subjective, no unanimity has been possible for devising an ideal index of comfort/discomfort. Hot humid conditions make humans susceptible to a number of infections and allergies due to the profuse growth of bacteria and insects.

Condensation

Condensation is a process opposite to that of evaporation, for here the change takes place from gaseous to the liquid or solid state. The mass of air, in case of condensation, should be cooled below its dew point. It also takes place by the cooling of unsaturated air, not exactly below its dew point, but by the presence of condensation nuclei, called aerosols, like common salt, specks of dust, pollen and negatively charged ions. Water vapour cool, as a result of radiation of heat from the surface of the earth, on a clear and calm night by the mixing together of two air currents of different temperatures, movement of warm air over a cold surface and by ascent. Different forms of condensation, floating and deposited, are produced by each of these cooling processes. The condensed particles of water and ice crystals are so minute that they float in the air as fog, mist and clouds. Large drops of water and ice crystals are deposited on leaves and grass as dew and frost.

Deposited Condensation

Dew

On a calm, clear night when the temperature falls, due to radiation, below dew point, the water vapour present in the layer of air resting on the ground is deposited in the form of dew on soil, vegetation and other objects. Conditions essential for the formation of dew are a warm day to increase the water vapour content of the air, a clear night to favour quick radiation and a calm situation to help in the condensation of water vapour.

Frost

When the dew point is below freezing, the moisture present in the air is deposited directly in the form of tiny crystals of ice. The silver white glistening powder is frost. It is the common form of deposited condensation noticed in Kashmir during its core winter. It gets carried into homes along with its unique vegetable of *Hak-sag.*

Floating Condensation

Fog

It is a low level stratus cloud with its base at or near ground level. Fog can be of radiation, advection and frontal type depending upon the cooling process involved. The thickness of the fog depends on the concentration of water droplets. In fog, visibility is less than one kilometre. In mist, which is a similar phenomenon as fog, the visibility is between one and two kilometres. Haze, a thin mist, has a visibility of 2 to 5 km.

Clouds

These are huge floating masses of tiny water droplets and ice crystals at an elevation ranging between ground level and a height of 12 km. These also consist of super cooled water droplets, which though cooled below freezing point retain their liquid form. It typifies an intermediate stage in the conversion of water vapour from the gaseous to the liquid or solid state. Clouds help us to know the processes at work in the atmosphere. To a scenic spot like Kashmir they contribute their share in enhancing its beauty and charm by the fantastic shapes and hues they acquire. Many a sunsets observed from the eastern shore of the Dal lake have been quite bewitching.

Different criteria have been adopted for the classification of clouds. One is based on their height, when clouds can be of high, medium or low altitude. Clouds which extend from the surface of the earth to a height of 2 km are called low clouds. *Alto* or the middle are formed between altitudes of 2 to 6 km. *Cirro* or the high clouds have their base at an elevation of 6 km. Low clouds are composed of droplets of water and high clouds of ice crystals, while the medium clouds are a mixture of both.

The second criterion is based on their form and structure. Clouds in the form of sheets of large extent are called *stratus*. Those of fibrous type are *cirrus,* wind torn and ragged *fracto*, and of heaped form cumulus. In the following discussion the symbol of each cloud type is given in parenthesis (Critchfield 1965).

Cirrus (C), a forerunner of a temperate cyclone, is feathery and fibrous which usually takes the form of locks of hair. *Cirrostratus* (Cs) is a cloud which appears as the milkness of the sky in which the halos of the sun and the moon can be seen. A series of rows of globular clouds with rippled appearance constitute *Cirrocumulus* (Cc). A thin cloud through which the sun and the moon assume a watery appearance is *altostratus* (As). *Altocumulus* (Ac) comprises patches of globular clouds arranged in the form of waves. A darker cloud very common in winter is *stratocumulus* (Sc). *Nimbostratus* (Ns) is known for its heavy rainfall. A low cloud of common occurrence in summer afternoon, formed as a result of convection, is *cumulus.* (Cu) This beautiful cloud has a horizontal base and round cauliflower – like heads. The horizontal base represents the level of condensation. By evening these flatten into *stratus* (St) on account of the decrease in temperature. These are brilliantly coloured by the setting sun. On a hot moist day when the ascending air currents in a cumulus cloud are strong it takes the form of an anvil shaped cloud called *cumulonimbus* (Cb). With it is associated heavy rain, hailstorm, lightning and thunder. A stratus cloud broken into patches is termed *fractostratus* (Fs).

Cloud observation aids weather forecasting. Cloud types are recorded at meteorological observatories by visible observations and expressed in eighths or oktas. A sky is overcast when the cloud number is eight oaktas. It is clear when the number of oktas is zero. Farmers have a keen sense of forecasting weather with the help of clouds. They smell weather, so to say, and start or abandon their operations accordingly. Even a layman is conversant with the following saying:

> Red morning is the shepherd's warning. Red evening is the shepherd's delight.

Precipitation

In the climatic study of any place precipitation, after temperature, is the most significant element. The minute droplets of water and or tiny crystals of ice in a cloud, under favourable conditions, collide and coalesce, grow bigger in size. Unable to float any longer, these fall earthwards under the force of gravity, in various forms of precipitation like drizzle, rain, hail, sleet and snow. Most of the precipitation takes the form of rain and snow but it is easy to measure rainfall. Hence precipitation is considered analogous to rainfall and is expressed in millimetres or centimetres.

Types of Rainfall

The processes of condensation and precipitation involve considerable ascent of air masses so that these get adiabatically cooled, reach the dew point, form clouds, get saturated and may ultimately, fall in liquid or solid form. This ascent or atmospheric lifting mechanism is brought about in three ways – orographic, convectional and frontal.

Orographic

When ascent of warm, humid air is caused by mountain barrier which is aligned at right angle to the path of the air current, the consequent precipitation is orographic in nature. Unstable air ascends more easily over an obstacle when the stable air has the tendency to move round it. It is on this account that more rain falls on the windward side of the mountain and less on its leeward side. In Jammu and Kashmir the Pir Panjal range acts as a climatic barrier between Jammu region and Kashmir. Poonch on windward side of the Pir Panjal receives 717 mm of rain from July to September when Gulmarg on its leeward side receives only 284 mm during the same period. The configuration of the mountain ranges, in the state, places Kashmir in the rain shadow of the Pir Panjal and Ladakh in the rain shadow of the Great Himalaya. The total annual rainfall received in the representative stations of these regions is 1156.7 mm in Jammu city, 698.3 mm in Srinagar and 81.9 mm in Leh.

The impact of relief on the precipitation is best exemplified by the transverse valley of the Sindh. The air currents readily enter this narrow valley, get entrapped, ascend to higher elevations and cause copious rainfall in the headwater region of the stream. Sonamarg, consequently, receives the highest rainfall, in Kashmir region, of 1815 mm.

Convectional

Dry air which is usually stable, becomes unstable when water vapour gets added to it. In summer, hot and moist air undergoes ascent due to the process of convection. This moisture-laden air expands, cools and becomes saturated followed by condensation and precipitation. The warm and damp rising air together with cold upper air create highly unstable conditions. Consequently, a cumulonimbus cloud is formed which stretches to a height of about 8 km. What follows is a thunder-storm. It is a local storm characterized by lightning, thunder, strong winds, a heavy downpour and even hail. Thunderstorms, are of two types – thermal and frontal. Thermal thunderstorms formed during summer, are restricted to land. These are formed on a hot humid day mostly in the afternoon. Frontal thunderstorms are formed when a cold air mass is undercutting and lifting a warm air mass. These occur in winter and are formed over land and sea.

The favourable conditions for the development of a thermal thunderstorm are a high temperature and high humidity of the surface air so that it furnishes cumulonimbus cloud with ample moisture. Secondly, the lapse rate must be steep so that a rapid fall of temperature is effected with the increasing height. The base of the cumulonimbus is formed of dark threatening clouds while at its top is an anvil shaped cirrus umbrella consisting of ice crystals. Inside it are present one or more chimneys or convective cells. Circulation in each is independent of the other. Thunder clouds attain a diameter of 8 to 40 km. In the chimney are found strong up and down currents. Warm moist air is carried upwards where it undergoes condensation to form droplets of water. Enormous heat energy is released as a result of condensation.

This local heating of air causes violent up draughts. The droplets coalesce to form bigger drops of water which tend to fall downwards but the up current is so strong that these drops of water are carried to very cold upper regions of this cloud where they freeze to form ice crystals. These ice crystals form the nuclei of hail stones. The strong up currents of air carry these ice particles upwards where supercooled water drops, freeze round them to give them a coat of opaque ice. The opacity of each hailstone is due to the air enclosed in the thin coat of ice. On its downward journey it again collects water droplets round it which assumes the form of transparent ice. The presence of onion-like alternate layers, of transparent and opaque ice, gives an idea about the number of times the rise and fall has taken place. Finally, when the strength of the chimney gets depleted a very heavy shower of rain or a hailstorm takes place. The rain drops are quite large so are the hailstones. Lightning and thunder are the essential associates of a thunderstorm. Lightning strikes a number of solitary objects like tall trees (sight encountered during the trek from Gulmarg to Khillanmarg), metallic objects, isolated structures in open spaces and mountain tops. It even kills animals and humans. Hailstorms destroy crops and damage fruit. Convectional precipitation, though heavy, is highly localized with minimum cloudiness.

Sometimes the downpour from a thunder cloud is in the sheet form, when it is referred to as cloudburst. In that case much loss of life and property is caused. A cloudburst took place in Pahalgam on 20 July 1963 at 5 pm. The scar left by it on the landscape of this tourist resort speaks for itself, the devastation caused by it. Cloudbursts are of common occurrence in the highlands of Jammu and Kashmir mostly in July and August. The worst cloudburst of Leh, of 5–6 August, 2010, followed by flash floods, which washed down mud and rock, claimed more than 250 lives and caused great loss of property and infrastructure.

The present writer had a first-hand brush with the aftermath of a cloudburst.

> On 15 July when the bus left Handwara for Wader, on way to Nichahom lignite deposits, the weather was clear but hot and humid. The road to Wader occupied a higher ground along the left bank of a stream. Its water was clear like other streams of the Valley. Four kilometres short of Wader our attention was arrested by the crying and wailing of a group of peasants on the right bank of the stream. To our astonishment we found the rivulet transformed into a gushing mud torrent.
>
> The large volume and swift current threatened to submerge and lay waste the well-grown paddy fields on its banks. In addition to a heavy load of

> coffee brown Lower Karewa clay the other tools of destruction carried by it were full-sized conifer trees, broken awkwardly during their downward journey, with each piece acting as a giant chisel. What was the reason? A cloudburst (Kashmiri-Aabi Treth). Where? In the catchment area of the of the stream. Close to Wader there is a sharp bend in the road to the right and before us floated, at a distance, clouds at tree top level. This was the site of the cloudburst. As it took place, it eroded and washed down the surface layers of the Karewa hill and its forest cover. This had taken place, probably, between 2:30 and 3 pm.
>
> The weather at Wader was fair and we took to a footpath to ascend the Lower Karewa upland. We hardly walked for about fifty minutes when clouds from nowhere appeared without any forewarning and poured their hearts out. The spot where we stood was Soyam, the area where the surface clay was baked red by subterranean thermal activity a century and a half ago. There was no shelter. Talking about the intensity of the rainfall it was simply a deluge. The ground became miry and the clay sticky, shoes water filled, clothes and body dripping wet, spectacles misty, the guide a local teenager physically responding to the instinct of self-preservation and wishing to leave but culturally reluctant to desert me in that wilderness ...*

In a thunderstorm when the water vapour content is low, showers do not take place. Instead, the downward squalls scoop up dust or sand in arid and desert regions which lead to the formation of a duststorm or a sandstorm. Visibility in a duststorm is nil hence it is called *aandhi.* These are of frequent occurrence in subtropical Jammu.

Frontal

The precipitation received in Jammu and Kashmir in January to May and November to December is of frontal origin. It is discussed in detail in the section on 'Western Disturbances' in this chapter.

Intensity of Rainfall

Rainfall intensity is defined as the total amount of rainfall received per unit of time. It is calculated with the help of the formula. I=P/N where I is the intensity of rainfall, P the precipitation in millimetres and N the number of days. The problems linked with it are absorption, run-off, soil erosion, flood control and evaporation. It is an aid to judge the nature of showers, whether heavy or light, regular or irregular.

Dryness and Wetness

For determining dryness or wetness of a particular month the following definitions of Bagnouls and Gaussen (1953, 1964) are being considered.

---

* The present writer is highly indebted to Khwaja Mohamad Mir, son of Gaffor of Dal, Wader, Nichahom for his affection and attention in that hour of distress.

(i) A month is very dry when its mean rainfall in mm is less than its mean temperature T in °C.

Very Dry, $P < T$

(ii) It is dry when rainfall is less than twice the temperature.

Dry, $P < 2T$

(iii) The month is sub-dry when rainfall is between two and three times the temperature.

Sub-Dry, P Between 2T and 3T

(iv) In sub-humid conditions precipitation is between three and four times the temperature.

Sub-Humid, P between 3T and 4T

(v) A month is humid when the rainfall is greater than four times the temperature.

Humid, $P > 4T$

Classification of Seasons

The preceding systematic study of the weather and climate of Jammu and Kashmir, clearly illustrates that climate of its three regions is distinctly dissimilar. In such a situation it is quite difficult to choose a scheme, out of the few available, for a description of its seasons. This problem seized the attention of present writer, in the seventies of last century, when an attempt was made to find a dependable basis of seasonal classification of Kashmir. This effort resulted in the publication of paper 'Seasons of Kashmir Valley', in the *Geographical Review of India.*

Certain geographical tenets deserve to be considered regarding yearly march of the seasons of a particular place. In temperate regions seasonal changes are temperature induced whereas, in tropical monsoon climes it is initiated by rainfall. The seasonal changes in the highlands are, also, brought about by temperature.

Modern geography in its explanatory descriptions advocates the adoption of a methodology which comprises the essentials of *literacy, graphicacy* and *numeracy.* In the quantitative appraisal of each available classification the first step involved is to find the temperature range of each season with the hap of mean monthly or 5-day normals data. It shall be followed by comparing these temperature values. The norm set up for accepting a particular scheme is that the temperature range of each season, in it, is uniform regardless of its duration. The seasonal classifications are presented in their historical order.

Traditional Classification

The first and the age-old, indigenous scheme, which forms part of Indian ethos and tradition, divides the year into six 'ritus' or seasons, each of two months duration. These are Vasanta (spring), Grishma (summer), Varsha (rainy season), Sharada (autumn), Hemanta (cool season), and Shishira (cold season). The Kashmiri equivalents of these terms, respectively, are *Sont, Gresham, Wahraat, Harud, Wandah* and *Shishur*. The two-month period of each season according to Gregorian calendar consists of second half of one month, full second month and the first half of third month. Use of monthly mean temperature in this case is not feasible. Instead, 5-day normals of mean maximum and mean minimum temperatures of Srinagar have been utilized. The results obtained are presented in Table 7.6. It is found that mean temperature range of 5.2°C. in summer is approximately equal to 5.5°C of cool winter. It is highest, 8.8°C in autumn and 7.3°C in spring. The rainy season and cold winter have the lowest range of 3.4°C and 4.3⁻°C, respectively. In spite of this two-season near equality of range of temperature, the overall picture is far from satisfactory. Range of temperature values of all the seasons are dissimilar. Hence, this classification is not worthy of acceptance. Traditional classification of seasons, is at best, qualitative in essence, for each name conveys the main attributes of the climate obtainable in that season. Varsha (Wahraat), for example, stands for the rainy season (July 16 to September 15), when the country is under the sway of south-west monsoon.

Table 7.6

Quantitative Appraisal of the Traditional Classification of Seasons of Srinagar

S. No.	*Season (Kashmiri Name)*	*Extent*	*Duration (month)*	*Mean Temperature (°C)*	*Temperature Range (°C)*
1.	Sont (Spring)	16 March to 15 May	2	10 to 17.3	7.3
2.	Grishum (Summer)	May 16 to July 15	2	19.1 to 24.3	5.2
3.	Wahraat (Rainy Season)	July 16 to September 15	2	21.6 to 25.0	3.4
4.	Harud (Autumn)	September 16 to November 15	2	9.7 to 18.5	8.8
5.	Wandah (Cool Winter)	November 16 to 15 January	2	1.0 to 6.5	5.5
6.	Shishur (Cold Winter)	January 16 to 15 March	2	3.0 to 7.3	4.3

Textbook Classification

This plan, of foreign origin, was introduced in India, by our erstwhile colonial masters from England through geography textbooks. It recognizes four seasons spring, summer, autumn and winter – each of three months duration. This classification has its roots in the two solstices and two equinoxes which happen during the annual march of our planet on its orbit, round the sun. It has a global application.

For determining its quantitative validity, mean monthly temperature data of Srinagar (Table 9.1) has been put to use. The results obtained find their place in Table 7.7. It is observed that there is some sort of similarity between the range of temperature of summer (2.2°C) and winter (2.6°C), but the autumn range of temperature of 12.5°C does not at all match with that of 8.5°C of spring. With range of temperature different for all the four seasons, it is evident that no system is exhibited by this classification for Kashmir. For want of uniformity in the required values, textbook classification, in the present form, is unacceptable.

Table 7.7

Quantitative Appraisal of Textbook Classification of Seasons of Srinagar

S. No.	*Season*	*Extent*	*Duration (months)*	*Mean Temperature °C*	*Temperature Range °C*
1.	Spring	March to May	3	8.7 to 17.2	8.5
2.	Summer	June to August	3	21.9 to 24.1	2.2
3.	Autumn	September to November	3	7.8 to 20.3	12.5
4.	Winter	December to February	3	1.0 to 3.6	2.6

Meher Homji's Seasonal Classification

The first quantitative and scientific classification of seasons of Srinagar has been attempted by V.M. Meher Homji, of the Institute Francais, Pondicherry (Puducherry). It forms part of the paper, 'The Climate of Srinagar and its Variability', published in *The Geographical Review of India.* The first outstanding feature of this classification is the breaking up of the three months duration girdle of seasons in the textbook classification, by assigning them periods of varying duration. According to this plan spring lasts for two, summer for five, autumn for one and winter for four months (Table 7.8). The second peculiarity is uniform mean temperature range of all the four seasons which is 6.5°C. It is worthy of acceptance on the basis of its merits.

On the face of it, there can be no challenge to these research based findings. But the only point of disagreement is longer duration of five months of summer in comparison to the four month span of winter. The actual field situation presents a reverse position, a winter longer than any other season including summer. Winter hangs quite heavy on the psyche of the people of Kashmir. It brings in its wake numerous problems for them. In the event of continued low temperature on either periphery of winter they continue to shiver with cold and complain of a *sheyiretun Wandah* or *satiretun wandah,* a winter of six or a winter of seven months or *puet wandah,* an extended winter. It is, therefore, contended that winter in Kashmir has a longer duration than summer. A need was, in this context, felt for yet another classification that could satisfy this basic requirement.

Table 7.8

Meher Homji's Seasonal Classification of Srinagar: 1971

S. No.	*Season*	*Extent*	*Duration in months*	*Mean Temperature Range °C*	*Seasonal Range of Temp. °C*
1.	Winter	January-February November and December	4	1 to 7.5	6.5
2.	Spring	March-April	2	8 to 14.5	6.5
3.	Summer	May to September	5	17.5 to 24.0	6.5
4.	Autumn	October	1	8 to 14.5	6.5

Kaul's Classification

This seasonal classification was attempted by the present writer after taking cue from Hadlow's Word-Scale for monthly mean temperatures (Table 7.9). With each temperature slab, in this scale, is given the climatic description associated with it. Climate is *very hot* when the

Table 7.9

Hadlow's Word-Scale For Monthly Mean Temperatures: 1956

°F	*°C*	*Climatic Description*
Over 86	Above 30	Very Hot
68 to 86	20 to 30	Hot
50 to 68	10 to 20	Warm
32 to 50	0 to 10	Cool
14 to 32	–10 to 0	Cold
Below 14	Below-10	Very Cold

monthly mean temperature is above 30°C, *hot* when it is between 20° and 30°C, *warm* between 10° to 20°, *cool* between 0° and 10°C, *cold* between 0° and –10°C, and *very cold* when it is below –10°C. In each slab, range of temperature is uniform. It is 10°C.

Seasonal classification of Srinagar given in Table 7.10 emerges when its monthly mean temperature is cast into Hadlow's frame. The year in Srinagar, according to this plan, comprises two main seasons a cool season of five and a hot season of four months followed by two warm seasons, the periods of transition from cold to hot and vice versa. Winter includes the months of January to March, November and December. The two spring months are April and May. June to September constitute summer and October the autumn. Among the main attributes of this classification are a uniform range of monthly mean temperature and a dissimilar length of the seasons.

Table 7.10

Kaul's Seasonal Classification of Srinagar: 1979

S. No.	*Season*	*Extent*	*Mean Temperature Range °C*	*Duration (No of months)*	*Monthly Mean Temperature Slab °C*	*Seasonal Range of Temperature °C*
1.	Cool (Winter)	January to March November, December	1.5 to 8.8	5	0 to 10	10
2.	Warm (Spring)	April – May	13.7 to 17.3	2	10 to 20	10
3.	Hot (Summer)	June to September	20.1 to 24.1	4	20 to 30	10
4.	Warm (Autumn)	October	13.9	1	10 to 20	10

What is common between Meher-Homji's and Kaul's classification of seasons of Srinagar? It is the extent of the spring (2 months) and autumn (one month), in each case. Where do these schemes differ? In the range of monthly mean temperature, 6.5° and 10°C. It is, also, in the spread of the summer and the winter. Further, spring though of two months duration includes a different set of months – March and April in Homji's and April and May in Kaul's.

To conclude, the system and clarity evinced by categorization of seasons based on Hadlow's Word-Scale furnished sufficient inducement for its adoption in the description of seasons, not only of Srinagar but also of other temperate stations of Qazigund and Banihal together with highland stations of Leh, Kargil and Dras. However, for subtropical Jammu city, with monsoon type of climate, the seasonal plan suggested by India Meteorological Department shall be valid and binding.

References

Books

Awasthi, Anandeshwari, (1995): *Indian Climatology,* APH Publishing Corporation, New Delhi.

Crictchfield, Howard J. (1965): *General Climatology,* Prentice Hall, New Delhi.

Das, P.K. (1995): *The Monsoons,* National Book Trust, New Delhi.

Hadlow, Leonard (1956): *Climate Vegetation and Man,* London.

Hardy, Ralph (1996): *Weather,* Teach Yourself Books, London.

Heintzalman, Oliver H. and Highsmith, Richard M. (1965): *World Regional Geography,* Prentice Hall, New Delhi.

Kaul, A.K. (1985): *Home Geography (Jammu and Kashmir),* Ambanju Publications, Srinagar/Vinod Publications, Ludhiana.

Menon, P.A. (1993): *Ways of the Weather,* National Book Trust, New Delhi.

Miller, Austin A. (1972 reprint): *Climatology,* B.I. Publications, Delhi.

Monkhouse, F.J. (1959): *The Principles of Physical Geography,* U.P.L.

Stringer, E.T. (1971): *Foundations of climatology,* W.H. Freeman & Co., London.

Paper and Articles

Kaul, A.K. 'Seasons of Kashmir Valley', *The Geographical Review of India,* Kolkata, Vol 41, No. 2, June 1979.

——. 'Monsoon Component of Rainfall of Kashmir Valley', *Vayu Mandal,* New Delhi, July–December 1980.

Krishnan, Anantha R., 'Monsoon of the World', *India Meteorological Dept.* 1960.

Lidoo, P.N. and Pradhan, S.K., 'A Climatological Study of Jammu and Kashmir', *The Civil Investigation and Design Dept.,* PDD, J&K Government, 1986.

Mason, Jeff, 'Panel Issues Warning on Meltdown', *The Hindustan Times,* Chandigarh April 2007.

Meher-Homji V.M., 'The Climate of Srinagar and its Variability', *The Geographical Review of India,* Kolkata Vol. XXXIII No. 1 March 1971.

Pillai, Madhvan Kutty, 'Spreading the Message, Face to Face with R.K. Pichauri', *The Readers Digest,* April, 2008.

Pradhan, S.K., Upadhaya, D.S. & Lidoo, P.N., 'Climatological Study of Jammu and Kashmir', Part I, unpublished, *India Meteorological Centre, Srinagar, 1979.*

Stern, Sir Nicholas, 'Freaky Weather', *The Sunday Hindustan Times,* June, 2007.

8

Weather and Climate

Subtropical and Temperate Jammu

Jammu region, because of its varied relief and relatively large extent, compared to Kashmir, ceases to be a single entity with regard to its weather and climate. A vivid understanding of the broad features of this element of its environment is obtained when, at the outset, we deal with its rainfall and temperature separately. In terms of rainfall the entire region exhibits homogeneity as it is lashed, up to its northern boundary, formed by the Pir Panjal range, by the south-west monsoon which reaches here unobstructed and in strength. With respect to temperature, the southern part of the region, comprising Jammu plain and Siwaliks, enjoy sub tropical conditions. This also includes Rajouri and Poonch in the north-west and Doda and Ramban in the north-east. This zone forms the northern limit in our state, of the tropical monsoon climate. Climatic data of Jammu city represents this subtropical zone.

In northern mountainous parts of Jammu region there are a number of places situated at an elevation of more than 1,500 metres, where definite impact of altitude on temperature is discerned. A few examples are Patnitop (1,950 m), Bhaderwah (1,634 m), Kishtwar (1,634 m) and Banihal (1,630 m). These are marked by moderate summer temperatures and snowfall in winter. This highland zone depicts temperate temperature characteristics. The climatic data of Banihal portrays the weather and climate of temperate Jammu.

Subtropical Jammu

Jammu City

Jammu city, the winter capital of the state, spread over the Siwalik slopes and Jammu plain, is situated at an altitude of 367 m. Its locational coordinates are 32° 40′N and 74° 50′E.

Air Temperature

Mean Monthly

January, in Jammu city, with a mean temperature of 13.2°C is the coldest month of the year (Table 8.1). Temperature begins to increase January onwards in varying proportions. There is a small increase of 2.3°C from January to February. March mean temperature of 19.8°C marks the beginning of hot weather conditions. A substantial increase of 5.5° and 4.7°C takes place in, following months of April and May. The temperature difference between May and June is 2.9°C. June with a mean temperature of 32.9° is the hottest month. Jammu city shares this attribute with other subtropical stations like Delhi (34.4°C), Meerut (33.5°C) and Agra (35°C).

Temperature begins to fall with the arrival of south-west monsoon when July mean is reduced to 29.5°C. In the hot-wet period of August and September the temperature remains almost the same. October continues to be hot at 24.7°C. Temperature drops below 20°C in the following months, with December mean temperature lowered to 14.7°C.

With a mean monthly temperature of 13.2° to 32.9°C, the subtropical Jammu experiences a year-round growing season. It is the only part of Jammu and Kashmir where the rabi crops grow to full maturity and with ease. (Figure 8.1)

According to Hadlow's Word-Scale of mean monthly temperatures, in subtropical Jammu, May and June with temperatures above 30°C are very hot; April, July, August, September and October are hot and January to March, November and December are warm months.

The highest mean maximum temperature of 39.9°C is observed in June and the lowest of 19.5°C in January. The extreme highest day temperature of 47.4°C was recorded on 31 May 1988. In mean monthly minimum temperature, too, June with 25.9°C and January with 7°C depict the highest and the lowest values. The extreme minimum temperature of 0.6°C was noticed on 11 January 1945.

Table 8.1

Jammu City: Air Temperature (°C)

Temperature	*J*	*F*	*M*	*A*	*M*	*J*	*J*	*A*	*S*	*O*	*N*	*D*	*Annual Mean*
Mean Maximum	19.5	22.2	26.7	32.5	37.4	39.9	35.2	33.5	33.7	31.8	27.2	21.2	
Mean Minimum	7.0	8.9	13.0	18.1	22.7	25.9	23.8	23.8	22.5	17.7	12.1	8.2	
Mean Monthly	13.2	15.5	19.8	25.3	30.0	32.9	29.5	28.6	28.1	24.7	19.6	14.7	23.5
Mean Range	12.5	13.3	13.7	14.4	14.7	14.0	11.4	9.7	11.2	14.1	15.1	13.0	Av. 13.1

Annual mean temperature of Jammu city is 23.5°C. According to earlier data slab of 1951–80 its mean temperature was 23.8°C.

Mean Range

Normal range of temperature of Jammu city is 32.9°C, which establishes continentality trait of its climate. Its annual average range of temperature (Table 8.1) is 13.1°C. For seven months in a year, February to June, October and November, it is above the annual average. The highest mean monthly range of temperature of 15.1°C is traced in November. Rainfall of 14.8 mm in this month is received in 1.1 normals of rainy days. It, therefore, is a month with a clear sky and with a large variation in day and night temperatures. On the contrary, the lowest range of temperature of 11.2°C is observed in September. The other months with the mean range of temperature below the annual average are January, July, August and December. In most of these months the sky is overcast leading to a small difference between maximum and minimum temperatures. The climate of Jammu city is subtropical monsoon continental.

Atmospheric Pressure and Winds

Station-Level Pressure

Annual mean station-level atmospheric pressure in Jammu city is 975 mb (or hPa). It is higher than that of Srinagar (840.5 hPa) and Leh (686.4 hPa) because of its lower altitude. January station level pressure is 983.2 hPa which gradually decreases to 965.6 hPa in June. (Table 8.2). It continues to be low in July also. June and July lowest atmospheric pressure is in tune with the existence of low pressure belt over north-western India. A perceptible upward trend is noticed, August onwards, to attain the peak value of 983.5 hPa in December.

Table 8.2

Jammu city – Station-Level Pressure* and Mean Wind speed

Particulars	*J*	*F*	*M*	*A*	*M*	*J*	*J*	*A*	*S*	*O*	*N*	*D*	*Mean Annual*
Station Level Pressure (hPa or mb)	983.2	981.0	978.2	974.2	970.0	965.6	965.8	967.7	972.1	977.6	981.5	983.5	975
Mean wind speed (kmph)	6.1	6.8	6.4	6.6	6.5	5.7	4.8	3.8	4.6	5.5	6.1	5.3	

* Station Level Pressure data provided by 23 Wing IAF.

The line graph (Figure 7.2) depicting the station level pressure of Jammu city acquires the shape of letter V which is broader at the bottom. The annual range of atmospheric pressure is 17.9 hPa.

Mean Wind Speed

The highest mean wind speed of 6.8 kmph is noticed in February and the lowest of 3.8 kmph in August. Mean wind speed below 8 kmph, according to Beaufort scale, is denoted as light air and its common effect is indicated by smoke drift. January to May and November have the mean wind speeds above 6 kmph. It is between 3 and 6 kmph in June, July, September, October and December. Jammu city, therefore, experiences light air in all months of the year.

Atmospheric Moisture

Humidity

The line graph representing relative humidity (Figure 8.1) assumes the shape, roughly, of letter 'W'. It decreases from 62 per cent in January (Table 8.3) to reach the lowest value, 29 per cent, in May. It increases to register the maximum value of 75 per cent, in August. August maximum commands much higher position compared to January–December maxima. The slide from August is smooth till the plateau is formed by October, November figures (of 52%). It rises again in December to 61%. Relative humidity is same in some pairs of months. It is 38 per cent in April and June, 52 per cent in October and November. It is 62 per cent in January and 61 per cent in December. Climograph of Jammu city reveals that weather is muggy in July to

Table 8.3

Jammu City Atmospheric Moisture

Particulars	*J*	*F*	*M*	*A*	*M*	*J*	*J*	*A*	*S*	*O*	*N*	*D*	*Mean Annual*
Rainfall (mm)	34.0	64.6	75.2	38.7	32.1	59.5	340.3	299.8	120.8	18.7	14.8	58.2	1156.7
No. of Normals of rainy days	2.3	3.9	4.7	3.0	2.6	4.0	10.8	12.0	4.7	1.3	1.1	2.6	53
Intensity of rainfall (mm/r.day)	14.8	16.5	16.0	12.9	12.3	14.8	30.5	24.9	25.7	14.3	13.4	22.3	18.2
Relative Humidity (%)	62	56	48	38	29	38	68	75	66	52	52	61	53.7
No. of days with Thunder storms	1.1	1.1	2.6	3.0	3.9	5.6	5.4	4.8	4.0	1.6	0.9	0.8	34.8
No. of days with dust storms	00	00	0.1	0.5	1.1	1.6	0.3	0.1	0.3	00	0.1	00	4.1

Figure 8.1

Jammu City: Weather and Climate

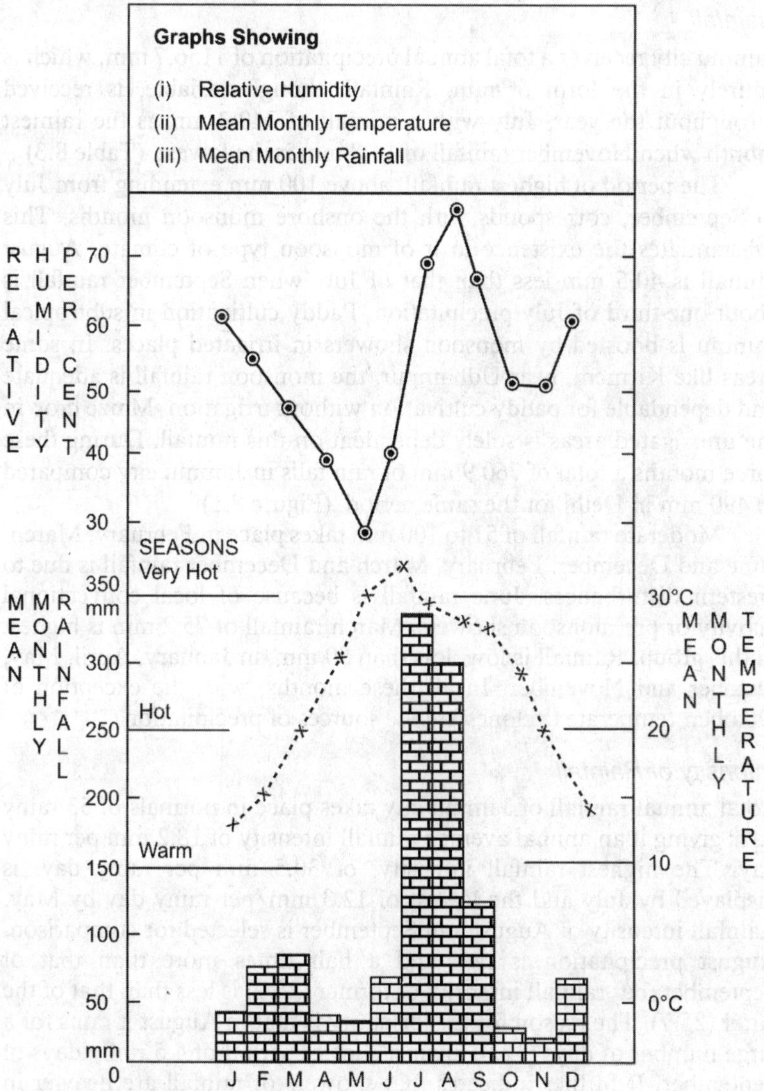

Altitude	:	367 m
Mean Annual Temperature	:	23.5°C
Normal Range of Temperature	:	32.9°C
Frost-free Period	:	365 days
Total Annual Rainfall	:	1156.7 mm

September, scorching in May–June, keen in April and raw in January–December.

Rainfall

Jammu city receives a total annual precipitation of 1156.7 mm, which is entirely in the form of rain. Rainfall, though variable, is received throughout the year. July with a rainfall of 340.3 mm is the rainiest month when November rainfall of 14.8 mm is the lowest. (Table 8.3)

The period of highest rainfall, above 100 mm extending from July to September, corresponds with the onshore monsoon months. This substantiates the existence in it of monsoon type of climate. August rainfall is 40.5 mm less than that of July when September rainfall is about one-third of July precipitation. Paddy cultivation in subtropical Jammu is boosted by monsoon showers in irrigated places. In some areas like Kirmchi, near Udhampur, the monsoon rainfall is adequate and dependable for paddy cultivation without irrigation. Maize crop in the unirrigated areas is solely dependent on this rainfall. During these three months a total of 760.9 mm of rain falls in Jammu city compared to 490 mm in Delhi for the same period. (Figure 8.1)

Moderate rainfall of 51 to 100 mm takes place in February, March, June and December. February, March and December rainfall is due to western disturbances. June rainfall is because of local convectional activity or pre-monsoon showers. March rainfall of 75.2 mm is highest in this group. Rainfall is low, less than 50 mm, in January, April, May, October and November. In all these months, with the exception of October, temperate cyclones are the sources of precipitation.

Intensity of Rainfall

Total annual rainfall of Jammu city takes place in normals of 53 rainy days giving it an annual average rainfall intensity of 18.2 mm per rainy day. The highest rainfall intensity, of 30.5 mm per rainy day, is displayed by July and the lowest of 12.3 mm/per rainy day by May. Rainfall intensity of August and September is selected for comparison. August precipitation is two and a half times more than that of September, but rainfall intensity of former (24.9) is less than that of the latter (25.7). The reason for this disparity is that in August it rains for a large number of days (12.0) against shorter period of 4.5 rainy days of September. It further indicates that showers of rainfall are heavier in September than in August.

Thunderstorms

Total number of days with thunderstorms recorded in Jammu city is 34.8. June leads with 5.6 days followed by July 5.4, August 4.8 and

September 4.0 days. All these are summer months when convectional activity is at its peak. In warm months of April and May it varies between 3.0 and 3.9 days. In winter months it is quite low ranging between 0.8 days of December and 2.6 days of March. Thunderstorms are of both thermal and frontal types. Monsoon season accounts for 40.8 per cent of total number of days with thunderstorms (Table 8.3).

The other weather phenomenon of convective occurrence is a duststorm. The dry hot months of April to June favour its development. The number of days with duststorms ranges from 0.5 in April to 1.1 in June. Other months with 0.3 days with duststorms are July and September. It is 0.1 days in March, August and November. These are not formed in the winter months of January, February, December and in October.

Dryness and Wetness

In order to determine the periods of dryness and wetness of Jammu city the scale based on the definitions of Bagnouls and Gaussen has been used and results presented in Table 8.4

Table 8.4

Jammu City: Periods of Dryness and Wetness

S. No.	*Month*	*Rainfall (mm)*	*Mean Month Temp. °C*	*Scale*	*Inference*
1	January	34.0	13.2	P between 2T & 3T	Sub-Dry
2	February	64.6	15.5	P > 4T	Humid
3	March	75.2	19.6	P between 3T & 4T	Sub-Humid
4	April	38.7	25.3	P less than 2T	Dry
5	May	32.1	30.0	P less than 2T	Dry
6	June	59.5	32.9	P less than 2T	Dry
7	July	340.3	29.5	P > 4T	Humid
8	August	299.8	28.6	P > 4T	Humid
9	September	120.8	28.1	P > 4T	Humid
10	October	18.7	24.7	P < T	Very Dry
11	November	14.8	19.6	P < T	Very Dry
12	December	58.2	14.7	P between 3T & 4T	Sub-Humid

The table reveals that in subtropical Jammu, February, July to September are humid as precipitation (in mm) in these months is more than four times the temperature in degrees Celsius. March and December are sub-humid because amount of precipitation is between 3 and four times the temperature. Remaining six months depict various degrees of dryness. January is sub-dry, April, May and June are dry when October and November are very dry.

Spatial Distribution of Rainfall (I) (Based on IMD Data)

Of the four stations of subtropical Jammu, for which data is provided by India Meteorological Department (Table 8.5), Kathua lies in the Jammu plain to the south of Jammu city, Chenani to its north, Nowshehra and Poonch to its north-west. The last three stations are situated in the trans-Siwalik region either close to or within the Jammu mountains.

Annual Rainfall

Poonch, in this group, receives the highest annual rainfall of 1474 mm, followed by Chenani 1436.6 mm, Kathua 1177.9 mm and Nowshehra the lowest of 981 mm. The highest rainfall of above 1400 mm in Poonch and Chenani is because of orographic effect. The months with maximum and minimum rainfall vary from station to station. July gets maximum rainfall in Poonch and Nowshehra when August is the rainiest month in Kathua and Chenani. The month with minimum rainfall is November in Kathua, Poonch, Nowshehra and October in Chenani.

Rainfall Intensity

Total annual rainfall of Chenani is received in normals of 58.8 rainy days giving it the highest average rainfall intensity of 22.7 mm per rainy day. Monsoon months of July and August together with June have higher rainfall intensity than the annual average, so have frontal months of January to March and December. Chenani, among all stations of subtropical Jammu, is a unique case where rainfall intensity of winter months alongwith June, July and August exceeds the annual average. In the remaining five months, April, May, September to November the intensity of rainfall is less than the yearly average.

Poonch receives the total annual rainfall in normals of 65.1 rainy days giving it the second highest rainfall intensity of 22.6 mm/r.d. In August rainfall intensity is higher and for remaining eleven months less than annual average. Annual average rainfall intensity of Nowshehra is 20.2 mm per rainy day as normals of rainy days, at this station, is 48.5. Intensity of rainfall is higher for three monsoon months of July to September and lower for remaining part of the year. Kathua has the least average rainfall intensity of 20.1 mm per rainy day, when normals of rainy days, here, is 50.4. Rainfall intensity values are higher during January, July to September and lower than the annual average during the remaining eight months. Not much variation in average annual rainfall intensity of these four stations is observed as these figures range between 20.1 and 22.7.

Table 8.5

Subtropical Jammu: Spatial Distribution of Rainfall (based on data from IMD, Srinagar)

Station		*Ap*	*M*	*J*	*J*	*A*	*S*	*O*	*N*	*D*	*J*	*F*	*M*	*Total Annual*
Kathua (alt. 325 m)	Monthly Mean Rainfall (mm)	27.4	17.0	51.1	339.9	352.5	14.7	21.3	5.6	34.3	72.6	62.7	52.8	1177.9
	Rainy Days (No.)	2.1	1.5	3.3	11.9	12.4	4.8	1.1	0.6	2.2	3.6	3.8	3.1	50.4
	Rainfall Intensity (mm/day)	13.0	11.3	15.4	33.6	28.2	29.3	19.3	9.3	15.5	20.1	19.3	17.0	20.1
	Seasonal Rainfall (%)		Pre-Monsoon 8.1			Monsoon 70.9		Post-Mons 2.2				Winter 18.8		
Chenani	Monthly Mean Rainfall (mm)	72.1	50.5	79.0	278.1	293.6	73.7	17.8	40.4	53.6	152.7	134.1	191.0	1436.6
	Rainy Days (No.)	4.0	2.3	3.2	10.8	9.6	8.9	1.1	0.5	1.8	4.8	5.6	6.2	58.8
	Rainfall Intensity (mm/day)	18.0	21.5	24.7	25.7	30.5	8.2	16.2	8.8	29.7	31.3	23.9	30.8	22.7
	Seasonal Rainfall (%)		Pre-Monsoon 14.1			Monsoon 45.7		Post-Mons 3.3				Winter 36.9		
Nowshehra	Monthly Mean Rainfall (mm)	43.4	31.0	55.9	253.0	239.0	97.3	18.3	7.4	35.6	66.5	70.9	62.7	981.0
	Rainy Days (No.)	2.8	2.6	3.6	10.3	10.1	4.4	1.1	0.5	1.8	3.8	4.0	3.5	48.5
	Rainfall Intensity (mm/day)	14.4	11.9	15.5	24.5	23.6	22.1	16.6	14.8	19.8	17.5	17.7	17.9	20.2
	Seasonal Rainfall (%)		Pre-Monsoon 13.2			Monsoon 60.1		Post-Mons 2.7				Winter 24.0		
Poonch (1002 m)	Monthly Mean Rainfall (mm)	93.7	67.6	90.6	300.5	299.8	116.8	32.3	16.8	62.2	127.6	127.8	138.9	1474.0
	Rainy Days (No.)	5.7	4.6	6.4	13.4	12.7	6.0	1.9	1.0	3.5	6.2	6.7	7.0	65.1
	Rainfall Intensity (mm/day)	16.4	14.7	14.1	22.4	23.6	19.4	17.0	16.8	17.7	20.4	19.0	19.8	22.6
	Seasonal Rainfall (%)		Pre-Monsoon 17.7			Monsoon 47.9		Post-Mons 3.5				Winter 30.9		

Seasonal Distribution

An appraisal of the given rainfall data, of these four stations, is also attempted on seasonal basis. In pre-monsoon season Kathua receives the least percentage of 8.1 of the total annual rainfall, when it is 13.2 in Nowshehra, 14.7 in Chenani and the highest of 17.7 per cent in Poonch. Rainfall is copious in monsoon season in all the four stations. Kathua receives the highest rainfall of 70.9 per cent of total annual followed in order by Nowshehra 60.1, Poonch 47.9 and Chenani, 45.7 per cent. Post-monsoon season is marked by a low rainfall in each station. It is 2.2 in Kathua, 2.7 in Nowshehra, 3.3 in Chenani and 3.5 per cent, of the total annual, in Poonch. The winter rainfall manifests the second maxima after summer monsoon but much less in comparison. Its highest percentage of 36.9 per cent is registered in Chenani followed by 30.9 in Poonch, 24.0 in Nowshehra and 18.8 per cent in Kathua. All these stations except Kathua get more winter rainfall than that of Jammu city (20%).

Compared to other four subtropical stations of Jammu city, Kathua, Nowshehra and Poonch, Chenani receives the least monsoon and the highest frontal rainfall. The question arises, why?

Spatial Distribution of Rainfall (II) (Based on IFCD Data)

Rainfall data of the following rain gauge stations of subtropical Jammu region is compiled by Irrigation and Flood Control Department (IFCD) of Jammu and Kashmir government. These are Mansar, Kishanpur, Akhnoor, Khore (the Siwaliks), Udhampur (the Dun), Mandi, Basohli and Rajauri (Jammu mountains). The data given consists of total rainfall and number of rainy days (Table 8.6).

Table 8.6

Subtropical Jammu: Spatial Distribution of Rainfall (based on IFCD data)

S. No.	*Station*	*Total Annual Rainfall (mm)*	*No. of Rainy Days*	*Intensity of Rainfall (mm/r.d.)*
1.	Akhnoor (345 m)	1,776.4	78	22.7
2.	Basohli (660 m)	1,511.0	53	28.5
3.	Mansar (666 m)	1,471.0	61	24.1
4.	Khore	1,268.0	48	26.4
5.	Udhampur (760 m)	1,158.8	67	17.2
6.	Mandi	929.0	77	12.0
7.	Kishenpur	745.0	64	11.6
8.	Rajauri (924 m)	605.0	35	17.2

Annual Rainfall

The given eight stations are tabulated in descending order of their total annual rainfall. Akhnoor rainfall of 1,776.4 mm is the highest followed by Basohli with 1,511 mm. The abundant rainfall of these two stations can be ascribed to their location in the Siwaliks and trans-Siwalik area and on the rivers Chenab and Ravi, respectively. Total annual rainfall of 1,471 mm is recorded in Mansar; 1,268 in Khore, 1,158 in Udhampur, 929 in Mandi and 745 mm in Kishenpur. Rajauri receives the lowest rainfall of 605 mm.

Rainfall Intensity

The varied amounts of rainfall of the above listed stations is received in unequal number of rainy days, thereby, assigning them a diverse rainfall intensity. It is high 28.5 in Basohli, 26.4 in Khore, 24.1 Mansar and 22.7 mm per rainy day in Akhnoor. It is moderate 17.2 mm per rainy day, each, in Udhampur and Rajauri. Mandi with 12 and Kishenpur with 11.6 mm per rainy day have the low rainfall intensity.

Seasons

The most dominating influence in the weather and climate of Indian subcontinent, including subtropical Jammu, is the south-west monsoon. It is imperative to present a seasonal pattern which is monsoon-centric. Such monsoon based seasonal classification, devised by Indian meteorologists, is given below:

	Seasons	*Months Included*	*Duration*
(i)	The Pre-Monsoon or Hot Dry Summer	April, May, June	3
(ii)	The Monsoon or Hot Wet Summer	July to September	3
(iii)	The Post-Monsoon	October–November	2
(iv)	The Winter	January to March, December	4

The Pre-Monsoon Season

In terms of seasonal pattern pre-monsoon begins in April but traditionally Holi, the festival of colours, marks the advent of summer when the woollens and quilts are packed for use in next winter. Snakes, scorpions, lizards, etc., that had gone into hiding due to earlier unfavourable cold season, it is believed, are let loose on *Shivratri.* They actually come on the scene by the time of Holi as the temperature, by then, is high enough to help them resume their food procuring and other vital activities.

A substantial increase in temperature is noticed in April and the ascending trend continues through May, till the peak is reached in June. Abundant convective activity takes place during this period which is manifest in the form of thunderstorms and duststorms. The rainfall received in June is either derived from thunderstorms or pre-monsoon showers. This season, in addition to high temperature is characterized by low rainfall making it a hot dry summer. Relative humidity is low and varies between 29 and 38 per cent.

The quick evaporation of perspiration leads to cooling of skin which makes dry heat less oppressive for the humans. Loss of water through sweating speeds up need for quenching the thirst. Hence *Chabeels* or drinking water storage and distribution facilities form an important feature of the dry summer scene. On *Nirjala Ekadashi,* in June, among other things, new earthenware pitchers filled with drinking water are offered in alms.

The blue of the sky is replaced by dark yellow haze. The landscape, except for evergreens, puts on a parched and brown appearance. Irrigated cropland in subtropical Jammu, at any point of time, is under one crop or the other. In April, rabi crops, wheat and oil seeds are in ripening stage and from *Basaikhi,* mid-April, onwards wheat harvest commences. In irrigated areas preparations are afoot for cultivation of next crop but in unirrigated places agricultural activities cease till the arrival of monsoons. Total rainfall of this season is 130.3 mm or 11.2 per cent of total annual precipitation.

The Monsoon Season

The south-west monsoon, by the middle of June, is active and vigorous in most parts of India except in its north-west. Monsoon winds arrive in Jammu in the first week of July. There are no India Meteorological Department (IMD) attempted, recognized and published dates of arrival and withdrawal of summer monsoons for this state. The meteorologists working in IMD. Srinagar, after the analysis of 50-year rainfall data, of 1927 to 1976, have arrived at the monsoon schedule for Jammu and Kashmir. Part of this schedule, that pertains to Jammu region, is given below:

Jammu Region: South-West Monsoon Schedule

Onset	*Retreat*
7 July: Kathua, Jammu city	13 September: Banihal
8 July: Udhampur, Reasi, Rajauri, Poonch	14 September: Reasi, Udhampur,
10 July: Banihal	Kathua, Jammu city, Rajauri, Poonch

Accordingly, summer monsoon arrives in Kathua and Jammu city on 7 July and Banihal within three days. Roughly, a week before actual onset of the monsoon, moisture in sufficient quantities penetrates into the atmospheric circulation of Jammu causing much unease, particularly during night. First showers, heralded by the 'burst of monsoon' usher in welcome relief from the scorching heat. The season, consequently, undergoes a change from dry-hot to hot-wet weather. Rainfall is widespread, showers are heavy but of short duration.

With the arrival of monsoon the highest mean monthly temperature of June drops to 29.5°C in July registering a fall of 3.4°C. But the decrease from July to August and August to September is quite marginal, 0.9° and 0.5°C, respectively. High temperature continues to be one of the traits of this season.

July rainfall is copious when it is plentiful in August. Comparatively, it is less in September. The rainy season in Jammu city works out to be 70 days when it is 100 to 120 days long in many parts of the country particularly in the south. In spite of its short duration, it outclasses the remaining three seasons in the amount of rainfall received. A total of 760.9 mm of rainfall, in the three monsoon months of July to September, accounts for 65.9 per cent of the annual total.

In this season the dry and the wet spells alternate with each other. During a wet spell, a fall in temperature is followed by a cool breeze which make the weather pleasant. But during a dry spell, the temperature again increases and so does the humidity making living conditions distressful. Heavy rainfall causes floods and landslides whereas, little or no rainfall causes drought. The rivers in Jammu region are generally in spate. The devastating flood in the Chenab, in September 1992, washed away the old historic iron bridge at Akhnoor. With the Tawi in flood, the island locality between its two branches gets threatened. The frequency of thunderstorms during this period is highest.

High temperature and high rainfall cause high humidity. A high percentage of 66 to 75 relative humidity is registered. Under such conditions air gets saturated with water vapour to the extent that the rate of evaporation gets sufficiently slowed down hence the feeling of *wetness*, which becomes a persistent bother of this season. To this may be added the scourge of skin allergies, viral fevers, snake bites and other water-borne diseases. This season favours prolific growth in number of mosquitoes which are carriers of the germs of diseases like malaria and dengue.

In unirrigated areas of the region 'Kharif' sowing gets initiated with the arrival of the monsoons. The crops raised are maize and legumes. The phenomenal transformation of the landscape from brown of hot-dry summer to verdure, soon after several days of monsoon rainfall is an alluring spectacle.

The luxuriant growth of vegetation, the formation of bowers and groves, the sky overcast with dark clouds, the soothing coolness of the moving air and the response, thereof, of humans, animals and birds, peacocks in particular, have inspired numerous Indian poets, since ages, to eulogize the entrancing panoramas of *Sawan* and *Bhadoon*. The *Meghdoot* of Kalidasa, in Sanskrit, is a classic on this theme. Artists have not lagged behind in this context. These panoramas were transferred by them to form the background of the world famous Pahari miniature paintings of different schools, including those of Jammu and Basohli.

The Post-Monsoon Season

This season comprises October and November. By October the sun has shifted to the south of the equator. The sun rays are more oblique and their heating power lessens. A fall of temperature takes place when mean temperature in October drops to 24.7° and in November to 19.6°C. October receives some amount of rainfall but November is nearly dry. Relative humidity is less than monsoon but more than pre-monsoon season. Dewali, the festival of lights, which generally falls in November, is the time for unpacking the woollens and quilts, in preparation for facing the winter cold. It also marks the time for hibernation of cold blooded animals. Post-monsoon season is harvest time of Kharif crops, particularly rice, and a busy time for the farmers. The cropland, soon after, is made ready for 'Rabi' sowing. Rainfall received amounts to 33.5 mm or 2.9 per cent of the annual total.

The Winter

In subtropical Jammu winter includes four months – January to March and December. January, as already mentioned, is the coldest month of the year and Lohri which falls on 13 January is considered to be the coldest day of the season. Ritual fires, using fuelwood, are lit at night, among other things, to ward off cold. Basant Panchmi, which follows Lohri, announces the arrival of spring. Yellow is the colour of the attire and food, which match with, mustard flowers in bloom at that time.

Days in this season are warm and nights are cool. The mean maximum temperature varies between 19.5° and 22.2°C. March with 26.7°C is an exception. The mean minimum temperature ranges from 7.0° to 8.9°C. Fair weather conditions are disturbed by the arrival of western depressions which at this time frequent the state repeatedly.

These temperate cyclones cause precipitation of varying amounts in all winter months. This frontal rainfall is a boon for the cultivation of winter crops, wheat and oilseeds, in unirrigated localities. When it rains in Jammu city in winter, snowfall takes place in the highlands. Soon after the first snowfall at Patnitop the tourist influx to this scenic spot begins. A thin veneer of snow, on such occasions, is observed on Trikuta peaks. Winter claims a share of 20 per cent of the total annual rainfall.

This season is the time in subtropical Jammu for staying and working outdoors during the sunny days. All convenient spots with a sunny aspect, including flat roofs of the houses, are thronged by people for basking in the sun, in order to avoid the cold of the interiors.

Jammu and Kashmir state has two capitals, the winter and the summer. Shifting of the secretariat from one capital to other previously, during the time of Maharajas, referred to as 'Darbar Move' has been in vogue for the last more than a hundred and fifty years. One, out of the many reasons cited for this office-move is to satisfy regional needs and aspirations of its populace. But, to all intents and purposes, geographical factor has been of paramount importance. It is to avail of the climatic virtues of either of the capital city, the warm winter of Jammu and the genial summer of Srinagar. The secretariat shifts to Jammu city in November and functions here up to May. During these six months, the sunny and warm weather provides better working environment to both the administrators and the bureaucrats.

Temperate Jammu

Banihal

Banihal serves as the representative station of temperate Jammu. It is the northernmost town of Jammu region which is situated at the foot of the Pir Panjal range and has a southern aspect. Its locational coordinates are 33°30′N and 75°10′E. It has an altitude of 1,630 m above sea level.

Air Temperature

Mean Monthly

The temperature values of Banihal given in Table 8.7 reveal that its monthly mean temperature is between 10° and 20°C for five months in a year. On the basis of the criterion set for temperature based climatic zones (Chapter 7), the climate of Banihal is temperate. In January, mean temperature is below 6.6°C, an indicator of real cold season, when plant growth ceases. It follows that the climate of Banihal is cool temperate.

July, with a mean temperature of 22.8°C is the hottest month of the year. June and August temperatures on either side of the peak are 1° and 0.4°C less respectively. January with a mean temperature of 4.7°C is the coldest month. Both these features are peculiar to temperate climates. January onwards the temperature tends to rise but February figures exceed it by 1.1°. The increasing trend continues through March to June taking it to 21.8°C in the latter month. The fall of temperature between August and September is small but substantial between September and December. In January, February and December mean temperature values vary between 4° and 7°C. (Figure 8.2)

A comparison of mean temperature figures of Banihal, with the other cool temperate station of Srinagar, at this stage, is revealing. Banihal which lies 43 m above Srinagar, registers a higher mean temperature of 4.7°C in January against 1.5°C of Srinagar. It may be because of the sunny aspect of Banihal. Further, July mean of Srinagar, 24.1°C, is higher than that of, 22.8°C of Banihal. Shall we attribute it to higher altitude of Banihal? The mean temperature data of these stations, thus, confirms that Banihal is warmer in winter and cooler in summer compared to Srinagar (Table 9.1).

Table 8.7

Banihal: Air Temperature (°C)

Temperature	*J*	*F*	*M*	*A*	*M*	*J*	*J*	*A*	*S*	*O*	*N*	*D*	*Mean Annual*
Mean Maximum	9.9	10.8	15.6	21.4	25.0	28.8	28.3	27.9	26.8	23.6	18.1	12.5	
Mean Minimum	–0.4	0.8	4.3	8.5	11.2	14.8	17.4	17.0	12.4	6.9	3.3	0.6	
Mean Monthly	4.7	5.8	9.9	14.9	18.1	21.8	22.8	22.4	19.6	15.2	10.7	6.5	14.4
Mean Range	10.3	10.0	11.3	12.9	13.8	14.0	10.9	10.9	14.4	16.7	14.8	11.9	12.6

The highest mean maximum temperature of 28.8°C is recorded in June and lowest of 9.9° in January. The extreme maximum temperature rose to 36°C on 7 June 1978. The highest and the lowest mean minimum temperature readings are 17.4°C and –0.4°C in July and January respectively. Extreme minimum temperature of –13.6°C was registered on 12 December 1964.

Annual mean temperature of Banihal is 14.4°C which was 14.3°C, according to earlier 1960–80 data set. The frost free period in Banihal is 334 days.

Mean Range

Normal range of temperature of Banihal is 29.2°C which testifies to its having a continental climate. Mean range of temperature is highest, 16.7°C, in October and lowest, 10°C, in February. October is a dry month with a least cloud cover hence a marked difference in the diurnal temperatures. Contrary to it, February is a rainy month with an expected cloud cover hence, a low range of temperature. Average annual range of temperature is 12.6°C. For six months (January, February, March, July, August and December) the range of temperature is less than annual average. This group includes the frontal rainfall and monsoon months. For the other six months it is above the annual average. (Table 8.7). Banihal has a cool temperate continental climate.

Station-Level Pressure

Annual average station-level pressure of Banihal is 836 hPa, which contrasts well with station-level pressure of Jammu city of 975 hPa. Station-level pressure of 837.8 mb in January falls to 837.1 mb in February. The decline is gradual up to May but steep from May to June. It acquires the least value of 829.0 hPa in July. After July station-level pressure displays an increasing trend (Table 8.8) and attains the highest value of 839.7 hPa in December.

Table 8.8

Banihal: Station-Level Pressure (hPa or mb)

J	*F*	*M*	*A*	*M*	*J*	*J*	*A*	*S*	*O*	*N*	*D*	*Annual Average*
837.8	837.1	836.8	835.8	834.0	830.3	829.0	830.4	834.1	838.1	839.5	839.7	836.0

Atmospheric Moisture

Humidity

The average annual relative humidity of Banihal is 62 per cent, with highest of 74 per cent recorded in August and lowest of 53 per cent in June. (Table 8.9). January and February relative humidity is same, 66 per cent. It declines through the following months up to June. With the arrival of monsoons it shoots to 70 per cent in July. Though July is the hottest month and it receives more rainfall than August, it is the latter that registers highest relative humidity. It drops again to the November minimum of 55 per cent. It rises for the second time to 58 per cent in December. January February relative humidity is higher than that of December. In June because of high temperature it is lower than that of November.

Figure 8.2

Banihal: Weather and Climate

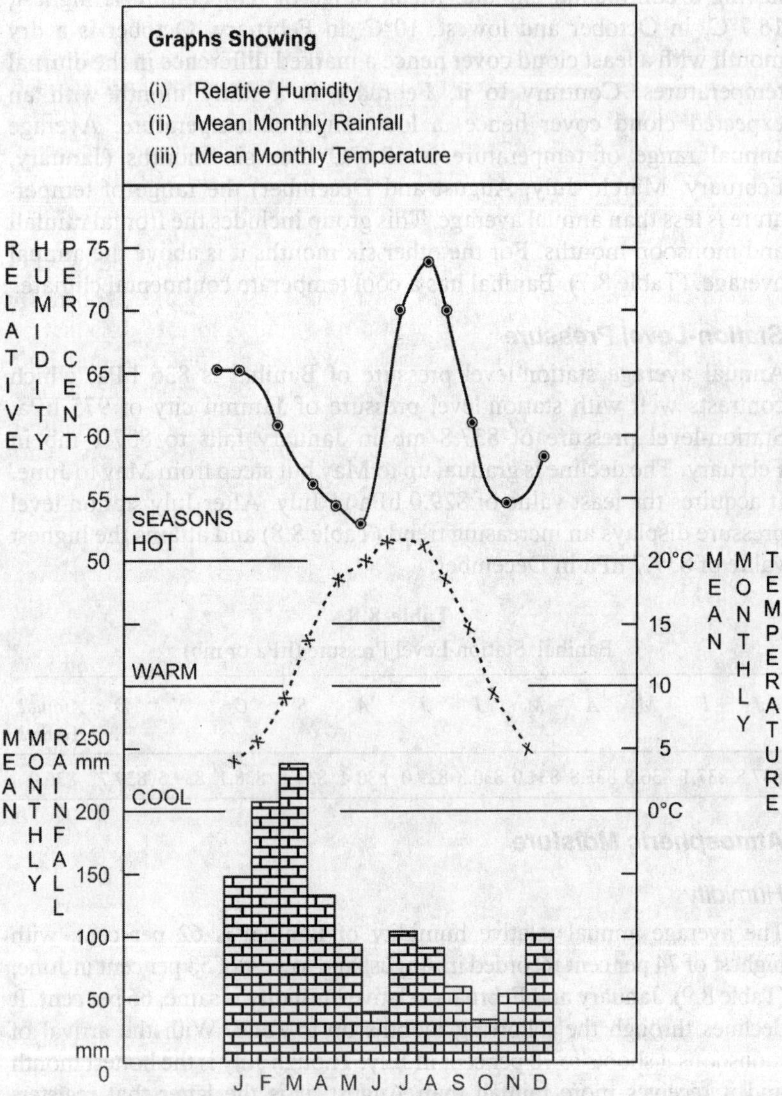

Altitude : 1630 m
Mean Annual Temperature : 14.4°C
Normal Range of Temperature : 29.2°C
Frost Free Period : 334 days
Total Annual Rainfall : 1317.8 mm

The pair of months with same relative humidity are July and September, January and February. (Figure 8.2)

Table 8.9
Banihal: Atmospheric Moisture

Particulars	*J*	*F*	*M*	*A*	*M*	*J*	*J*	*A*	*S*	*O*	*N*	*D*	*Total/ Mean Annual*
Total monthly rainfall (mm)	141.6	201.1	242.6	132.3	92.5	45.3	106.1	91.4	60.5	38.5	58.5	107.4	1317.8
No. of rainy days	7.0	8.7	10.4	8.4	6.5	3.4	8.0	6.1	3.6	2.4	3.2	4.9	72.6
Intensity of rainfall (mm/day)	20.2	23.0	23.3	15.7	14.2	13.3	13.2	15.0	16.8	16.0	18.2	21.9	17.5
Relative humidity (%)	66	66	62	56	54	53	70	74	70	61	55	58	62
No. of days with thunder storms	0.6	2.1	4.6	7.3	11.2	8.3	6.1	3.4	4.5	3.2	1.1	0.7	53.1

Annual Rainfall

Total annual rainfall received in Banihal is 1317.8 mm which is, roughly, 1.1 times more than total annual rainfall of Jammu city and twice that of Srinagar. The cause for this high precipitation is orographic, situated as it is on the windward slope of the Pir Panjal Range. Banihal rainfall exceeds that of Qazigund, 1246.1 mm, as the latter station lies on leeward side of this mountain range. In each of the eight months, in a year, the rainfall received is more than 91 mm.

Two rainfall maxima, in a year are observed at this station, one each, during the sway of temperate cyclones and the prevalence of monsoon winds. Total amount of frontal rainfall received in 7 months is 976 mm and the monsoon rainfall of 3 months adds up to 258 mm. The average per month rainfall is 139.4 mm during the time of western disturbances and 86 mm in the monsoon months. It follows that Banihal has more rainfall due to mid-latitude cyclones than through monsoons. March, like other temperate stations, is the rainiest and October the lowest rainfall month. (Figure 8.2)

Intensity of Rainfall

Total annual rain in Banihal falls in normals of 72.6 rainy days assigning it an average rainfall intensity of 17.5 mm per rainy day. Intensity of rainfall is higher than annual average in January to March, November and December. It is less than the annual average for remaining seven months of the year. Rainfall intensity of January to March and December is above 20 mm per rainy day. It is lowest, 13.2 mm/rainy day, in July. Table 8.9 further shows that the intensity of rainfall is high in case of frontal rainfall months whereas, it is low in the three monsoon months of July to September. It follows that showers of rain are heavier during the winter than those of the summer months.

Thunderstorms

A total of 53.1 days with thunderstorms, in a year, is registered in Banihal. Most of this convectional activity is experienced from April to July as number of days with thunderstorms is highest in these months, with May accounting for 11.2, June 8.3, April 7.3 and July 6.1 days. It is between one and five days in February, March and August to November. Number of days with thunderstorms is less than one, in January and December. These are of thermal as well as of frontal types. Thunderstorms of April to June make sizeable contribution to the rainfall of these months.

Spatial Distribution of Rainfall – Bhaderwah

Bhaderwah, a mountain girdled valley, of Jammu region, lies at an altitude of 1,634 m. Its locational co-ordinates are 32° 59′N and 75° 43′E. It receives a total annual precipitation of 1123.2 mm which is about, 20 per cent less than of the other temperate station of Banihal. The line graph showing precipitation assumes the form of letter W. There are two maxima of rainfall – one in January and the other in July and two minima of rainfall one each in June and November. For seven months in a year the rainfall is above 90 mm. These are January to April, July, August and December. Frontal rainfall claims a share of 65.5 per cent and monsoon rainfall totals 26.2 per cent. June and October which lie outside the above stated wind systems contribute 8.3 per cent of the total annual rainfall. It follows that frontal rainfall in Bhaderwah is two and a half times the monsoon precipitation. This establishes its closeness to the rainfall pattern of Banihal and its place in temperate segment of Jammu region.

Table 8.10

Bhaderwah: Precipitation (mm)

J	*F*	*M*	*A*	*M*	*J*	*J*	*A*	*S*	*O*	*N*	*D*	*Total Annual*
159.3	156.0	145.5	94.5	61.5	55.9	128.5	117.6	49.0	36.3	24.1	95.0	1,123.2

Wetness and Dryness

The scale based on the definitions of Bagnouls and Gaussen has been used to compute the periods of wetness and dryness in Banihal and results presented in Table 8.11. It shows that in Banihal rainfall in nine months of the year is four times higher than the temperature. Only June and October are sub-dry months whereas, September is sub-humid. The remaining nine months are humid. It is the copious rainfall of these months which is responsible for the humid conditions for three-fourths of the year at this station.

Table 8.11

Banihal: Periods of Wetness and Dryness

S. No.	*Month*	*Rainfall (mm)*	*Temperature (°C)*	*Scale*	*Inference*
1	January	141.6	4.7	P > 4T	Humid
2	February	201.1	5.8	P > 4T	Humid
3	March	242.6	9.9	P > 4T	Humid
4	April	132.3	14.9	P > 4T	Humid
5	May	92.5	18.1	P > 4T	Humid
6	June	45.3	21.8	P between 2T & 3T	Sub-Dry
7	July	106.1	22.8	P > 4T	Humid
8	August	91.4	22.4	P > 4T	Humid
9	September	60.5	19.6	P between 3T & 4T	Sub-Humid
10	October	38.5	15.2	P between 2T & 3T	Sub-Dry
11	November	58.5	10.7	P > 4T	Humid
12	December	107.4	6.5	P > 4T	Humid

Seasons

For a station, with a temperate climate like Banihal, the seasonal classification is based on Hadlow's Word Scale of monthly mean temperatures. The four seasons, their duration and temperature characteristics is given in Table 8.12. Winter includes four, spring two, summer three and autumn three months.

Table 8.12

Banihal: Seasons

Mean Temp. Range (°C)	*Climatic Description*	*Months Included*	*Name*	*Duration*
0–10	Cool	January, February, March, December	Winter	4
10–20	Warm	April, May	Spring	2
20–30	Hot	June, July, August	Summer	3
10–20	Warm	September, October, November	Autumn	3

The Winter

During January the mean minimum temperature recorded is sub-zero. Night frosts in this coldest month are common. The mean monthly temperature ranges between 4.7° and 9.9°C. Winter precipitation received is 692.7 mm or 52.5 per cent of the total annual. March is the rainiest month. Winter precipitation exceeds that of all the three other seasons. It is of frontal type. Most of it is in the form of snow which does not stay on the ground for much time. The national highway is cleared of accumulated snow regularly to keep it traffic worthy.

The Spring

April and May constitute first transition period from winter to summer. It is spring in Banihal. Mean monthly temperatures in this season range between 14.9 and 18.1°C. The deciduous trees are in leaf and fruit trees bring forth blossoms. Mountain slopes, with a soil cover, are carpeted with grass and wild flowers. Agricultural operations begin from first week of April. Kharif sowings consist of rice and maize, the former is raised in the irrigated land, often terraced, and the latter on rainfed slopes. Amount of precipitation received in this season is 224.8 mm or 17.0 per cent of the total annual. Out of the total of 53.1 days of thunderstorms 18.5 are experienced in this season.

The Summer

Monthly mean temperatures of summer months of June to August vary between 21° and 23°C. The highest number of days with thunderstorms is 8.3 in June but the number dwindles to 6.1 in July and 3.4 in August. July is the rainiest among summer months. A total of 242.8 mm of rain falls in this season which works out to 18.6 per cent of the total annual. Most of it is derived from summer monsoon and the rest from convectional activity.

The Autumn

Second transition period from summer to winter includes months of September to November. The monthly mean temperature decreases from 19.6°C in September to 15.2°C in October and to 10.7°C in November. Autumn is characterized by the least rainfall of 157.5 mm or 11.9 per cent of the total. It is harvest time and that of leaf fall. The dry sunny weather is a boon for the farmers, particularly in September and October.

Sources of Data

1. Tables 1,3,4,7,8,9,11 and 12 are based on the climatological tables for Jammu and Banihal supplied by IMD Srinagar. It is the latest available data set which pertains to 1961–90.
2. Data, for Table 2, on 'Station-Level Pressure', for the period 1971–2005, was provided, on written request, by the 23 Wing, Air Force, to the present writer for which he is grateful to the concerned. The said data is not available at IMD, Srinagar.
3. Rainfall data for Tables 5 and 10 for the period 1901–1950 has been taken from *A Climatologic Study of J&K* by M/s Lidoo and Pradhan, (December, 1986). The civil Investigation and Design Department, P.D.D., J & K Govt.
4. Table 6 contains the data compiled by the Irrigation and Flood Control Dept., J & K Govt., published in the Digest of Statistics D.O.E.S. (1995–96) for the period 1986 to 1995.

9

Weather and Climate

Temperate Kashmir

Admitted that weather in Kashmir for eight months in a year is endurable and also favourable for carrying out primary activities but it can, at times, turn unreliable with disastrous consequences in view of its single crop economy. This environmental restriction has made an average person in Kashmir quite weather conscious. A farmer working in his field or a boatman rowing on a lake often forecasts ensuing weather, with sufficient accuracy. The practice, here, of propitiating local saints, during spells of incessant rain or continued drought, detrimental to the standing crops, is exciting and unique.

The systematic observation of elements of weather, with the aid of scientific instruments, took place in Kashmir when a meteorological observatory was set up at Lal Mandi, in Srinagar, in the year 1891, during the reign of Maharaja Pratap Singh. With the arrival of Europeans into the Valley, after the construction of Jhelum valley road, who opted for Gulmarg as the place of their sojourn, a seasonal meteorological observatory came up here which functioned from June to October. In April 1954, the meteorological observatories of the state became part of the India Meteorological Department (IMD). Meteorological observatories were also established at Qazigund in 1955, Hyderpora, in Srinagar on the airport road, in 1961, Kupwara in 1977, Pahalgam and Kokernag in 1978. Rain gauges at twenty-two places have been installed by the state government.

Temperate Kashmir

The surrounding mountain fortification, its small extent, compared to Jammu or Ladakh, and a small variation in the elevation of its floor has given Kashmir Valley a homogenous climatic constitution. The climate is cool temperate and the two representative stations selected are Srinagar and Qazigund.

Srinagar

Srinagar, the summer capital of the state, is situated in the middle of the Valley, close to the Himalayan flank, at an elevation of 1587 m. Its locational coordinates are 34° 05′N and 74° 50′E.

Air Temperature

Mean Monthly

July, in Srinagar, with a mean temperature of 24.1°C, is the hottest month. January, on the other hand, with a mean temperature of 1.5°C is the coldest. This temperature pattern is in consonance with the conditions obtainable in modified subtropical or temperate climates where maxima and minima of temperature are reached in the months following the two solstices.

Single digit values of mean monthly temperature are observed in January to March and November to December when for rest of the year these are in double digits. Temperature increases from January onwards to attain the peak in July, after which it declines to reach the lowest in December. Increase is small from January to February but substantial from February to March and March to April. Rise in temperature varies between 3.6° to 4.6°C from April to May and May to June. June temperature increases by 2.2°C to reach the July maximum. July and August are almost equally hot as temperature difference is only 0.5°C (Table 9.1). Fall of temperature is 3.5° between August and September. A reduction of 6°C brings temperature of following two months down to 7.9°C in November. December mean of 3.1°C is less than November but higher than that of January.

Table 9.1

Srinagar: Air Temperature (°C)

Temperature	*J*	*F*	*M*	*A*	*M*	*J*	*J*	*A*	*S*	*O*	*N*	*D*	*Mean Annual*
Mean Maximum	5.5	8.1	13.9	19.7	24.1	29.2	30.1	29.7	27.8	22.0	14.9	7.9	
Mean Minimum	–2.4	–0.5	3.7	7.8	10.6	14.7	18.1	17.5	12.4	5.9	1.0	–1.6	—
Mean Monthly	1.5	3.8	8.8	13.7	17.3	21.9	24.1	23.6	20.1	13.9	7.9	3.1	13.3
Mean Range	7.9	8.6	10.2	11.9	13.5	14.5	12.0	12.2	15.4	16.1	13.9	9.5	12.1

In Srinagar the highest maximum temperature of 30.1°C is observed in July. Extreme maximum temperature of 38.3°C was recorded on 10 July 1946. In January, February and December the mean minimum temperature varies between –0.5° to –2.4°C. Extreme minimum temperature of –14.4 was noticed on 31 January 1893.

The mean annual temperature of Srinagar is 13.3°C. It was 13.2°C according to the earlier data-set of 1951–80.

Mean Range

Normal range of temperature of Srinagar is 32.5°C. Temperature range of this magnitude is an indicator of continental type of climate. This is substantiated by the use of five layers of clothing, mostly woollen, in December-January to a single cotton garment in July–August. The lowest mean monthly range of temperature is 7.9°C in January. Whereas it is highest, 16.1°C, in October. In January the sky is mostly overcast which results in a small difference between the mean maximum and mean minimum temperature. October, on the other hand, is a dry month, when the sky, by and large, is clear, both, during the day as well as at night. The diurnal temperature difference, therefore, is large. The climate of Srinagar is cool temperate continental.

Vertical Distribution

For elucidation of vertical distribution of temperature in Kashmir, comparison is made between the temperature data of Srinagar situated at a lower altitude with that of Gulmarg, which occupies a terrace of the Pir Panjal range at an altitude of 2,655 m.

Table 9.2

Gulmarg: Air Temperature (°C)

Element	*J*	*F*	*M*	*A*	*M*	*J*	*J*	*A*	*S*	*O*	*N*	*D*	*Mean Annual*
Mean Maximum	0.8	0.2	6.2	10.9	15.3	20.0	21.4	20.3	18.2	14.0	9.7	1.0	
Mean Minimum	–8.2	–9.3	–3.9	2.6	4.1	6.9	10.5	10.2	5.5	2.2	–2.3	–4.3	
Monthly Mean	–3.7	-4.5	1.1	6.7	9.7	13.4	15.9	15.2	11.8	8.1	3.7	–1.6	6.4

Table 9.2 reveals that the lowest mean maximum temperature of Gulmarg is 0.8°C in January and the highest 21.4°C in July. The mean

minimum temperature is sub-zero for five months in a year during January to March and November to December. Lowest mean minimum temperature of –9.3°C is recorded in February and the highest of 10.5°C in July.

Mean monthly temperature of Gulmarg is below freezing in January, February and December. From –4.5°C in February the mean temperature rises to 15.9°C in July. According to Hadlows word scale there is no hot season (above 20°C) in Gulmarg. Warm season (10 to 20°C) includes June, July, August and September. Cool season months are March, April, May, October and November. January, February and December constitute cold (0° to –10°C) season. The annual mean temperature of Gulmarg is 6.4°C.

It is evident that an increase of 1,068 m in altitude of Gulmarg above Srinagar has reduced its annual mean temperature by almost one-half compared to the latter. It corroborates the existence of inverse relationship between altitude and temperature. The vertical zonation of climate has been rightly summed up by Lawrence when he remarks, 'Every hundred feet of elevation brings some new phase of climate and vegetation and in a short ride of thirty miles one can pass from overpowering heat to climate delightfully cool or can escape from wearisome wet weather to a dry summer atmosphere'.

Inversion of Temperature

In intermontane valleys, on winter nights when sky is clear, air is dry and wind is absent, rapid radiation from the ground and layers of air, near it, takes place. The cooled air becomes dense and heavy and rests on the ground for a number of days. Under such conditions, layers of the air close to the ground are at a lower temperature compared to layers above which are warm and at a higher temperature. Here is a case of cool below and warm above in lower layers of the air. It is a reversal of the vertical distribution of temperature. This atmospheric phenomenon is called inversion of temperature.

Kashmir Valley experienced such an occurrence in November-December 1980. From 26 November a spell of intense cold sent its people shivering but the temperature was not below freezing. Bright sunshine was reported in highland stations of Gulmarg and Pahalgam when it was bleak and dismal in the Valley floor. The maximum temperature recorded in Srinagar and Pahalgam from 6 to 14 December 1980 is given below:

Maximum Temperature (°C)

Date	*Srinagar*	*Pahalgam*
December 6	2.6	3.0
December 7	2.1	3.2
December 8	1.6	2.9
December 9	1.2	3.5
December 10	0.8	3.5
December 11	1.9	3.3
December 12	2.0	2.4
December 13	2.5	3.5
December 14	3.2	5.0

On 14 December faint sunlight appeared at 1330 hrs. It was followed by a clear sky when the sun appeared after nineteen days. A high speed upper air wind was responsible for unsettling this inversion layer.

Atmospheric Pressure

Station-Level Pressure

Mean monthly station-level pressure of Srinagar at 0830 (I) and 1730 hrs (II) is given in Table 9.3. There is a difference of 2 to 3 mbs in the two readings as atmospheric pressure in the morning is higher than that in the evening.

It is highest (846 hPa) in December, followed by 844.3 hPa in January. It falls gradually up to May. The descent is steep from May to June but gentle from June to July. July is the month of minimum station-level pressure of 833.5 hPa. July onwards it exhibits an ascending trend. The increase from July to August is small but it is considerable between August and September and September and October. It further increases to 845.4 hPa in November. The line graph (Figure 7.2) depicting the station-level pressure of Srinagar presents a V-shape with a pointed base. The mean annual station-level pressure is 840.5 hPa.

Table 9.3

Srinagar: Station-Level Pressure (mb or hPa) and Mean Wind Speed (kmph)

Elements	*Hrs*	*J*	*F*	*M*	*A*	*M*	*J*	*J*	*A*	*S*	*O*	*N*	*D*	*Mean Annual*
Station level pressure	0830	845.2	843.7	843.2	842.4	840.8	836.8	834.9	836.1	840.7	844.8	846.8	847.0	
	1730	843.4	841.9	841.1	839.9	838.5	833.9	832.2	833.2	837.2	841.8	844.0	845.0	
Monthly mean		844.3	842.8	842.1	841.1	839.6	835.3	833.5	834.6	838.9	843.3	845.4	846.0	840.5
Mean wind speed		2.6	3.4	4.1	4.6	3.9	3.6	3.5	3.0	2.9	2.8	2.3	2.1	

Mean Wind Speed

The mean wind speed data in Table 9.3 indicates that not much surface air motion is discerned in Srinagar throughout the year. Mean wind speeds up to 8 kmph, according to Beaufort scale, is designated as light air. Maximum light air speeds of 4.1 to 4.6 kmph are noticed in March and April, corresponding to the month of *Chaet* (or *Chither* in Kashmiri) of the Bikrimi calendar hence the local name *Chittrun Wav* – the wind of *Chaet*. It marks the transition period from winter to spring. Mean wind speeds of 3 to 3.9 kmph are found in February and May to August. The remaining months of the year have wind speeds of 2.1 to 2.9 kmph. The sluggish wind speeds of 3.5 and 3.0 kmph in July and August make the humid heat oppressive in Srinagar.

Thunderstorms are, generally, accompanied by strong gusty winds though of short duration. These can be so strong as to uproot trees and cause other forms of damage. In such a situation, six huge Chinars were uprooted in Shalimar garden in June 1978. People visiting the Mughal gardens of Nishat or Shalimar, in summer, in flat bottomed residential boats, called *doongas,* often, face odds on their return journey, in the evening, because of strong wind which raises high waves in the Dal lake. The Wular lake, by tradition, has to be crossed, before noon in summer, in usual flat bottomed boats. The lake surface gets disturbed in the afternoon because of the squalls sweeping down the surrounding mountain ranges. Specific names have been assigned to these local winds depending on their direction. Eastern wind is called *Sindabat,* western *Nat,* northern *Nagakhon,* north-eastern *Vijiwav* and north-western *Kamaraez* (Lawrence, 1895).

A local wind specific to Baramulla town needs a mention here. It is a gentle breeze that blows during the day in summer. It is formed because of the situation of this town at the head of the Jhelum gorge. The hills and mountains of the town stand in a manner so as to form the head of a funnel, while its long stem is constituted by the gorge. The breeze is caused by thermal contrasts of the gorge walls and consequent up slope flow of air. It is the valley breeze or anabatic wind caused on a clear summer day in settled weather. This valley breeze provides much needed comfort in the otherwise sultry weather of this season.

Atmospheric Moisture

Humidity

A remarkable feature of the weather and climate of Srinagar is its high relative humidity. (Table 9.4). It is above 55 per cent throughout the year. It is highest in December (83%) and lowest in June. The other month with humidity of more than 80 per cent is January. In the remaining cold months of February, March and November it is between 71 and 78 per cent. Temperature is low but precipitation is high during these months which results in humid cold. The relative humidity is between 65 and 69 per cent in the summer months of July to September and also in October. It is low between 61 to 63 per cent in April and May. In spite of the fact that July is the hottest month, it is August heat that causes much discomfort because of its higher humidity. In June with mean temperature of 21.9°C and the least humidity of 55 per cent, the weather indicated in the climograph is scorching.

Precipitation

Srinagar receives a total annual precipitation of 698.3 mm. (Table 9.4). It is distributed throughout the year but not evenly. March is the rainiest month with 114.2 mm when November, with 27.8 mm, claims the least precipitation of the year. The next highest rainfall month is April followed by May. A close relationship is found between the number of western disturbances (Table 9.10) arriving in a particular month and the amount of precipitation received. January onwards the rainfall increases and the first maxima is registered in March. It decreases during the following months of April and May. The dominating influence in the weather of Srinagar during these five months is the western disturbances. June denotes the first minima of rainfall. Rainfall again shows an increasing trend when the second maxima is reached in August. This is the period of onshore monsoon. The next downward slide of precipitation commences in September when the second rainfall minima is noticed in November. Whereas, the first maxima of rainfall is much higher than the second, the second minima is marginally less than the first. (Figure 9.1)

Table 9.4

Srinagar: Atmospheric Moisture

Element	*J*	*F*	*M*	*A*	*M*	*J*	*J*	*A*	*S*	*O*	*N*	*D*	*Annual Total*
Total Monthly Rainfall (mm)	45.3	69.2	114.2	94.3	68.8	39.4	55.6	63.6	29.0	35.1	27.8	56.0	698.3
Normals of Rainy days (No.)	4.2	5.6	8.0	7.3	6.0	3.7	5.0	4.9	2.5	2.3	2.0	3.5	55
Rainfall Intensity (mm/r. day)	10.7	12.3	14.2	12.9	11.4	10.6	11.1	12.9	11.6	15.2	13.9	16.9	12.8
Relative Humidity (%)	82	78	71	63	61	55	66	69	65	68	76	83	M.A. 69.7
Days with Thunderstorms (No.)	0.0	0.3	1.7	4.2	8.0	6.2	6.0	5.5	3.4	1.5	0.3	0.0	37.1

Figure 9.1

Srinagar

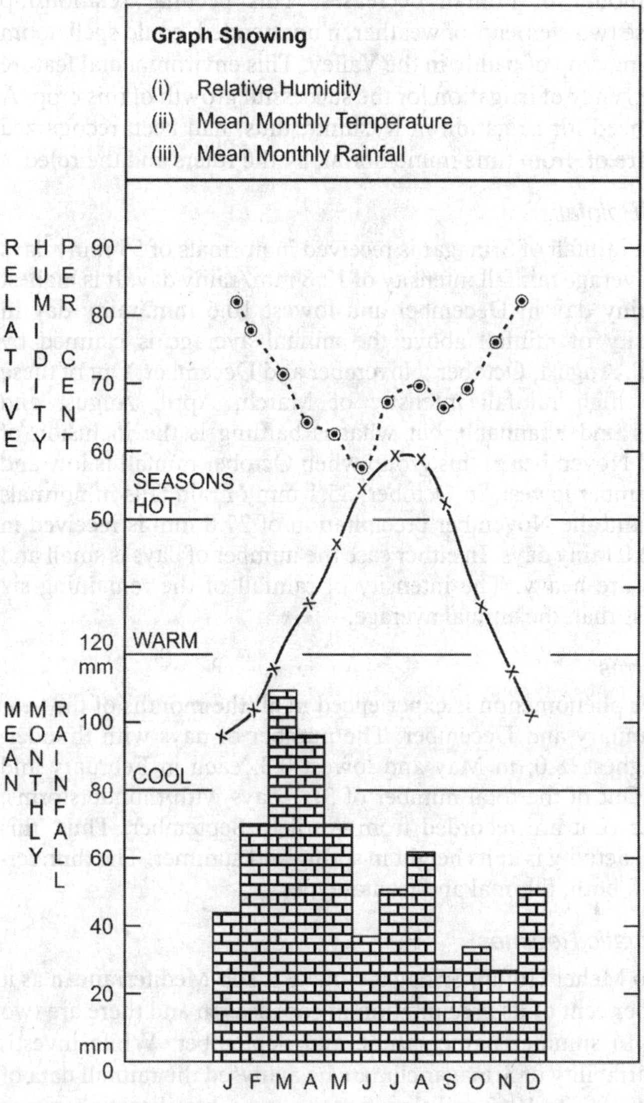

Altitude	:	1587 m
Mean Annual Temperature	:	13.3°C
Normal Range of Temperature	:	32.5°C
Frost Free Period	:	273 days
Total Annual Rainfall	:	698.3 mm

By comparing mean monthly temperature data of Srinagar with that of rainfall, it is evident that as the temperature increases, May onwards, amount of rainfall decreases. This peculiar relationship between these two elements of weather, if unattended, could spell doom on the growing crop of paddy in the Valley. This environmental feature created an urgency of irrigation for the successful growth of this crop. A compelling need for irrigation in Kashmir, thus, had been recognized and taken care of, from time immemorial, by the rulers and the ruled.

Intensity of Rainfall

Total annual rainfall of Srinagar is received in normals of 55 rainy days giving it an average rainfall intensity of 12.8 mm/rainy day. It is highest 16.0 mm/rainy day in December and lowest 10.6 mm/rainy day in June. Intensity of rainfall above the annual average is claimed by March, April, August, October, November and December. Out of these months the high rainfall intensity of March, April, August and December is understandable but what is baffling is the inclusion of October and November in this group when October rainfall is low and that of November lowest. In October, 35.1 mm of rain falls in normals of 2.3 days and the November precipitation of 27.8 mm is received in normals of 2.0 rainy days. In either case the number of days is small and the showers are heavy. The intensity of rainfall of the remaining six months is less than the annual average.

Thunderstorms

This weather phenomenon is experienced in all the months of the year except in January and December. The number of days with thunderstorms is highest, 8.0, in May and lowest 0.3, each in February and November. Out of the total number of 37.1 days with thunderstorms, about 90 per cent are recorded from April to September. Thus, this convectional activity is at its height in spring and summer. The thunderstorms are of, both, thermal and frontal types.

Rainfall Climatic Regimes

According to Meher Homji, Srinagar climate is sub-Mediterranean as it receives 62 per cent of its precipitation in cool season and there are two dry months in summer namely June and September. While investigating the variability of Srinagar climate he analysed the rainfall data of 72 years from 1892 to 1963 and classified the years into climatic regimes like unixeric or mediterranean, bixeric or sub-mediterranean, trixeric and quadrixeric. An appraisal of the monthly rainfall of these 72 years revealed that twelve years or 16.6 per cent of the total period under study are typically mediterranean as there is only one dry period during summer and precipitation is mostly in cool season. The bixeric (two dry periods) regime is noticed in thirty-two (or 44.4%) years out of which six years have a tendency towards mediterranean climate. Years with three dry periods (trixeric), total 19 or 26.4 per cent. Six years have quadrixeric regime while four years do not fit into any aforesaid regimes (Table 9.5).

Table 9.5

Srinagar: Rainfall Classification of Years 1892–1963
According to Regimes by Meher Homji

Bixeric	*Bixeric with Med. Tendency*	*Mediterranean Unixeric*	*Trixeric*	*Quadrixeric*	*Unclassified*
1892, 1893, 1894,	1910, 1912	1896, 1899,	1895,1901,1908,	1898,1904,	1907
1897, 1902, 1903,	1932, 1939,	1900, 1914,	1909,1911,1923,	1921,1938,	1948
1905, 1906, 1913,	1949, 1963	1915, 1918,	1929,1930, 1931,	1955,1962	1951
1916, 1917, 1919,		1920, 1934,	1933,1937,1941,		
1922, 1924, 1925,		1936, 1945,	1944,1947,1952,		
1926, 1927, 1928		1946, 1961	1954,1956,1958,		
1935, 1940, 1942,			1960		
1943, 1950, 1953,					
1957,1959					
26 years	6 years	12 years	19 years	6 years	3 years

On the basis of his findings Meher Homji concludes, 'Mediterranean years may be of rare occurrence in Srinagar … Srinagar may lay claim to several types of climate, temperate, Mediterranean, tropical, bixeric, trixeric quadrixeric, according to years but it seems best to classify it in the group of irregular climate, with strong variation from year to year'.

Snowfall

Snow is a type of frozen precipitation. Water vapour in a cloud on cooling below O°C get converted into ice. These tiny crystals of ice, hexagonal in shape, coalesce to form white flakes of snow, a centimetre or more in size. In order to prevent melting of snowflakes during their earthward journey the layers of the air must be below freezing point of water. When the temperature is very low, instead of snowflakes, spicules of ice, called Kathkosh in Kashmiri, glide down.

The first snowfall of the season known as *Nausheen* is an occasion of rejoicing. It breaks the prevalent spell of dry cold. Snowfall, in the Valley, takes place from December to March. The crestline of the mountain rim receives the first snow cover in late October. Snow may fall earlier as it did in September 1957. The standing crop of paddy was completely destroyed and Kashmir plunged into famine. Such calamities have taken place on a number of occasions in the history of this region. Even at present, when national highway gets closed for vehicular traffic due to heavy snowfall, a pall of gloom descends on the Valley inhabitants for fear of scarcity of essential goods and the concomitant price escalation. Snow can fall beyond March also as it happened on 29 April to 1 May 1969. In winter, overall availability of water in the tributaries and the master stream is far from satisfactory. This reduced water flow becomes a major hindrance in the generation of hydroelectricity to its full potential which results in decreased power production when it is needed most. Snow cover at Gulmarg has proved a blessing as the place has emerged as a venue of winter sports. Here, the slopes are favourable for skiing and so is the thickness and hardness of snow.

Snowfall at Srinagar

A study of snowfall at Srinagar for the fifteen-year period, from 1939 to 1953, has been made by Bhan (1956) of the Meteorological Centre, Srinagar. During this period snow fell during January to March and October to December. It took place on 153 occasions in January (Table 9.6), 99 in February and 59 in December. Number of days with snowfall is least in the months of March (20), October (2) and November (8). Same pattern holds true for the total amount of snowfall. January records the highest average snowfall of 500 mm followed in order by February 432 mm and December 279 mm. It is too small for the remaining three months. It can be inferred that snow, in Srinagar, mostly falls during January, February and December and that March, October and November are the lean months of this form of precipitation.

Snow is mostly accompanied by sleet and rain. Number of snowy days with sleet and rain is highest in February (36) and least in October (2). From the percentage frequency of these occasions it is evident that less sleet and rain is associated with snow during the cold months of January (22), February (36) and December (46). It is mostly sleet and rain during the less cold months of March (85), October (100) and November (75). Total snowfall received during the period under study is 1393 mm. A total of 87 per cent snow fell during January, February and December. Out of the three lean months March leads with 9.4 per cent.

Table 9.6

Snowfall at Srinagar (1939–53)*

Sr. No.	*Subject*	*Jan.*	*Feb.*	*March*	*Oct.*	*Nov.*	*Dec.*
1	No. of days with snowfall (a)	153	99	20	2	8	59
2	No. of snowy days with sleet and rainfall (b)	33	36	17	2	6	27
3	Percentage frequency (b/a)	22	36	85	100	75	46
4	Average snowfall (inches, mm)	19.7 (500)	17.4 (432)	5.2 (132)	0.1 (2.54)	1.9 (48)	11.0 (279)
5	Highest snowfall (inches, mm)	17.5 (445)	24.5 (622)	10.2 (259)	1.0 (25.4)	13.6 (345)	21.6 (549)
6	Date and year	7–1952	3–1949	21–1950	27–1939	28–1946	26–1953

* After S.N. Bhan (1956)

The timing of snowfall is, also, interesting. On 169 occasions snowfall has taken place between 0431 and 0830 hrs (I.S.T.) and on 183 occasions between 0831 and 1230 hrs. During January and February the usual period of snowfall was between 0831 to 1230 hrs and in December it took place between 0431 to 0830 hrs. The highest snowfall of 622 mm was received on February 3,1949, 549 mm on December 26, 1953 and 445 mm on January 7,1952. In the lean months highest snowfall of 259 mm was registered on March 21, 1950, 25.4 mm on October 27, 1939 and 345 mm on November 28, 1946.

Cloud Phenomenon

During the field work attention of the present writer was drawn, at Verinag, to a special cloud phenomenon, which occupies crestline of the Pir Panjal range to the east of Banihal pass, called *Wavmaal.* The phenomenon commences by 15 June every year and lasts up to the end of August, roughly coinciding with the time of south-west monsoon. Unlike usual cumulus clouds, which hang on the mountain tops in summer, these woolly forms are in constant motion horizontally. Their western and eastern limits are fixed between the peaks of the Pir Panjal above the villages of Manzmuh and Chouhan. They appear to roll horizontally like cylinders between these two bounds. The clouds are dirty white in colour with dark streaks present in certain parts. The breeze set in by these clouds, in and around Verinag, blows in the direction away from the mountains. But more often, the breeze is erratic and assumes a swirling movement. This results in constant stirring of standing field crops. The farmers working in the fields opined that this breeze helps in timely awning of paddy in the area, which experiences a short growing season due to its proximity to the Lesser Himalayan range. They wait, anxiously, every year for the occurrence of this weather phenomenon.

Dryness and Wetness

Periods of dryness and wetness of Srinagar have been computed with the help of the scale based on the definitions of Bagnouls and Gaussen and the results presented in Table 9.7.

Table 9.7

Srinagar: Periods of Dryness and Wetness

S. No.	*Month*	*Precipitation (mm)*	*Mean Temperature (°C)*	*Scale*	*Inference*
1	January	45.3	1.5	P > 4T	Humid
2	February	69.2	3.8	P > 4T	Humid
3	March	114.2	8.8	P > 4T	Humid
4	April	94.3	13.7	P > 4T	Humid
5	May	68.8	17.3	P between 3T & 4T	Sub-Humid
6	June	39.4	21.9	P < 2T	Dry
7	July	55.6	24.1	P between 2T & 3T	Sub-Dry
8	August	63.3	23.6	P between 2T & 3T	Sub-Dry
9	September	29.0	20.1	P < 2T	Dry
10	October	35.1	13.9	P between 2T & 3T	Sub-Dry
11	November	27.8	7.9	P between3T & 4T	Sub-Humid
12	December	56.0	3.1	P > 4T	Humid

Table 9.7 reveals that in Srinagar, five months January to April and December, are humid. May and November are sub-humid, July, August and October are sub-dry and June and September are dry months. There is no month which is very dry.

Spatial Distribution of Rainfall (I)

Distribution of rainfall at a particular place varies both in time (seasonal) and space (spatial or areal). The first attempt for finding spatial distribution of precipitation, in Kashmir, is based on the data of seven stations recorded by IMD Srinagar.

Total Annual Precipitation

Out of the seven stations, listed in Table 9.8, Sonamarg, situated in the headwater region of the Sindh stream, receives the highest rainfall of

Table 9.8

Kashmir Region: Spatial Distribution of Precipitation (in mm) and Normals of Rainy Days (No.) (Based on IMD Data)

Station & Location		*J*	*F*	*M*	*A*	*M*	*J*	*J*	*A*	*S*	*O*	*N*	*D*	*Total*	*Annual Rainfall Intensity*
1. Srinagar	Ppt	70.4	73.7	94.2	90.2	59.7	34.3	56.1	62.7	39.9	27.7	12.7	37.3	658.9	
34°0′5N 74°-50E	No.	6.2	6.2	7.5	7.8	5.6	3.4	4.8	5.3	3.4	2.4	1.1	3.1	57.1	11.4 mm/r.d.
2. Anantnag	Ppt	74.4	82.0	82.3	84.8	54.6	33.0	39.7	59.7	49.3	26.4	12.9	43.9	663.0	
33°43′N, 75°-09°E	No.	5.6	5.5	6.2	6.8	4.5	2.8	4.5	4.4	2.5	1.7	1.2	3.4	49.1	13.5 mm/r.d.
3. Baramulla	Ppt	118.9	120.1	163.6	134.1	89.1	52.6	49.5	32.1	39.4	34.4	25.4	67.1	955.3	
34°12′N, 74°22′E	No.	8.0	7.1	9.5	8.6	6.6	9.6	4.1	4.2	3.2	3.2	2.0	4.9	66.0	14.4 mm/r.d.
4. Sopore	Ppt	106.9	106.7	139.5	93.9	70.4	43.7	45.5	35.8	35.1	35.8	17.8	51.3	782.0	
34°18 N, 74°24E	No.	7.1	7.3	8.4	6.9	5.5	3.8	4.3	3.6	2.7	2.7	1.5	3.7	57.5	13.6 mm/r.d.
5. Uri	Ppt	137.9	142.7	180.0	145.3	99.3	80.5	100.6	96.8	71.6	54.9	26.7	82.0	1227.3	
34°03′N, 74°′02′E	No.	7.7	7.5	9.2	8.6	6.7	5.9	7.7	7.3	5.1	3.4	2.0	4.5	75.6	16.2 mm/r.d.
6. Gurez	Ppt	144.5	191.8	222.5	155.2	119.4	68.6	55.1	79.0	61.0	69.3	28.5	118.9	1314.8	
34°38′N, 74°51′E	No.	10.2	10.1	11.1	11.0	9.4	5.9	6.0	6.9	5.4	5.3	3.1	7.1	91.5	14.3 mm/r.d.
7. Sonamarg	Ppt	254.3	237.0	232.5	246.1	146.8	76.5	93.0	93.5	90.4	58.4	45.0	142.0	1815.5	
34°19′N, 75°19′E	No.	11.5	9.0	12.5	12.0	10.1	7.3	8.7	9.1	7.0	4.8	3.2	7.5	103.6	17.5 mm/r.d.

Ppt – Precipitation

1815.5 mm. The orography of the area is mainly responsible for this high precipitation as the moisture-laden winds get entrapped within the gorge above Gagangir. The other two stations of high rainfall are Gurez and Uri. Baramulla also gets high precipitation of 955.3 mm against 782 mm at Sopore. Rainfall of Anantnag is nearly the same as that of Srinagar.

A significant outcome of this study is that stations situated in highlands, like Sonamarg, Gurez and Uri are favourably placed in terms of precipitation. Compared to other lowland stations of Sopore, Anantnag and Srinagar, Baramulla with high rainfall is an exception on account of its nearness to the Jhelum gorge. Srinagar in the middle of the Veth plain receives the least precipitation.

Intensity of Rainfall

The highest rainfall of Sonamarg takes place in normals of 103.6 days thus assigning it a rainfall intensity of 17.5 mm/ rainy day (r.d.). This highest rainfall intensity implies that the showers are heaviest here. Uri holds second place with 16.2 mm/r.d. It is 14.4 mm/r.d. in Baramulla, 14.3 in Gurez, 13.6 in Sopore and 13.5 in Anantnag. Intensity of rainfall of 11.4 mm/r.d. is lowest in Srinagar.

Rainfall Characteristics

In the seven months, January to May and November to December, of frontal rainfall, the month with the highest rainfall is March in Srinagar, Baramulla, Sopore, Uri and Gurez; April in Anantnag and January in Sonamarg. These figures also denote the highest rainfall month of the year in each case. November in each case is the month with minimum precipitation.

Frontal rainfall claims a share of 66.8 per cent of the total annual rainfall of Srinagar. These figures for other station are Anantnag (65.7), Baramulla (75.1), Sopore (75.0), Uri (67.1), Gurez (74.5) and Sonamarg (72.3%). The highest frontal rainfall is received in Baramulla and the lowest by Anantnag.

July to September is the period of monsoon rainfall. July rainfall is highest in Baramulla, Sopore, and Uri when it is highest in August in the remaining stations. Monsoon rainfall is highest, 28.1 per cent of the total annual rainfall of Srinagar. It is lowest, 12.8 per cent in Baramulla.

Spatial Distribution of Rainfall (II)

A second attempt on areal distribution of rainfall in Kashmir region, involving 22 rain gauge stations, is based on the rainfall data recorded by the Irrigation and Flood Control Department of Jammu and Kashmir Government, given in Table 9.9. The list of stations includes that of Srinagar with data from IMD. The large number of stations is an asset in delimiting precipitation zones of this region. Out of the listed stations, Gulmarg received the highest annual precipitation of 1213.0 and Tral the lowest of 330.4 mm. Three major precipitation zones are identified in Kashmir.

Precipitation Zones

High precipitation zone includes stations with more than 901 mm of rainfall. These are Gulmarg, Qazigund, Verinag and Sogam. These stations are situated either on or near the surrounding mountain rim. Here the orographic factor is the main cause of high precipitation.

Table 9.9

Kashmir Region: Spatial Distribution of Precipitation (mm), Number of Rainy Days and Intensity of Rainfall (Based on IFCD Data)

S. No.	*Station*	*Total Annual Rainfall (mm)*	*No. of Rainy Days*	*Rainfall Intensity (mm per rainy day)*
1.	Anantnag	419.5	44	9.5
2.	Arizal	355.9	43	8.2
3.	Babapora	603.3	40	15.0
4.	Bandipora	732.3	54	13.5
5.	Baramulla	609.2	43	14.1
6.	Budgam	636.4	53	12.0
7.	Chrari-Sharief	628.8	54	11.6
8.	Dachigam	829.0	57	14.5
9.	Ganderbal	495.9	50	9.9
10.	Gulmarg	1213.0	73	16.6
11.	Handwara	841.0	55	15.2
12.	Kokernag	888.5	61	14.5
13.	Kulgam	677.5	48	14.1
14.	Pahalgam	635.2	84	7.5
15.	Pulwama	547.7	41	13.3
16.	Qazigund	1039.7	58	17.9
17.	Shopian	743.9	53	14.0
18.	Sogam	925.9	67	13.8
19.	Sopore	679.3	48	14.1
20.	Srinagar (IMD)	599.1	47	12.7
21.	Tangamarg	352.6	39	9.0
22.	Tral	330.4	36	9.1
23.	Verinag	967.8	58	16.6

More than half of the total number of stations with total annual rainfall of 601 to 900 mm constitute the *medium precipitation zone.* These are Pahalgam, Kokernag, Kulgam, Shopiyan, Handwara, Bandipore, Chrari-sharief, Budgam, Sopore, Baramulla, Babapora and Dachigam. This zone covers a large area in the north of Kashmir.

Low precipitation zone covers the middle and southern parts of the region where the annual rainfall is less than 600 mm. It extends from Ganderbal to Anantnag. The other stations are Arizal, Pulwama, Srinagar, Tangamarg and Tral. Within this zone can be delineated a dry or drought prone zone with a rainfall of less than 360 mm. It is bounded by Arizal and Tangamarg in the west and Tral in the east.

Based upon the analysis of the above mentioned spatial precipitation data several relationships are unfolded. Areas of high precipitation have a peripheral location. There is a well defined and contiguous area of low rainfall in the middle of the Valley, around Srinagar, marked by its southward extension. This is encompassed by a zone of medium rainfall with a northward bulge. It can safely be concluded that site factor and orography play a vital role in the distribution of precipitation in Kashmir.

Intensity of Rainfall

Rainfall intensity is highest (17.9 mm/r.d.) in Qazigund and lowest (8.2 mm/r.d.) in Arizal. Gulmarg, with the highest rainfall is relegated to second position because of its large number (73) of rainy days compared to 55 days of Qazigund. Showers of rainfall are heavier in Qazigund than those at Gulmarg. Like the zones of total annual precipitation the intensity of rainfall of these 23 stations (Table 9.9) lends itself to threefold division. it is less than 10 mm per rainy day in Anantnag, Arizol, Ganderbal, Tangamarg, Tral and Pahalgam. First Five Stations of this category receive least rainfall and their presence in this group is expected. Inclusion of Pahalgam, with medium rainfall, in this category is surprising. Rainfall intensity of Pahalgam is decreased because of the large number, 84, of normals of rainy days. Such group variations can be detected in other categories also. Intensity of rainfall is between 10.1 and 15 mm per rainy day in Babapora, Bandipore, Baramulla, Budgam, Chrari-Sharief, Dachigam Kokernag, Kulgam, Pulwama, Shopian and Srinagar. Gulmarg, Handwara, Qazigund and Verinag claim the highest rainfall intensity of more than 15.1 mm per rainy day.

Seasons

The two main seasons of Srinagar (Table 7.10), based on Hadlow's Word-Scale of mean monthly temperatures, are a long summer and a longer winter, each followed by a warm transition season, a short spring and a shorter autumn. The changes brought about by annual march of seasons in its natural environment are distinct and striking. Use has been made, wherever necessary, of 5-day normals of the mean maximum and mean minimum temperatures of Srinagar in the explanation of these seasons.

The Winter

This season of longest duration includes January, February, March, November and December. High precipitation, high humidity, overcast sky and snowfall are some general features of Kashmir winter. Fall onwards the common deciduous trees like chinar, poplar willow and the like, together with fruit trees stand in a state of utter helplessness because of the absence of their foliage. Dark and grey are the predominant colours with an occasional white mantle of snow. Winter here is not uniformly monotonous but exhibits some variety. It can easily be split up into three well-defined segments, of varying attributes, like low precipitation winter, severe winter and mild wet winter.

Temperature Status

Mean maximum temperature of January is 5.5°C which increases through February to attain the value of 13.9°C in March. November mean maximum of 14.9 decreases to 7.9°C in December. Mean minimum temperature of –2.4°C of January increases to –0.5° in February and to 3.7°C in March. On the contrary, the mean minimum temperate of 1° of November falls to –1.6°C in December. Mean monthly temperature ranges between 1.5° to 8.8°C. Two conclusions drawn from this description are that the season experiences a fall as well as a rise of temperature, and that sub-zero night temperatures prevail in three out of five winter months.

Low Precipitation Winter

The first fifty days of the winter from November 1, to December 20, are characterized by low precipitation. November receives minimum precipitation, as the western disturbances which arrive at this time are mostly in an occluded form. December rainfall for the first three weeks happens to be meagre. Cold, cough and other pulmonary diseases are rife. This part of the winter is marked by only a general decrease in temperature.

Severe Winter

This second segment of winter in Kashmir has a duration of 70 days from 21 December to end of February. On winter solstice the sun shines vertically over the Tropic of Capricorn. This results in the lowest altitude of the sun and shortest length of the day in the northern hemisphere. These, aided by persistent cloud cover in Kashmir, lead to low insolation making January the coldest month. As is well known, cold intensifies in temperate regions in the month following winter solstice.

According to local tradition the severest part of the winter begins on 21 December and lasts for 40 days. This period is referred to as

Chillai Kalan or senior frigid phase. The mean maximum temperature of 7.9° in December declines to 5.5°C in January. The minimum temperature falls from –1.6° to –2.4°C. The night temperature remains below freezing throughout this stretch of 40 days.

The first snowfall in the Valley floor, generally takes place around Christmas, which ushers in a welcome change in the earlier dry cold spell. January precipitation is mostly in the form of snow. The climograph of Srinagar reveals that the weather associated with January February and December is raw. Raw or damp cold is much more exacting than dry cold, as damp air is a good conductor of heat and it allows the escape of heat from the body.

The sub-zero temperature at night gives rise to frost, particularly when the sky is clear. Snow cover or its melt on the ground freezes hard making all kinds of movement – human, animal or vehicular, difficult. Potable water in overground pipes also freezes on such occasions. The prevalence of cold wave conditions reduce the temperature by 6°C. In that case the water of the Dal lake freezes hard. *Kangri,* the indigenous portable fire pot is a friend indeed, in this inclement weather, but if not handled with care it causes much damage. The gliding, dancing snow flakes, on their earthward journey, during a snowfall, the white, soft snow blanket that covers all objects, useful or useless, and the long icicles hanging from the eaves are some of the fascinating winter scenes.

The second part of the severe winter is designated as *Chillai Khurd* or junior frigid phase. It lasts, from 31 January to 19 February, for a period of 20 days. As the name implies it is less harsh than the preceding phase. The mean maximum temperature increases from 5.5° to 8.1°C and mean minimum temperature which continues to be sub-zero, rises to 0.5°C. Precipitation mostly takes the form of snow and sleet. Frosts are frequent in the first fortnight. Temperature exhibits an increasing trend.

The last part of the severe winter, which lasts for ten days, is called *Chillai Baccha* or minor frigid phase. The increasing trend of the temperature continues and the cold is less severe. Precipitation is in the form of sleet.

The Mild Wet Winter

March is the last month of the winter. In terms of temperature and precipitation it is a winter month with a difference. The mean maximum temperature increases at the rate of 1°C in the first fortnight and at 2°C in the second, thereby raising it from 11° to 17°C. Mean minimum temperature increases from 2° in the beginning, to 5°C by its end. In the last ten days the mean monthly temperature is 11°C, one degree Celsius more than the upper limit of the cold season.

March claims the largest share of western disturbance, with both warm and cold fronts, and consequently, highest amount of rainfall. In association with rising temperature, these heavy showers of rain initiate revival of vegetation. Narcissus flowers are first to greet us. These frequent showers help in the thaw, reduce the sting in the cold and soften sods in the cropland.

Spring equinox, 21 March when the sun is positioned vertically over the equator, is celebrated as *Nauroz* in Kashmir. The day is significant in the context of agricultural operations which, after a holiday of several months, commence for the ensuing growing season from this day.

Winter Season: An Appraisal

Winter precipitation in Srinagar is highest in both relative and absolute terms. It is this cold season precipitation which has prompted some scholars to trace mediterranean traits in Kashmir climate. As plant growth ceases when the soil temperature drops below 5.5°C, this copious precipitation of winter is directly of little significance for crop cultivation. But indirectly, it is a major contributor to dependable and thriving agriculture, in the favourable season by building reserves of snow on the mountains and by restocking subsoil water reserves. The snowmelt feeds the streams, springs, lakes and wetlands for which Kashmir is famous. It is carried to the cropland through a network of canals.

The period of sub-zero temperatures begins from the second week of November and lasts up to the middle of February. Frosts exist for normals of 15 days in November, 31 days in December, 31 days in January and 15 days in February (based on 5-day normal data). This adds up to 92 days which curtails the growing season to 273 days. Agriculture, therefore, observes a holiday during these 92 winter days. In such a situation double cropping becomes rather difficult. This cessation of cultivation forces tens of thousands of farm hands into idleness. Similar is the case of workers engaged in other primary activities. A large number of such workers migrate to the neighbouring states to become economically productive.

To combat winter cold fuel, charcoal, dried leaves and twigs and host of other materials are to be stored. All these inflammable substances make the dwellings, generally made of timber, susceptible to fire. The loss of property in that case is enormous. Burns due to Kangri are painful and leave the skin scarred.

Production of world renowned Kashmir handicrafts receive impetus in the warm interiors of the workplaces resounding with melodious *Chakkri* strains. This congenial working environment prompts an artisan for strenuous efforts, the outcome of which is a bewitching and an unrivalled quality product.

Gulmarg as an ideal ski resort, with attendant infrastructure in place, is attracting tourists and sports persons. An era of winter tourism, with its economic benefits, appears to have dawned in Kashmir.

The Spring

The first transition season from winter to summer includes the months of April and May. The sun has crossed the equator and is on its apparent northward journey towards the Tropic of Cancer. The days are of more than 12 hours duration and there is a noticeable increase in the angle of inclination of the rays of the sun.

Spring is a warm season with mean monthly temperature varying between 13.7° and 17.3°C. The mean maximum temperature increased from 19.7° in April to 24.1°C in May. Mean minimum temperature is 7.8° in April and 10.6°C in May.

The weather in this season, in continuation of the winter, is under the sway of western disturbances. More rain falls in April than in May. April rainfall is only 20 mm less than that of March. Spring rainfall, aided by warm sunshine becomes instrumental in the thawing process on the mountains, where the snow has frozen hard due to winter frosts. The tributary streams consequently regain their original volume of water. Canals drawn from these streams carry water to the cropland where it is badly needed for raising paddy nurseries and for the preparation of rice paddies. Land which lay fallow since last harvest, in October-November, is opened by two or more ploughings, clods are broken, farmyard manure is added, water directed into the fields and the soil worked in to a slush, levelled and kept ready for the transplantation of paddy seedlings. The latter operation has to be completed by summer solstice. The warmth and moisture favour growth of vegetation. The naked deciduous trees acquire a light green foliage. The fruit trees like almonds, apple, peach, plum, etc., bring forth blossoms before they are in leaf. Bird migration to Kashmir takes place with the arrival of swallow, hoopie, starlings, wagtails and others.

Houseboat owners and *shikarawallas* get busy renovating their respective floating structures. Same holds true for hoteliers. Mughal gardens are thrown open to public on *Baisakhi,* 13 April. This also marks the inauguration of the tourist season. Spring brings hope and cheer and the people of Kashmir look forward to a year of promise and fortune, be it the peasant or the orchardist, a businessman or a transporter, a houseboat or a hotel proprietor, a shikarawalla or a pony man, a tourist guide or a tour organizer. In spring pink, pearl, light green and yellow are the hues of the landscape. In consequence of frequent showers of rain in the last week of March and most of April, puddles are numerous, roads and lanes become miry, and clothes get wet and mud-stained. For this reason this period is nicknamed, *Ganda Bahar,* the dirty spring.

The Summer

In Srinagar four months from June to September, with mean monthly temperature between 20° and 30°C, constitute the hot season or the summer. Mean maximum temperature of 29.2°C in June increases to 30.1°C in July, which drops to 29.7°C in August and 27.8°C in September. From 14.7° in June, the mean minimum temperature rises to 18.1°C in July. It declines to 17.5°C in August and to 12.4°C in September. The monthly mean temperature varies from 20.1° to 24.1°C. July serves as the temperature divide. This season registers rise as well as fall of temperature.

High temperature and long hours of sunshine favour execution of all primary activities including farming. A study of the temperature rainfall graph of Srinagar (Figure 9.1) reveals that May onwards when there is substantial increase in air temperature, the amount of rainfall diminishes. For productive agriculture the short supply of rainwater is to be compensated by water through irrigation. Compared to two other regions of state – Jammu and Ladakh – Kashmir with least geographical area supports the largest population. Among other factors, one of the reasons for this area – population anomaly is the dependable and thriving agriculture made possible by ample cropland, fertile soils, propitious temperature regime and an assured supply of water through canal irrigation (Table 6.2 at Annexure-1).

By April end, the entire irrigated cropland gets water filled, an essential requirement of paddy cultivation. This together with the lakes, wetlands, master stream and its tributaries presents the appearance of a vast sheet of water. With available high temperature, evaporation is brisk and widespread. The state of atmosphere, at this stage, favours convectional lifting of moisture-laden air. Thunder storms are common throughout the summer. The peak temperatures of July and August cause a very high incidence of evapo-transpiration which makes weather sultry.

Monsoon in Kashmir

Many authors and scholars deny the arrival of onshore monsoon in Kashmir. There are two main reasons responsible for this negation. The first is the averment of some academicians that south-west monsoon fails to reach Kashmir because of the barrier effect of the Pir Panjal range. The second is the omission of dates of onset and withdrawal of summer monsoon in Jammu and Kashmir in the Forecasting Manual of India Meteorological Department, Part IV, 18.1, 1967 which tantamount to non-recognition, by this apex body on weather and climate, of the arrival of monsoon currents into Jammu and Kashmir.

There is no denying the fact that the Pir Panjal is a climatic divide between the subtropical Jammu and temperate Kashmir. But at the same time we should not disregard the reality that the Pir Panjal (the Lesser Himalaya) is not as formidable a barrier as the Great Himalaya. In this connection, de Terra asserts that monsoon currents are guided by morphologic depressions such as the Kashmir Valley and the transverse gorges of the Pir Panjal slope. These depressions act like 'wind funnels' admitting the south-west winds into the mountains, where they finally sweep into the valley by way of 'certain' low ridges and passes like the Banihal, Tosamidan and the Jhelum gorge. According to him Kashmir owes some of its attractive features like the dense forests on the valley facing slopes of the Pir Panjal to this southern wind. It also carries the suspended silt in the air across this barrier and drops it in the Valley to enrich its soils.

In the words of Lidhoo and Pradhan the south-west monsoon on its onward march towards north-west India in July is pulled into Jammu and Kashmir … and enters as a south-easterly current through the trenched valleys. The north-west to south-east orientation of mountains ridges, in spite of their height, do not cut off completely the rain bearing monsoon winds. So it is contended that the Pir Panjal does not completely prevent the entry of monsoon currents into Kashmir. These winds even reach Ladakh, as explained in the following chapter.

Monsoon Schedule

After acknowledging the arrival and withdrawal of south-west monsoon in Jammu and Kashmir, an attempt was made at Meteorological Centre, Srinagar to fix the respective dates of onset and retreat of Monsoons for different stations. (Pradhan et al., 1978). These were computed from the 50-year rainfall data (1927–76), collected from IMD observatories in the state and also from functional rain gauges of I & FC Department. The outcome of this attempt for Kashmir is tabulated below.

Kashmir: South-West Monsoon Schedule

Onset	*Retreat*
10 July: Qazigund, Anantnag, Srinagar, Gulmarg, Baramulla	11 September: Anantnag, Srinagar, Gulmarg, Baramulla 13 September: Qazigund

Affirmation

Evidences, both traditional and scientific shall be presented in support of the claim regarding the arrival and impact of summer monsoon in Kashmir.

Folk Traditions

One of the six seasons, in the traditional classification, (Table 7.6), is *Wahraat* which stands for rainy season. A Kashmiri proverb, '*Baechan duen hinz her gayi Wahraach hund rood*', or the quarrel between a married couple is like a (short lived) wahraat (monsoon) shower. It manifests the impact of this weather phenomenon on their ethos. Since ancient times, its presence has been recognized and accepted by its scholars and laymen, and adopted in its folklore.

There is an age-old practice, an environmental compulsion, of sun drying of vegetables like brinjal, tomato, gourd, bitter gourd, etc., available in abundance in summer, for use in winter when fresh vegetables are in short supply. Drying of these vegetables is avoided in Wahraat as the air is damp and the showers are frequent. Growth of fungus, under such atmospheric conditions, affects the quality of the product making it, even, unfit for human consumption.

The Season

This first scientific evidence is based on the duration of the Wahraat season, source of rainfall and its impact on vegetation. In the first instance, not much variation exists between the extent of Wahraat, from 16 July to 15 September based on tradition and the dates of the onset and withdrawal of monsoon, 10 July to 11 September, arrived at by modern systematic investigation.

The rainfall regime of Srinagar depicts second rainfall maxima in August. Why this high rainfall? When onshore monsoon is active and vigorous in north-western India, including Jammu region as far as Banihal, Reasi, Rajouri and Poonch on the south of the Pir Panjal, how can Kashmir be an exception to its sway. The growth of the growing flora is accelerated by the monsoon showers but the change here is not from brown to verdure but from light green to its darker shades.

Humidity

In the three monsoon months, relative humidity varies between 65 to 69 per cent. High temperature and high humidity result in sweltering weather. It causes much human discomfort. Clothes are reduced to minimum and cottons predominate.

Rainfall

Monsoon component of Kashmir rainfall was computed by the present writer and published in the *Vayu Mandal* (1980). With the help of tables of daily normal rainfall of Srinagar (Bhan, 1954) the total amount of rainfall received in this season and its percentage in relation to total annual rainfall is found.

(a) Based on traditional Wahraat. The rainfall received from 16 July to 15 September adds up to 128.2 mm out of a total annual precipitation of 638.8 mm. Here the share of monsoon rainfall is 20 per cent.

(b) Based on IMD, Srinagar schedule. The monsoon rainfall received from its onset on 10 July to 11 September is 127.2 mm. It works out to 19.9 per cent of the total annual rainfall of 638.8 mm.

(c) Based on seasonal distribution of rainfall worked out by Pradhan et al. (1978). The total monsoon rainfall from July to September is 85.1 mm, when the total annual rainfall is 395.1 mm. The percentage of monsoon rainfall in this case is 22.

Thus, the monsoon component of rainfall in Kashmir varies from 20 to 22 per cent.

Floods

Floods occur in summer months of July to September. During this period streams are almost full of water. Spells of rainfall in the catchment area of the master stream are the main cause of floods. Depressions originating from the Bay of Bengal and moving over the axis of monsoon trough in west to north-westerly direction, under certain favourable conditions recurve and find their entry into Kashmir region causing heavy rainfall. Another occasion of abundant rainfall is when the oscillating monsoon trough shifts close to the Himalayan foothills. In either case, the heavy rainfall affects the river level which rises to danger mark within 36 hours. Devastating floods are caused depending on the duration and intensity of rainfall. Two worst floods have taken place, in the post-Independence era, on 20 September 1950 and 9 September 1992.

Conclusion

The preceding discussion establishes that south-west monsoon reaches Kashmir as a weak current despite the barrier effect of the Pir Panjal. Its dates of arrival and withdrawal have been worked out and fixed. Its presence and impact has been identified by its people since ancient times. Thus, like *Barsaat* in north-western India the *Wahraat* in Kashmir is the season of south-west monsoon. About one-fifth of the total annual rainfall is contributed by these winds. At times, these cause ravaging floods. According to P.K. Das (1995), by mid-July the monsoon extends into Kashmir and the remaining parts of the country but only as a feeble current because by this time it has shed most of its moisture.

The Autumn

The second transition and warm season is autumn, which is of one month duration. It comprises the month of October. The maximum and the minimum temperatures of this season are 22° and 5.9°C respectively. The mean monthly temperature is 13.9°C. A total rainfall of 35.1 mm is received in normals of 2.3 days.

Autumn the season of 'mellow fruitfulness and maturing sun', locally called *Harud,* is a hectic time for the peasants. Reaped paddy is stacked, threshed and stored to make the granary full. Ripe and succulent apples are picked, graded and packed for export. Vegetables are to be threaded in the form of garlands for drying. It is a common sight to find the scarlet of the chillies, purple of the brinjals, red of the tomatoes and green of the gourd adorning the sunny side of the houses. Fodder, feed and fuel is to be stored for ensuing winter.

Climatic conditions become unfavourable for deciduous vegetation and leaf fall sets in. It is a gradual process in which the leaves change colour from green to yellow before they fall to the ground. The most spectacular sight is presented by the giant Chinar where the green leaves first turn yellow and then red. Birds that had migrated into the Valley, in spring, return to warmer climes. Yellow and brown are the hues of the landscape. Autumn in Kashmir is unique because of its salubrious climate, ripe juicy fruit and tranquil setting.

Productive Period

In terms of region's economy the productive period in Kashmir sums up to eight months – two of spring, four of summer, one of autumn and one fortnight each at the either end of winter. All primary activities like cultivation, grazing, lumbering, horticulture, mining and quarrying which had come to a stand still during winter are resumed and worked to full capacity. Tourism, a major industry, on which depend great number and variety of workers, booms during this period.

Seasonal Distribution of Rainfall

Table 9.10 gives the monthly and seasonal precipitation and frequency of western disturbances in Srinagar.

The Winter

During this season the entire north-western India is under the influence of temperate cyclones. Out of the total of 28 western depressions, 20 or 71.4 per cent arrive during this season. Rainfall of the period claims a

Table 9.10

Srinagar: Seasonal Distribution of Precipitation (mm) and Frequency of Western Disturbances (No.)

Seasons	*Winter*					*Spring*		*Summer*				*Autumn*	*Total*
Months	*J*	*F*	*M*	*N*	*D*	*A*	*M*	*J*	*J*	*A*	*S*	*Oct.*	
Frequency of western Disturbances	4	5	6	2	3	5	3	0	Monsoon			0	28
Total Seasonal Numbers & Percentage	20 Nos. or 71.4 per cent					8 Nos. or 28.6 p.c.		Nil				Nil	
Mean Monthly Precipitation	45.3	69.2	114.2	27.8	56.0	94.3	68.8	39.4	55.6	63.6	29.0	35.1	698.3
Total seasonal Precipitation & Percentage	312.5 or 44.7 p.c.					163.1 or 23.3 p.c.		187.6 or 26.8 p.c.				35.1 or 5.2 p.c.	

share of 44.7 per cent of total annual precipitation. A close relationship is identified between the frequency of western disturbance and the amount of seasonal rainfall.

The Spring

Eight out of twenty-eight western disturbances arrive in this season giving a total spring precipitation of 163.1 mm or 23.3 per cent.

The Summer

The peripheral months of this season June and September receive marginal rainfall but it is substantial in the core months of July and August. From mid-July to mid-September the rainfall is due to south-west monsoon. Summer rainfall share is 26.8 per cent.

The Autumn

October, like June, lies outside the purview of either of above noted wind systems. Very little rain, 5.2 per cent, falls in this season. It is the harvest time and dry weather is ideal for this purpose.

Qazigund

Qazigund is situated, in south Kashmir at an elevation of 1,739 metres, 14 km short of Jawahar tunnel on national highway, 1 A. It occupies a flat-topped Karewa which forms part of Valley floor. It is located on 33° 35' N latitude and 75° 05' E longitude.

Air Temperature

Mean Monthly

January with a mean monthly temperature of 0.6°C is the coldest month. There is a marginal increase in temperature from January to February, when it is substantial from February to March. The increasing trend of temperature continues as the year advances when it reaches 20.7°C in June. It attains the peak, 22.4°C, in July. In this case too, like Srinagar, July functions as the temperature divide. A small difference of 0.3°C marks the August temperature. If July is the hottest, August is the next hottest month. The fall of temperature is 3.3°C between August and September when it is about 5°C in each of the consecutive months. It finally drops to 3.1°C in December. (Table 9.11)

Mean temperature in Qazigund is between 10° and 20°C for four months in a year. It, therefore, has a temperate climate. It is cool temperate for in three months the temperature is below 6.6°C.

Table 9.11

Qazigund: Air Temperature (°C)

Element	*J*	*F*	*M*	*A*	*M*	*J*	*J*	*A*	*S*	*O*	*N*	*D*	*Annual Mean*
Mean Maximum	5.1	8.0	13.6	19.4	23.1	27.7	28.0	27.9	26.4	21.6	15.4	8.2	
Mean Minimum	–3.8	–1.6	2.7	7.0	9.9	13.8	16.9	16.3	11.1	5.8	1.1	–2.0	
Mean Monthly	0.6	3.2	8.1	13.2	16.5	20.7	22.4	22.1	18.8	13.7	8.3	3.1	12.6
Mean Range	8.9	9.6	10.9	12.4	13.2	13.9	11.1	11.6	15.3	15.8	14.3	10.2	12.2

The mean maximum temperature rises to 28°C in July. The extreme maximum temperature of 34.5°C was recorded on 11 July 1988. In January the mean minimum temperature drops to –3.8°C. The other months with sub-zero temperatures are February and December. The extreme minimum temperature registered on 3 February 1964 was –16.7°C.

The mean annual temperature of Qazigund is 12.6°C which is slightly less than that of Srinagar. This may be attributed to its higher elevation.

Mean Range

The normal range of temperature of Qazigund is 31.8°C. This high range depicts a continental type of climate. The mean range of temperature is below 12.2°C in January to March and December. All these are winter months when the sky generally remains overcast. Not much difference is noticed in their mean maximum and mean minimum temperatures. It is highest 15.8°C in October, followed by 15.3°C in September. These are comparatively dry months with clear sky, resulting in large variation in diurnal temperatures. The remaining six months hold an intermediate position in this regard. Qazigund, thus, has a cool temperate continental climate.

Atmospheric Moisture

Humidity

The relative humidity of Qazigund is highest, 80 per cent, in January and lowest, 59 per cent, in June. It is above 70 per cent in the winter months of January to March and December and also in the monsoon months of July and August. It is below 70 per cent in the remaining months of the year. Mean annual relative humidity is 69 per cent, which is almost the same as that of Srinagar (Table 9.4).

Precipitation

This station gets a total annual rainfall of 1,246 mm. It is nearly twice than that of Srinagar rainfall. March, as in case of Srinagar, is the rainiest month, with a total rainfall of 211.5 mm. October, on the other

Table 9.12

Qazigund: Atmospheric Moisture and Mean Wind Speed

Element	*J*	*F*	*M*	*A*	*M*	*J*	*J*	*A*	*S*	*O*	*N*	*D*	*Annual Total/ Mean*
Mean Monthly Rainfall (mm)	127.1	177.9	211.5	137.6	111.1	62.1	96.8	69.8	57.9	48.4	48.9	97.0	1246.1
Normal of Rainy Days (Number)	6.8	8.5	9.4	8.3	7.9	4.2	7.0	5.7	3.5	2.9	2.7	4.9	71.8
Intensity of Rainfall (mm per rainy day)	18.7	20.9	22.5	16.5	14.0	14.8	13.8	12.2	16.5	16.6	18.1	19.8	17.3
Relative Humidity (%)	80	78	70	62	62	59	70	72	65	61	69	77	69
No of Days with Thunder storms	0.4	1.3	4.8	8.2	13.0	9.8	9.3	7.3	6.0	3.4	1.2	0.3	65
Mean Wind Speed (kmph)	2.3	2.7	3.0	2.7	2.5	2.8	3.7	3.3	3.0	2.6	2.1	2.0	

Figure 9.2

Qazigund

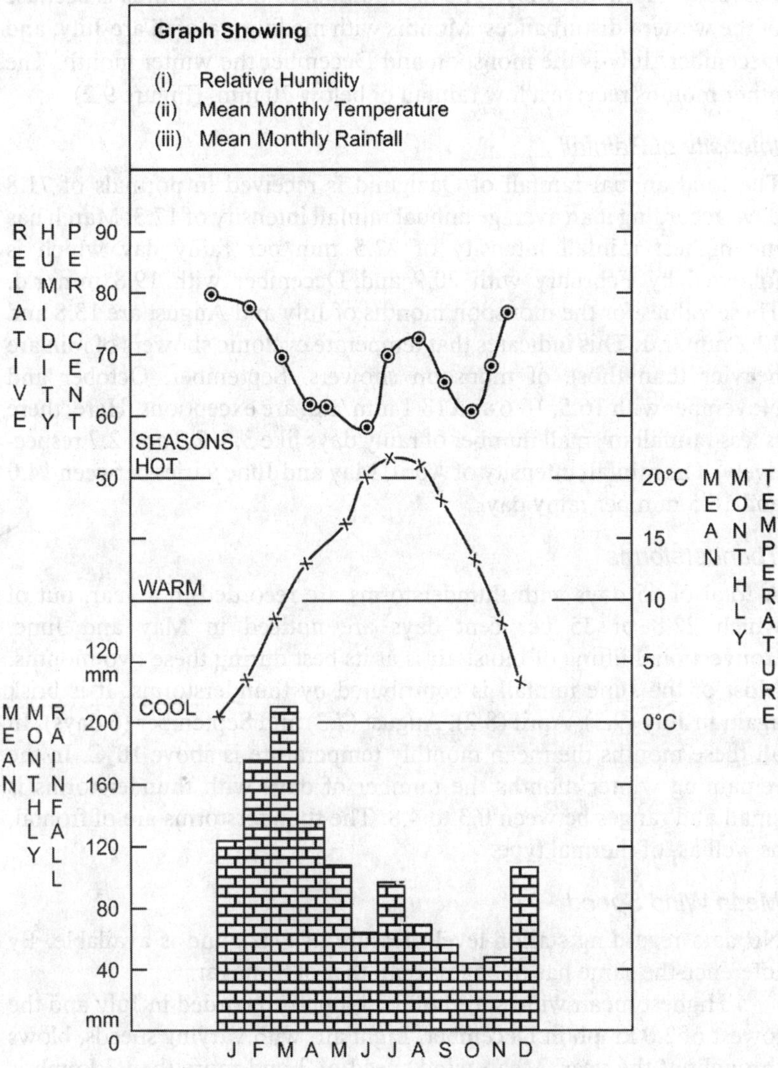

Altitude	:	1739 m
Mean Annual Temperature	:	12.6°C
Normal Range of Temperature	:	31.8°C
Frost-free Period	:	275 days (approx)
Total Annual Rainfall	:	1246. mm

hand, is the month with least rainfall of 48.4 mm. Months with the high rainfall of more than 110 mm, in addition to March, are January, February, April and May. The high rainfall of these months is because of the western disturbances. Months with medium rainfall are July, and December. July is the monsoon and December the winter month. The other months receive a low rainfall of below 70 mm. (Figure 9.2)

Intensity of Rainfall

The total annual rainfall of Qazigund is received in normals of 71.8 days according it an average annual rainfall intensity of 17.3. March has the highest rainfall intensity of 22.5 mm/per rainy day which is followed by February with 20.9 and December with 19.8 mm/r.d. These values for the monsoon months of July and August are 13.8 and 12.2 mm/r.d. This indicates that temperate cyclonic showers of rain are heavier than those of monsoon showers. September, October and November with 16.5, 16.6 and 18.1 mm/r.d. are exceptions. Here, there is less rainfall in small number of rainy days like 3.5, 2.9 and 2.7 respectively. The rainfall intensity of April, May and June varies between 14.0 and 16.5 mm per rainy day.

Thunderstorms

A total of 65 days with thunderstorms are recorded in a year, out of which 22.8 or 35 per cent days are noticed in May and June. Convectional lifting of moist air is at its best during these two months. Most of the June rainfall is contributed by thunderstorms. It is brisk again in July (9.3), April (8.2), August (7.3) and September (6 days). In all these months the mean monthly temperature is above 10°C. In the remaining winter months the number of days with thunderstorms is small and ranges between 0.3 to 4.8. The thunderstorms are of frontal, as well as, of thermal type.

Mean Wind Speed

No data regarding station-level pressure of Qazigund is available. By inference the same has to be less than that of Srinagar.

Highest mean wind speed of 3.7 kmph is recorded in July and the lowest of 2.0 kmph in December. Light air, with varying speeds, blows throughout the year. Mean wind speed of 3 and more than 3 kmph is observed in March, July, August and September. It is less than 3 kmph in the remaining months of the year. Qazigund is a zone of calm air.

In the month of February when heavy snowfall had taken place on Kashmir side of the Pir Panjal the national highway was closed for vehicular traffic. All the motor vehicles coming from Srinagar were stopped at Qazigund for the night. The night wind was so strong that it literally shook the parked taxi, with five occupants, off the ground several times. Could it be katabatic wind or the wind that accompanies a western disturbance?

Seasons

Based on Hadlows Word-Scale of monthly mean temperatures, a year in Qazigund comprises two major seasons, five month long winter and a summer of three months. Each is followed by a warm, transition season of two months. (Table 9.13).

Table 9.13

Qazigund: Seasons

S. No.	*Mean Monthly Temp. Scale*	*Season*	*Extent*	*Duration (Months)*
1.	0–10	Cool (Winter)	January to March November, December	5
2.	10–20	Warm (Spring)	April, May	2
3.	20–30	Hot (Summer)	June to August	3
4.	10–20	Warm (Autumn)	September, October	2

The Winter

Like Srinagar, the winter in Qazigund is of five months duration and includes the same months. The mean monthly temperature in this season ranges from 0.6° to 8.3°C. Sub-zero night temperatures prevail for three months – January, February and December. Precipitation is high throughout the season except in November. It takes the form of snow which stays on the ground for a long time due to frosts, except on the national highway where it is cleared regularly for the uninterrupted flow of vehicular traffic. March and November precipitation is sleet or rain. The seasonal precipitation received is 662.4 mm or 53.1 per cent of the annual total. Agriculture enjoys a holiday and the idle farmers of this and other adjacent tehsils migrate to Jammu and the neighbouring states. Some of the stay-at-homes indulge in making of baskets and *Kangris*, weaving of woollen cloth for blankets and production of Kashmir handicrafts.

The Spring

Monthly mean temperature in this season varies from 13.2° to 16.5°C. It is high enough to revive vegetation. Agricultural operations are launched from spring equinox onwards. Rainfall of this season amounts to 248 mm or 19.9 per cent of the total annual precipitation. The rise in temperature is as much responsible for the seasonal change as is the high rainfall.

The Summer

Unlike Srinagar, the summer in Qazigund is only of three months duration. Mean monthly temperatures hover close to the lower limit (20°C) of the temperature range of this season. These range between 20.7° and 22.4°C. Summers are short and mild, too. This may be ascribed to its altitude and closeness to the Lesser Himalayan range. Rainfall of June is less than that of July and August. High July rainfall is due to monsoons. Withdrawal of monsoon at this station takes place two days later than its retreat from other parts of Kashmir. The total rainfall of summer is 228.8 mm or 18.7 per cent of the total annual precipitation. Cultivation of crops is in full swing, so are other primary activities.

The Autumn

Autumn in Qazigund, unlike Srinagar lasts for two months, September and October. Mean monthly temperature varies from 13.7° to 18.8°C. Rainfall is moderate, 106.3 mm or 8.3 per cent of the total annual precipitation. The weather in second fortnight of September and October is favourable for crop harvest.

A Climatic Study of Kashmir Valley

A comprehensive climatic study of Kashmir is only feasible when the data of all the five, existing, meteorological stations, located in it are scrutinized. The said data, of Pahalgam, Kokernag and Kupwara, for the years 1978–81, not withstanding its limitations, has been selected for this study. The related figures of Srinagar and Qazigund, for the same period for making the entire data compatible, have been incorporated with it (Table 9.14). It shall be used for the seasonal classification based on Hadlow's plan, for finding mean annual temperature and other temperature and precipitation attributes.

Climatic Characteristics

At the outset the climatic characteristics of each station shall be presented.

Pahalgam

Monthly mean temperature of Pahalgam is between –0.8°C in January and 18.6°C in July. Its mean annual temperature is 9.4°C. The seasons are:

(i)	Warm season (10° to 20°C)	April to October	7 months
(ii)	Cool season (0° to 10°C)	February, March November, December	4 months
(iii)	Cold season (–10° to 0°C)	January	1 month

There are only three seasons in Pahalgam warm, cool and cold. Subzero mean temperature in January results in cold season of one month.

Kokernag

The monthly mean temperature of this station is 1.3°C in January and 21.6°C in July. Its annual mean temperature is 12.2°C. The seasons are:

(i)	Hot season (20° to 30°C)	July, August	2 months
(ii)	Warm Season (Autumn)	September, October	2 months
(iii)	Cool Season (Winter)	January to March, November, December	5 months
(iv)	Warm Season (Spring)	April to June	3 months

In Kokernag, four seasons of varying duration are identified. Mean temperature in no month is below zero. Unlike Pahalgam there is no cold season. The hot season lasts for two months and the cool season for five months.

Qazigund

The highest mean temperature of Qazigund is 22.4°C in July and the lowest of 2.0°C in January. The annual mean temperature is 12.6°C. The seasons are:

(i)	Hot season	June to August	3 months
(ii)	Warm season (Autumn)	September, October	2 months
(iii)	Cool season	January to March, November, December	5 months
(iv)	Warm season (Spring)	April, May	2 months

Unlike Kokernag, summer in Qazigund has a three month term. The winter here is of the same duration and includes the same months as that of Kokernag.

Kupwara

January in Kupwara registers the least monthly mean temperature of 3°C and July the highest of 22.5°C. Its annual mean temperature is 12.7°C. The seasons are:

(i)	Hot	July, August	2 months
(ii)	Warm (Autumn)	September, October	2 months
(iii)	Cool	January to March, November, December	5 months
(iv)	Warm (Spring)	April to June	3 months

The seasonal pattern of Kupwara resembles that of Kokernag, both in their duration and months included.

Srinagar

Monthly mean temperature in Srinagar is 2.7° in January and 24.5°C in July. It has an annual mean temperature of 13.7°C. The seasons, on the basis of data given in Table 9.14, are:

(i)	Hot	June to August	3 months
(ii)	Warm (Autumn)	September October	2 months
(iii)	Cool	January to March, November, December	5 months
(iv)	Warm (Spring)	April, May	2 months

Seasonal pattern of Srinagar is similar to that of Qazigund, where summer lasts for 3, autumn for 2, winter for 5 and spring for 2 months (Figure 9.3).

Discussion

Altitude Temperature Relationship

In Table 9.14 the five stations are arranged in descending order of altitude. Pahalgam, with the highest elevation, of 2,130 m, registers the lowest annual mean temperature of 9.4°C. Contrary to it, Srinagar with the lowest height above sea level, of 1,587 m, has the highest annual mean temperature of 13.7°C. Kupwara, at an altitude of 1,615 m has the annual mean temperature of 12.7°C. These figures for Qazigund and Kokernag are 1,739 m and 12.6°C, 1,860 m and 12.2°C, respectively. It reveals a decrease of temperature with the increase in elevation. This is in accordance with the principle of normal lapse rate of temperature.

The other inference drawn from this analysis is that Pahalgam with the highest altitude manifests an entirely different seasonal scenario compared to other four stations of lower elevation. Pahalgam, situated in the side valley of the Lidder, with given altitude, can be termed as a highland station and demands a separate treatment. The other four stations constitute the Valley stations.

Table 9.14

Kashmir Valley: Areal Distribution of Temperature (°C) and Precipitation (mm.)

Station	*Elements*	*J*	*F*	*M*	*A*	*M*	*J*	*J*	*A*	*S*	*O*	*N*	*D*	*Ann. Mean Temp. (°C)*	*Total Ann Precipitation (mm)*
1. Pahalgam (2,130 m)	Mean Max	4.6	5.5	9.0	18.2	20.6	24.4	24.6	25.1	22.8	19.4	12.6	5.5		1339
	Mean Min	–6.2	–5.0	–1.7	3.6	5.9	8.8	12.6	12.0	7.7	3.7	–0.7	–4.6		
	Monthly Mean	-0.8	0.2	3.6	10.9	13.2	16.6	18.6	18.5	15.2	11.5	5.9	0.4	9.4	
2. Kokernag (1,860 m)	Mean Max	5.4	6.3	10.9	19.9	22.2	26.0	26.9	27.6	24.9	21.1	16.9	5.6		1033
	Mean Min	–2.7	–1.6	2.1	6.1	9.8	13.7	16.3	14.9	10.8	7.2	2.5	–1.4		
	Monthly Mean	1.3	2.3	6.5	13.0	16.0	19.8	21.6	21.2	17.8	14.1	9.7	2.1	12.2	
3. Qazigund (1,739 m)	Mean Max	6.9	7.7	11.7	20.5	23.3	27.1	27.9	28.0	26.1	22.7	15.2	7.2		1343
	Mean Min	–2.8	–1.6	2.2	7.1	9.8	13.2	16.9	14.9	9.6	5.8	1.6	–1.6		
	Monthly Mean	2.0	3.0	6.9	13.8	16.5	20.1	22.4	21.4	17.8	14.2	8.4	4.4	12.6	
4. Kupwara (1,615 m)	Mean Max	7.4	7.9	12.2	21.5	27.2	26.1	28.7	29.6	27.2	23.7	15.4	7.7		1319
	Mean Min	–1.3	–0.1	2.1	7.0	9.8	12.1	16.3	14.6	9.7	5.2	1.1	–0.9		
	Monthly Mean	3.0	3.9	7.1	14.2	18.5	19.1	22.5	22.1	18.4	14.4	8.2	3.4	12.7	
5. Srinagar (1,587 m)	Mean Max	6.9	8.5	13.4	22.4	24.9	29.7	30.5	29.8	27.0	22.7	14.7	7.0		707
	Mean Min	–1.4	0.7	3.5	8.5	11.3	15.0	18.6	16.9	11.4	6.3	1.9	–1.3		
	Monthly Mean	2.7	4.6	8.4	15.4	18.1	22.3	24.5	23.3	19.2	14.5	8.3	2.8	13.7	

Note: The temperature and rainfall data of Srinagar and Qazigund used in this table is restricted to this study. The latest 30-year normal data of these two stations is given in Tables 9.1, 9.4, 9.11 and 9.12

Highland Station

High altitude of Pahalgam has wiped out hot season from this station. It enjoys a continuous spell of warm weather from April to October. July mean temperature of 18.6°C, in comparison to July mean of 24.5°C of Srinagar, results in its bracing climate in summer. It is the only station, in this group, with sub-zero mean temperature in January.

Valley Stations

As already mentioned, the valley stations are situated at different altitudes varying from 1,587 to 1,860 m. These also have different locations in the Valley floor. Kokernag lies in the south-east, Qazigund in the south, Kupwara in the north-west and Srinagar in the middle. Similarities and differences in the extent of the seasons, mean temperature and precipitation are identified in these four stations.

Similarities

(a) No Valley station experiences a cold season. In each case the lowest monthly mean temperature is above freezing point. It is 1.3° in Kokernag, 2.0 in Qazigund, 2.7° in Srinagar and 3°C in Kupwara.

(b) The cool season or winter is of five months duration in each Valley station. Even the months included are the same, viz., January to March, November and December. This finding upholds the earlier claim of the present writer, regarding the five months duration of the winter, during the appraisal of the Meher Homji's seasonal classification (Table 7.8). It is, however, surprising to find that even the highland station of Pahalgam has a winter of five months, one cold plus four cool months.

(c) Autumn in each station comprises two months of September and October.

(d) July is the hottest and January the coldest months in all the four Valley stations.

Differences

(a) The duration of the *hot season* varies from one pair of Valley stations to the other. Two months, July and August, constitute it in Kokernag and Kupwara. It lasts for three months in Qazigund and Srinagar.

(b) In one pair of stations like Kokernag and Kupwara the *spring season* has a spread of three months which include April, May and June. In the other pair it lasts for only two months, April and May.

Figure 9.3

Homogeneity of Kashmir Climate

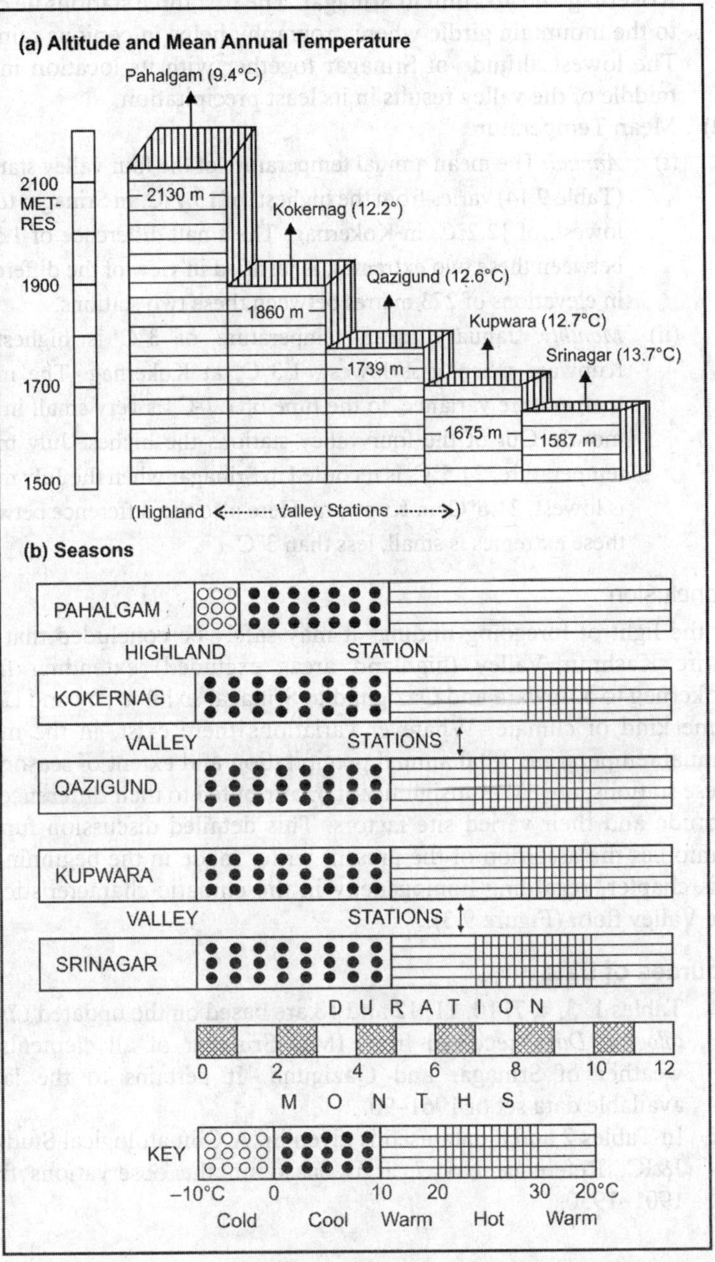

(c) Total annual *precipitation* of the valley stations, in descending order, is 1,343, in Qazigund, 1,319 in Kupwara, 1,033 in Kokernag and 707 mm in Srinagar. The first three stations lie close to the mountain girdle where orography helps in copious rainfall. The lowest altitude of Srinagar together with its location in the middle of the valley results in its least precipitation.

(d) Mean Temperature

(i) *Annual:* The mean annual temperature of the four valley stations (Table 9.14) varies from the highest, of 13.7°C, in Srinagar to the lowest, of 12.2°C, in Kokernag. The small difference of 1.5°C, between these two extremes, is justified in view of the difference in elevations of 273 metres between these two stations.

(ii) *Monthly:* January mean temperature of 3°C is highest in Kupwara when it is lowest, 1.3°C, at Kokernag. The mean temperature variance, to the tune of 1.7°C, is very small in this month. Out of the four valley stations the highest July mean temperature, 24.5°C, is recorded in Srinagar when the July mean is lowest, 21.6°C, in Kupwara. Here also the difference between these extremes is small, less than 3°C.

Conclusion

In the light of foregoing findings it may safely be concluded that the entire Kashmir Valley (highland areas excluded) extending from Kokernag to Kupwara and Qazigund to Srinagar exhibits, by and large, same kind of climate. Whatever variations there exist, in the mean annual temperature, total annual precipitation and extent of seasons at these stations, are either insignificant or attributed to their differences in altitude and their varied site factors. This detailed discussion further reinforces the assertion of the present writer made in the beginning of this chapter, regarding homogeneity in the climatic characteristics of the Valley floor (Figure 9.3).

Sources of Data

1. Tables 1, 3, 4, 7, 10, 11, 12 and 13 are based on the updated *Climatological Data,* received from IMD Srinagar of all elements of weather of Srinagar and Qazigund. It pertains to the latest available data set of 1961–90.
2. In Tables 2 and 8 data used is given in 'A Climatological Study of J&K', Reference No: 7. It is based on the observations from 1901–1950.

3. Table 9 data has been taken from the *Digest of Statistics (1995–96),* DOES, J&K Govt. It is for the period 1986–95.
4. Other Tables:
   5 – Meher Homji, 1971.
   6 – S.N. Bhan, 1956.
   14 – IMD, Srinagar, 1982.

References

Books

Das, P.K. (1995), *The Monsoons,* NBT, New Delhi.

Lawrence, Walter R. (1895), *The Valley of Kashmir,* O.U.P. (1967 reprint), Kesar Publications, Srinagar.

Papers and Articles

Bhan, S.N. 'A Study of Fifty-year Rainfall of Srinagar (1901–50) and Jammu (1893–1942)', *Memoirs of IMD,* Vol. XXXI, Part IV, New Delhi, 1954.

——. 'Snowfall at Srinagar (1939–1953)', *The Indian Journal of Meteorology and Geophysics,* vol. 7 No. 3, July 1956.

——. 'Thunderstorms at Srinagar', *The Indian Journal of Meteorology and Geophysics,* 1957.

——. 'Rainfall in the Upper Catchment of the Jhelum', *The Indian Journal of Meteorology and Geophysics,* vol. 9, No. 1, January, 1958.

Kaul, A.K. 'Monsoon Component of Rainfall in Kashmir Valley, *Vayu Mandal,* July–December, 1980.

Lidhoo, P.N. and Pradhan, S.K. (1986), *A Climatological Study of J & K,* The CI & DD of PDD, J&K Govt. (unpublished).

Meher Homji, V.M. 'The Climate of Srinagar and its Variability', *The Geographical Review of India,* Kolkata, March 1971.

Pradhan, S.K., Upadhaya, D.S. and Lidhoo, P.N. (1978), *Climatological Study of J& K,* Part I, IMD, Srinagar (unpublished).

10

Weather and Climate

Cold Highland Ladakh

This regional study of weather and climate of cold highland Ladakh includes three stations: Leh, Kargil and Dras. With their trans-Himalayan situation, the climatic features of these places display broad similarities but not without striking differences. In highlands, altitude and aspect play a vital role in influencing temperature.

Cold Higland Ladakh

Leh

Leh is situated on the south-facing slope of the Ladakh range at an altitude of 3,514 m. It is located on the latitude of 34° 09' N and longitude of 77° 34' E.

Air Temperature

Mean Monthly

The coldest month in Leh is January with a mean temperature of –6.8°C, when July, with 21.5°C, is the hottest. Leh shares this temperature characteristics with Srinagar and all other stations with modified subtropical climate. The other months with subzero temperatures are February, March and December. A small increase, of 3.4°C and 3.2°C in the mean temperature, is discerned in the months of February and March. But the rise is substantial, 8°C, from March to April. There is an increment of 4.2°C and 5.1°C in the two consecutive months taking the temperature of June to 17.1°C. It falls 4.4°C short of July mean. (Table 10.1).

Fall of temperature takes place after July. August mean is 0.6°C less than that of July. But the decline in temperature is steep 5.3°C between August and September, 8.1°C between September and October and 8.4°C between October and November. The mean temperature finally settles down at –3.9°C in December.

The highest mean maximum temperature of 27.9°C and the lowest of 0.5°C are noticed in July and January respectively. Extreme mean maximum temperature of 35°C, in Leh, was recorded on 14 July 1973. July registers the highest mean minimum temperature of 15.1°C and January the lowest of –14.1°C. Extreme mean minimum temperature plunged to –30.2°C on 25 January 1976.

Table 10.1

Leh: Air Temperature (°C)*

Element	*J*	*F*	*M*	*A*	*M*	*J*	*J*	*A*	*S*	*O*	*N*	*D*	*Annual Mean*
Mean Maximum	0.5	3.1	7.3	14.7	18.9	23.9	27.9	27.6	22.8	15.7	9.7	4.0	
Mean Minimum	–14.1	–10.0	–7.8	1.0	5.1	10.4	15.1	14.2	8.5	–0.6	–7.8	–11.8	
Mean Monthly	–6.8	–3.4	–0.2	7.8	12.0	17.1	21.5	20.9	15.6	7.5	0.9	–3.9	7.4
Mean Range	14.6	13.1	15.1	13.7	13.8	13.5	12.8	13.4	14.3	16.3	17.5	15.8	14.5

* Data on request supplied by Met Flight, 21 Wing, Air Force.

Subzero mean minimum temperature is observed in six months, namely, January to March, and October to December. This leaves Leh with a frost-free period of 183 days. Making allowance for the period of thaw and for attainment of right soil temperature of 5.5°C, so essential for plant growth, length of growing season gets sufficiently curtailed. Cognizance, in this matter, has to be taken of the minimum temperature of April (1.0°C) and May (5.1°C). The length of the growing season, under these circumstances, is 122 to 137 days from mid-May to end of September. This short growing season permits cultivation of a single and quick ripening crop in a year. The cereal that has succeeded in such a harsh environment and sustained its people, for millennia, is grim. It has, in most cases, shared cropland with peas. In Leh, mean temperature is between 10° to 20°C for three months in a year. On account of this attribute Leh climate is cold highland type and not arctic (or polar) as suggested by some writers.

Annual mean temperature of Leh is 7.4°C. It is quite low because of its altitude. According to earlier data set of 1951–80, of IMD, Srinagar, its annual mean temperature was 5.7°C.

Mean Range

Normal range of temperature of Leh is 42°C which indicates that its climate is extremely continental. This is justified by its situation, far inland, in the heart of the continent of Asia. The average yearly range of temperature is 14.5°C (Table 10.1). The mean monthly range of temperature is above this annual average in January, March, October to December. In the remaining months it is less than this average. The range of temperature is highest, 17.5°C, in November and lowest, 12.8°C, in July. November sky, with a low rainfall, is mostly cloudless and allows a free flow of solar energy during the day and that of terrestrial radiation at night, resulting in sharp difference in diurnal temperatures. July, a monsoon month, with a cloud cover, does not permit free flow of energy either way, hence has the least range of temperature. Climate of Leh is cold highland continental.

Temperature Characteristics

The sky, for most part of the year, in Leh is clear. Its atmosphere is rarefied in view of its elevation. It is, almost, free of greenhouse gases. The insolation received is intense which results in a sharp rise of its day temperature. It is followed by unobstructed radiation at night when the fall of temperature is considerable. This abrupt and substantial change between day and night temperatures is the basic cause of rock disintegration, a conspicuous feature of Ladakh landscape. Other outcome is the jagged peaks. Heat during the day becomes oppressive because of its reflection from the bare rocky surfaces. A high proportion of ultraviolet rays causes sun burns and skin tan. At the same time, these rays are a great help in stimulating plant life. Difference between the sunshine and shade temperature is too high. It is best illustrated through a local adage which says that a person with feet in the shade and head in the sun can get frostbite and sunstroke simultaneously.

Atmospheric Pressure

Station-Level Pressure

Mean annual station-level pressure of Leh is 686.4 hPa, which is 154.1 hPa less than that of Srinagar because of its higher elevation. Low atmospheric pressure makes air thin which results in it of a reduced proportion of oxygen. More air has to be breathed in so as to get the required amounts of oxygen. This environmental constraint creates a need for acclimatization for those who visit Leh for the first time. Low air pressure also causes reduced boiling point of water.

Mean monthly station-level pressure is maximum (689.0 hPa) in October and lowest (682.5 mb) in July, giving it an annual range of pressure of 6.5 mb. (Table 10.2). The line graph of the mean monthly station level pressure acquires the shape of a sinusoidal curve with two distinct crests and troughs; with the second crest higher than the first and second trough deeper than the first (Figure 7.2).

Table 10.2

Leh: Station-Level Pressure (hPa or mb) and Mean Wind Speed (kmph)

Particulars	*J*	*F*	*M*	*A*	*M*	*J*	*J*	*A*	*S*	*O*	*N*	*D*	*Ann Average*
Station Level Pressure (AF)	688.0	686.1	686.5	686.9	686.6	684.2	682.5	683.6	686.4	689.0	688.5	688.6	686.4
Mean Wind Speed (IMD)	4.0	4.7	6.1	7.2	7.4	7.0	5.8	5.6	5.5	5.5	5.6	4.6	

In the said line graph the two maxima of pressure are observed in October (689 hPa) and January (688 hPa) and the two minima in July (682.5 mb) and February (686.1 mb). The pressure graph indicates higher pressure values in the latter part and in the beginning of the year. The station-level pressure is higher in the cool months of October to December and January and lower in the warm months of July and August. This is in accordance with the presence of the pressure systems of the period over Central Asia and north-west India, respectively.

Mean Wind Speed

Mean wind speed, in Leh, is highest (7.4 kmph) in May and lowest (4.0 kmph) in January which shows that it experiences light air (according to Beaufort scale) throughout the year. The wind speeds are between 7 to 7.5 kmph in April to June, between 6 to 7 kmph in March and between 5 to 6 kmph in July to November. It is less than 5 kmph in January, February and December.

In parts of Ladakh region, like other highlands of the world, local winds, like mountain and valley breezes, are produced as a result of rugged terrain and differential heating of the land surface. At night, mountain tops lose heat and cold air flows down the slopes as katabatic wind. It is strong and gusty. During the day, air moves uphill due to the heating of the mountain tops. It is anabatic wind. It is of low intensity. Constant fluttering of streamers, of different colours, atop *pagodas* and *Chortens,* at vantage points and mountain passes testifies high wind speeds. For high plains of Ladakh like Lingzhitang, Depsang and

Aksaichin the common appellation used is '*wind-swept*' which also denotes the presence of strong winds in Ladakh. Regarding the night winds above Nimu, Ahluwalia (1987) writes, 'The silence was broken by the noise of the swift and harsh winds which sometimes broke into a howl. But suddenly the fierce wind would die down into a gentle breeze and it would be calm again. This phenomenon continued throughout the night. In the morning air was fresh and bracing'.

Atmospheric Moisture

Humidity

January, in Leh, has the highest relative humidity of 56 per cent and July the lowest of 23 per cent. The other months with a high relative humidity of 50 to 56 per cent are February and December. The high relative humidity of these three winter months is related to the arrival of the western disturbances and the consequent precipitation. It is between 40 and 49 per cent in March and November. Both these months are under the sway of the western disturbances. Relative humidity ranges between 30 to 39 per cent in April, May, June, August, September and October. It is below 30 per cent in July. (Table 10.3) A noticeable increase in humidity in the warm months of August and September corresponds to the influx of moisture into Ladakh region due to the onset of south-west monsoon in the Indian subcontinent. July is an exception probably because of the late arrival of these winds.

Table 10.3

Leh: Atmospheric Moisture*

Contents	*J*	*F*	*M*	*A*	*M*	*J*	*J*	*A*	*S*	*O*	*N*	*D*	*Annual/Total Mean*
Mean Monthly Rainfall (mm)	14.6	6.6	14.4	3.6	3.3	2.7	7.6	12.1	6.5	1.6	3.4	5.5	81.9
Relative Humidity (%)	56	53	44	37	35	30	23	37	35	37	43	50	40
Days with Thunder-storms (No.)	–	–	–	–	1	1.5	1.5	2	2.5	–	–	–	8.5

* Data from Met Flight, 21 Wing, Air Force.

The highest relative humidity in January undergoes a fall in subsequent months to drop to the lowest value in July. July onwards it increases in steps to attain the value of 50 per cent in December. In no month, in Leh, relative humidity is more than 56 per cent, when in

Figure 10.1

Leh

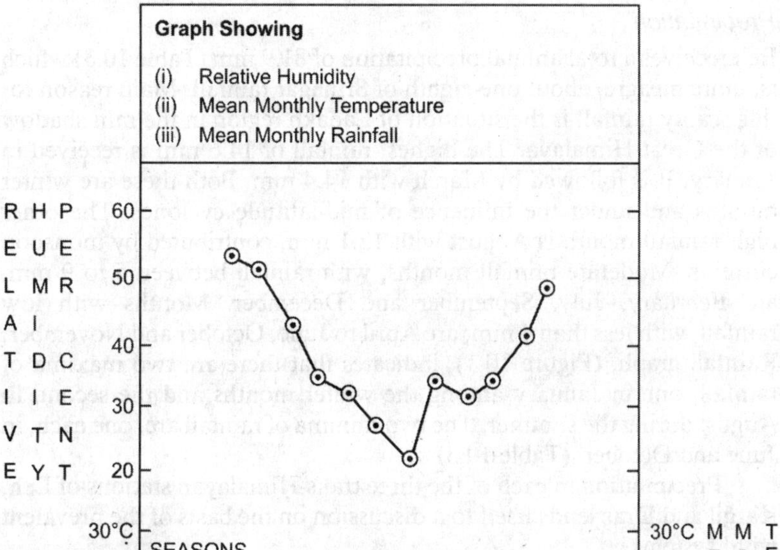

Altitude	:	3514 m
Mean Annual Temperature	:	7.4°C
Normal Range of Temperature	:	42°C
Frost-free Period	:	183 days
Total Annual Rainfall	:	81.9 mm

Srinagar its least value is 55 per cent. This bespeaks a dry climate of Leh aggregating to aridity (Figure 10.1). This is further attested by its annual average relative humidity of 40 per cent.

Precipitation

Leh receives a total annual precipitation of 81.9 mm (Table 10.3) which is, quite meagre, about one-eighth of Srinagar rainfall. Main reason for this scanty rainfall is the situation of Ladakh region in the rain shadow of the Great Himalaya. The highest rainfall of 14.6 mm is received in January. It is followed by March with 14.4 mm. Both these are winter months and under the influence of mid-latitude cyclones. The other high rainfall month is August with 12.1 mm, contributed by monsoon currents. Moderate rainfall months, with rainfall between 5 to 9 mm, are February, July, September and December. Months with low rainfall, with less than 4 mm, are April to June, October and November. Rainfall graph, (Figure 10.1), indicates that there are two maxima of rainfall, one in January among the winter months and the second in August during the summer. The two minima of rainfall are, one each, in June and October. (Table 10.3)

Precipitation in each of the three trans-Himalayan stations of Leh, Kargil and Dras lends itself to a discussion on the basis of the prevalent wind systems.

Western Disturbances

Extra-tropical cyclones arrive in Jammu and Kashmir from January to May, November and December. Within these seven months, Leh receives a total rainfall of 51.4 mm or 62.7 per cent of total annual precipitation. It is mostly in the form of snow. Western disturbances cause a heavy snowfall in all the mountain ranges of Ladakh region. The significance of this precipitation particularly in the Karakoram range, the home of gigantic glaciers, can be judged from the fact that south-west monsoon does not reach this part of Ladakh. The reserves of ice and snow in the Great Himalaya, the Zanskar, the Ladakh and the Karakoram ranges feed a myriad of water channels, streams and rivers. The glaciers and the snowfields, in this arid region, thus serve as the main sources of much needed water for use at far away places. Hamlets have come up where water courses serve alluvial fans. Winter snowfall, contributed by the temperate cyclones, consequently, is the chief source of water in this region.

South-West Monsoon

The dates of onset and retreat of monsoon, in Leh, are 11 July and 11 September respectively. Total rainfall received in July to September is

26.2 mm. It works out to 32.0 per cent of the total annual precipitation. This rainfall is quite useful in the further growth of the field crops.

June and October are an exception as neither falls in the above stated wind systems. The combined rainfall of these two months is 4.3 mm or 5.3 per cent of the total annual.

Aridity

A dry month is one with less than 25 mm of rain (Miller). All the twelve months in Leh, according to this criterion, are dry months. Cold highland climate of Leh, in view of aforesaid scarce precipitation, is further characterized by aridity. Aridity has a far-reaching impact on animate and inanimate elements of the environment, as well as, on the humans occupying that space. Low temperature and very low precipitation do not favour plant growth. Growth in plants ceases when soil temperature drops below 5.5°C and no appreciable vegetation, including trees, is possible when rainfall is less than 250 mm. Mountain slopes and other surfaces in Ladakh region are, therefore, bare and devoid of any natural vegetation. Whatever vegetation present is sparse and stunted and comprises hardy bushes and shrubs with necessary modifications for adaptation to such rigorous climatic conditions. These patches of vegetation exist close to the sources of water – a glacier, a spring or a stream. Ladakh region has a specific set of domestic animals in the form of yak, dzo, demo and dzomo, well adapted to this peculiar environment.

In the absence of erosive action of running water the landscape is littered, *in situ,* with rock waste and sand. The cumulative effect of its scanty precipitation, absence of natural vegetation, rock waste strewn landscape, as mentioned earlier, have shaped Ladakh into a cold highland desert.

Aridity and fierce heat cause dehydration in the humans and is, consequently, a health hazard. The human response to this environmental constraint, in this subregion, lies in the constant use of butter, which constitutes an essential item of daily diet. *Gurgur Chai,* an enjoyable and commonly used beverage, involves churning of butter with the brew.

Aridity leads to lack of cloud cover which permits an uninterrupted run of solar radiation. Solar radiation in this cold highland region constitutes a significant source of non-conventional energy. With the aid of solar thermal devices it is used for heating, cooking and drying. It is also converted into electricity through solar photo-voltaic technology. The appliances in use, in this regard, are domestic lights, street lights and solar lanterns. Abundant sunshine of the region is trapped in the south facing glass-panelled room to create a greenhouse effect, within the home, as a protection against cold. Greenhouses constructed by farmers, for raising vegetables, have proved very beneficial as these have extended span of the growing season. Low cost greenhouses are also erected by using heavy duty polythene.

Thunderstorms

Thunderstorms in Leh are experienced for a total of 8.5 days. Out of these, 6 days of thunderstorms take place from July to September. These are of thermal type. To this group may be added 1.5 days of June. May registers only one day with thunderstorms. It is of frontal type. Thunderstorm activity is restricted to summer months when temperature is high enough for their formation. It is more in the regime of monsoons than in that of western disturbances. This convectional phenomenon is not reported in January to April and October to December.

During last few decades, heavy showers of rain, of short duration, fell in some hamlets in Ladakh. This local convectional activity plays havoc with the fragile settings of the region, be it the cropland on the slopes or the sun-dried brick dwellings and other structures. This unusual rainfall is ascribed, by some people, to the increasing number of tree plantations. A ravaging weather phenomenon of this kind is despised by the inhabitants who even suggested cutting down of these precious plantations, a product of human endeavour and perseverance. What the people of Ladakh ardently wish is not a heavy shower of rain but a very hot sun to help in the melting of snow in the upper reaches, with the snowmelt moving through well laid out water courses, creations of native ingenuity, to the farms without any damage to their dwellings, cropland or surroundings.

A weather occurrence of similar nature but of enormous magnitude struck Leh town on the intervening night of 5th and 6th August, 2010. Here a cloudburst was followed by flash floods which caused the sliding down of huge masses of rock and mud that buried, downhill, the dwellings and their occupants. In consequence, there was a great loss of life and property. In addition, the landscape became disfigured as it got encrusted with a large thickness of eroded rubble. The dread of this disastrous weather phenomenon is likely to persist in the minds of the sufferer-survivors for a long time to come.

Seasons

On setting monthly mean temperature of Leh in Hadlow's Word-Scale frame, the following pattern of its seasons emerges:

Table 10.4
Leh: Seasons

Mean Monthly Temperature °C	*Climatic Description*	*Calendar Months*	*Duration (months)*	*Name*
20–10	Warm	September	1	Autumn
20–30	Hot	July-August	2	Hot Summer
10–20	Warm	May-June	2	Spring
0–10	Cool	April, October, November	3	Cool Winter
–10 to 0	Cold	January, February, March, December	4	Cold Winter

The year in Leh is divisible into a winter of seven months followed by a warm season of two months; a summer of two months followed by a warm season of one month. Winter comprises a cold and a cool component.

The Winter

The Cold Winter

Included in this season are January, February, March and December. Mean monthly temperature varying from –6.8° to –0.2°C make cold winter harsh and rigorous. Severity of the cold can be envisaged by considering mean minimum temperatures which range between –14.1° and –7.8°C. Even the day temperature in January drops to 0.5°C. It follows that subzero temperatures dominate weather in this season. This cxtremely low temperature regime is typical of a highland area situated in the middle of the Asian continent and under the influence of the Siberian high. Leh, during this period is also exposed to severe cold waves.

The precipitation is in the form of snow and this season at Leh claims a share of 50.2 per cent of the total annual precipitation. At times, crystals of ice in a snow flake are frozen hard due to the intense cold when these assume the form of a powder. This type of snowfall, often scant, when experienced in Leh and other inhabited places, is swept off, as the practice goes, with a broom from the flat roof of a house and other surfaces of accumulation.

The Cool Winter

April, October and November constitute cool winter. Mean temperature in no month of this season is below freezing. It ranges between

0.9° and 7.8°C. The increase of mean maximum temperature is sharp and steep from March to April when it gets doubled from 7.3° to 14.7°C. It is 15.1° in October and 9.7°C in November. Mean minimum temperature except in April is subzero. Winter continues to be severe in this season too, but it has lost the sting of the earlier cold winter. Precipitation for most of the time is in the form of snow. Share of precipitation contributed by this season is 10.5 per cent of total annual.

For these seven months of winter, whether cold or cool, iron stoves using hard coke are in continuous use for keeping the interiors of the houses, offices and other work places warm. The stove is recharged with a fresh stock of fuel after every eight hours. It also serves as a hearth for cooking meals and boiling water. The other place in the house where the family members like to sit, wherever such facility exists, is the greenhouse – the glass panelled room in the south.

People of Ladakh region have rightly responded to the environmental limitations associated with harsh, monotonous and prolonged winter by celebrating, during this period, a number of festivals and fairs linked with various monasteries. Participation in such functions draws them out of their homes and provides them occasions for worship, social interaction and enjoyment. Buddhist new year, *Losar,* falls just around winter solstice. It is again a week-long event of offerings and festivities.

Continuous subzero temperatures during the winter causes the freezing of liquid substances. Even the upper surface of a river freezes hard be it the Indus or Zanskar. The Chaddar trek through the frozen Zanskar river links Padam with Leh. The diesel in buses and trucks freezes and in order to make it a functional fuel a defreeze has to be added to it. An egg freezes hard and has the same impact as a pebble of its size and weight.

As vehicular traffic on both highways remains suspended from October to June the only link with the rest of the country, during winter is through airways. Some visitors arrive here for Chaddar trek.

The Warm Seasons

The first warm season or the spring includes the months of May and June when the mean temperature ranges between 12.0 and 17.1. May in Leh is of same significance as March in Srinagar. Its mean maximum temperature of 18.9°C is high enough to initiate thawing process. The day temperature of 23.9°C in June further speeds up melting of snow in the higher reaches. So, during this warm season the volume of water in side streams and channels gets increased. The other noticeable temperature characteristics is that the mean minimum temperature is much above the freezing point which plays a vital role in increasing soil temperature. The prevalent temperature, mid-May onwards, is high enough for the germination of the seeds and plant growth. The total precipitation received in this season is 6.0 mm or 7.3 per cent of the total annual. The planted deciduous trees are in leaf.

The autumn or the second warm season is restricted to one month – September, with a mean temperature of 15.6°C. The day temperature of 22.8°C is high enough to continue the melting of ice and maintaining the volume in water channels. It also, during the first fortnight, helps in the ripening of the field crops. The amount of rain that falls in this season is 6.5 mm or 7.9 per cent of the total annual. This season marks the harvest time of the area and the leaf fall of deciduous plantations.

The Hot Summer

Mean temperature of 21.5° in July and 20.9°C in August are the borderline cases which for the first time constitute hot summer in Leh. (According to earlier IMD data set of 1951–80 no such season existed. Instead, there was a warm season of four months – June to September). The day temperature increases to 27°C. The precipitation received is 19.7 mm or 24.0 per cent of the total annual. Both these weather conditions aid the growth and maturing of the sown crops.

The combined summer and warm seasons extend over a period of five month and excluding first half of May, coincides with the growing season of Leh. Farming operations are in full swing. Field Research Laboratory has developed improved varieties of vegetable seeds and locality-based farming practices. Greenhouses have been erected to augment the length of the growing season. The outcome of these innovations has been the cultivation of vegetables of large size and weight. Steps have been undertaken for production of a wide range of exotic vegetables for the consumption of civil population as well as for supply to armed forces.

Summer and warm seasons coincide with the road-open period when truckloads of essential commodities and development related materials arrive in Leh. For the people of Ladakh region, this period is an environmental asset. In addition to being the growing period of cereals, vegetables and fruit it is the period of hectic outdoor gainful activities. All development projects planned by the administration are executed in this season. Festivals in some of the *Gompas* are held in summer.

The summer is the time for the arrival of tourists. By now tourism is a well-established and lucrative industry in Leh providing employment to an assortment of local workers, including those of paying guest households. With its unblemished azure sky, a barren landscape of amazing hues and shapes, a challenging and provocative terrain for the adventurous, a cultural landscape embellished with Buddhism related signs and structures, the tourists depart from Leh entranced and gratified.

Kargil

Kargil is situated, close to the Zanskar range, at an elevation of 2,750 m. Its locational coordinates are 34° 34' N and 76° 08' E.

Air Temperature

Mean Monthly

January, with a mean temperature of –8.7°C, is the coldest month in Kargil. Subzero temperatures are also noticed in February and March. April is the first month of the year with a mean temperature above the freezing point of water. It registers a temperature increment of 9°C over that of March. Mean temperature takes another leap of 6.8°C from April to May. May mean of 15.5°C rises in two steps of 4°C each to reach 23.7°C in July. July is the hottest month.

Table 10.5

Kargil: Air Temperature (°C)

Element	*J*	*F*	*M*	*A*	*M*	*J*	*J*	*A*	*S*	*O*	*N*	*D*	*Annual Mean*
Mean Maximum	–4.2	–1.6	4.7	14.0	21.6	25.7	29.7	28.9	24.9	18.5	10.4	1.2	
Mean Minimum	–13.3	–12.1	–5.3	3.4	9.4	13.4	17.7	17.2	12.5	5.4	–1.3	–7.9	
Monthly Mean	–8.7	–6.8	–0.3	8.7	15.5	19.5	23.7	23.0	18.7	11.9	4.5	–3.3	8.8
Mean Range	9.1	10.5	10.0	10.6	12.2	12.3	12.0	11.7	12.4	13.1	11.7	9.1	11.2

July denotes temperature divide (Table 10.5) with August mean less by 0.7°C. A small decrease of 4.3°C brings down September mean to 18 7°C. A steep fall of temperature to the extent of 6.8° and 7.8°C between the consecutive months, September onwards results in December mean temperature of –3.3°C. Mean monthly temperature in Kargil is between 10° to 20°C for four months in a year which assigns it a cold highland climate.

In Kargil, highest mean maximum temperature of 29.7°C is recorded in July and the lowest of –4.2°C in January. Mean maximum temperature continues to be subzero in February also. Kargil, thus, has two such months with below freezing mean maximum temperatures which reflects the severity of winter climate. It is because of the thick snow cover in and around Kargil and in the surrounding mountain ranges.

The mean minimum temperature is subzero in January to March and November to December. This gives Kargil a frost-free period of seven months or 214 days.

These frost-free months extend from April to October. If first half of April, with a mean temperature of 8.7°C, is reserved for thaw and in helping the soil acquire appropriate temperature, Kargil is left with a precise growing season of six-plus months or about 200 days. Not only the long span of growing season but also high mean monthly temperature of these months allow cultivation of two crops in a year.

Mean annual temperature of Kargil is 8.8°C.

Mean Range

Normal range of temperature of Kargil is 43°C, which testifies to its highly continental climate. Average annual range of temperature is 11.2°C. The range of tempcrature is above this annual average in May to July and September to November, and for the remaining six months it is below the annual average. The range of temperature is low in the cool months of January to April and December. It is lowest in January and December. Range of temperature is medium in May to September. October, a warm month, registers the highest range of temperature. Kargil has a cold highland continental climate.

Atmospheric Moisture

Humidity

Highest relative humidity of 76 per cent and a lowest of 54 per cent is recorded in Kargil in April and October respectively. Relative humidity of more than 54 per cent, exhibits almost absence of aridity, and its high values of 70 to 76 per cent is indicative of humid traits in its climate. In this respect, too, Kargil is favourably endowed than Leh.

Months with high relative humidity (above 70%) are January to April and December. All these are winter months of high precipitation and low temperature (Figure 10.2). August and November have medium (60 to 70%) relative humidity. Low relative humidity (below 60%) is observed in May to July and September to October. It may safely be concluded that winter months are characterized by high and the warm months by low relative humidity (Table 10.6). Its average annual humidity is 65.4 per cent, which is only 4.3 per cent less than that of Srinagar.

Figure 10.2
Kargil

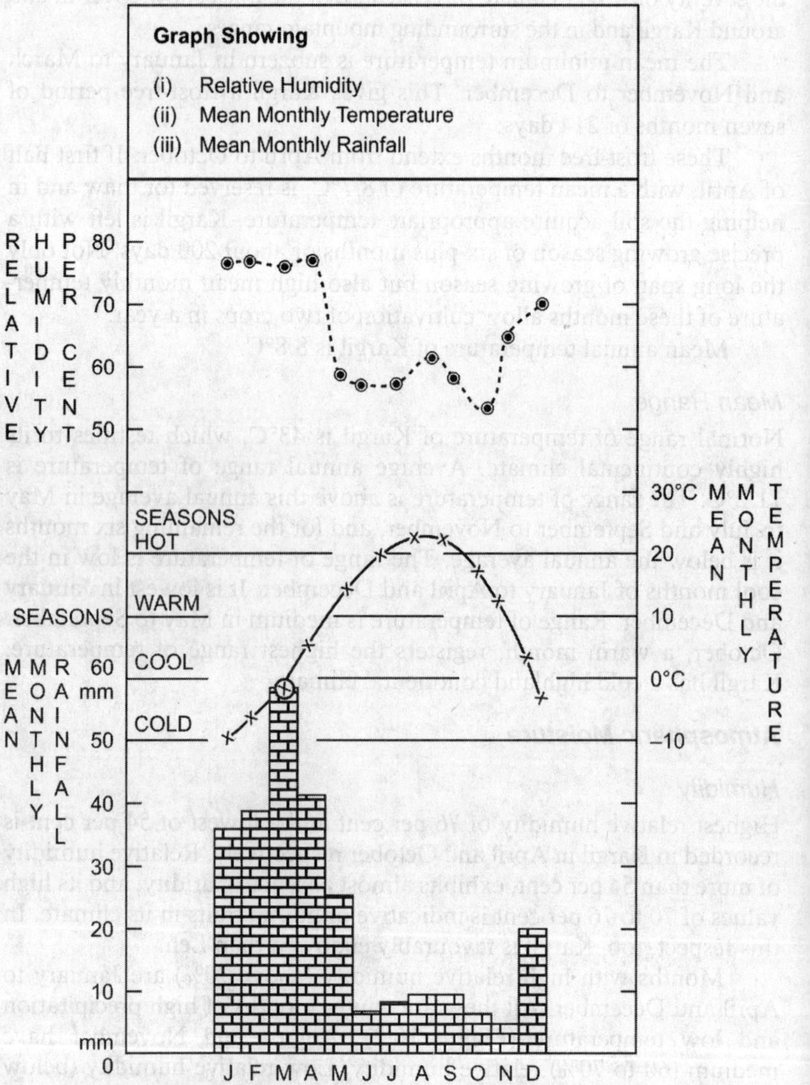

Altitude : 2750 m
Mean Annual Temperature : 8.8°C
Normal Range of Temperature : 43°C
Frost-free Period : 214 days
Total Annual Rainfall : 264.5 mm

Table 10.6
Kargil: Atmospheric Moisture

Element	*J*	*F*	*M*	*A*	*M*	*J*	*J*	*A*	*S*	*O*	*N*	*D*	*Annual Total Mean*
Precipitation (mm)	36.8	38.3	59.7	42.4	24.9	6.6	6.9	9.7	9.7	5.8	3.1	20.6	264.5
Relative Humidity (%)	74	75	75	76	58	57	57	63	59	54	66	71	65.4

Precipitation

Kargil receives a total annual precipitation of 264.5 mm. It is three times the precipitation registered in Leh. The rainfall data reveals a definite pattern. In the first five months of the year and in December the precipitation is denoted in double digits. It varies between 59.7 mm in March to 20.6 mm in December (Table 10.6). Like Srinagar, March is the rainiest month. The remaining and latter six months from June to November are marked by single digit rainfall values ranging between 9.7 mm each in August and September and 3.1 mm in November.

The distribution of precipitation is presented in the light of prevailing wind systems.

Western Disturbances

Precipitation received in January to May, November and December, under the influence of western disturbances is 85.3 per cent of the total annual. It causes heavy snowfall in and around the town and in the surrounding mountains. The meltwater of the glaciers and snowfields directed through water courses to the cropland, together with relatively high temperature, contribute to its thriving agriculture. In this district, too, cent per cent arable land is irrigated. Impact of availability of ample water is evident from the growth of bushes which have, to a large extent, enhanced expanse of verdure in its landscape. The girth and the height of the willow and poplar trees is quite large. It is also demonstrated by the preponderance of apricot trees.

South-West Monsoon

The normal dates fixed for the arrival and retreat of summer monsoon in this trans-Himalayan area are July 11 and September 11, respectively. Rainfall during three summer months of July to September is 9.9 per cent of the total annual. This lack of rainfall during the hot months, when water requirements of plants are on the increase, could damage standing crops but for assured irrigation facility which rescues agriculture from chances of crop failure. Rainfall in June and October is 4.8 per cent of the total annual. These months lie outside the above-noted two regimes of precipitation.

Seasons

For Kargil, the following seasonal pattern (Table 10.7) is unfolded when its monthly mean temperature is arranged in Hadlow's Word-Scale frame. Kargil has five distinct seasons. These are a half-year long winter with cold and cool components, a hot summer of two months and two warm seasons of two months each.

Table 10.7

Kargil: Seasons

S. No.	*Mean Temp. Range °C*	*Climatic Description*	*Calendar Months*	*Name*	*Duration (months)*
1.	10–20	Warm	September, October	Warm Season or Autumn	2
2.	20–30	Hot	July, August	Hot Summer	2
3.	10–20	Warm	May, June	Warm Season or Spring	2
4.	0–10	Cool	April, November	Cool Winter	2
5.	–10 to 0	Cold	January to March and December	Cold Winter	4

The Winter

Winter in Kargil extends from January to April and November to December. It has two constituents; the cold and the cool.

The Cold Winter

In this 4-month long cold winter, mean temperature is below the freezing point. The months included are January to March and December. In this harshest part of winter, night temperatures vary between –5° and –13.3°C. Even the day mean temperatures in January and February are –4.2° and –1.6°C respectively. Precipitation received is in the form of snow and amounts to 155.4 mm or 58.8 per cent of the total annual. This season claims the highest share of precipitation. The snow exposed to night frosts freezes hard and stays on the ground till the temperature is high enough to melt it.

The Cool Winter

In cool winter of April and November, monthly mean temperature is 8.7° and 4.5°C, respectively. Further, April in terms of temperature has an edge over November, as in this month the mean maximum, mean minimum and monthly mean temperatures are above zero degree Celsius. In latter month, mean minimum temperature is below freezing. The steep rise of temperature from March to April, by 9°C, aids thawing process. November nights continue to be cold with frequent frosts. April in the seasonal pattern of Kargil has the same significance as March in Srinagar and May in Leh. Precipitation is ample in April when November with least precipitation is almost a dry month. It accounts for 17.3 per cent of total annual and takes the form of snow and sleet. Relative humidity in five out of six months of entire winter, both cold and cool, is above 71 per cent. Winter climate of Kargil, consequently, can be termed as cold and humid. Iron stoves burning hard coke or dried cowdung bricks constitute the essential means of keeping off cold in homes and work places.

The Spring

May and June with mean monthly temperatures of 15.5° and 19.5°C form first warm season. The temperature is high enough to allow such agricultural operations as ploughing and sowing and to favour germination of seeds and growth of plants. Fruit trees are in blossom and deciduous trees in leaf, Spring rainfall is 11.9 per cent of the total annual precipitation. Relative humidity is 58 and 57 per cent.

The Hot Summer

Mean monthly temperatures of the two hot summer months are 23.7° and 23.0°C respectively. July and August temperatures are sufficiently high for speeding up growth and ripening of the first crop, thereby sparing land under cultivation for second sowing. Hot summer season by contributing only 6.2 per cent of total annual rainfall is a rain deficient period of the year. This is despite the fact that onshore monsoon is active in rest of the state and country. Relative humidity is 57 and 63 per cent, which makes summer neither dry nor sultry. This low rainfall and high temperature above 20°C justifies the urgency of cent per cent irrigation of its cropland.

The Autumn

This second warm season of the year is spread over September and October which register a mean temperature of 18.7° and 11.9°C. This season receives the least rainfall of 5.8 per cent of the total annual. Relative humidity is lowest, 59 and 54 per cent respectively. This warm and dry season favours growth and ripening of the second crop. It is also ideal for drying apricots which are generally spread over rocky surfaces for this purpose. This is the time for leaf fall.

This combined period of two warm seasons and one hot summer is an environmental asset of Kargil. It has a definite and remarkable effect on agricultural production. Crops cultivated include wheat, grim, peas and a variety of vegetables. The high temperature of this 6-month period subscribes to the surplus production of cereals and plentiful growth and proper ripening of the apricots.

This warm period, extending from May to October in duration, slightly exceeds road-open time. Apart from cultivation it is the time for remunerative outdoor pursuits, implementation of development works and handling of imported goods, including the necessaries of life. These require distribution and storage within the Kargil district and in the Zanskar sub-district. Trekkers and mountaineers arrive in connection with expeditions in the valleys of the Suru and the Zanskar. Tourists have started coming, lately, to get the firsthand feel of the outposts of Kargil war.

A suitable temperature of the warm and hot seasons together with the copious precipitation of the winter have blessed this areal unit with sufficient verdure to make it look distinct from other two subregions of Ladakh.

Dras

Dras, considered to be the second* coldest, permanently inhabited, place in the world, is situated midway between Zoji la and Kargil, in the Great Himalayas at an altitude of 3,066 m, a.s.l. It is located on the latitude of 34° 26' N and 75° 46' E longitude.

Air Temperature

Monthly Mean

The warmest month in Dras, with a mean temperature of 17.1°C is July whereas, the coldest month with –15.6°C is January. This temperature trait, of July highest and January lowest, Dras shares with Banihal, Srinagar, Qazigund, Leh and Kargil. Here five months in a year have a mean monthly temperature of less than 0°C. These are January to March, November and December. February mean temperature is 1.6°C higher than January mean (Table 10.8). An increase of 5.5° and 8.6° between the following months carries April mean to 0.1°C. It further increases to 8.3° in May and to 13°C in June. With an increment of 4.1°C, over the mean temperature of June, it attains peak in July. July and August temperature, differ by 0.1°C. A marked downward trend is observed after August when it ends up in December at –10.4°C. Highest

* Verkhoyansk, situated in Siberia, Russia is the coldest place in the world. This cold pole of the earth is located at 67°35'N latitude and 133°23'E longitude. Its altitude is 137 metres a.s.l. It lies within the Arctic Circle.

rise or fall of more than 8°C is observed in the pair of months of March–April, April–May and November–December.

Table 10.8

Dras: Air Temperature (°C)

Elements	*J*	*F*	*M*	*A*	*M*	*J*	*J*	*A*	*S*	*O*	*N*	*D*	*Annual Mean*
Mean Maximum	–9.0	–6.7	–2.0	5.4	15.1	20.5	23.7	23.6	19.6	12.8	4.3	–4.0	
Mean Minimum	–22.2	–21.4	–15.0	–5.2	1.5	5.6	10.6	10.5	6.9	–1.1	–8.6	–16.9	
Mean Monthly	–15.6	–14.0	–8.5	0.1	8.3	13.0	17.1	17.0	13.2	5.8	–2.1	–10.4	2.0
Mean Range	13.2	14.7	13.0	10.6	13.6	14.9	13.1	13.1	12.7	13.9	12.9	12.9	13.2

Mean maximum temperature is subzero in January to March and December. This is the first indication of intense cold in Dras even during the day. Mean minimum temperature of seven months is below freezing. Lowest minimum temperature of –22°C is recorded in January. For other months it varies between –1.1°C in October to –21.4°C in February. July registers the highest mean minimum temperature of 10.6°C. Harshness of winter cold, particularly at night, during the months of January, February and December is demonstrated by the temperature variation of –16° to –22°C. The extreme minimum temperature of –52°C was recorded in February, 1982.

Eight months in a year, in Dras, are unfavourable for plant growth. These include seven months with mean minimum temperature below freezing, and May with mean minimum temperature of 1.5°C. The massive accumulation of snow on the ground takes the full month of May for melting it. The growing season is, therefore, reduced to four months. However, a clear picture will emerge after the perusal of the 5–day normals data in the part of this chapter on seasons.

The annual mean temperature of Dras is 2°C, against 8.8°C of Kargil and 7.4°C of Leh. Higher mean temperature of Kargil is justified by its lower elevation compared to Dras. What about Leh which lies at a higher altitude vis-à-vis Dras? Can it be the southern aspect of Leh? Annual mean temperature of Verkhoyansk is –15.2°C.

Mean Range

The normal range of temperature of Dras is 45.9°C, which is the highest compared to the other stations of Jammu and Kashmir. This indicates that the climate of Dras is extremely continental. The yearly average range of temperature is 13.2°C. Monthly range of temperature above it is observed in January, February, May, June and October. For the other months of the year it is below annual average. The highest range of temperature is discerned in June and the lowest in April. Mean monthly range of temperature is above 14°C in February and June, between 13° and 14°C in January, March, May, July, August and October, and below 13°C in April, September, November and December. In each set, both cold and warm months are included. No definite pattern is identified in the mean range of temperature of Dras.

Mean temperature of Dras is between 10° and 20°C for four months in a year which accords it a cold highland climate. The cold is severe as the mean monthly temperature for five months is subzero.

Dras, therefore, has a very cold, highly continental highland climate. But it is not arctic or polar where monthly mean temperature for all the twelve months has to be below 10°C.

Atmospheric Moisture

Humidity

Mean relative humidity of Dras is 73.1 per cent. Considering the relative humidity values of Dras, Kargil (65.4) and Leh (40%) it is evident that among these three trans-Himalayan stations, Dras is the most humid.

November, in Dras, has the highest relative humidity of 81 and June the lowest of 61 per cent. It is 80 per cent, each, in March, April and December. It varies from 73 to 77 per cent in January, February and October. May to August have relative humidity between 61 and 69 per cent (Table 10.9). Low humidity months have the distinction of being warm months with mean monthly temperature between 13° to 17°C and a low rainfall of 13 to 57 mm. High humidity months of 77 to 81 per cent have a low mean temperature and high precipitation.

Precipitation

Dras receives the highest annual precipitation of 673.0 mm, compared to 264.5 mm of kargil and 81.9 mm of Leh. It is nearly the same as that of Srinagar. What Dras loses in temperature it gains in precipitation (Table 10.9). This high precipitation takes place mostly in winter (Figure 10.3).

The first four months of the year receive precipitation of more than 100 mm, each, with March registering the highest precipitation of 146.8 mm. March is also the rainiest month in Kargil and Srinagar. Moderate precipitation of 50 to 60 mm is experienced in May and December. For

Figure 10.3

Dras

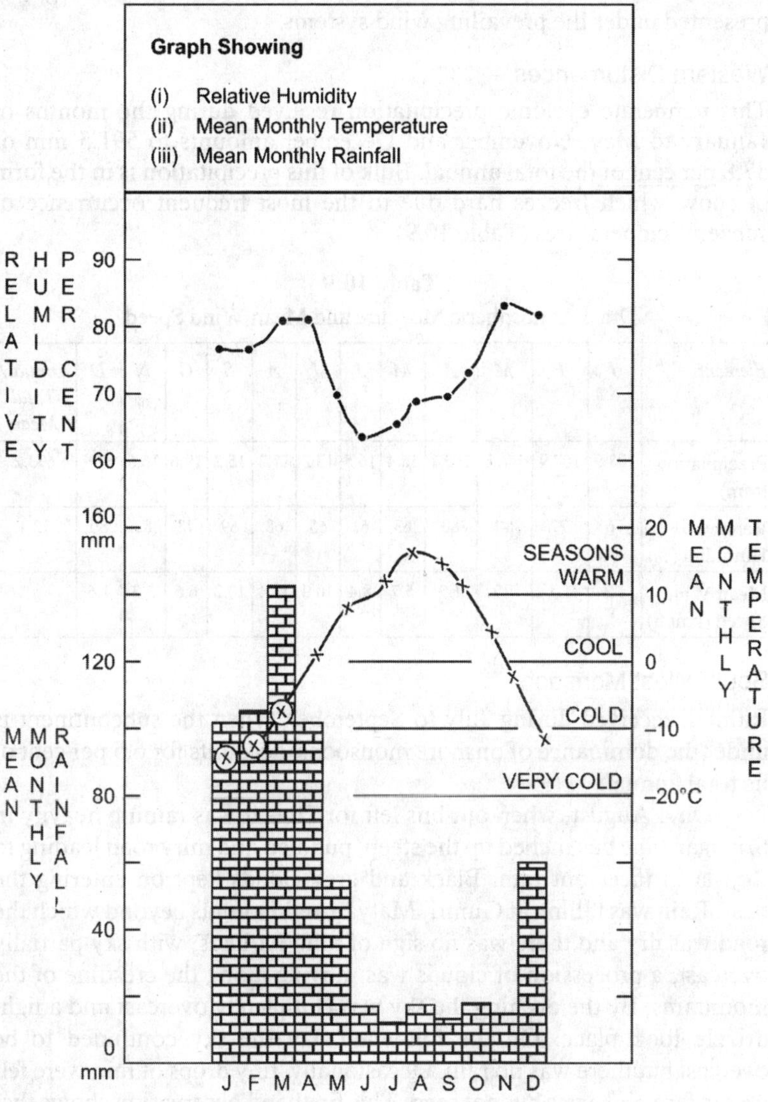

Altitude	:	3066 m
Mean Annual Temperature	:	2°C
Normal Range of Temperature	:	45.9°C
Frost-free Period	:	157 days
Total Annual Rainfall	:	673.0 mm

the remaining months it is less than 20 mm. July records the least rainfall of 13.2 mm.

Distribution of precipitation in Dras, like Leh and Kargil, is presented under the prevailing wind systems.

Western Disturbances

This temperate cyclonic precipitation received during the months of January to May, November and December amounts to 591.5 mm or 87.8 per cent of the total annual. Bulk of this precipitation is in the form of snow which freezes hard due to the most frequent occurrence of subzero temperatures (Table 10.9).

Table 10.9

Dras: Atmospheric Moisture and Mean Wind Speed

Element	*J*	*F*	*M*	*A*	*M*	*J*	*J*	*A*	*S*	*O*	*N*	*D*	*Annual/ Total Mean*
Precipitation (mm)	103.9	107.9	146.8	102.1	56.4	16.5	13.2	17.2	15.2	19.6	16.5	57.9	673.2
Relative Humidity (%)	76	77	80	80	68	61	65	68	69	73	81	80	73.1
Mean Wind Speed (kmph)	1.3	1.1	1.7	1.9	5.7	8.4	10.0	11.4	10.2	6.6	3.3	1.6	

South-West Monsoon

Rainfall received during July to September, when the subcontinent is under the dominance of onshore monsoons, accounts for 6.5 per cent of its total annual.

On 4 August, when our bus left for Dras it was raining heavily in Srinagar. The bus inched up the steep, puddled and miry road leading to Zoji la in incessant rain. Black and grey clouds kept on entering the pass. Rain was falling at Gumri, Matyan and Pandras beyond which the road was dry and there was no sign of rain. At Dras, with sky partially overcast, a procession of clouds was moving along the crestline of the mountains. By the evening the sky was completely overcast and a light drizzle took place. On the following day the sky continued to be overcast but there was no rain. Occasionally, tiny drops of rain were felt on the face and arms but not seen. This firsthand observation shows that monsoon winds enter the Dras valley, through Zoji la, but without resulting in much rainfall as is attested by the rainfall figures of this period. May be, the monsoon winds move in a direction parallel to the alignment of the mountain ranges in Dras.

Rainfall of the remaining two months of June and October contributes 5.7 per cent of the total annual.

Mean Wind Speed

In Dras, mean wind speed of 1.1 to 3.3 kmph is noticed in cold months of January to April, November and December. It is 5.7 to 8.4 kmph in May to June and October. Warm months of July to September experience light breeze (Beaufort scale) with wind speeds of 10.0 to 11.4 kmph (Table 10.9).

Seasons

Based on Hadlow's Word-Scale of mean monthly temperatures the following scheme of seasons of Dras, given in Table 10.10, manifests. There are two seasons in Dras – a long winter of eight months and a warm summer of four months.

Table 10.10

Dras: Seasons

Mean Monthly Temperature range (°C)	*Climatic Description*	*Calendar Months*	*Name*	*Duration in Months*
10 to 20	Warm	June to September	Warm Summer	4
0 to 10	Cool	April, May, October	Cool Winter	3
–10 to 0	Cold	March, November	Cold winter	2
–20 to –10	Very cold	January, February, December	Very cold winter	3

The Winter

Winter in Dras extends from January to May and October to December. The principal attributes of the winter are a continuous very low temperature, below freezing for most of the time, a high precipitation and high relative humidity. Help shall be taken from the table of 5-day normals of mean maximum and mean minimum temperature in the description of these seasons.

The Very Cold Winter

Months with mean temperature below –10°C constitutes very cold winter. This season includes January, February and December in which the mean temperature varies from –10.4° to –15.6°C. The mean maximum temperature of –8°C on first of January falls to –9°C on the 6th and continues to be same throughout the month. In February, it rises from –8°C on first of February to –5°C by its end. In December the mean maximum temperature of –1°C in the beginning of the month decreases to –7°C by its end. It follows that January and December exhibit a fall and February a rise in mean maximum temperature.

A very low mean minimum temperature of –21°C in the beginning of January falls to –22C and continues to be so throughout the month. This lowest temperature of –22°C continues during the first ten days of February which then rises to –21°C during the next ten days and finally settles at –19°C by the close of the month. December again indicates a descending trend from –15° to –21°C. Dras, therefore, experiences below freezing temperatures, both in the day as well as at night during the very cold winter.

A comparison with other two stations of Ladakh region makes the rigours of cold in Dras explicit. This very cold season does not exist in Kargil or Leh. The lowest mean minimum temperature of –22° in Dras, –13.3° in Kargil and –14.1°C in Leh (in January in each case) shows that this part of winter in Dras is much more severe than at these other two stations. In view of the above listed considerations Dras, undoubtedly, claims to be the second coldest permanently inhabited place in the world.

Precipitation in this season is heavy and entirely in the form of snow. It adds up to 269.7 mm and constitutes 40 per cent of the total annual. Snow usually accumulates on the ground to a height of two to three metres, when the entire ground floor of the house gets blocked. Movement of the occupants takes place through the windows of the first floor. Snow also collects on the flat roof of a house when it is removed, after every snowfall, with the help of a shovel, to prevent roof collapse due to its heavy weight. Recently, corrugated iron sheets have been used as the roofing material in some buildings. Snow clearance is carried out to keep the road open for vehicular traffic between Matyan and Kargil.

Here is an innovation worth reporting. Near the house is built a large bin of sun-dried bricks and mud for storing dried fodder for the use of the livestock in winter. This bin is lidless because of the paucity and high cost of timber. Soon after the first snow fall, the fodder filled bin at the top gets covered by a layer of snow which subsequently freezes hard to serve as a lid. The fodder is taken out of this bin through an opening near the bottom. This ice-slab lid protects the contents of the bin against dampness till the thaw sets in by the end of winter. By that time the stored fodder is completely consumed.

Like other places of Ladakh region, people of Dras have to store their eatables, for winter use, including pulses and meat. The killed sheep is exposed to frost so that meat gets frozen, which is used piecemeal throughout the long winter.

The Cold Winter

It includes March and November with mean temperatures of –5.8° and –2.1°C respectively. Mean maximum temperature of March at the beginning of the month is –4°C which increases to 1°C by its end. In November, it decreases from 8° to 0°C. The rise in March temperature is 5° but the fall in November is 8°C.

Mean minimum temperature of March increases from –17° to –11°C and that of November declines from –6° to –13°C. A scan of the mean maximum and minimum temperatures reveals that in the cold winter season, temperature on all the sixty nights and twenty days is less than 0°C. A temperature of above zero degree for forty days of the season indicates a slight reduction in the severity of cold.

Precipitation continues to be heavy in March but is scant in November. The combined precipitation in this season amounts to 163.3 mm which accounts for 24.1 per cent of the total annual.

The Cool Winter

This season, in Dras, comprises April, May and October with monthly mean temperature of 0.1° to 8.3°C from April to May and 5.8°C in October (Table 10.8).

Mean maximum temperature increases from 3° in April to 18°C in May and drops from 15° to 9°C in October. It follows that day temperatures in all these months are above freezing point of water. Mean minimum temperature of –9°C in the beginning of April increases to 4°C by the end of May. In October it falls from 1°C to –5°C. Mean minimum temperature is subzero in 55 days of this season. It is zero degree and above it for the remaining period.

Against the cool winter of three months in Dras, it lasts for two months in Kargil and three in Leh. Monthly mean temperature of April, which is part of the cool season in all the stations, is 0.1° in Dras, 8.7° in Kargil and 7.8°C in Leh.

Below freezing temperatures prevail for all the ninety days of the very cold, sixty-one days of the cold and fifty-five days of the cool winter seasons which adds up to 206 days. This leaves Dras with a frost-free period of 159 days in a year. But, no ploughing or sowing is possible before the accumulated snow on the ground melts completely. It creates problems because of its quality and quantity. Continuous subzero temperature for more than six months freezes it hard. Melting of snow and acquisition of the right soil temperature is completed by the end of May. Sometimes, when snow continues to cover the arable land, sods are thrown on it which hastens its melting. The growing season in Dras lasts only for 106 days from 8 June to 22 September.

As in other places in Ladakh region, an iron stove, using hard coke or dried cowdung bricks, is kept ignited throughout day and night, to ward off cold. The room where the stove is kept has an opening in the ceiling to allow escape of smoke and fumes. The stove is also used for household cooking.

The Warm Summer

June to September is the warm season in Dras when the mean monthly temperatures vary from 13° to 17.1°C. The temperatures of the peripheral months, of June and September, are almost equal (13°C) and so is it for the core months of July and August (17°C). Temperature rises from June to reach the peak in July and falls August onwards.

Precipitation received during these months is in the form of rain. It contributes 9.6 per cent of total annual precipitation. August, with 17.0 mm, receives the highest rainfall of the season. Relative humidity ranges between 61 and 69 per cent. It is least in June but increases through the monsoon months of July and August to 69 per cent in September. The climate of Dras in warm summer is characterized by a moderate temperature, scant rainfall and low relative humidity.

The prospect of agriculture in this very cold place, surrounded by towering ridges, is by and large grim. Crops raised are peas and grim. Pea pods are small so are the peas. The grim crop may or may not ripen depending upon the weather conditions in September. Huge reserves of snow in mountain recesses favour growth of grasses on melting. Availability of these grazing plots on the lower slopes encourage rearing of animals. Livestock rearing, with the predominance of sheep, in Dras is taken more seriously than cultivation. 'Dras on a sunny day in summer presents the aspect of a lovely pleasant pastoral retreat offering a complete contrast to the savage face it wears in winter when it witnesses the heaviest snowfall and the lowest temperature in the region' (Kaul and Kaul, 1992).

Ladakh Region

An Appraisal of its Precipitation

A scrutiny of the mean rainfall data of the three stations of Ladakh region, for the same period, 1901–50, bares factual relationships which invite our attention.

Mean Rainfall

Let us, at the outset, take up mean annual rainfall of each station. It is highest, 673 mm, in the southernmost station of Dras, and decreases to 264.5 mm in Kargil, situated 58 km to the north of Dras, and is further reduced to 92.6 mm in Leh, which lies 288 km to the north-east of Dras. The trend discerned is in accordance with the general observation that in western Himalayas, precipitation decreases as one proceeds from south to north (Figure 10.4).

The mean annual rainfall is analysed for its sources in the prevailing wind systems, like western disturbances and south-west monsoon. The percentage proportion of rainfall derived from each source has been computed and the findings tabulated below:

S. No.	*Station*	*Rainfall (%)*			
		Frontal (January to May, Nov–Dec) (7)	*Monsoon (July to Sept.) (3)*	*Others (June, Oct.) (2)*	*Total*
1.	Dras	87.8	6.5	5.7	100
2.	Kargil	85.3	9.9	4.8	100
3.	Leh	50.1	41.4	8.5	100

Western Disturbances

Like other parts of the state Ladakh region is under the domination of western disturbances from January to May, November and December. Precipitation on account of extra-tropical cyclones accounts for 87.8 per cent of the total annual precipitation of Dras. Related values for Kargil and Leh are 85.3 and 50.1 per cent respectively. These figures also exhibit a descending trend in the percentage of frontal precipitation from south to north (Figurc 10.4).

Monsoon Rainfall

For this purpose the rainfall of three months, July to September, in each station, has been considered despite the fact that onset and withdrawal of the monsoon takes place on 11 July and 11 September. The percentage of monsoon rainfall is 6.5 in Dras, 9.9 in Kargil and 41.4 in Leh. The pattern that emerges in monsoon rainfall is that of increase in the percentage amount from south to north. The rainfall also is disproportionate. The increase in the percentage of this summer rainfall is small between Dras and Kargil but it is substantial between these two stations and Leh.

Here a question arises. Why is the percentage of monsoon rainfall highest in Leh when it lies far inland in comparison to two other

Figure 10.4

Ladakh Region: Precipitation Attributes

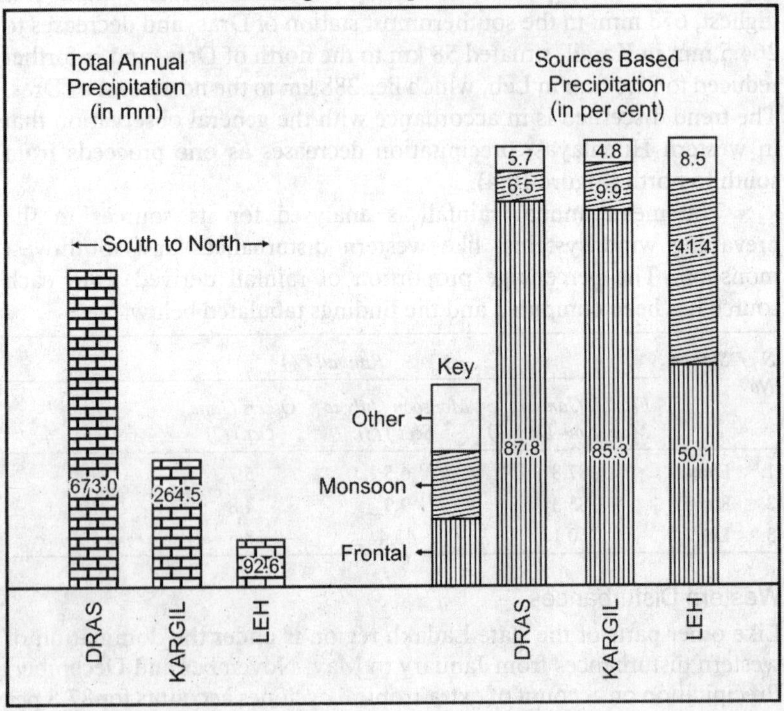

stations, Dras and Kargil. Can it be ascribed to the different directions, north-west and south-west, of the prevailing wind systems and the barrier or facilitator effect of the existing mountain ranges? Or what?

Sources of Data

1. Tables 1 to 4 are based on the climatological Data of Leh, supplied on request by Met Flight, 21 Wing, Air Force. The data set pertains to 1973–2010. (My sincerest thanks to the concerned authorities).
2. For Tables 5 to 10, data has been obtained from *A Climatological Study of Jammu and Kashmir,* by Lidhoo and Pradhan, C.I and D.D., J & K Govt., 1986.
   (a) Mean maximum and mean minimum temperature data used in Tables 5,7,8 and 10 are for the years 1931–60.
   (b) Mean rainfall data in the Tables 6 and 9 are for the years 1901–1950.

References

Ahluwalia, Major H.P.S. (1987): *Ladakh Nubra, The Forbidden Valley,* Himalayan Books, New Delhi.

Chaurasia, O.P., Bhat, B.B. and Singh, Col. D.V. (2000): *Ethnobotany of Ladakh Himalaya,* in Jina, Prem Singh: Ladakh, Past and Present, Gyan Publishing House, New Delhi.

Dwivedi, S.K. and Singh, Col. D.V. (2000): *Recent Advances in Horticultural Research in Ladakh* in Jina, Prem Singh.

Kaul, Shridar and Kaul, H.N. (1992): *Ladakh Through the Ages Towards a New Identity,* Indus Publishing Company, New Delhi.

Annexure – I

Natural Vegetation

The statement that Ladakh is a cold, dry and barren region devoid of vegetation carries the impression that natural vegetation does not at all exist here. If that is the case, how are about 2 lakh livestock, including Pashmina goats, reared in this area. For carrying out pastoral activities, the basic requirement is the presence of large number of pastures. Natural vegetation in Ladakh, because of its climate, is scant but in no case absent. Natural vegetation zones, comprising grazing areas, are found in the highlands where water is available for plant growth.

Vegetation Zones

These are situated in the alpine sections of the mountains of Ladakh above an altitude of 4,300 metres. Some of these lie on the slopes while others occupy the level land. The sloping meadows lie almost close to snow line where meltwater of glaciers percolates through soil to nourish the plants. In level surfaces these meadows are found where the ground remains snowbound for at least six months in a year. Here water of the rills and springs fulfils the water needs of the plants.

No natural tree growth is expected in this zone. The vegetation consists of annual and perennial herbs, shrubs and bushes. With the approach of summer when the snow begins to melt, vegetal cover gets revived. Three factors responsible for its revival are a scorching hot sun, the presence of extra amount of ultraviolet rays in it and the plentiful moisture in the soil. This herbaceous vegetation completes its full life cycle within this short summer. The pastures are full grown by August and degeneration sets in by the end of September. The plants survive in rigorous climatic conditions of such high elevations because of adaptations of different types. The other striking feature of this highland vegetation is its vegetative propagation (Chaurasia, et al.).

On the basis of their utility, the high alpine zone vegetation is listed in the following types.

Fodder Plants

These mostly consist of legumes and grasses. Alfa alfa, locally called 'ole' is the most common legume the other being wild gram. The other fodder plants are *Jamakh, Wakung, Seri, Ticktima, Iteming, Khros, Prangos, Yakjak,* etc. Some of these are reaped and dried for use in winter. Some long grasses like *Shyeong* and *Pili* also contribute their share of winter fodder.

Medicinal Plants

Like in many tribal and far flung areas, people in Ladakh also use wild growing medicinal herbs as remedy for the treatment of body ailments. The local practitioners of Tibetian system of medicine, called *Amchis,* prescribe these herbs for the treatment of different diseases. Of late, the system has been revived with many qualified professionals manning a number of dispensaries. Some of the medicinal plants collected from highland meadows are *Buma, Chhapat, Chikmo, Gotils, Khamchu, Khampa, Pahal Kutch,* etc.

Edible Plants

Some wild growing herbs are consumed by humans as part of their food. These edible plants are *Chhermang, Dyat, Elm, Kabra, Kala Zeera, Lamanchu, Stokche,* etc.

Fuel Bushes

Besides timber, the other scarce commodity in Ladakh region is fuel wood. The requirements of fuel are partly met with by utilizing dwarf bushes like *Ayuk, Burtse, Juniper, Khiaption, Longzey,* etc. *Hippophae* scrub or sea-buckthorn, which grows in wild profusion in the Nubra valley, is known for its soil and water conservation peculiarities. This quick growing weed is used as a fuel. Its berries are rich in vitamin C. This important fuel bush is being planted in other suitable areas of Ladakh region, with a view to mitigate the scarcity of fuel wood.

11

Jammu and Kashmir

Geology

Why is there a chapter on geology in a book on geography? Simply, because the term ge, meaning the earth, is the object of study of both these disciplines. Geography is an explanatory description of the earth's surface, which is the home of humans where they live and earn a living. Geology is the study of the structure of the earth – in particular, its rocks and minerals and its history and origins. Methodology of either branch of knowledge is different because geography is a spatial or a chorological science while geology is a systematic science. If geography is the study of interaction between humans and their environment, geological structure constitutes an important element of the physical environment. If geography is the study of areal differentiation of the earth, geological structure of the area is a vital cause for its differentiation. So in either case, geology (stratigraphy in particular) offers essential setting for geographical exposition.

Procedure

The age of our planet is estimated to be 4.5 billion years. All knowledge about past history of life on the earth and its physical conditions is obtained from the study of sedimentary rocks. The pages of the geological history are constituted by these rocks of specific composition, belonging to a particular sequence, together with the fossil flora and fauna contained in them. The age of the unfossilifesous rocks is determined by their stratigraphical position or by comparison with the similar strata elsewhere. The first five-sixths of the earth's history are, seemingly, clueless in the sense that the rocks of this period are without fossils (azoic). A satisfactory fossil record is available for the past, about, 600 million years. This stands as the *terra firma* for the commencement of the earth history. Geology has its own time scale. Here the entire geological time is first divided into *eras,* which are further subdivided into *periods, epochs* or *systems.* Table 11.1 presents the geological time scale based on radioactive findings.

Table 11.1
Geological Time Scale

	Era	*Period or Epoch*	*Age (million yrs)*
5	Psychozoic	Recent or Holocene	0.01
	(Reasoning Life)	III Glaciation	0.3
	or Quaternary (Fourth)	Glacial or Pleistocene	1.0
4	Cainozoic	Pliocene	11
	(Recent Life)	Miocene	25
	or Tertiary	Oligocene	40
	(Third)	Eocene	60
		Paleocene	70
3	Mesozoic	Cretacious	135
	(Middle Life)	Jurassic	180
	or Secondary	Triassic	225
	(Second)		
2	Palaeozoic	Permian	270
	(Ancient Life)	Carboniferous	350
	or Primary	Devonian	400
	(First)	Silurian	440
		Ordovician	500
		Cambrian	600
1	Proterozoic	Pre-Cambrian	
	(Azoic)	Archaean	

STRATIGRAPHY

Pre-Cambrian Basement

The Archaean System

It is constituted of a crystalline complex of rocks like granites, gneisses and schists. Most of the Ladakh region from the Great Himalaya to the Zanskar range the Ladakh range and up to the Karakoram is composed of these rocks. Minor intrusions are found in the Pir Panjal but these crystallines are fairly present in the Kaz Nag range and in the mountains at Padar. The Salkhala series of this system has been found to be of pre-Cambrian origin. It forms the basement on which the subsequent sediments are deposited.

Dogra Slates

The fossiliferous Palaeozoic sedimentary strata, in certain localities, does not rest directly on the Salkhala series but upon a rock formation called Dogra slates. The series consists of black and grey cleavage slates, which bear ripple marks but are unfossiliferous. These are widely distributed in the Pir Panjal range and Kishenganga valley. Typical areas of development are Poonch and Ramban in Jammu and Marinag in Kashmir.

The Palaeozoic Era

The Palaeozoic trench in Kashmir extends from its north-west, near Handwara, to the north-east in the Lidder valley. It runs parallel to the general strike of the Himalayas to the north of the Veth plain. The best exposures of the Palaeozoic marine sedimentary deposits are found in Handwara, Shams Abari anticline (between Wular and Titwal), Basmai anticline (between Sonamarg and Kolahoi), Lidder anticline near Aishmuqam, Naubug valley and in mountains of Vihi area between Zewan and Barus.

The Cambrian

Rocks of this group include limestones, greywacks, arenacious beds and clays. The Cambrian is best observed in Handwara and Kupwara areas where the Dogra slates are conformably succeeded by clay slates and the fauna is rich in *Trilobites* and *Brachiopods.* This strata is not well developed in other parts of Kashmir.

The Ordovician

Limestones and slates are the rocks of the Ordovician series. These are distributed in the north limb of Shams Abari anticline near Trehgam and in Basmai anticline in the Sindh valley. In this strata are present some species of *Orthis.*

The Silurian

Sandy shales or shaly sandstones are the rocks of this system. These are distributed in Marhom, Shams Abari, Gagangir, Harpatnar, Gugaldar, Naubugh and Margan pass. An ideal site is provided by the Lidder anticline from Aishmuqam to Lutharwan in the Warwan valley. Fossil fauna of this series includes *Orthis, Brachiopods, Cephalopods* and *Corals.*

The Devonian

The Devonian strata consists of massive and hard white quartzites, called Muth quartzites. These are found in Warwan valley, Naubug, Shams Abari and on either flank of Lidder anticline. These are unfossiliferous and their age is determined by their stratigraphic position. Kenlung formation of Zanskar, comprising thick bands of pure white to cream coloured quartizites, is considered equivalent to Muth quartzites.

The Carboniferous

This epoch is divided into three subgroups – Lower, Middle and Upper.

The Lower Carboniferous

Overlying the Muth quartzites is a thick strata of limestones which abound in *Brachiopods,* particularly of genus *Syringothyris cuspidata,* after which the series is designated as Syringothyris limestone. The other fossil present is *Productus cora.* These beds are well exposed at Marbal pass, Gugaldar, Gagarpathri, Ichnar, Kotsu, Aishmuqam, Sindh valley and Banihal. Aishmuqam and Kotsu provide ideal sites for collection of fossils. Even stones paved in the lanes of Mattan town, brought from Aishmuqam quarry, bear these fossils. This series is absent from Handwara.

The Middle Carboniferous

The Syringothyris limestones are overlain by Fenestella shales of the Middle Carboniferous period. This series is restricted to the north-western part of Lidder anticline. The exposures are observed in Lehindajjar, Bugmore, Yanzar, Khirram and Ainu in Anantnag district and Banihal and Budhil passes in the Pir Panjal range. In the west of Tral valley near Prongam and Mandakpal shales, cherts and limestones are crowded with *Fenestella* and other fossils. These rocks are absent from the Sindh valley and Handwara.

The Upper Carboniferous

Marine sedimentation proceeded quietly in the Palaeozoic trench from the Cambrian to the Middle Carboniferous. Kashmir, then, witnessed a massive volcanic activity resulting in change in its physical geography. It reached its peak in the Permian and continued in Gurez area up to the Upper Triassic times. This volcanic phenomenon is connected with post orogenic movements of the Hercynian activity (Wokhalio, 1972).

The venue of the volcanic extrusion was the submarine shelf where, through cracks, large quantities of ashes and tuffs were extruded. These were followed by basic lava flows. During this period deposition of detritus continued without break. In this way sedimentary strata got mixed with volcanic material. A set of volcanic islands emerged, out of sea water, which resulted in the formation of an archipelago.

Panjal volcanics is the name assigned to these volcanic products of Upper Carboniferous period. These are divided into the 'Lower

Agglomeratic Slates' and the 'Upper Panjal Traps'. Either of these is widely distributed in hills and mountains of Kashmir. Both these rock series constitute the serrated crestline of the Pir Panjal. Its highest peak, Mt. Tratakuti, is made of agglomeratic slate permeated by intrusive sills of dolerite (Pascoe). Panjal traps form the peaks from Shin Mahinyu to Apharwat. Most of the Pir Panjal range is constituted of these rocks by virtue of which it is called 'the Panjal series'.

These also constitute peaks in the Himalayan flank from Shams Abari to Mt. Kolahoi. The mountains around the Dal lake, including the Shankaracharya hill, are formed of the Panjal volcanics. The isolated hills like the Ahateng, Baba Shakur-ud-Din, Magam and Shupiyan are composed of these rocks. The Panjal volcanics are also distributed in mountains enclosing the valleys of the Sindh and the Lidder, and the mountains bordering the Wular lake, on the east and the north.

The Agglomeratic Slates

These consist of thick series of pyroclastic slates, conglomerates and agglomeratic products. With a dark grey colour these slates disintegrate rapidly on weathering and acquire a brownish tint. In the Shankaracharya hill, out of a total thickness of the Panjal volcanics of 421 metres, agglomeratic slates account for 93 metres. (Loan, 1973).

These rocks are generally unfossiliferous but at Brein (on the eastern shore of the Dal) and Nagmarg (north of the Wular lake) the series contains Lower Gondwana plants associated with sandstones and shales containing a marine *Polyzoa* and *Brachiopod* fauna and *Eurydesma.* A few specimens of plant fossils of generic name cordaites were found at Singhpora, in north-western Kishtwar on the border with Kashmir. (Wokhalio and Dhar, 1968).

The Panjal Traps

These comprise a great thickness of lava flows, andesitic to basaltic in composition. As many as fourteen lava flows have been counted in the Shankaracharya hill (Loan, 1973). The traps are of a dark or greenish colour and are either compact or amygdaloidal. At Gagribal, in the northern spur of Shankaracharya hill, the traps are metamorphosed along with the agglomeratic slates. Rhyolites an acid variety of volcanic rocks constitute the Wasterwan spur, Athwajan and Pantachok quarries and Hari Parbat hillock. Near Buniyar is a plug of gabbro surrounded by doleritic masses. Thick beds of limestone of Permian/Triassic age are found within lava flows near Bandipore and Uri. The Panjal trap, locally called *Phandayi Kaen,* after due dressing is extensively used in the construction of the plinths of houses in Srinagar. The Rinam volcanics of Zanskar are considered contemporaneous with the Panjal volcanics of Kashmir. In the Suru valley it overlies the Zanskar crystallines.

The Gondwana Beds

The extrusion of large quantities of magma during the Upper Carboniferous epoch paved way for prevalence of continental conditions in Kashmir and its subsequent link with the Gondwanaland. Land plants, insects and cartilaginous fish appeared on the scene at this stage. The plant fossils are of seed ferns like Gangamopteris (*Gangamopteris Kashmirensis)* and Glossopteris* *(Glossopteris indica).* Lower Gondwana plant bearing beds are of Permo-Carboniferous age and consist of shales, cherts and sandstones. These beds are found in the Valley facing slopes of the Pir Panjal range near the passes of Banihal and Golabgarh, near the peaks of Tratakuti and Apharwat. The other localities are Vihi (near Srinagar), Marhom (Bijbehara) and Nagamarg (north of Wular). In Vihi area the plant beds lie between the Panjal volcanics and Permian limestones. Here important places of exposure are mountain spurs of Risin, Zewan, Ludov, Barus and Guruyul ravine (above Khonamuh). In Guryul ravine the section offers an interesting study where the Panjal volcanics are overlain in sequential order by Gangamopteris beds, Zewan series and Lower Trias. Indistinct plant impressions are found in the slates above Nishat Bagh.

The Permian

Kashmir, in the following epoch, witnessed marine transgression of the Permian sea which cut short its continental phase. Henceforth, Kashmir got linked with the Tibetian zone of the Himalayas. The Permian deposits of Kashmir are better known as Zewan series. In the Guryul ravine these beds have a thickness of 70 metres. The series consist of shales and limestones which abound in fossils of *Brachiopods* and *Polyzoa.*

In Zanskar this fossil-bearing Permo-Carboniferous series extends from Yunam Tso valley through Tanse to Lunak valley. The limestones are creamy dark to bluish grey in colour. Fossils of *Brachiopods, Gastropods, Lamellibranchs* and corals are found in this series. Gypsum deposits occur within the limestones near the village of Kurgiak.

* The presence of Glossopteris plant fossils in peninsular India, Falkland islands, Antarctica, South America and south Africa was one of the evidences put forth by Alfred Wegner to support his Theory of Continental Rift and Drift.

In sub-Himalayan Jammu unfossiliferous limestone of Permian or Permo-Carboniferous age is exposed at a number of places extending from Reasi to Poonch. Due to the removal of the overlying strata of the Eocene and the Murrees, the limestones got exposed. This dolomitic limestone, also called Reasi limestone, is white or bluish grey in colour. A celebrated eminence of these rocks is the Trikuta hill near Katra. These limestones contain sulphide ores of zinc, copper, lead and nickel.

The Mesozoic Era

The Triassic

Rocks of the Triassic system consist of limestones of a light blue or grey tint, compact and homogenous. In some cases these are dolomitic in composition. The Upper Trias is unfossiliferous but fossils of *Cephalopoda* abound in the Middle and the Lower Trias. These Triassic formations with their graceful folds present a captivating sight in Kashmir landscape.

The series is widely distributed in the valleys of the Sindh and the Lidder. It covers the volcanic beds of the Pir Panjal range from Kishtwar to Uri. In Anantnag district most of the ridges and spurs are composed of the Triassic limestone. From the foot of these ridges gush forth springs of large volume. The prominences in the Vihi area stand in the form of a semicircle which opens towards the Veth. The series extends through Khonamuh, Nagabaran, Lam, Mandakpal and Narasthan. At Pahalgam it forms a number of ridges and peaks. The Amarnath ridge and cave are formed of the Upper Triassic limestone and dolomite which at some places has changed into gypsum. In Gurez, the Kishenganga has cut a gorge in the Triassic limestone. In central Ladakh the series extends up to the Karakoram and Lingzhitang plains.

This greyish-blue massive limestone, locally called *Diwer Kaen,* lends well to chisel and hammer. In the ancient period it was extensively used in the construction of such imposing edifices as the temples of Martand, Awantipore, Paraspore, Tapar, Pattan, Narasthan, etc. (now in ruins). In mediaeval times it has been used in the construction of magnificent mosques. It can be shaped into pillars, tombstones, corner and pavement stones. At present, it is used in the construction of private and public buildings. It forms the basic raw material in the manufacture of cement in Kashmir.

The Jurassic

Limestones, sandstones and shales, containing fossils *Cephalopods* and *Lamellibranchs,* constitute the Jurassic system. Exposures are few within

Kashmir. These are found on the Valley-facing side of the Banihal pass, in Srinagar-Leh road above Baltal, in the Sindh valley above Sonamarg and in the Amarnath valley. Deposits of the Jurassic period are widely distributed in Ladakh. These overlie the Triassic limestones of central and southern Ladakh. They also form a part of the broad basin of the Mesozoic rocks along the inner edge of the Zanskar range.

The Cretacious

Rocks of this system have not so far been noticed in Kashmir. The Cretaceous strata has been found in the Zanskar range and in the Rupshu plateau. It consists of unfossiliferous limestone, of which some of the peaks of the range are formed. This epoch is characterized by another rock series the Cretaceous volcanics. It consists of basalts, granites, agglomerates and gabbro. This formation extends from Dras to Kargil and is distributed in the valley of the Indus. Serpentine and mineral chromite is found in these rocks.

The Cainozoic Era

By the close of the Cretaceous epoch the sea of Tethys had completely retreated from Kashmir region and with it ceased, therein, the period of marine sedimentation. Consequently, the Tertiary strata is absent in this part of Jammu and Kashmir. Sections of the sea continued to exist, one each, in the north of the Great Himalaya and to the south of the Pir Panjal range. So, for Tertiary rock formations our focus of study shifts to trans-Himalayan Ladakh and sub-Himalayan Jammu.

The Eocene

Ladakh

A long stretch of the Eocene formation is found in the southern part of Ladakh along with the Permo-Carboniferous, the Triassic, the Jurassic deposits and the Cretaceous volcanics. The Lower Tertiary zone of Ladakh extends from Dras to Kargil, Leh and Hanle. Purple and green shales form the base of these deposits which, in turn, are overlain by blue limestones which contain *Nummulites.*

Jammu

In sub-Himalayan Jammu the Eocene is present in two well-defined zones. The first consists of a 200 km long narrow belt of Nummulitic limestones and other associated rocks extending from the Ravi to the Jhelum along the foot of the Pir Panjal range. The second consists of Nummulitic limestones which lie close to the Permo-Carboniferous limestones and extends from Reasi to Poonch. In this Eocene strata are found ores of iron and aluminium and seams of coal.

The Oligocene

The rocks of this period are absent in Jammu and Kashmir.

The Miocene

This epoch is characterised by two types of deposits marine (the Muree Series) and fresh water or sub-aerial (The Siwalik Series).

The Lower Miocene

In the mountain (*Pahar)* region of Jammu the Eocene is overlain by alternating beds of sandstones and shales, called the Murree series. On lithological basis the series is divisible into the upper and the lower stages.

The Lower Murree Series

This formation consists of purple and red sandstones, purple shales, deep red clays and pseudo-conglomerates. The Lower Murrees are unfossiliferous.

The Upper Murree Series

It comprises soft brown, coarse sand-stones, with grey interior, red and purple shales and nodular clays. These contain leaf impressions of mono- and di-cotyledons.

Middle Miocene to Lower Pleistocene

During Middle Miocene, second Himalayan upheaval took place and the sea of Tethys completely retreated from North India. Marine sedimentation was replaced by cstuarine and fluvitile deposits of the following epochs. Soon after its emergence, the Himalayan mountain system was exposed to the forces of denudation. The rock waste, so produced, was transported by the fast flowing streams and deposited in the estuary of the Indobrahm (or the Siwalik) river. This alluvial deposition was subjected to folding and was uplifted by the latest phase of Himalayan orogeny. This outermost foothill region of the Himalayas runs all along its length. These are called the Siwaliks. About 500 metres of the Siwalik strata overlie the Murree series. These are divisible into three stages the Lower, the Middle and the Upper.

The Lower Siwaliks

Rocks of the Lower Siwaliks resemble those of the Murree series with which they are in close contact. These consist of brown sandstones, red and purple nodular clays. Fossil assemblage in the lower part comprises plants and bones of fish, birds and reptiles. In the upper part are found several species of antelopes, giraffes, apes and other mammals.

The Middle Siwaliks

These comprise massive beds of coarse, micaceous sand of pepper and salt colour. In the absence of some cementing material it crumbles into sand at the end of a shower or when in contact with running water. It is, therefore, termed as sand rock. The fossil remains include those of apes, elephants and rodents.

The Upper Siwaliks

Boulder conglomerates, beds of sand, grit and clay constitute the Upper Siwaliks. The old quarters of Jammu city occupy the Upper Siwalik strata which is now completely obliterated by the buildings and the roads. The massive deposits lie exposed on its Tawi-facing slopes. The preponderance of boulder conglomerate, in the earlier times, gave the city an appellation of '*Wattan da Shehr*'.

The Psychozoic Era

The Glacial or the Pleistocene System

In early part of the Quaternary era North America, Europe and other northern regions of the world experienced very low and freezing temperature conditions when thick and vast sheets of ice covered these areas. These frigid climatic conditions lasted for less than a million years. This period is referred to as the Ice Age or the Glacial Epoch. In India the sphere of influence of this Ice Age was the Himalayas.

Evidences

Moving ice, as an effective tool of earth sculpture, gave final touches to the physiography of Jammu and Kashmir which had, by then, evolved as a result of Himalayan orogeny. The pyramidal peaks, serrated ridges, U-shaped valleys, erratic boulders, polished and striated rocks, moraines, glacio-fluvial deposits, rock basins, cirques, *roches moutonnees* and unique fossil lake beds, the Karewas, are the evidences of the Pleistocene glaciation. Cirques filled with water have formed the tarns. In the mountain girdle, hollows formed by past glaciers and filled with moraines and fluvio-glacial outwash deposits, have given rise to a number of *margs* and *pathris*. Such features on the Valley-facing slopes of the Great Himalaya are Sonamarg, Minimarg, Lidderwat and Bod Bongus and on the Pir Panjal flank are Tosmaidan, Ludrmarg and Gulmarg.

Two sets of moraines are observed all along Kashmir Himalayas. Those of existing glaciers lie at a higher elevations close to them. These seldom occur below 4,300 metres. The moraines of the past glaciation are found at heights far below the lowermost limit of the present glaciers. Drew observed *roches moutonnees* at village Hari, near Gund, at an elevation of 1,918 m. The two transverse valleys of Sindh and Lidder provide model locations for the study of impact of the Quaternary glaciation.

Divisions

The Pleistocene Ice Age, according to Richard Carrington, commenced more than 600 thousand years ago and lasted as far back as ten or twenty thousand years. It was characterized by alternate periods of ice advances and retreats. The first ice advance lasted for 60,000 years, while the second and third, each, were of 40,000 years duration. The interglacial periods were longer than the glacial and stretched for 100,000, 200,000 and 100,000 years for the first, second and the third respectively. The second interglacial was longer than the first and the third. The longer duration of interglacial period allowed a certain amount of weathering and erosion of the deposits.

Quaternary Ice Age Deposits

The Ice Age deposits in Kashmir are the Karewas. Karewa* is a Persian term for a landform which is neither too high nor too low. These consist of partly consolidated silts, sands, clays and boulder gravels of fluvio-glacial, lacusrine and eolin origin. These were divided into the Lower and the Upper Karewas by Lydekker (1883) on the basis of their age and mode of formation. According to de Terra, the former were deposited during the First Interglacial in a vast and deep lake when the climate was warm and wet, hence their great thickness. The deposition of the latter took place when the lake was smaller in size and shallow and the climate on certain occasions was dry. An unconformity separates one from the other, and the Upper Karewas rest on the eroded surface of the folded Lower Karewas.

The Lower Karewas

These extend along the Pir Panjal over a distance of about 150 kms, with a width varying from 12 to 25 kms. Exposures of the series are found in Sedau (the Vishau), Hirpur (the Rembiar), Abhom and

* *Tarikh-i-Hassan*, in Persian, written by Pir Ghulam Hassan (of Khuyihom), the famous, historian of Kashmir, comprises four volumes, out of which one volume deals with the geography of Kashmir. In it the term Karewa is used in the description of its uplands.

Sangerwani (the Romshi), Gogjipathri (near Nilanag), Ludrmarg (above Yusmarg) Botapathri (the Ningle), Laridura (near Baramulla) and Nichahom (near Handwara).

The thickness of the Lower Karewas is estimated to be 1,600 metres. For such a massive sedimentation two causes, one geographical and other geological, are held responsible. The unobstructed monsoon currents because of low elevation of the Pir Panjal during the First Interglacial, resulted in heavy and widespread rainfall which drenched every nook and corner of the Great Himalayan flank. Consequently, immense load of eroded material was washed down these mountain slopes and deposited in the still waters of the lake. As the mountain slopes had a thick forest cover the humus present in the soil helped in the formation of clay. Besides, the extent of the lake increased due to the sinking of the rock basin of Kashmir in relation to its rising mountain flanks.

Towards the close of the First Interglacial, with the uplift of the Pir Panjal, the lake beds got compressed, resulting in the slight folding of these beds in the basin and faulting along the mountain slopes. These were, also, raised to their present elevations and became tilted. The uplift was followed by erosion when a large thickness of these beds was removed.

de Terra and Paterson have identified four lithozones of the Lower Karewas. The clay zone at the base contains a thin layer of lignite. It is followed by an upper lignite zone, with thick deposits of lignite found in brown sand. The association of lignite with river sand indicates that the formation took place when the lake was in existence and heavy delta deposition was taking place. The next is the clay layer which abounds in fossils of leaves, wood and spores of trees like oak, birch, apple, poplar, spruce, juniper, walnut and berberis and of such plants as rose, trapa and lotus. This fossil bed is overlain by gravel and sand.

Sombur Exposure

Sombur quarry is situated about 20 km to the south-east of Srinagar on the right bank of the Veth. The river at this place has exposed a large platform of the Triassic limestone overlain by the Pleistocene beds. On the platform rests breccia consisting of angular limestone fragments. Over it lies a layer of conglomerate which is considered to be the outwash of the I Glaciation. A thin bed of clay, about 30 cm in thickness, rests on the conglomerate. It is designated as the bone bed in view of the presence in it of fish, bird and animal bones. In this bed of yellowish clay are found fish bones, broken bones of extinct mammals, remains of elephants, fresh water shells and plant parts. de Terra found a well preserved tusk of *Elephas cf hysudricus*, belonging to the oldest of the Pleistocene Indian elephants. This find has enhanced the significance of this Lower Karewa bed. The presence of bones in this bed indicates that deposition took place in quiet waters of the lake shore. On the basis of the articles collected from the bone bed, palaeontological evidence for the existence of the Pleistocene elephant in Kashmir got established.

The Upper Karewas

These Pleistocene Ice Age deposits have a thickness of about 300 metres. These consists of varved clays, yellow marls, silt and sand. Exposures of the Upper Karewas are widely scattered in the valley floor and easy of access. Loessic silt and laminated clays with marl beds are found at the foot of the Shankaracharyal hill, at Gagribal and in palace premises. The upper several metres of Upper Karewas of Burzahom consist of loess. The upper Karewa beds are well exposed along the western shore of the Mansbal lake. Here the gravelly sand, marl bearing silt and sand, and yellow loessic silt is clearly seen. At Paraspore are observed whitish grey silts with fine bedding and horizontal position. The isolated hill at Magam has a cover of this series. Conglomerate and green sand are found below the laminated clays and silts in Budgam.

Clay forms base of the Upper Karewa series. Generally, it is of grey colour but much of it is ochreous. It contains remains of fresh water plants like broken stems of rushes and grass. Contrary to their abundance in the Lower Karewas, these are bereft of tree leaves. The predominance of grass and rushes along with fresh water shells indicate quiet water deposition in a shallow lake. The clay beds are overlain by stratified yellow silt and sand which form the bulk of this series. The lower group is formed by laminated silt with alternate layers of marl and concretionary clay. The marl, usually, is mixed with oxides of iron and manganese. Good exposures are found to the south of Pampore town along the national highway. Presence of five to eight marl layers testify fluctuations in the lake level. The upper group is of loessic origin. Some of the silt layers are cemented to form siltstones. It may safely be concluded that lacustrine, fluvial, glacial and eolian agencies, too, were responsible in the formation of Upper Karewas.

The horizontal surface of the Upper Karewas is best perceived on the Pampore Karewa where the surface is patterned into square beds for saffron cultivation or on the Damodar *Wudar* where the Srinagar airport is located. An ideal section of this Pleistocene formation extends from the *Baal* hill in Anantnag town towards east, beyond the ruins of the Martand temple.

Recent or Holocene

These deposits include recent alluvium and younger loam found in many parts of the Valley. Younger alluvium also occurs in river valleys where it was formed in recent times.

QUATERNARY GLACIATION

Based on the study of moraines, Dainelli identified four distinct stages of glaciation and three interglacial epochs in the north-western Himalayas, which were further supported by the findings of Helmut de Terra.

The glacial cycle in Kashmir, according to de Terra, is tabulated below:

Period	*Pleistocene*
Upper	*IV Ice Advance:* Terminal moraines at 2,700 to 3,600 m. The Pir Panjal rises to present elevation.
	Third Interglacial: Intense erosion.
	III Ice Advance: Terminal moraines at 2,100 m.
Middle	*Long Second Interglacial:* Upper Karewa beds, erosion.
	II Ice Advance: Boulder clay and gravel in Karewa beds, Sharp rise of the Pir Panjal.
Lower	*First Interglacial:* Lower Karewa beds, erosion, first mild uplift of the Pir Panjal.
	I Ice Advance: Terminal moraines at 1,675 m.

I Glaciation

The physical geography of Kashmir before I Glaciation presented a different picture compared to the present. This intermontane basin was bounded in the north by the towering Great Himalaya but in the south the Pir Panjal stood at a lower elevation. This southern rampart of Kashmir was then too low to act as a monsoon barrier. Consequently, strong south-west monsoon currents entered the Valley unobstructed to thoroughly drench the Himalayan slopes as is evident from the intensity of the I Glaciation on this side. Against the vigorous glaciation of the Himalayan, it was feeble on the Pir Panjal side. The glaciers that occupied the valleys of the Sindh and the Lidder extended to their respective valley outlets. The coarse outwash aprons were spread in each valley.

First Interglacial

Uplift of the Pir Panjal, during the First Interglacial, caused the damming of the Upper Jhelum in Kashmir. Reversal of the course of the master stream and, also, melting glaciers resulted in the creation of a vast, inland, fresh water lake.

In this lake were deposited enormous quantities of eroded and other materials derived from different sources. In still waters of the lake entered rock flour, silt and sand washed down by running water from the moraines of I Glaciation. Bulk of the sediment was contributed by the Himalayan slopes. It was followed by wind-blown loess carried from the Punjab plains in the south. Chemical precipitates also contributed their share. The immensity of the deposits establishes the maximum inundation of the Valley. Towards the close of this epoch, uplift of the Pir Panjal took place which compressed the Karewa beds that were carried upwards along its slopes.

II Glaciation

An increase in the height of the Pir Panjal range resulted in adequate glaciation on this Lesser Himalayan range for the first time. It continued to be strong on the Great Himalayan range but not as considerable as during the I Glacial. Huge quantities of rock debris were stocked on either side. Streams carried down this glacial gravel and deposited the same on the tilted Karewa beds forming large boulder fans. The deposition of loessic matter, which was a regular feature of the Pleistocene Ice Age, continued during the II Glacial as well.

The other peculiarity of the II Glaciation is the absence of the terminal moraines on either flank of the Valley. It appears that the glaciers of the time moved close to the water's edge and offloaded outwash gravels and moraines directly into the Karewa lake and on top of Lower Karewas. The lake waters entered the Sindh valley and submerged the moraines of I Glaciation. The Sindh glacicr floated over this inundation and icebergs that were severed from it floated in the Karewa lake and left the moraines into it or carried the erratics as far as Baramulla.

Second Interglacial

On account of its long duration the Second Interglacial was a period of complete deglaciation. Its main outcomes are deposition of Upper Karewa beds, erosion and formation of terrace one.

At the beginning of this epoch the Karewa lake with diminished area deepened because of mountain uplift and its level fell due to subsidence of its bottom. This situation helped in the deposition of second group of sediments comprising sands and silts over the boulder gravel of II Glaciation. This was followed by decreased inflow of river water and snowmelt into the Karewa lake because of spells of dry climate. The water of the shallow lake became alkaline when marls and concretionary materials got deposited. These shell-bearing soft rock beds received a thick cover of yellow coloured loessic material brought by the dust storms coming from the south. The Jhelum, then, excavated its channel through the blockade and the lake was permanently drained. The streams cut their channels in this fluvio-glacial debris. A stage came when the down cutting of the streams was replaced by lateral cutting which gave rise to the formation of the first terrace.

III Glaciation

Moraines of this glaciation are mostly found at an elevation of 2,100 metres and are generally covered by pine forests. This period was marked by diminished glaciation when some valleys were glacier-free. In other valleys, lakes were formed due to blockade of the meltwater in their upper parts. Three to four boulder ridges are found in the terminal moraines of this period. Terrace two, of aggradational type, was formed by the redeposition of the moraines of the third glacier.

Third Interglacial

This was the period of intense stream erosion when their channels were deepened and the third terrace was formed.

IV Glaciation

It was the least significant among all the stages of ice advances in Kashmir. The glaciers were small, occupied upper parts of the stream valleys, melted quickly and deposited the terminal moraines at altitudes of 2,700 and 3,600 metres. The moraines near the Gangabal lake are supposed to belong to this period. The glaciation produced sufficient detritus to form the fourth terrace.

The Karewa Lake or the *Satisara*

The preceding discussion on the Quaternary Glaciation reveals the existence of a vast, deep and fresh water lake in the rocky basin of Kashmir during the first two interglacial epochs. This lake served as a settling tank for the denuded materials of the I and II Glaciations, which resulted in the formation of the Karewa series. This was the Karewa lake of the geologists and the 'Satisara' of the classical writers. The factors responsible for its creation were the uplift of the Pir Panjal, consequent blockade of the Jhelum outflow channel and the warm interglacial period of melting ice.

Formation of the Lake

The uplift of the Pir Panjal range is testified by the direction of tilt of the Lower Karewa beds, which slope everywhere towards the Valley and also by the presence, at an elevation of about 3,000 metres, of fossils of plants which, at present, grow in the Wular lake and the Valley floor at an altitude of less than 1,580 metres. The only feasible explanation can be that these clay beds, containing fossils, were carried to their present locations by imperceptibly ascending mountain range.

The spillway of the Karewa lake is said to have been situated at Sheri Narwav, between Baramulla and Rampur. The area is prone to seismic disturbances as is evident from the earthquake of 1884, when nearby village of Laridura was completely wrecked or the earthquake of 2005 which rocked the adjacent locality of Uri. It is surmised that the formation or the removal of blockade, of the master stream, was the result of some seismic activity. Kashmir, as remarked by Prof. Katsumasa Abe of Tokyo University, Earthquake Research Institute, is liable to earthquakes because it lies at the collision point of the Eurasian and the Indian tectonic plates.

The sequence of events, that led to the formation of the Karewa lake, is, justly, presented by de Terra. Before him Godwin Austen and Lydekkar had stated that the lake was formed because of the rise of the Pir Panjal. Dainelli had expressed that the lake had its spillway below Baramulla. All of them had agreed to the formation of the lake but none of them explained how it was formed. According to him the first mild elevation of the Pir Panjal range, during the First Interglacial, blocked the outflow channel of the Jhelum. Its backward flow caused the flooding of the rocky basin of Kashmir. This is exhibited by the sudden change in the deposits of the period from coarse sand to clay. The extent of the lake so formed was further increased several fold by pouring into it of profuse quantities of the meltwaters of the glaciers occupying the slopes of its mountain rim. Towards the close of the First Interglacial, a channel carved through the spillway resulted in the first partial draining of this Karewa lake. This occurrence is marked by the deposition of green sand along the Himalayan flank and upper lignite bearing sand along the Pir Panjal side. At the time of the II Glaciation, the lake was considerably reduced in size and its level fell due to the subsidence of the bottom of Kashmir basin. The second Interglacial witnessed a conspicuous rise of the Pir Panjal range which tilted the lower Karewa beds and pushed the lake towards the opposite side. It was a smaller lake compared to the earlier one. By the end of the long second Interglacial the outflow channel got restored and the lake was gradually drained.

Dimensions

The Karewa lake at the height of the Ice Age, according to Wadia (2004), occupied an area of not less than 7,800 sq km. The lake, opines de Terra and Paterson (1939), must have been 305 metres above the Valley floor. Drew (1875), asserts that the level of the lake was 2,133 metres a.s.l. Sir Hayden observed, '... and the whole valley was filled what must have been the most lovely lake in the world ... twice the length and three times the width of the lake Geneva and completely encircled by mountains high and higher than Mont Blanc, while in the following glacial period mighty glaciers came wending down, the Sindh, the Lidder, the Lolab and the other valleys, even to the very edge of the water. 'To Nilamatapurana the Satisara was', deep like the sky, bright with lotuses, containing cool and clear water, it is the most charming (lake) on the whole Earth'. To a palaeontologist, like Vishnu Mittre, (1964) 'the Karewa lake was a quiet sheet of water inhabited by free floating plants of *Trapa natans,* along the shores of which the reed swamps were largely made up of typha'.

Legends

A legend about the presence and the desiccation of this prehistoric lake is given in the Nilamatapurana (circa 8th century AD) and repeated in somewhat modified form in Kalhana's Rajatarangini (12th century AD). Here is a resume of this lengthy legend. During ... the land in the womb of the Himalayas was filled with water. This was Satisara, the lake of *Sati (Siva's* consort). In this lake a wicked demon *Jalodhbhava* had taken shelter. He harassed the people of neighbouring areas by his devastations. Sage Kasyapa learnt about this distress. He took to severe penance and implored the Hindu trinity for help. The gods arrived and occupied vantage positions on the three peaks of the Brahma Shikhar, in the Pir Panjal range, above Kounser Nag. The demon while hiding in water was invincible. So *Visnu* directed his brother Balbhadra to pierce the mountains, in the west, with his personal weapon the plough. The thrust of ploughshare created an opening in mountains through which escaped the lake water. The lake was drained and the demon killed. Then Kasyapa settled the land so evolved.

Equally fascinating, though different, is the Buddhist version recorded by Hiouen Thsang. Kashmir was a dragon lake. Lord Buddha while passing over the lake country told his disciple, Ananda, that Madytyantica would find a kingdom in this land, pacify the people and spread the *dharma.* On hearing this prophecy Madytyantica, the *arhat,* with unsurpassed spiritual prowess proceeded to Kashmir. There he took his seat on a mountain peak and exhibited his spiritual charms. The dragon was impressed and asked the *arhat* what he desired. The *arhat* told the dragon that he needed a piece of land, in the middle of the lake, just big enough for his knees to sit on. The dragon responded by withholding water from the middle of the lake for a piece of land to appear for the *arhat* to sit on. But the *arhat,* by his supernatural might, increased the size of his body to the extent that the dragon had to withdraw the entire volume of water. By doing so the lake was completely drained of water and dry land appeared.

Another version of the legend is found in the history books of the medieval period, written in Persian, including Haider Maliks', *Tarikh,* from where it was adopted by Wilson (1960), in his History of Kashmir. Here Kasyapa is a *deo or a dgin* with great miraculous powers, whose efforts led to the draining of the lake.

Fiction and Fact

The legend regarding the *Satisaras* is likely to be considered as a piece of fiction. But how akin is this fiction to the fact has been best elucidated by Frederic Drew (1875), in the following words, 'The traditions of the natives, tend in the same direction ... Agreeing, as I do, with the conclusion, I cannot count the traditions as perceptibly strengthening it, I have little doubt they themselves originated in the same physical evidence that later travellers have examined, they do not, therefore, afford independent support to the theory but are valuable rather as showing how in early times some races of mankind had learnt to interpret aright geological records of the history of their dwelling places'. Similar views are expressed by G.T. Vigne (1842) when he remarks, 'For the foregoing reasons, I fully believe in the tradition of the natives, as to the valley having been originally a lake of 300 to 400 feet in depth. But I also believe its drainage to have been the work of time.'

Evidences

Following geological and glacial evidences corroborate the existence of this Quaternary Ice Age lake in Kashmir.

Karewas

The composition and the mode of formation of the Karewa series is the first convincing proof in this regard. 'The present view', writes Wadia (2004), 'regards the Karewas the surviving remnants of deposits of a lake or series of lakes which once filled the whole valley basin from end to end'. According to Bhat (1976), 'the Karewa lake formed the sedimentational basin for the Hirpur (Lower Karewa) formation .... The graded nature of varved laminae, the crowding of lacustrine fresh water gastropod shells in some clay beds and the presence of trapa in some others are evidence for lacustirine origin of Hirpurs'. '... It thus seems that in the basin of a large cool lake fed with numerous streams, the lacustrine facies of Nagum (Upper Karewa) formation was deposited' (Bhat and Chatterji, 1976). Wakefield (1879), in this regard, avers, ... 'Kareewahs or prominences that form so striking a feature in the topography of the valley whose characteristic flat and uniformly even surface can only be attributed to their having been submerged for ages beneath the still calm waters of a deep vast lake'.

Bore-Hole Data

During the seventies of the last century, ONGC had selected two sites in the Valley for drilling operations. One was at Chattergam (on Srinagar-Khandah road) and the other at Narabal (Srinagar-Gulmarg road). The bore-hole data was, on request, made available to the present writer by the Deputy Director General, ONGC, Dehradun. It lays bare the following details in connection with the composition of the Karewas.

Karewas

Type	*Deposits*	*Thickness in Metres*
Upper	*Clay,* ash grey to dark grey bentonitic, plastic 5–10 metres thick, Bands of *conglomerate* with pebbles of trap	60
Lower	*Clay,* ash grey to greenish grey bentonitic plastic.	30
	Siltstone, grey and compact.	4
	Clay, grey to dark grey soft, plastic, bentonitic with fossil wood.	60
	Alternations of light green to dark green, medium to fine grained *sand* and grey to dark grey, soft plastic, bentonitic *clay*.	
	Grit, very coarse to *pebbly fragments* of limestone, trap and quartzite.	106
	Basal Rocks: Triassic limestone or Panjal trap.	04

Several pertinent inferences can be drawn from this data. Allowing margin for the denudation of both the Karewas, the thickness of the Upper Karewas (60 m) is small compared to 204 m thickness of the Lower Kerawas. This upholds the earlier assertion regarding the relative size of the lakes during the First and the Second Interglacial epochs. Second, the dominance of clay of various hues with a sprinkling of sand and silt stones. Third, the deposition of the heavy materials comprising pebbly fragments of limestones, trap and quartzites at the bottom of the clay beds could only be possible in a sedimentation tank, where so to say, sorting of the material, prior to deposition, took place.

Formation of Beaches

Shingle beaches and gravel strewn shorelines of the Satisara have been traced at a number of places in the Valley, mostly on the Himalayan flank. In the Shankaracharya hill, Dainelli had observed several beach lines. One of these is on the northern slope of the hill, facing Gagribal, 165 metres above the boulevard. The beach is cut into the trap and is strewn with gravel. The second is seen near the top of the hill, 88 metres above the aforementioned one, where the TV tower is erected. The platform has a mantle of yellow loam of eolian origin (raw material for the preparation of *Parthishvar* on *Shravan Poornima*). To the south of Brein village, on the eastern shore of the Dal, is a long spur. Here a set of gravel strewn beaches is found at an elevation of 120 metres.

One such beach slopes awkwardly on the spring-facing slopes of the *Baal* hill in Anantnag town. Here are rounded pebbles of limestone and sand cemented together by calcarious mud. 'There can be no doubt', contends Drew, 'these pebble-beds were the shingle beach formed when the hill was part of the shore of the lake of such a size that its waves had the power to fashion beaches out of the waste of the rocks'. Beaches are observed on the limestone mountains above the holy spring of Mattan and Bumzu caves. Here the horizontal layers of the beaches are observed on the mountain slopes, which at places carry ripple marks. Beach lines have been identified in the Ahateng (in Mansbal lake) at Gundi-Sadrkut and Gnor (on the eastern shore of the Wular lake), and Wodhpur (on the Pohru stream). On the Pir Panjal flank solid masses of shingly conglomerate are observed near Hirpur.

Fossil Assemblage

Out of the many plant fossils found in the Lower Karewas special interest was evinced by aquatic plants like trapa, nelumbium and *Euryale ferox* which at present grow in wild profusion on the waters of the Wular and other lakes. All these fossil plant sites lie 500 to 1500 metres above the Wular lake and at a distance of more than 15 km from its nearest shore.

Major Godwin Austin for the first time, in 1864, reported the presence of plant fossils in the clay deposits of Gogjipathri (near Nilnag) and Ludrmarg (west of Yusmarg). Later on, many fossil studies were conducted in Kashmir by a number of investigators. These include B. Prasad (fresh water mollusca), Dr Caulson (plant fossils), R.P. Wodehouse (tree pollen), Middlemiss (leaf fossils) and S.K. Mukerji (forest trees and shrubs). Studies of the fossil flora were undertaken by the scholars of Prof. Birbal Sahni Institute of Palaeontology, of

Lucknow University, at several places like Ludrmarg (2,032 m), Botapathri (2,987 m) and Laridura (2,032 m). Fossil analysis carried out by Vishnu Mittre, et al., (1971) reported the existence of leaf impressions, in specimens collected, to the tune of 209 at Ludrmarg, 193 at Laridura, 120 at Dangerpur, 103 at Botapathri and 60 at Nichahom. In all the cases the impressions were of broad leaved trees.

Lignite

Large deposits of lignite, in the Lower Karewas of Kashmir, are found in Raithan and Nichahom. A luxuriant growth of vegetation, particularly in swamps, is expected in warm humid environment. Before uplift of the Pir Panjal such conditions were prevalent here. Rushes, sedges, grasses and peat moss, the basic materials for lignite formation had, it is said, a lush growth before being embedded in clay. The peripheral location of these beds implies shallow water along the western shore of the Karewa lake and consequent bog conditions. Abundance of trapa and leaf impressions of oak and willow are found in these fuel deposits.

Varves

In the lakes fed by glacial streams more material is transported in summer than in winter for obvious reasons. The coarse material settles down quickly while the finer stuff remains in suspension for a long time. In such lake deposits the coarse and light coloured sediment (of summer) forms the lower part and the dark coloured material (of winter) the upper, thereby giving rise to varves. These varved or laminated clays are characteristic of glacial regions. We are quite sure about the occurrence of glacial epoch in Kashmir when the other requisite is a water body. It existed in the form of Satisara. Varved clays constitute a principal feature of the Karewas. Dr Birbal Sahni had observed varves, as early as 1934, in a narrow ravine at Hajbal and Botapathri near Gulmarg.

Identical Strata

For citing an example of strata formed under similar conditions as the Karewas of Kashmir, the geological history of Kathmandu valley in Nepal is relevant. The vale is an exposed lake basin almost circular in shape. It was occupied by a lake, in the prehistoric times, formed by the damming of the river Bhagmati, in the south, near Chobar, by the uplift of the Lesser Himalayas, called here as the Mahabharat range. The river later on cut through the obstruction of crystalline limestone and carved a gorge as an escape route for itself. The legend ascribes the cutting of the gorge by Lord Manjushree, with his sword. The deposits of the lake are known as Tanr. These are found as terraces along the rim of the valley when in the middle these have been eroded by the Bhagmati. The Tanr consists of gravel, sand and clay. Springs abound where the clay and the sand layers are in contact. In the Tanr are found peat and phosphatic deposits, together with the remains of the mammals. On one terrace is situated Kathmandu airport. A close similarity is discerned in the geological history of Kathmandu and that of Kashmir. The scale is different but the geological formations are identical.

Conclusion

This discussion on the presence in Kashmir of the Karewa lake or the *Satisara,* in the prehistoric times is concluded with the following observation of Sir Edwin H. Pascoe, former Director, Geological Survey of India, 'Landslips are frequent especially during the earthquakes which so often visit this region and in some cases cause the formation of mountain lakes of varying permanency. Lakes, some of them of large size, are produced in this way or by dams of moraine material and occupy some of the longitudinal valleys. When drained by cutting back of some stream, they leave behind the wide, flat alluvial valleys which offer such a contrast to the drainage elsewhere. The valley of Kashmir is a worthy instance of such a lake basin, in this case not completely drained ...'.

Quaternary Glaciation at the Regional Level

In the following pages is given the gist of the Quaternary Glaciation in the three regions of Jammu and Kashmir, based on the studies of de Terra and Paterson (1939), who in turn have incorporated the observations of Drew (1875), Lydekkar (1878), Oestreich (1906), Dainelli (1922), and Norin (1925).

Kashmir Region

The Sindh Valley

For the study of past glaciation this river valley is divided into three parts, the lower from Manigam to Hari, the middle from Hari to Gagangir and the upper from Gagangir to Sonamarg and Baltal.

The terminal moraines of I Glaciation are found at Manigam on the left bank of the Sindh. These, lying at an elevation of 1,676 metres, are the earliest and the lowest glacial deposits. The erratics present in the stream bed are derived from the trap rocks of Gagangir and the Triassic limestones of Sonamarg. The other glacial deposits which overlie Manigam moraines is the conglomerate. This outwash apron of I Glacial extends up to Malshahibag. It consists of small rounded pebbles cemented by a hard calcarious substance.

As already mentioned, there are no terminal moraines of II Glaciation because the snouts of the glaciers of this period terminated at the shores of the Karewa lake. A typical formation of this period is the yellow-brown clay which contains angular and sub-angular boulders of sandstone, trap and white quartzite. Exposures of it are seen in Wayil, Nunar and Ganderbal. Shaping of the U-shaped valleys has probably taken place during the first two glaciations, at Hari, Mamar, Margund, Kangan and Wusan. Deposits of the second Interglacial are the clay series which constitute the Upper Karewas. The terminal moraines of III Glaciation are found in the middle section of the Sindh at Gund (2,070 m) Pharo (2,011 m), Rewan and Gagangir (2,346 m).

In the upper section of the Sindh Sonamarg is an anticlinal shaped out of Triassic limestones. Here the moraine mounds, 9 to 12 metres high, lie to its west. The valley was flooded after the II Glaciation by the damming of the stream due to uplift. Large erratics of breccia which had moved down during the III Glaciation lie at the confluence of the Sindh with the Lashimarg rivulet. The cemented conglomerate which extends from the said confluence to Baltal is likely to belong to this period. Moraines of the IV Glacial were laid at Gagangir gorge, Shitkari and Nilagrar.

The Lidder Valley

The Lidder Valley, in connection with the past glaciation, is divided into two sections, one from Pahalgam to Sheshnag and the second below Pahalgam. The upper Lidder is characterized by a narrow width, a steep slope and a number of gorges. Lower Lidder is wide, has a mild slope and constitutes an area of deposition.

More than a kilometre above Ganeshbal, on the left bank of the stream, is a thick heap of avalanche material. It overlies a yellow-brown clay sand matrix which contains angular and sub-angular boulders of white quartzite, and sand stone which is presumed to belong to I Glaciation. Resembling the cemented conglomerate of Malshahibag, is the cemented conglomerate at Krungus to Kanjdori and on the Baal hill in Anantnag town. This is considered to be the outwash apron of the I Glacial.

Deposits of II Glaciation are found in a hollow at Nunwan. Moraines of the II Glaciation are overlain by the deposits of Second Interglacial in Pahalgam at the confluence of the east and west Lidder.

These morain heaps have a thickness of about 155 metres. The erratics are present in the stream bed near Pahalgam village. Brown granular clay, with a thickness of 150 m formed during the second Interglacial lies between the Baal hill and Kanjdori. The glacial deposits of the III and IV Glaciations are confined to upper Lidder. The III Glacial has left moraines at Nekabatun (2,286 m) and Phraslun (2,481 m). At Burzakot and the outlet of Sheshnag the moraines found are supposed to belong to IV Glacial.

The Vishau Valley

The II Glaciation caused the formation of cirques and hanging valleys in the Vishau where it is joined by the Harseni stream. In this river valley, Sedau locality is of great significance. Here is observed warved clay lying over ground moraines which in turn is overlain by Upper Karewa clay. This indicates that the area happened to be the estuary of the Karewa lake into which eroded material was deposited by the II Glacier. It is also marked by the formation of terraces. Five terraces are identified here which are so well developed that it may be considered a type locality for the same.

The Rembiar Valley

A huge pile of gravel which runs 16 kms upstream of Shupiyan town is a conspicuous remnant of glaciation of the Rembiar Valley. The gravel terrace has a thickness of 3.6 metres on the left bank of the river at Shupiyan. In it are found angular and sub-angular boulders. Its location between the Lower Karewa and the Upper Karewa beds shows it to be a representation of Karewa gravel. The stream bed is littered with huge erratics.

The Sukhnag Valley

It is presumed that glaciation in the Sukhnag valley was intense with the main valley and the side valleys covered by glaciers. The tongue of the main glacier was 24 km long. Coarse boulder moraines and erratics are present up to Khag and Drang, which belong to I Glaciation. The Valley outlet lies at Zugu Kharyan where arrangement of the beds, bottom upwards is the Lower Karewa clays, boulder gravel and the Upper Karewa beds. The II Sukhnag glacier is believed to have terminated at Raiyar Yech. At Drang, lateral moraines of the III Glaciation occupy slopes to the north of the village. Boulder heaps are found to the north of Shungilipore. Three ridges of terminal moraines are observed at Khag. The IV Glaciation was not of much significance in this valley.

The Ferozepur Valley

Two gravel terraces lie on the left bank at Goiran. The lower one represents the ground moraines of III Glaciation, while the upper one belongs to the Third Interglacial. Ferozepur stream has the outlet at Tangamarg. Here on terrace one, Srinagar–Gulmarg road is constructed. It lies between Karewa gravel and the Upper Karewa silt. The Upper Karewa silts are exposed on the road below Tangamarg. They are brown and show layers of dark soil, the carbonaceous matter in the latter is rich in conifer pollen.

Gulmarg

From Khillanmarg a glacier descended towards the edge of the Gulmarg basin, the boulder moraines of which are found at an altitude of 2,900 metres. Water channels flowing downhill have dissected this moraine heap and detached the erratics. The morainic matter carried down the slope filled Gulmarg basin which in turn was covered by the Karewa beds which have resulted in its undulating surface. These glacial and lacustrine deposits have concealed the geology of this upland meadow. At Tilwanmarg, the thickness of the Karewa beds exceeds 30 metres. These consist of laminated ochre-coloured silt underlain by bluish grey clay with plant remains.

The Ningle Valley

A glacier descended from the Apharwat peak along the valley of the Ningle. At the top it scooped a cirque which is filled by Alpather lake. Downhill lies a clay moraine, of 3 to 15 metres in thickness, exposed on the bank of the stream. It probably belongs to I Glaciation. Some distance downstream, on the right bank are found erratic boulders which increase in number towards Dhobighat. At Dandamuh, on the right bank are long boulder ridges. This seems to be the halting place of III glacier. In nearby Botapathri are found plant fossil beds which are in an excellent state of preservation.

The Jhelum Gorge

The Pleistocene glaciation in Jhelum gorge is confined to the area between Rampur and Uri. At Rampur the side valley is slightly U-shaped. Here on higher slopes are present erratics. Near Chandenwari, across the Jhelum, on its right bank, is village Nur Khwah. In the approach way to the village is a large accumulation of huge granite erratics. The right bank tributary of the Jhelum near the village is called Lachipur nala (or Nilnag stream). Its source lies in the KazNag range and the valley of this stream appears to be the path followed by KazNag glacier. It was reported that there are three moraine heaps in the Lachipur nala valley. The first is at Bijehama, 4 km uphill of Nur Khwah, second at Lachipora and third at Payass. Massive granite boulders are found along the left bank of the Jhelum, in the fields and hamlets up to Uri.

Jammu Region

The Chenab Valley

The part of the Chenab valley above Kishtwar, in Jammu and Kashmir, called Padar, has witnessed heavy glaciation during the Pleistocene period. In this area, terrace remnants are found at an elevation of 120 to 180 metres above the river level. The valley fill comprises coarse boulder conglomerate of reddish colour in which angular blocks lie in a matrix of silt and gravel. This deposit is likely to belong to II Glaciation.

The Tawi Valley

In its longitudinal section, from Seoj to Chenani, the river valley was occupied by a glacier. Its impact is observed in the undulating surface of the meadow of Seoj formed due to the deposition of moraines. The meadow is also littered with erratics. At Chenani (983 m) the terrace deposit consists of rewashed and partly residual ground moraines mixed with landslide material. The presence of erratics upstream of Chenani, at a low altitude of 1,068 metres, is ascribed to glacial action.

Poonch Valley

A characteristic feature of the mountains of Poonch is the presence of canyon-like valleys with a depth of about 610 metres. Two such valleys are those of the Lohrin and the Palera. These are separated by flat inter-stream ridges which merge with the southern slopes of the Pir Panjal range. Moraines of the II Glaciation lie scattered over these flat topped ridges. In the Lohrin stream bed, below Mandi, at an altitude of 1,370 m, is an accumulation of erratics.

Poonch town lies in a wide valley in which terraces are noticed in the western part. These are formed because of the deposition o glacio-fluvial outwash. Terrace 2, which lies at the top was probab formed during II Glaciation. It is composed of sandy yellow cl Terrace 3, at the middle level, assigned to III Glacial, consists redeposited conglomerate with red clay matrix. Stratified red, pink and sand constitute the terrace 4, which lies below terrace 3. I considered deposited during the IV Glacial.

Ladakh Region

Kargil

During the Pleistocene epoch, Kargil presented the appearance of a depression. The imprint of I Glaciation is discerned in remnants of high glacial troughs. II Glaciation has been quite vigorous in this area. The deposits of the period include boulder gravel and ground moraines. Also present is the upper gravel associated with a thick deposit of laminated lacustrine silt. The glacier streams of the time, it appears, were dammed by tributary glaciers to give rise to a number of lakes which were younger than the Karewa lake of Kashmir. The silt is considered to be of glacial as well as eolian origin. It was derived from the rock meal of ground moraines. The rest of it was wind blown material brought from the south by the monsoon currents. This wind blown material also found its way into the deposits of Lamayuru and the Indus valley. The lake beds comprising of white lacustrine silt and boulder sand is linked with glacio-fluvial outwash of III Glaciation. During the IV Glacial, Kargil was ice free but the terminal moraines in the side valleys are linked with this epoch.

The Indus Valley

It is presumed that vast sheets of ice covered the plateaus of Rupshu and Deosai during the I Glaciation. The First Interglacial experienced the uplift of the mountains which was followed by erosion. This period saw the entrenchment of all the rivers of this region including the Indus at Skardu.

Glaciation was strong in the Himalayas and the Karakoram during the II epoch. The Indus glacier, is believed to have extended up to the plains of north-west Punjab where the erratics were carried by it. In this river valley between Nurla and Leh, thick gravel deposits are encountered. The older cemented boulder gravel is expected to belong to II Glaciation. These beds, in Spituk rest against the enormous fan of Leh. This epoch marks the first stage of fan formation when glacial troughs were filled to a great extent with the glacio-fluvial outwash. Old cemented gravel or breccia represents the fan debris which in case of Leh acquires a thickness of 305 metres. The other factor responsible for his huge fan deposit is the uplift of the Ladakh range.

The origin of the upper Indus lake silt is ascribed to the damming glacial streams by ice-barriers giving rise to lakes into which was osited air borne loess from the Indian plains brought by the soon winds. Pangong basin at that time was covered by a glacier which has left behind ground moraines and glacio-fluvial cemented gravels. Only half of the area of the Indus valley was glaciated during II Glaciation.

III Glacial saw the damming of the Skardu lake by tributary glaciers. Lakes were found in Baltistan and near Leh. A second stage of fan formation was presumed and the debris comprised younger loose gravelly sand which was deposited over the early organic matter. This period saw the glaciation of only 30 per cent area of the Indus valley. Lake silt in Lamayuru belongs to this period. It has a thickness of 137 metres.

IV Glaciation deposits consist of young terminal moraines and fans. A young moraine found about 138 metres below the top surface of the lake bed at Lamayuru is assigned to this glacial period. Only 20 per cent of the total area of the Indus valley was glaciated at this stage.

References

Books

Beal, Samuel (1958 Reprint): *Travels of Hiouen Thsang,* Sushil Gupta, Kolkata.

Carrington, Richard (1956): *A Guide to Earth History,* Chatto and Windus, London.

de Terra, H. and Paterson, T.T. (1939): *Studies on the Ice Age and Associated Human Cultures,* Carnegie Institute of Washington, Publication No. 493.

Drew, Frederic, (1875): *The Jummoo and Kashmir Territories,* E. Stanford, London.

Hassan, Pir Ghulam; *Tarikhi-i-Hassan, A History of Kashmir,* Vol. I-IV, Ghulam Mohd Noor Mohamad, Srinagar.

Kumari, Ved (1968): *The Nilamata Purana,* J & K Academy of Art, Culture and Languages, Srinagar/Jammu.

Negi, S.S. (1995): *Cold Deserts of India,* Indus Publishing Company, New Delhi.

Pascoe, Sir Edwin H. (1973): *A Manual of the Geology of India and Burma,* Third Edition, Controller of Publications, Govt. of India, Delhi.

Stein, M.A. (1900): *Kalhana's Rajatarangni,* A Constable & Company, London (1961 Reprint, Motilal Banarasidas, Delhi).

Vigne, G.T. (1842): *Travels in Kashmir, Ladakh and Iskardo,* Henry Colburn, London.

Wadia, D.N. (2004): *Geology of India,* 21st Reprint, Tata McGraw Hill Publishing Company, New Delhi.

Wakefield, W. (1879): *The Happy Valley,* Sampson Low, London.

Wilson, H.H. (1960): *Hindu History of Kashmir,* Sushil Gupta, Kolkata.

Papers and Articles

Bhat, D.K., 'Stratigraphical Status of Karewa Group of Kashmir', *Himalayan Geology,* Vol. 6, 1976.

Bhat, D.K. and Chatterji A.K., 'An Appraisal … on the Geology of the Karewa Group', *Proc. VI Indian Coll. Micropal Strat,* 1976.

'Burzahom Excavations, A Review (1961–62)', 1962–63 *Indian Archaeologist,* pp. 17–21, & 9–10.

Khazanchi, T.N. 'Developments in Science of Archaeology in Kashmir', *Koshur Samachar,* September, 2004.

Loan, M. Faroaq (1973), 'Petrological Studies of Shankaracharya Hill', Unpublished Dissertation in part fulfilment of M.Sc. Degree, Dept. of Geology, Jammu University.

Mittre, Vishnu, 'Floristic and Ecological Reconsiderations of the Plant Impressions from Kashmir', *Palaeobotanist,* 1964.

Sahni, Prof. Birbal, 'The Karewas of Kashmir', *Current Science* Vol. 5, No. 1, 1936.

Sankalia, H.D., 'Early Man in Ice Age of Kashmir', *Science Today*, December, 1969.

Wokhalio S.N and Dhar B.L., 'On a New find of Fossil Flora', *University Reviews,* J & K University April–May, 1968.

Wokhalio, S.N., 'Hercynian Vulcanicity in Kashmir,' *University Review,* Jammu University, Feb-March, 1972.

Annexure – I
The Soyam

In the pargana of Uttar Machipora, three-quarters of a kilometre to the south-west of Nichahom, lies the site of the *Svayambhu* or Soyam. From ancient times the place has been in the limelight as a *tirtha* (a place of pilgrimage). On account of the heating of the ground Kalhana, in the first book of his history (I–34) records, 'There the "Self Created Fire" rising from the womb of the earth receives … the offerings of the sacrificers'. Occurrence of this phenomenon, during the modern times is referred to by Vigne (in *Travels* …, 1842: ii–280) and Dr Falconer (in *The Valley of Kashmir* by Lawrence). Abul-Fazl (Ain II – 365) has also written about this event at Soyam. Stein during his visit to this spot in 1892 had observed the soil to be bright red like burned clay in shallow hollows.

It was last observed in 1876. In 1875 the soil at Soyam became heated and the Hindus flocked to the place to offer *shradas* to their dead. They placed brass pots, filled with water and rice, in shallow pits, till the rice got boiled. That year the occurrence lasted for thirteen months.

In this connection Vigne reports, 'About 36 years ago, an intense heat was found to issue from the spot. The soil, which is a mixture of clay and sand, has been fused by the heat from below ... but no fire, or sulphurous smell was perceivable and no fissures opened in the ground. No earthquake took place at the time ... no noises were heard ...'

Hardened lumps of clay of light red colour are still found at the spot as observed by the present writer. This phenomenon could be attributed to the burning of the underground deposits of lignite. But how was the fire caused?

Annexure – II
Early Man in Kashmir

Dr H.D. Sankalia, Professor of Proto-Indian and Ancient History at the Deccan College Post-Graduate Research Institute, Pune visited Pahalgam, in 1969, to make an on spot study of the glacial deposits described by de Terra and Paterson. He was accompanied by several research scholars and two experts, R.K. Pant and Sardari Lal. The moraine heaps, on the right bank of the East Lidder near its confluence with the West Lidder, were further exposed due to the widening of the road to the race course.

This moraine bed comprises two distinct layers. The thicker one consists of whitish boulder conglomerate, containing angular stones of trap and quartzite. This according to Paterson was deposited during the II Glacial epoch. This is overlain by a layer of brownish clay, which belonged to Second Inter-glacial. After a vigorous search by Dr Sankalia and his team a huge massive flake of black Panjal trap, about 25.5 cm by 10 cm, was found in this conglom-erate bed at a height of about 16 m above the stream level. It had two distinct flake scars, one on each edge. This massive flake, to all intents and purposes, was a manmade artefact. This discovery encouraged the group to continue the search for more finds.

It was several days later that a flake star was noted on a stone embedded at a much higher level between the zone of contact of boulder-conglomerate and brown clay. It was photographed *in situ.* On extraction it turned out to be a different type of a tool. It was smaller in size, made on yellowish quartzite and worked all over. It was a crude, pear shaped, bifacial tool with a blunt point, usually called as hand axe.

Dr Sankalia, on the basis of these two finds concludes, 'Archaeology has now shown that it was sometime during the first Interglacial that the first man appeared in Kashmir. Environmentally this was the most ideal time for the existence of Man ...'. The wait is on for the skeletal remains of this Kashmir Man to fall in the hands of the researchers to ascertain this claim.

Annexure – III
Neolithic Culture in Kashmir

It is to de Terra and Paterson that we owe the discovery of early human settlements in Kashmir. During their exploration in search of early man in this glaciated region, in 1936, they found the megalithic site of Burzahom and hinted at its significance. The excavation of Burzahom was undertaken by Archaeological Survey of India from 1960 to 1971. This was followed by similar type of excavations at Gofkral in Tral and Semthan in Bijebehara.

The Quaternary Ice Age in Kashmir was followed by a forest period, when conditions were ideal for early settlers. At all the three sites, cited above, the neolithic settlers had opted for Karewas, for their merits. A nearby stream provided them stones for making tools in addition to fishing and fowling activities. The forests served as the hunting grounds. These neolithic settlers lived in pits and a total of sixteen pits were excavated. The stone tools made by these pit-dwellers included axes, adazes and chisels, whereas awls, needles and harpoons were made of bones. The use of metal was unknown at that stage. Thirteen skeletons have been collected from the pits, of which eight are human and the rest, those of animals. In the human burials of Phase II, red ochre was used on bones. Sometimes, a skeleton of a pet animal was also found near the human skeleton.

In the following period pits were abandoned and replaced by mud and mud-brick structures. Pottery wheel was introduced. Polished stone and bone tools were used on a large scale. Wood was cut with the help of the stone axe. Bone tools, besides hunting and fishing, were used for cleaning skins. Bone needles helped in the stitching of the cleared skins which were used as garments. The presence of mat impressions on pottery depicts that they knew weaving also.

The other sites of neolithic culture identified are Thajwor, Jaya Devi Wudar, Begagund, Hariparigom, Olchibag, Panzgam, Pampore and Sombhur, situated in south Kashmir. The other such locations are Aripanthan (near Magam) Damodar Wudar (Budgam), Duviekampore (Gulmarg), Ganderbal (Sindh valley), Gurhoma Sangri (Wular lake), Putkhai (Sangrama) and in Wangat nala (above Kangan). This wide distribution of settlements indicate that Kashmir was inhabited by a large number of neolithic settlers.

Neolithic was followed by megalithic period demonstrated by the erection of menhirs, when a new wave of people arrived in Kashmir and started living with early settlers. The period saw the wheel-made dull red pottery. In addition to bone and stone tools, use was made of iron and copper. They lived in rubble and mud structures. Rice cultivation, in the valley, was introduced by them. The full story is yet to be told for 'In spite of scientific outputs from various research institutes there are wide gaps in the story of early man in Kashmir … . Extensive field work is required to solve this problem and to fill in the gaps' (Khazanchi, 2004).

Index